The Natural World and God:
Theological Explorations

Denis Edwards

Scholars Collection

1. *Opening the Scripture*, 2014, Antony Campbell SJ

2. *Amplifying that Still Small Voice*, 2015, Frank Brennan SJ

3. *Gospel Interpretation and Christian Life*, 2017, Francis J Moloney SDB

The Natural World and God:
Theological Explorations

Denis Edwards

Adelaide

Text copyright © 2017 remains with Denis Edwards for all papers in this collection. All rights reserved. Except for any fair dealing permitted under the Copyright Act, no part of this book may be reproduced by any means without prior permission. Inquiries should be made to the publisher.

Unless noted otherwise, the Scripture quotations contained herein are from the New Revised Standard Version of the Bible, and the Revised Standard Version of the Bible copyright © 1989, and are used by permission. All rights reserved.

Creator: Edwards, Denis, 1943- author.

Title: The natural world and God: theological explorations
/ Denis Edwards.

ISBN: 9781925643053 (hardback)
       9781925643046 (paperback)
       9781925643060 (ebook : epub)
       9781925643077 (ebook : pdf)

Series: Scholars collection.
Notes: Includes index.

Subjects: Nature--Religious aspects.
Nature in the Bible.
Natural theology.
Religion and science.

Cover art work Think stock Cover design by James Brownridge.

Layout, in Minion Pro 11, by Extel Solutions, India.

Published by:

An imprint of the ATF Press Publishing
Group owned by ATF (Australia) Ltd.
PO Box 504
Hindmarsh, SA 5007
ABN 90 116 359 963
www.atfpress.com
Making a lasting impact

Table of Contents

Introduction	vii
Acknowledgments	xi
A. Ecology, Evolution and Theology	**1**
1. Creation Seen in the Light of Christ: A Theological Sketch	3
2. The Attractor and the Energy of Love: Trinity in Evolutionary and Ecological Context	23
3. Sketching an Ecological Theology of the Holy Spirit and the Word of God	43
4. Humans, Chimps and Bonobos: Towards an Inclusive View of the Human as Bearing the Image of God	55
5. 'Every Sparrow that Falls to the Ground': The Cost of Evolution and the Christ-Event	75
6. 'Sublime Communion': The Theology of the Natural World in *Laudato Si'*	99
7. 'Everything is Interconnected': The Trinity and the Natural World in *Laudato Si'*	119
B. Creation, Eucharist and Spirituality	**135**
8. Eucharist and Ecology: Keeping Memorial of Creation	137
9. Celebrating Eucharist in a Time of Global Climate Change	157

10. Planetary Spirituality: Exploring a Christian Ecological Approach — 173

11. Experience of Word and Spirit in the Natural World — 187

C. Divine Action — **203**

12. Exploring How God Acts: *God, Grace & Creation* — 205

13. Why is God Doing This? Suffering, the Universe and Christian Eschatology — 227

14. Miracles and the Laws of Nature — 253

15. Towards a Theology of Divine Action: William R Stoeger, SJ, on the Laws of Nature — 269

D. In Dialogue with Karl Rahner — **293**

16. Resurrection and the Costs of Evolution: A Dialogue with Rahner on Non-Interventionist Theology — 295

17. Resurrection of the Body and Transformation of the Universe in the Theology of Karl Rahner — 317

18. Teilhard's Vision as Agenda for Rahner's Christology — 345

19. Climate Change and the Theology of Karl Rahner: A Hermeneutical Dialogue — 361

E. In Dialogue with Athanasius — **381**

20. Athanasius: The Word of God in Creation and Salvation — 383

21. Incarnation and the Natural World: Explorations in the Tradition of Athanasius — 405

22. Athanasius's *Letters to Serapion*: Resource for a Twenty-First Century Theology of God the Trinity — 423

23. Where on Earth is God? Exploring an Ecological Theology of the Trinity in the Tradition of Athanasius — 445

Indices

Index of Authors — 467

Index of Biblical References — 471

Index of Subjects — 477

Introduction

When I was invited by Hilary Regan to contribute a volume to the ATF Scholars Collection, it was soon clear to me that I would like to gather some of my writings on the theology of the natural world. Two reasons have guided my focus in this work. One is the fact that our twenty-first century worldview has been radically changed by recent science. Cosmology now gives us a picture of the observable universe as containing something like two trillion galaxies, and as expanding and growing in complexity from its origin 13.8 billion years ago. Evolutionary biology presents us with a story of life in which all of the diverse creatures of our planet have evolved, by means of natural selection, from the first microbial live that emerged on Earth 3.7 billion years ago. It is an urgent matter for theology to engage with this large scientifically shaped worldview that many people take for granted today.

Even more urgent for theology, I am convinced, is the imperative to respond to the human-induced crisis of life on our planet. We live in an extraordinary moment in the history of life Earth, a time that scientists have begun to call the Anthropocene, a period when the human impact on other species, and on the systems that support life on the plant, has reached a new, critical level. Human actions are contributing to climate change that brings extreme weather events, inundation of low-lying land, destruction of crops, desertification, and the extinction of species. We are polluting the land, rivers, and seas, destroying habitats, and rapidly diminishing the biodiversity of the planet.

Both the scientific worldview of our time and the ecological crisis we face require a renewed theology of the natural world. Sadly, it must be admitted that Christian theology and preaching had, until recently, largely ignored, or lost sight of the natural world. I am using the words *natural world* in this context to refer to the world of plants, animals, rivers, seas, mountains, stars, and galaxies. I include humans as part of the natural world, but I use the expression *natural world* to point beyond the human to the rest of nature. Much of traditional Christian theology, whether biblical, patristic, or medieval, included the natural world. It concerned three realities, human beings, the rest of the creation, and God. But, tragically, this threesome was reduced to a twosome in Western theology through the late medieval, Reformation, and Enlightenment periods, when a theological approach to the wider creation largely disappeared. This reduction of theology persisted into the late twentieth century.

In this context, it became clear to me that the priority in my theological research needed to be on contributing to the development of a theology that fully embraced the natural world. But I took this option as part of a community of theologians. The articles and chapters represented here are part of something far bigger, as theologians around the world engage in dialogue with science and seek to contribute to an ecological theology that is so much needed. An enormous step in this work, of course, has been *Laudato Si'*, and Pope Francis's clear positions on the value and meaning of the natural world, the sublime communion between human beings, other creatures, and God, Earth as our common home, and ecological conversion and action.

A central emphasis of my own work has been the attempt to locate a theology of the natural world right at the heart of Christian faith. It has never seemed sufficient to me simply to see ecological theology as an offshoot of the doctrine of creation. And it certainly has not seemed appropriate to concentrate on creation over against incarnation and redemption. Rather I have thought it important to keep creation and incarnation together as aspects of God's loving self-giving to creatures, and to see redemption, or salvation in Christ, as embracing not just human beings but the whole of creation. So the kind of ecological theology that I have worked on in these essays is one that seeks to embrace the natural world within a fully Trinitarian theology of creation and incarnation.

This book is divided into five sections. The first section is concerned with a theology of the natural world that is both evolutionary and ecological. The second section explores the place of the natural world in our eucharistic theology and in Christian spirituality. The third section focuses on the issue of divine action in an evolutionary universe. A central concern is the way suffering, predation, death, and extinction are built into an evolutionary world. How does theology deal with this intensification of the problem of evil? The fourth and fifth sections deal with my attempts to build upon a contemporary theology of nature in dialogue with the thought of Athanasius of Alexandria and Karl Rahner. It has seemed important to me to harvest the trajectories in the Christian theological tradition that can open out into a contemporary ecological theology. Of course, there is overlap between the sections of this book. And there is some repetition, which I hope is helpful in following the development of the theology rather than simply distracting.

I am very grateful to Hilary Regan, the Chief Executive Officer of ATF Publishing Group, for suggesting this collection, and to Hilary and all at ATF for bringing this work to completion. It is a joy and an honour to be part of the ATF Scholars Series.

Acknowledgments

The articles in this volume are based on the following original articles and I am grateful to the editors and publishers for having them in this volume.

Ecology, Evolution and Theology

'Creation Seen in the Light of Christ: A Theological Sketch', in *Creation is Groaning: Biblical and Theological Perspectives*, edited by Mary L Coloe (Collegeville, Minnesota: Liturgical Press, 2013).

'The Attractor and the Energy of Love: Trinity in Evolutionary and Ecological Context', in *The Ecumenical Review*, 65/1 (March 2013): 129–144.

'Sketching an Ecological Theology of the Holy Spirit and the Word of God', in *Concilium* 4 (2011): 13–22.

'Humans, Chimps, and Bonobos: Towards an Inclusive View of the Human as Bearing the Image of God', in *Turning to the Heavens and the Earth: Theological Reflections on a Cosmological Conversion: Essays in Honor of Elizabeth A Johnson*, edited by Julia Brumbaugh and Natalia Imperatori-Lee (Collegeville, MN: Liturgical Press, 2016), 7–25.

'Every Sparrow that Falls to the Ground: The Cost of Evolution and the Christ-Event', in *Ecotheology*, 11/1 (March 2006): 103–23.

'Sublime Communion: The Theology of the Natural World in *Laudato Si*', in *Theological Studies*, 77 (June 2016): 377–391.

'Everything is Interconnected: The Trinity and the Natural World in *Laudato Si*', in a forthcoming issue of *Australasian Catholic Record*.

Creation, Eucharist, and Spirituality

'Eucharist and Ecology: Keeping Memorial of Creation', in *Worship* 82/3 (May 2008): 194–213.

'Celebrating Eucharist in a Time of Global Climate Change', in *Pacifica* 19 (February 2006): 1–15.

'Planetary Spirituality: Exploring a Christian Ecological Approach', in *Compass* 44/4 (Summer 2010): 16–23.

'Experience of Word and Spirit in the Natural World', in *The Nature of Things: Rediscovering the Spiritual in God's Creation,* edited by Graham Buxton and Norman Habel (Pickwick Publications 2016), 13–26.

Divine Action

'Exploring How God Acts', in *God, Grace & Creation*, edited by Philip J Rossi (Maryknoll, NY: Orbis Books, 2010), 124–146.

'Why is God Doing This? Suffering, the Universe, and Christian Eschatology', in *Physics and Cosmology: Scientific Perspectives on the Problem of Natural Evil*, edited by Nancey Murphy, Robert John Russell and William R. Stoeger (Vatican City: Vatican Observatory; Berkeley CA: Center for Theology and the Natural Sciences, 2007), 247–66.

'Miracles and the Laws of Nature', in *Compass* 41/2 (2007): 8–16.

'Towards a Theology of Divine Action: William R. Stoeger, S.J. on the Laws of Nature', in *Theological Investigations,* 76/3 (September 2015): 485–502.

In Dialogue with Karl Rahner

'Resurrection and the Costs of Evolution: A Dialogue with Rahner on Noninterventionist Theology', in *Theological Studies,* 67/4 (December 2006): 816–33.

'Resurrection of the Body and Transformation of the Universe in the Theology of Karl Rahner', in *Philosophy and Theology,* 18/2 (2006): 357–83.

'Teilhard's Vision as Agenda for Rahner's Christology', *From Teilhard to Omega: Co-creating an Unfinished Universe,* edited by Ilia Delio (Maryknoll, NY: Orbis, 2014), 53–66; and in *Pacifica,* 23/2 (June 2010): 233–235.

'Climate Change and the Theology of Karl Rahner: A Hermeneutical Dialogue', in *Confronting the Climate Crisis: Catholic Theological Perspectives,* edited by Jame Schaefer (Milwaukee, Marquette University Press, 2011), 233–51.

In Dialogue with Athanasius

'Athanasius: The Word of God in Creation and Salvation', in *Creation and Salvation: Volume 1: A Mosaic of Selected Classic Christian Theologies,* edited by Ernst M Conradie (Zurich: LIT, 2012), 37–51.

'Incarnation and the Natural World: Explorations in the Tradition of Athanasius', in *Incarnation: On the Scope and Depth of Christology,* edited by Niels Henrik Gregersen (Minneapolis: Fortress Press, 2015), 157–176

'Athanasius's *Letters to Serapion*: Resource for a Twenty-First Century Theology of God the Trinity', in *Phronema,* 29/2 (2014): 41–64.

'Where on Earth is God? Exploring an Ecological Theology of the Trinity in the Tradition of Athanasius', in Ernst M Conradie, Sigurd Bergmann, Celia Deane-Drummond and Denis Edwards, editors *Christian Faith and the Earth: Current Paths and Emerging Horizons in Ecotheology* (London: Bloomsbury, 2014), 11–30.

A. Ecology, Evolution and Theology

Creation Seen in the Light of Christ: A Theological Sketch

Is there anything specific to the Christian understanding of creation? Christianity certainly shares with Judaism, and with Islam, a great deal. From the ancient faith of Israel it learns that there is only one transcendent God who is Creator of absolutely everything; that this transcendent God is immanently present to all creatures; that this God not only creates things in the beginning, but is their constant source of existence, life and fruitfulness; that this Creator delights in the goodness of creation; that the fruitfulness of creation is a result of divine blessing; that humans are uniquely made in the image of God (Gen 1:1–31).

The common biblical tradition teaches that human beings are called to till and to take care of creation (Gen 2:15), that human sin damages creation, but that God, nevertheless, commits God's self to creation by an everlasting covenant (Gen 9:8–17). It sees humans as standing before a Creator, and a creation, far greater than anything humans can grasp, as called to cosmic humility, and to the recognition that other creatures have their own proper relationship to their Creator not mediated by human beings (Job 38:39–12). This same ancient biblical tradition locates human beings within an interrelated community of creation, a community of praise and thanksgiving (Ps 104; Ps 148; Dan 3:51–90).[1]

All this and much more belongs to the common biblical tradition. What then is specific to the Christian view of creation? In what follows, I will attempt a partial response to this question; first, by proposing

---

1. This biblical line of thought has been explored by Richard Bauckham in his *Bible and Ecology: Rediscovering the Community of Creation* (London: Darton, Longman & Todd, 2010), 37–102.

that the Christian theology of creation begins from the resurrection of the crucified one; second, by arguing that creation and incarnation can be understood as united in one divine act of self-giving love; third, by outlining four characteristics of creation understood in the light of Christ, as enabling creaturely autonomy, empowering evolutionary emergence, accepting the limits of creaturely processes and suffering with suffering creation; fourth, by suggesting that in spite of all ambiguity in our experience of the natural world, the revelation of God in Christ enables us to claim that creation is an act of divine love.

Beginning from the Resurrection of the Crucified Jesus

A specifically Christian theology of creation begins only with the resurrection of Jesus. Those who had loved Jesus in his lifetime, investing all their religious hopes in him and leaving all to follow him, caught up in his vision and in his person, had lost everything in his condemnation and death on a Roman cross. For Peter, Mary Magdalene and the other disciples, to meet Jesus risen from the dead transformed in the glory of God, was a radically new experience of forgiveness, peace and hope. In the risen One, they knew God. In the transfigured Jesus, the fullness of God was revealed. In him, they experienced the boundless love of God and were caught up in a joy that echoes through the centuries in the life of the church.

In some way, they knew then that all sin, all the violence of the world, and death itself, were transformed by God's saving act. They experienced themselves as brought from death to wonderful new life, participating in the life of the risen Christ by the Spirit of God. For them, God would forever be God revealed in Jesus and in the Holy Spirit given in his name. The crucified and risen Jesus would be forever the human face of God.

Jesus, in his life and even in his death, above all in his death, is revealed as 'God-with-us' (Matt 1:23). Jesus' cruel, ugly, death now becomes the radical sign of hope, the unthinkable expression of divine forgiveness and love without limits. And it becomes the expression of God-with-us and the promise of life in all our experiences of suffering, no matter how devastating. The disciples saw the light of God in the risen One and they knew his divinity in a way not possible during his lifetime.

The disciples of Jesus had to find words to speak of what was beyond words. They needed ways to express what they knew in the risen Christ, that he is from God the Creator, that he is God-with-us. They found a fruitful insight in the biblical concept of Wisdom—a deeply traditional way of speaking of God's presence and action. In the biblical tradition, Wisdom (Gk *Sophia*) is personified as God's companion in the creating and sustaining of all things (Prov 8:22–31; Sir 24:3–7; Wis 8:1–4). This ever-creative Wisdom of God comes to live with human beings. She makes her home among them, and invites them to come to her table to share the food and drink she provides (Prov 9:1–6; Sir 24:8–22; Wis 8:16–21).

Jewish thinkers could see Wisdom come to us as Torah (Sir 24:23). The early Christians, in the light of resurrection, saw Jesus as the Wisdom of God come to us in the flesh. *Sophia*, the one through whom everything in the universe is created, has now come to be with us in Jesus. The true Wisdom of God is revealed in the human face of Jesus, in his life and ministry, in his death and resurrection. Paul tells us that it is Christ crucified who is the true Wisdom of God (1 Cor 1:24) and he can say that everything is created in Christ (1 Cor 4:6). In John we find that, like Wisdom who comes from God to feed us at her table, Jesus-Wisdom feeds the five thousand on the mountain side; he himself is the very bread of life, that living bread that comes down from heaven to give life to the world (Jn 6:5).[2]

A Jewish writer like Philo of Alexandria could use both Wisdom (*Sophia*) and Word (*Logos*) language to speak of God's creating and revealing presence. So in New Testament hymns, such as the prologue of John's Gospel and the opening of Hebrews, we find Christ as the Word of God, in texts with a Wisdom structure of thought, and in language that echoes biblical Wisdom hymns (Jn 1:1–14; Heb 1:1–3). For John, Jesus is clearly and ambiguously the creative Wisdom/Word of God—'all things came into being through him' (Jn 1:3)—now made flesh in our midst.[3] In the late Pauline corpus, Christ is understood, like Wisdom, as the one in whom all things are created, the one in whom all things hold together and as 'the firstborn

---

2. On the Wisdom theme in John 6, see André Feuillet, *Johannine Studies* (Staten Island, NY: Alba House, 1964), 76–102.
3. For a commentary that traces the theme of Wisdom across the entire gospel, see Ben Witherington III, *John's Wisdom* (Louisville: Westminster/John Knox, 1995).

from the dead', the one in whom all will be reconciled (Col 1:15–20) and recapitulated (Eph 1:20–22).

In this biblical theology, there is an inner relationship between creation and the incarnation. Everything in the universe is created by God through the eternal Wisdom/Word of God. This Wisdom/Word of God is made flesh in Jesus in order that the whole creation might participate with human beings in the salvation and fulfilment of all things promised in the resurrection of Jesus. Early theologians, like Athanasius, see Christ as the one true Word, Wisdom and Radiance of God, made flesh.[4] He writes of John 1:3 as the 'all-inclusive' text: 'All things came into being through him, and without him not one thing came into being'.[5] He sees the Word of creation as becoming flesh in order that humanity might be deified, transformed by grace so that it might partake in the divine life of the Trinity. In his anti-Arian writings, he uses frequently both the verb *theopoieō*, and the noun he coins, *theopoiēsis*, to defend the eternal divinity, and divine condescension, of the Word, who is made flesh to bring about our deification: 'So he was not a human being and later became God. But, being God, he later became a human being in order that we may be deified'.[6]

The Word/Wisdom of God is made flesh for the deifying transformation of human creatures and with them of the whole universe of creatures. So Athanasius writes of the Father's love for humanity, 'on account of which he not only gave consistence to all things in his Word but brought it about that the creation itself, of which the apostle says that it 'awaits the revelation of the children of God', will at a certain point be delivered 'from the bondage of corruption into the glorious freedom of the children of God' (Rom 8:19, 21).[7]

Creation and Incarnation: God's Self-Bestowal

Is there a way of summing up in a few words what is most central to the specifically Christian view of God? With Karl Rahner, I see the

---

4. Athanasius, *Orations Against the Arians* 1:46, translated in Khaled Anatolios, *Athanasius* (London and New York: Routledge, 2004), 103.
5. Athanasius, *On the Incarnation* 2, translated in RW Thompson, *Athanasius, Contra Gentes and de Incarnatione* (Oxford: Clarendon Press, 1971), 139.
6. *Orations against the Arians* 63, translated in Anatolios, *Athanasius*, 96.
7. Athanasius, *Orations against the Arians* 2:63, translated in Anatolios, *Athanasius*, 157.

concept of divine self-communication, or divine self-bestowal, as an encapsulation of what God does for us in Christ and the Spirit.[8] The Christian experience is fundamentally of a God who gives God's self to us two ways: 1. God gives God's very self explicitly and irrevocably to creatures in the humanity of Jesus, in all that makes up his life, death and resurrection; 2. This same God gives God's self to creatures in the Holy Spirit in the free and abundant gift of grace, and in the Pentecostal experience constitutes the community of disciples into the church of Jesus Christ.

God gives God's self to us in the Word made flesh and in the Spirit poured out in grace. Paul speaks of two divine 'sendings': 'But when the fullness of time had come, God sent his Son, born of a woman, born under the law, in order to redeem those who were under the law, so that we might receive adoption as children. And because you are children, God has sent the Spirit of his Son into our hearts, crying, 'Abba! Father!' So you are no longer a slave but a child, and if a child then also an heir, through God' (Gal 4:4–5). The concept of divine self-bestowal in Word and Spirit can be seen as a brief summary of the central doctrines of Christian faith, of Christology, Pneumatology and Trinitarian theology. It expresses what we experience of God in the economy of salvation and, because God is faithful, we rightly hold that the God we experience in our history, as giving God's self to us in the Word made flesh and the Spirit poured out, represents the true nature of God as Trinity.

What is revealed in the Christ-event is a God who gives God's self to creatures. Based on this revelation in Christ, Rahner sees divine self-bestowal as defining every aspect of God's action, in creation, redemption in Christ and final fulfilment.[9] He sees creation itself as an act of self-giving love that reaches its goal only in the self-giving of the incarnation and in the final transformation of all things in the risen Christ. The creation of the universe of creatures is the first element in the free and radical decision of God to give God's self in love to that which in not divine. When God freely to bestow God's self in love, creation comes to be as the addressee of this self-bestowal.

---

8. See, for example, Karl Rahner, *Foundations of Christian Faith: An Introduction to the Idea of Christianity* (New York: Seabury, 1978), 136.
9. Karl Rahner, 'Christology in the Setting of Modern Man's Understanding of himself and of his World' in *Theological Investigations* 11 (New York: Seabury Press, 1974), 219.

This means that God's self-giving in Christ is the real foundation of the history of the natural world. The mystery of God's will, we are told in Ephesians, has been revealed to us 'according to his good pleasure that he set forth in Christ, as a plan for the fullness of time, to gather up all things in him, things in heaven and things on earth' (Eph 1:9–10). It is not simply that the event of Jesus Christ unfolds against the background of nature. The story of the natural world, and everything that science can tell us about its evolution, is part of a larger vision of divine self-bestowal.[10] The big bang and the expansion of our universe from a small dense hot state 13.7 billion years ago, and the evolution of life since its beginning on Earth 3.7 billion years ago—this whole story exists *within* the vision of the divine purpose.

Harvey Egan has said that the briefest possible summary of Rahner's theological enterprise in found in 'his creative appropriation of Scotus's view that God creates in order to communicate *self* and that creation exists in order to be the recipient of God's free gift of self'.[11] While one line of Christian theology has held that the incarnation comes about simply as a remedy for sin, another, associated with Eastern Christianity, particularly with Maximus the Confessor (580–662), and in Western theology with Franciscan theology, exemplified in Duns Scotus (1266–1308), sees the incarnation as always the divine intention in the creation of a universe of creatures.

The incarnation, then, is not simply a remedy for sin or a corrective for a creation that has gone wrong. Once sin exists, of course, the incarnation expresses divine forgiveness in a most beautiful and radical way, but the incarnation is not something added on to creation; it is not a kind of back-up plan. The Incarnation is the meaning of creation. God freely chooses, from the beginning, to create a world in which the Word would be made flesh and the Spirit poured out.[12] The incarnation expresses the divine purpose in creating, which is the divine self-bestowal. Creation and incarnation are united in the one act of God: they are 'two moments and two phases of the *one* process

---

10. Karl Rahner, 'Resurrection: D Theology', in *Encyclopedia of Theology: A Concise Sacramentum Mundi* (London: Burns and Oates, 1975), 1442.
11. Harvey D Egan, 'Theology and Spirituality', in Declan Marmion and Mary E Hines, *The Cambridge Companion to Karl Rahner* (Cambridge: Cambridge University Press, 2005), 16.
12. Karl Rahner, 'Christology within an Evolutionary View of the World', in *Theological Investigations* 5 (Baltimore: Helicon Press, 1966), 184–7.

of God's self-giving and self-expression, although it is an intrinsically differentiated process'.[13] The creation of the universe and all its creatures and the Incarnation are to be seen as distinct dimensions of the one act of divine self-bestowal in love. In the next three sections, I will explore briefly three characteristics of God's creative act understood as divine self-giving.

Enabling Creaturely Autonomy

How should we think of the Creator's inter-relationship with the world of creatures? Are we to think of God as constantly intervening in the laws and conditions of the natural world (sometimes called 'occasionalism') or as intervening at certain points in the process of evolution (as proponents of 'intelligent design' seem to think)? Or are we to think of God as setting the processes of the natural world in place and then allowing things to run their course (the position of 'deism')? Aquinas offers a far richer theology of creation than either interventionism or deism, a response I see as a fundamental basis for contemporary dialogue between science and theology, with his metaphysical understanding of the relationship between primary and secondary causality.

Primary causality for Aquinas is simply God's creative act that enables all creatures to exist and to act. God is unlike all creatures, in that it is God's very nature to exist. The One whose nature is to exist causes existence (*esse*) in all other things. Creation is the interior relationship between the Creator and each creature by which the creature is held in being. If God were not interiorly present to each creature enabling it to be, it would be nothing. Aquinas sees all things in the universe existing in the community of creation only as created by God *ex nihilo* at each moment, and as dependent on God entirely for their existence and action at every point. He sees God's providence as governing all creation to its final end, which is participation in the goodness of God. To speak of God's creative act as primary cause is to use the word 'cause' in an analogical fashion. God's creative act is radically unlike creaturely causality, radically beyond empirical observation, and radically beyond human comprehension.

---

13. Rahner, *Foundations*, 197.

In Aquinas's thought, all the interacting agents at work in the empirical world are seen as secondary causes. This includes literally everything that can be studied by the natural and social sciences. God as primary cause is always and everywhere creatively and providentially at work in all creaturely interactions, in all the conditions, constants, contingencies and laws of the natural world. God is not a cause like creaturely causes in the world and is never to be thought of as one amongst such causes. God acts creatively in and through creatures that are themselves truly causal. Aquinas sees the Creator as respecting the proper dignity of created causes because of 'the abundance of his goodness imparting to creatures also the dignity of causing'.[14]

God's respect for creation's autonomy is such that God wants creation to have its own pattern of causality. Aquinas's theology leads to a genuine respect for the proper integrity and independence of the natural sciences. There is never a resort to the 'God of the gaps' to solve a scientific problem. One who follows Aquinas would not be inclined to search for a place where God intervenes in creation because God is found in every dimension of creation: God 'acts interiorly in all things', because 'God is properly the universal cause of *esse*, which is innermost in all things'.[15]

The divine act of creation is unique. On the one hand, creation is a relationship of absolute nearness and real dependence, where each creature is dependent on God for its existence and capacity to act. On the other hand, God establishes the creature in genuine difference from God's self, and in the relationship of creation, because of God's love and respect for creatures, each creature has its own otherness, integrity and proper autonomy.

A fundamental principle of this relationship, one grounded in Aquinas's thought and often articulated by Karl Rahner, is expressed in the axiom: radical dependence on God and the genuine autonomy of the creature are directly and not inversely related.[16] In everyday experience, it seems that the more one thing depends upon another,

---

14. Thomas Aquinas, *Summa Theologiae*, 1a.22.3, translated by Thomas Gilby, *St Thomas Aquinas Summa Theologiae*, volume 5 (Cambridge: Blackfriars, 1967), 99.
15. Thomas Aquinas, *Summa Theologiae*, 1a.105.6, translated by TC O'Brien, *St Thomas Aquinas Summa Theologiae*, volume 14 (Cambridge: Blackfriars, 1975), 79.
16. See, for example, Rahner, *Foundations*, 789.

the less autonomy it has. The relationship of creation is the opposite: the closer creatures are to God, the more they can be truly themselves. We humans know this from the experience of grace: the closer we are drawn into the love of God, the freer we are. In relation to God, 'radical dependence grounds autonomy'.[17] Creaturely integrity is not diminished because a creature's existence is dependent on God, but flourishes precisely in this dependence. This is true not only in the divine relationship to human beings, but also in God's interaction with all the dynamics of the natural world, including the emergence of our universe and the evolution of life on Earth.

Empowering Evolutionary Emergence

One of the radical changes in our view of reality since the time of Aquinas springs from the nineteenth century discovery by Charles Darwin and Alfred Russel Wallace not only of the large-scale evolution of life on our planet, but also of the fundamental role played by natural selection in the evolutionary emergence of insects, eagles, whales and human beings, and of their wings, eyes and brains. Then, in the twentieth century, building on Einstein's general relativity and the astronomical observations of Edwin Hubble, cosmologists discovered that the universe is not static, but dynamic and expanding, and that it has emerged from an unthinkable small, hot and dense state over the last 13.7 billion years.

How is this dynamic, evolutionary understanding of reality to be understood in relationship to God's creative act? In Aquinas's view, God's creative act sustains all creatures in existence (*conservatio*) and enables them to act (*concursus*). Clearly in the light of insights into the emergent nature of reality, Aquinas's view needs further development. It needs to be a theology of God's creative act as enabling and empowering of the evolutionary becoming of the interconnected world of creatures. This task was taken up by Karl Rahner. He saw the need for a theology of creation that can account for the emergence of the new, as in the transitions from inert matter to living creatures, and from living creatures to self-conscious human beings.

---

17. Rahner, *Foundations*, 79.

Rahner sees the self-bestowal of the transcendent God as 'the most immanent factor in the creature'.[18] What is the effect of this presence of God? A fundamental effect of God's creative self-giving presence, Rahner holds, is that creation itself has the capacity for emergence, to become more, to become what is new. Rahner calls this dynamic capacity for the new 'self-transcendence'. The two concepts of divine self-bestowal and creaturely self-transcendence are inter-related: it is God's self-bestowal that enables and empowers creaturely self-transcendence. This means that God's creative, immanent presence to all things not only enables them to exist, and to act, as theologians like Aquinas taught, but also to evolve into the new. This idea of creaturely self-transcendence is worked out in Rahner's anthropology and in his evolutionary Christology, but it plays a fundamental systematic role in many aspects of his theological work.[19]

The 'self' in self-transcendence means that the evolutionary capacity is truly intrinsic to creaturely reality. It comes from within the natural world. This means that the emergence of the new is completely open to explanation at the scientific level. God's creative presence operates at a strictly metaphysical and theological level. Just as God's creative act enables creatures to exist, so this same creative presence of God enables the new to emerge from within the natural world itself, according to the natural world's own processes and laws. Emergence is a creaturely reality, but it exists only because of God's creative act. God's presence in self-bestowing love enables creatures to exist, to interact, and to evolve.

Rahner links this pattern of self-transcendence to Christology, seeing Jesus Christ as both God's self-bestowal in the Word made flesh to the universe of creatures and, in his humanity, as the self-transcendence of the created universe to God. I believe it needs to be linked more fully to pneumatology as well, so that the emergence of the new, as when life first appears in a lifeless universe, can be seen as given through the Word and in the Holy Spirit. As Athanasius says,

---

18. Karl Rahner, 'Immanent and Transcendent Consummation of the World', in *Theological Investigations*, 10 (London: Darton, Longman & Todd), 281.
19. See, for example, Rahner's *Hominisation: The Evolutionary Origin of Man as a Theological Problem* (London: Burns and Oates, 1965); 'Christology within an Evolutionary View of the World', in *Theological Investigations* 5 (Baltimore: Helicon, 1966); 'Immanent and Transcendent Consummation', 273–89; and various passages in his *Foundations*.

'The Father creates and renews all things through the Word and in the Spirit'.[20] He sees the Spirit is the one who 'binds creation to the Word'.[21] Much more recently, Walter Kasper has written of the Creator Spirit:

> Since the Spirit is divine love in person, he is, first of all, the source of creation, for creation is the overflow of God's love and a participation in God's being. The Holy Spirit is the internal (in God) presupposition of communicability of God outside of himself. But the Spirit is also the source of movement and life in the created world. Whenever something new arises, whenever life is awakened and reality reaches ecstatically beyond itself, in all seeking and striving, in every ferment and birth, and even more in the beauty of creation, something of the being and activity of God's Spirit is manifested.[22]

The Spirit of God is the Life-Giver who enables and empowers the emergence of galaxies and stars, the Sun and its solar system, with Earth placed at the right distant from the Sun to enable life, the first forms of prokaryotic life, more complex life forms, the extraordinary flourishing of sea creatures, flowering trees and shrubs, the diversity of land animals, mammals and human beings with their extraordinarily complex brains. God's presence through the Word and in the Spirit enables the universe of creatures to exist, to interact and evolve within the one community of life on Earth within a dynamic, evolutionary universe. God seems prepared to create through long, complex processes of emergence, respecting the processes rather than through constant intervention. How might we think theologically of the power of God at work in all of this?

Accepting the Limits of Creaturely Processes

In the Christ-event, self-giving love is revealed as the way of God. The Incarnation and, above all, the cross of Jesus, reveal a God who enters into the vulnerability of love in a kenotic way (Phil 2:7). Paul sees

---

20. Athanasius, *Serapion* 1:24, in Anatolios, *Athanasius*, 224.
21. Athanasius, *Serapion* 1:25, in Anatolios, *Athanasius*, 225.
22. Walter Kasper, *The God of Jesus Christ* (London, SCM, 1983), 227.

Christ crucified as the very 'power of God and the wisdom of God' (1 Cor 1:24). For Christian theology, the absolutely vulnerable human being on the cross is the true revelation of God. As Walter Kasper has said, in the extreme vulnerability of the cross we do not find the loss of divinity, nor the absence of divinity, but the true revelation of divinity.[23] In Jesus crucified, divine power is revealed as the boundless power of unthinkable love. It is revealed as the omnipotence of love. The power of God revealed in the cross is not a power to dominate but a power-in-love.

The resurrection of the crucified reveals the power of this divine love to heal, liberate, and bring creation to transfigured new life. Divine power-in-love is not only capable of the vulnerability of the cross, but also of bringing forgiveness, participation in divine life and resurrection life to human beings. The resurrection promises fulfillment to the whole interconnected creation (Rom 8:19–25). To believe in God as all-powerful is to believe in the omnipotence of divine love and its eschatological victory over sin, violence and death. The vulnerable self-giving love of Christ gives expression in our finite, creaturely world to the divine nature. This self-bestowing love, revealed in Jesus' life and death and culminating in the transforming power of the resurrection, is the true icon of the Triune God in our world, and the true revelation of divine omnipotence.

This same pattern of divine power-in-love discovered in the Christ-event can be read back into the divine act of creating a universe of creatures. Power-in-love can be thought of as characterising the whole divine act of creation, God's original creation, God's ongoing creative act, and God's eschatological fulfillment of creation. In all of this, God freely creates in a way that respects the limits and integrity of creaturely processes. This means that we can think of God as waiting upon the proper evolutionary unfolding of these finite processes.

In his late work, Edwards Schillebeeckx has written on the defenselessness and vulnerability of God. He discusses this divine vulnerability at three levels: God's defenselessness in creation, God's defenselessness in Jesus Christ, and the Holy Spirit's defenselessness

---

23. Kasper, *God of Jesus Christ*, 195.

in the church and in the world.²⁴ He explains that he speaks of the defenselessness of God rather than of divine powerlessness, because powerlessness and power contradict one another, whereas defenselessness and power need not: 'We know from experience that those who make themselves vulnerable can sometimes disarm evil!'²⁵ In creation, he sees a kind of divine yielding on God's part, as God makes room for the other, and in creating human beings, God makes God's-self vulnerable to human freedom. Schillebeeckx sees God's act of creation as 'an adventure, full of risks'.²⁶ This does not do away with divine creative and saving power. This creative power, however, does not break into creation from outside. It comes from within creation and shows itself as 'the power of love which challenges, gives life and frees human beings'.²⁷

To say that God waits upon creatures is not to suggest that God is simply allowing things to run their course. God was with Jesus in his cross, holding him in love, and acting powerfully in the Spirit, transforming evil and death into the source of healing for the world. In creation, too, divine power can be seen as the transcendent power-in-love that has an unimaginable capacity to respect the autonomy and independence of creatures, to work with them patiently, and to bring them to their fulfillment. This is not divine passivity, but the creative and powerful waiting on another. God works with creaturely limits and waits upon them with infinite patience. By creating in love, God freely accepts the limitations of working with finite creatures.

Based upon the Incarnation, and the cross of Christ, it can be said that there may be circumstances when God freely accepts the limitations of creating in and through finite entities and processes, because of God's love and respect for finite creatures and for creaturely processes. God achieves the divine purposes, not in ways that override the proper autonomy of creaturely processes, but by an infinite power-in-love that lives within the process and accompanies creation in love, promising to bring it to healing and fulfilment in Christ.

---

24. Edward Schillebeeckx, *For the Sake of the Gospel* (New York: Crossroad, 1990), 88–102.
25. Edward Schillebeeckx, *Church: The Human Story of God* (New York: Crossroad, 1990), 90.
26. Schillebeeckx, *Church*, 90.
27. Schillebeeckx, *Church*, 91.

Suffering with Suffering Creation

Evolution is a costly process, involving not only co-operation and symbiosis, but also creatures preying on other creatures and competing for resources. Random mutations provide novelty that enables evolutionary emergence, but they more often bring damage and suffering. Death is intrinsic to the pattern of evolutionary emergence that can occur only through a series of generations. The costs of evolution, and above all the terrible costs of human violence, have raised important theological questions not only about God's power, but also about God's engagement with the suffering of creatures.

Does God suffer with suffering creatures? For thinkers like Irenaeus and Athanasius, the concept of divine impassibility defends the biblical and Christian concept of the radical transcendence of God and does this precisely in opposition to Hellenistic views. At the centre of their thought is the Christian concept of *creatio ex nihilo*. Because God is radically other than all creatures, God can enable the whole world of creatures to exist constantly and faithfully. God's impassibility defends divine otherness against tendencies to see God as trapped within the vicissitudes of creation, as at the mercy of changing human emotions, or as arbitrary and fickle like pagan gods or human tyrants. It points to the constancy and fidelity of divine love in creation, salvation and final fulfilment.

These are fundamentals of Christian theology that must, and can, be safeguarded, I believe, in a contemporary theology of a God who suffers with suffering creation. The way forward is by reflection on the Trinitarian, eternal, constant passion of love that freely chooses to create a world of creatures, and to embrace these creatures in the incarnation. The particularity of the incarnation can teach us that this divine passionate love is not only general, but engages with the particular and the concrete. Divine passionate love embraces each specific creature in the divine act of creation and new creation in Christ. In the light of the Incarnation and the cross, it is appropriate to speak of God's compassionate suffering with suffering creation as long as compassionate suffering with creatures is affirmed of God by way of analogy and where it is understood that God's capacity for feeling with creation, springing from eternal divine passionate love, is a capacity that God possesses in a completely transcendent way, infinitely beyond human capacities for empathy with others.

Walter Kasper points out that to speak of divine suffering with creation is not the expression of a lack in God, but the expression of a capacity to love in a transcendent and divine way. God does not suffer from lack of being, but suffers out of love that is the overflow of the divine being.[28] Suffering does not befall God, but expresses the divine freedom to love. A self-giving love involves allowing the other to affect oneself. Thus, 'suffering and love go together'.[29] This is not a passive being-affected, but a free, active allowing the other to affect oneself. Because God is love, God can suffer with us. For Elizabeth Johnson, too, analogical speech about the suffering of God does not mean that God suffers because of some intrinsic deficiency, or because of some external force. It does not mean that God suffers by necessity or that God suffers passively. It points, rather, 'to an act of freedom, the freedom of love deliberately and generously shared'.[30] Divine suffering with us springs from the compassionate loving act of the triune God in creating a world of creatures and embracing them in redemptive love.

Christian believers are surely right to see in the cross the symbol of a God who loves us with a love that involves a compassion, a suffering with us, beyond any human capacity for being with another in their pain. It is not that the human physical and emotional states of Jesus are simply transferred to the life of the eternal Trinity. It is rather that the passionate love of God-with-us expressed in the cross represents the truth of the transcendent God's capacity to be with creatures in boundless passionate love. The Gospel tradition of the glorious risen Christ still bearing the wounds of the cross suggests that the sufferings of creation are forever remembered and taken up in the healing, compassionate love of God.

Beauty and Violence in Nature and the Work of Love

Annie Dillard's *Pilgrim at Tinker Creek* is a powerful reflection on the natural world, based on a year of living quietly at Tinker Creek,

---

28. The Jewish theologian, Abraham Heschel, contrasts the biblical theology of divine pathos, expressed in the prophetic literature, with the Greek philosophical concept of God's immutability; see Abraham J Heschel, *The Prophets*, volume 2 (New York: Harper & Row, 1962) 1–47.
29. Kasper, *God of Jesus Christ*, 196.
30. Elizabeth Johnson, *She Who Is: The Mystery of God in Feminist Theological Discourse* (New York: Crossroad, 1992), 266–7.

in the Roanoke Valley of Virginia, observing nature closely, backed by wide reading in the sciences and in theology.³¹ Her work asks fundamental questions: Is the natural world unutterably beautiful, so that if we took the time to really see we would be transformed? Or is it extremely wasteful and violent in a way that we seldom face? The same questions arise for many who watch the brilliantly executed television documentaries on the natural world presented by David Attenborough and others.

I am convinced that the natural world is profoundly beautiful, and that its beauty has always nourished human existence, art and spirituality. Over and over again, in ever new ways, it is experienced as absolute gift. But it is also deeply ambiguous. No one can delight in the predation, the pain and the enormous scale of loss in nature. In our time, we know, in a way that earlier generations did not, that the costs are not extrinsic but profoundly built into evolutionary emergence and the way the natural world functions. The beautiful and the violent are in many cases two sides of the one reality. As Holmes Rolston puts it, 'The cougar's fangs have carved the limbs of the fleet-footed deer, and vice versa.'³²

So can we affirm without reservation, simply from observation, that the natural world is unambiguously good? I think that, from empirical observation alone, this could be said only with important reservations. Biblical faith, of course, does pronounce creation as good. But as Christopher Southgate notes, in his important treatment of these issues, biblical faith actually affirms both the 'good' and the 'groaning' of creation.³³ Without revelation, simply on the basis of observation and reason, it is possible to come to the conclusion that there is a Creator, and to believe in the goodness of the Creator. But there are also real obstacles in the way of these positions because of the ambiguity and violence in the natural world, of which we humans are a part.

For Christianity, the affirmation that creation is unambiguously the work of love is an affirmation that comes from revelation in Christ. It is affirmed on the basis of faith in the God revealed in Christ and in

---

31. Annie Dillard, *Pilgrim at Tinker Creek* (New York: HarperPerennial, 1974, 1999).
32. Holmes Rolston III, *Science and Religion: A Critical Survey* (1987; repr., Philadelphia and London: Templeton Foundation Press, 2006), 134.
33. Christopher Southgate, *The Groaning of Creation: God, Evolution and the Problem of Evil* (Louisville: Westminster John Knox Press, 2008), 1–18.

hope in this God's eschatological healing and fulfilment. The nature of God is revealed in Jesus of Nazareth, in his life, death and resurrection, as a God of radical love. On this basis, on faith, we can affirm not only the unqualified goodness of the Creator, but also the unqualified goodness of creation when it is fulfilled in Christ. Meanwhile creation is 'groaning in labor pains until now, and not only the creation, but we ourselves, who have the first fruits of the Spirit, groan inwardly while we wait for our adoption, the redemption of our bodies' (Rom 8:22–23). The rest of the natural world, too, needs redemption, healing and transfiguration in Christ. What is not obvious to empirical observation can be affirmed in the light of Christ: the natural world is entirely the work of divine love, destined for fulfilment in God. It was long ago affirmed on the basis of Jewish faith by the author of the Wisdom of Solomon:

> For you love all things that exist,and detest none of the things that you have made,for you would not have made anything if you had hated it. How would anything have endured if you had not willed it? Or how would anything not called forth by you have been preserved?
> You spare all things, for they are yours, O Lord, you who love the living.
> For your immortal spirit is in all things (Wis 11:24-12:1).

Bibliography

Aquinas, Thomas, *Summa Theologiae*. In *St Thomas Aquinas Summa Theologiae*, Volume 5, translated by Thomas Gilby (Cambridge: Blackfriars, 1967). In *St Thomas Aquinas Summa Theologiae*, Volume 14, translated by TC O'Brien (Cambridge: Blackfriars, 1975).

Athanasius of Alexandria, *Orations against the Arians*, translated in Khaled Anatolios, *Athanasius* (London and New York: Routledge, 2004).

Athanasius of Alexandria, *On the Incarnation*, translated in RW Thompson, *Athanasius, Contra Gentes and de Incarnatione* (Oxford, Clarendon Press, 1971).

Athanasius of Alexandria, *Letters to Serapion*, translated in Anatolios, *Athanasius*.

Bauckham, Richard, *Bible and Ecology: Rediscovering the Community of Creation* (London: Darton, Longman & Todd, 2010).

Dillard, Annie, *Pilgrim at Tinker Creek* (New York: HarperPerennial, 1974).

Egan, Harvey, 'Theology and Spirituality', in *The Cambridge Companion to Karl Rahner*, edited by Declan Marmion and Mary E Hines (Cambridge: Cambridge University Press, 2005), 13–28.

Feuillet, André, *Johannine Studies* (Staten Island, NY: Alba House, 1964).

Finch, Jeffrey, 'Athanasius on the Deifying Word of the Redeemer', in *Theōsis: Deification in Christian Theology*, edited by Stephen Final and Vladimir Kharlamov (Cambridge, UK: James Clarke & Co, 2006), 104–21.

Johnson, Elizabeth, *She Who Is: The Mystery of God in Feminist Theological Discourse* (New York: Crossroad, 1992).

Kasper, Walter, *The God of Jesus Christ* (London, SCM, 1983).

Rahner, Karl, *Hominisation: The Evolutionary Origin of Man as a Theological Problem* (London: Burns and Oates, 1965).

Rahner, Karl, 'Christology within an Evolutionary View of the World', in *Theological Investigations* 5 (Baltimore: Helicon Press, 1966), 157–92.

Rahner, Karl, 'Immanent and Transcendent Consummation of the World', in *Theological Investigations* 10 (London: Darton, Longman & Todd, 1973), 281–89.

Rahner, Karl, 'Christology in the Setting of Modern Man's Understanding of himself and of his World', in *Theological Investigations* 11 (New York: Seabury Press, 1974), 215–29.

Rahner, Karl, 'Resurrection: D Theology', in *Encyclopedia of Theology: A Concise Sacramentum Mundi*, edited by Karl Rahner (London: Burns and Oates, 1975), 1440–2.

Rahner, Karl, *Foundations of Christian Faith: An Introduction to the Idea of Christianity* (New York: Seabury, 1978).

Rolston, Holmes, *Science and Religion: A Critical Survey.* 1987. Reprint, (Philadelphia and London: Templeton Foundation Press, 2006).

Schillebeeckx, Edward, *For the Sake of the Gospel* (New York: Crossroad, 1990).

Schillebeeckx, Edward, *Church: The Human Story of God* (New York: Crossroad, 1990).

Southgate, Christopher, *The Groaning of Creation: God, Evolution and the Problem of Evil* (Louisville: Westminster John Knox Press, 2008).

Witherington III, Ben, *John's Wisdom* (Louisville: Westminster/John Knox, 1995).

The Attractor and the Energy of Love: Trinity in Evolutionary and Ecological Context

In the Greek-speaking world in which the Gospel was first preached and the doctrine of the Trinity emerged, permanence and stability were highly prized. Amidst the turmoil of personal and political life, the world itself seemed relatively stable. Our twenty-first century worldview is radically different. After Einstein and Hubble, we know that we are part of an observable universe made up of more than a hundred billion galaxies, all of them in motion, a dynamic universe that has been expanding and evolving from a tiny, dense and hot state over the last 13.7 billion years. And after Darwin, we know that all life on Earth has evolved by means of natural selection from the first forms of microbial life that appeared on our planet about 3.7 billion years ago. At the same time, we face a looming crisis of life on our planet because of human actions.

Stability no longer characterises our worldview. We belong to a universe of constant motion and emergent processes. We are confronted by the reality that we are contributing to global climate change and to an increasing loss of Earth's biodiversity. How is the Christian community to speak of its God in this new context? What difference does it make to our classical understanding of the Trinity to think about such a God in relation to an evolutionary worldview? How might this theology of God inform our ecological action? I will begin to explore these questions by briefly outlining a theology of the Trinity that I find meaningful in this context, that of Athanasius. Then I will explore three theological developments of the classical tradition for an evolutionary and ecological context: 1. The Word as Attractor and the Spirit as the Energy of Love in evolutionary emergence; 2. The Costs of Evolution and the Divine Passion of Love; 3. The Defencelessness of the humble God in creation.

Athanasius: Creation and Deification through the Word, In the Spirit

For Athanasius, the universe of creatures is continually held in being over an abyss of nothing by God's creative Word. Creatures exist only because they participate in God, by partaking of the creative Word:

> But being good, he governs and establishes the whole world through his Word who is himself God, in order that creation, illuminated by the leadership, providence and ordering of the Word, may be able to remain firm, since it shares in the Word who is truly from the Father and is aided by him to exist, and lest it suffer what would happen, I mean a relapse into nonexistence, if it were not protected by the Word.[1]

Creatures exist because they 'share in' or 'partake of' the Word. After not paying much attention to the Holy Spirit in his early works, Athanasius makes it clear in his later writings that he sees the Spirit as fully divine immanent presence of God, as the divine energy and the bond that unites creatures to the Word. It is, then, in the Holy Spirit that creatures partake of the Word. For Athanasius, both creation and deification occur through participation in the triune God: 'The Father creates and renews all things through the Word in the Spirit'.[2] Before turning to Athanasius's theology of deification, I will discuss three aspects of his theology of creation that I find meaningful in an evolutionary and ecological context.

The first is the immediacy of the triune God to creatures. For Athanasius's opponents, the divine dignity of the Creator rules out a direct relationship with creatures. For them, the created Word serves as a 'buffer' between God and creation.[3] But for Athanasius, by con-

---

1. Athanasius, *Against the Pagans,* 41. Translations of *Against the Pagans* (*C gent*) and *On the Incarnation* (*Inc*) are taken from Robert W Thompson, *Athanasius: Contra Gentes and De Incarnatione,* (Oxford: Clarendon Press, 1971).
2. Athanasius, *Letters to Serapion on the Holy Spirit,* 1.24. Translations of Athanasius's *Letters to Serapion* (*Ep Serap*), *Orations Against the Arians, and Letter 40: To Adelphius* are taken from Khaled Anatolios, *Athanasius* (Routledge, London and New York: Routledge, 2004). Hereafter abbreviated as '*C Ar*' and '*Ep Ad*', respectively.
3. Peter J Leithart, *Athanasius* (Grand Rapids, Michigan: Baker Academic, 2001), 91.

trast, there is no such buffer. He agrees with his opponents on the radical otherness of the Creator and on the biblical conviction that God engages with creation through the Word. But he will not accept their view of the Word as a created intermediary. He insists that the Word shares fully the Father's very essence. And it is precisely as fully divine that the Word can bridge the gap between Creator and creatures in loving condescension.[4] The ontological distinction between God and all creatures is bridged solely from God's side, in loving divine generosity, and not by any intermediary. Because Word and Spirit are one with the Father's essence, the Word's mediation in the Spirit involves the immediacy of the Father.[5] The triune God is immediately present to each creature through the Word and in the Spirit, present in self-humbling love, immanent to it in a way that no creature could ever be. This view of the immediacy of God to creatures has consequences for the way we value and treat other creatures.

Second, Athanasius sees the fruitfulness and diversity of creation as springing from the dynamic fruitfulness of the Trinity. He asks: If God is simply a monad, if there were no dynamism in God, no generation of the other, how could we possibly account for the creation of a world of creatures? He asks: 'But if, according to them, the divine essence itself is not fruitful but barren, like a light that does not shine and a fountain that is dry, how are they not ashamed to say that God has creative energy?'[6] It is only because of the generativity of the divine life, where the light shines brilliantly and the fountain flows freely, that God then freely creates a world of creatures in the Word and in the Spirit. The fruitfulness of the evolutionary processes at work on Earth are all grounded in the dynamic fruitfulness of the Trinity, the divine Fountain, endlessly pouring forth the River of Living Water, from which all creation drinks in the Spirit.

Athanasius's third insight is his situating of creation within the joyful relations of the divine persons. Athanasius recalls the words of Wisdom, God's companion in the creation of all things, from Proverbs 8: 'then I was beside him, like a master worker; and I was daily his delight' (Prov 8:30). He sees the biblical teaching of God's delight in Wisdom as pointing to the eternal delight within the life of the

---

4. *C Ar*, 2.64.
5. Khaled Anatolios, *Athanasius: The Coherence of his Thought*. (London and New York: Routledge, 1998), 113.
6. *C Ar*, 2.2.

divine persons and he locates God's joy in creation within this divine delight. His argument is that Wisdom cannot be thought of as being created and having a beginning, but must always have been God's delight:

> When was it then that the Father did not rejoice? But if he has always rejoiced, then there was always the one in whom he rejoiced . . . For he did not delight in this way by acquiring delight as an addition to himself, but it was upon seeing the works that were made according to his own image, so that the basis of this delight also is God's own Image.[7]

Creation takes place within the mutual love and delight of the divine persons. God's delight in creatures is enfolded within the mutual delight of the Father and the Son.[8]

This rich, Trinitarian theology of creation is profoundly interconnected with Athanasius's theology of the incarnation. The Word in whom all things are created is the Word of the Cross. In the sacrificial Word of the Cross we find our forgiveness, the overcoming of death and the true revelation of God. In his theology of the cross, Athanasius takes up various images and concepts of salvation from Paul and from Hebrews. But he also builds on Irenaeus to offer an overarching theory of salvation as deification: 'For he became human that we might become divine.'[9]

This theology of deification is closely linked to the Pauline idea that by the grace of the indwelling Spirit we are adopted into the life of God (Gal 4:7; Rom 8:16) and transformed in Christ (2 Cor 3:18). By the grace of the Holy Spirit, we participate in the crucified and risen Christ. We are enfolded in the inner life of the Trinity, and as adopted daughters and sons are taken up in the position of the Word in relation to the Father.[10]

For Athanasius, deification is a radical ontological transformation in creaturely reality. Because of the incarnation, there is a divine transformation already at work in humanity and not just in humanity but in the whole creation. Athanasius's concern, of course, is not that

---

7. *C Ar*, 2:82.
8. Anatolios, 118, 153–4, 288.
9. *Inc*, 54.
10. *C Ar*, 1:46; 2:59. See Anatolios, 125.

of a twenty-first century ecological theology. His concern is with the full divinity of the Word made flesh, the divinity of the one in whom we participate and are deified. While Athanasius's direct focus is on humanity, he sees the whole creation as in some way sharing with humanity in deification and final fulfilment. He speaks frequently of the deification of creation, without distinguishing between humans and other creatures.

At times, he explicitly includes the rest of creation in liberation in Christ. He speaks, for example, of Christ as 'the Liberator of all flesh and of all creation'.[11] He refers to Colossians 1:15–20 and Romans 8:19–23 and writes of the Father's philanthropy, 'on account of which he not only gave consistence to all things in his Word but brought it about that the creation itself', of which the apostle says that it 'awaits the revelation of the children of God', will at a certain point be delivered 'from the bondage of corruption into the glorious freedom of the children of God' (Rom 8:19, 21).[12]

I see Athanasius as offering the basis for a renewed theology of creation and salvation that involves the whole creation, but one that needs to be developed in the light of evolution emergence and our twenty-first century ecological context. I will take up three of these developments, concerning, first, the roles of the Word and the Spirit in evolutionary emergence, second, the divine passion of love for creatures and, third, the humility of the Creator in accepting the limits of creaturely processes.

The Word as Attractor and the Spirit as Energy of Love

The evolutionary nature of the universe invites us to think again about God. It suggests that we need a theology in which the triune God is seen not only as the source of the existence of the natural world but also of its wonderful fruitfulness, creativity and novelty. We need a theology of a God who, like Mother Carey in Charles Kingsley's *The Water Babies*, 'can make things make themselves'.[13] I will outline such a theology, in Trinitarian terms, with the Holy Spirit understood as

---

11. *Ep Ad*, 4.
12. *C Ar*, 2.63.
13. Charles Kingsley, *The Water-Babies: A Fairy Tale for a Land-Baby* (New York: Hart Publishing Company, 1977), 255–6.

the immanent Energy of Love and the Word of God as the divine Attractor in evolutionary emergence. In taking this approach, I hold to the traditional view that the Trinity's actions with regard to creation are one and undivided, but also propose that something specific can be said of the persons in the unity of their one act.[14]

The Spirit as the Energy of Love in Evolutionary Emergence

Karl Rahner has made an important contribution to theology in an evolutionary context with his idea of the Creator enabling the active 'self-transcendence' of creatures.[15] The effect of God's creative presence to creatures is that it gives them the capacity to become something new, to transcend themselves. It is God who enables this process. But the God-given capacity for emergence truly belongs to the creaturely world. It occurs through all the processes of evolutionary emergence studied in the sciences. Rahner's insight transforms the classical theology of creation, enabling it to function in a new, evolutionary era. I am proposing two modifications of Rahner's theology. First, instead of 'self-transcendence' I will speak of the natural world's own 'evolutionary emergence'. By the relationship of creation, the Creator, then, confers on the creaturely world the capacity for its own evolutionary emergence. Second, I will explore this as a Trinitarian theology of the Spirit, envisioning the Spirit as the Energy of Love enabling the evolutionary emergence of our universe and all its creatures.

The proposal, then, is to see this Spirit as immanently present to all the entities of our universe, enabling creatures to exist, to interact and emerge into the new by means of the laws of nature and the processes discussed in the natural sciences. The capacity for emergence, for increase in complexity through self-organisational processes at work throughout the universe, and for the evolution of life on Earth by means of natural selection, is interior to creaturely reality. It belongs to the natural world. The capacity for emergence comes from within.

---

14. I have argued this in some detail in my *Breath of Life: A Theology of the Creator Spirit* (New York, Maryknoll: Orbis, 2004).
15. Karl Rahner, *Foundations of Christian Faith: An Introduction to the Idea of Christianity*. (New York: Seabury Press, 1978), 183–7.

At the empirical level of science, the emergence of the new is completely open to explanation at the scientific level.

The Spirit's presence and action operates at a level that entirely transcends the empirical. In *A Brief History of Time*, physicist Stephen Hawking asks a famous question:

> Even if there is only one possible unified theory, it is just a set of rules and equations. *What is it that breathes fire into the equations* and makes a universe for them to describe? The usual approach of science of constructing a mathematical model cannot answer the questions of why there should be a universe for the model to describe. Why does the universe go to all the bother of existing?[16]

Theology does have its response to this question. It sees God as breathing the fire of the Spirit into the equations. It sees the Holy Spirit as breathing life into the laws of nature and the natural processes by which the universe and life emerge. The Spirit can be imaged as the blazing flame that confronts Moses in the burning bush (Ex 3:2), the whirlwind that is the place of God for Job (38:1), and in 'the sound of sheer silence' that is the sign of the divine presence for Elijah (1 Kgs 19:12). The Spirit is the Breath of Life of the Scriptures (Gen 2:7; Job 34:14–15; Ps 33:6; Ps 104:27–30; Ez 37:3–10) and the Life-Giver of the Creed.

The Holy Spirit can be understood as the dynamic life-giving presence of God to the whole process of the emergence of a universe, uniting it, and every part of it, to the Word in the relationship of continuous creation. It is this relationship that enables the existence of entities and their becoming. Without this relationship, there is no existence and no emergence. The relationship with the Spirit enables both.

Emergence is a creaturely reality, but it occurs because of God's ongoing creative presence in the Spirit. It is God's immediate Trinitarian presence in the life-giving Spirit that enables creatures to exist, to interact and to emerge into the wonderfully new. The Spirit is at work in the emergence of the first atoms of the early universe, the birth of galaxies and stars, the development of our solar system around the

---

16. Stephen Hawking, *A Brief History of Time: From the Big Bang to Black Holes* (New York: Bantam, 1988), 174.

young Sun, the origin of the first microbial life on Earth, the flourishing of life in all its diversity and the emergence of humans with their highly developed brains.

The Risen Christ as Divine Attractor in Evolutionary Emergence

What can be said about the relationship between the Word that is made flesh in Jesus and the evolving universe? I find a beginning in a proposal of the Polish philosopher and Archbishop of Lublin, Jósef Życiński (1948–2011). He argues that an evolutionary view requires us to go beyond the traditional idea of God as the divine planner. He suggests replacing this image with an analogy taken from the role of an attractor in dynamic systems, so that God is thought of as the 'Cosmic Attractor' of evolution.[17]

Życiński takes the analogy of the attractor from its use in mathematics and physics. In mathematics, it names a set or a point that 'attracts' points from its surroundings. In physics it is used to describe the thermodynamic evolution of physical systems, where the system is directed toward a state that appears to be attracting the whole system to itself.[18] Although Życiński does not refer to it, the idea of the attractor is also found in astronomy, where the 'Great Attractor' names a part of the universe that exercises a powerful gravitational pull on the Milky Way and thousands of other galaxies—although more recently it has been discovered that much of this gravitational attraction comes from a massive cluster of galaxies beyond the Great Attractor.

I will take up Życiński's analogy in a Trinitarian and Christological way, proposing that the eternal Word of God can be imaged as the divine Attractor in the emergence of the universe and of its individual entities, and that the Word made flesh, Jesus crucified and now risen from the dead, can be thought of as the Attractor not only of evolutionary emergence but also of the final transformation and fulfilment of the whole creation. It is, of course, important to insist that this attraction is not any kind of physical action, but the divine act that

---

17. Jósef Życiński, *God and Evolution: Fundamental Questions of Christian Evolutionism* (Washington, DC: The Catholic University of America Press, 2006), 161.
18. Życiński, *God and Evolution*, 162.

we call God's creation of a world of creatures. The power of attraction is the bond of divine creative love, the presence and action of the indwelling Spirit. The Holy Spirit, the power of the new, *is* this indwelling attraction, drawing all things to the Word of God.

Earlier, I discussed Athanasius's view of each creature as existing by partaking of the Word through the indwelling Spirit. In evolutionary terms, Athanasius's idea can be developed so that the Word is understood as the divine Attractor, drawing into existence galaxies, stars and planets, and then, on Earth, calling into existence through evolutionary processes all the diverse species of microbes, insects, birds, fish, and animals, including human beings. The divine Word draws each species to its own identity and place in evolutionary emergence. Not only each species, but each member of each species, each sparrow, is held in the divine memory and embraced in the divine love, as a word of the Word, an expression of divine Wisdom in our world.

The incarnation of the Word is, then, the incarnation of the Attractor of evolutionary emergence. As John's Gospel tells us, all things were made through the Word (Jn 1:3) and this Word of creation is made flesh in our midst (Jn 1:14). In this line of thought, there is a profound connection between the evolutionary emergence of a universe of creatures and what happens in the birth, life, death and resurrection of the Saviour. In the theology of John's Gospel, and in the subsequent Christian theology of the incarnation, the whole creation is directed towards this event in some way, and is transformed by it.

In the resurrection of the crucified Jesus, the Word of God is forever flesh, but earthly, bodily reality, now transfigured in glory. The risen Christ is the promise and the beginning of new creation for the whole of reality. The incarnate Word, the crucified and risen Christ, can thus be seen as the Attractor of the whole creation, not just to its evolutionary existence, but to its transfiguration and fulfilment. And the Holy Spirit is the enabling power at work in this whole process—the very attraction, the drawing power of love, the life-giving presence at work in it all.

To say that the risen Christ is the Attractor of the whole process of evolutionary emergence is to speak in evolutionary terms about the promises of a future for all things in Christ that are already contained in the Scriptures (Rom 8:21; Col 1:19–20; Eph 1:8–10). One of the advantages of the analogy of the Attractor is its not-anthropomorphic character. It points to the fulfilment and transfiguration of a creaturely and cosmic world far beyond the human. But I see it as having the further advantage that it can also be understood in a personal way as offering meaning for human beings on their journeys. The gospels tell us of a Jesus who attracts great crowds in Galilee, who draws followers to himself, who involves them in a life-long relationship, and calls them to become active participants in his mission on behalf of the kingdom of God. Jesus attracts not only adults but also the children and tells those who would move them away: 'Let the little children come to me; do not stop them; for it is to such as these that the kingdom of God belongs' (Mk 10:14).

In the Wisdom books of the Bible, the Wisdom of God is presented as an attractive Woman, who invites all to the feast she has prepared: 'Come, eat of my bread and drink of the wine I have mixed' (Prov 9:5); 'Come to me, you who desire me, and eat your fill of my fruits' (Sir 24:19). In the New Testament, Jesus-Wisdom invites to his inclusive table all those in need, including the poor, the sinners, the socially unacceptable. In a particular way, he reaches out to draw to himself all those who struggle in life with weariness, pain and grief: 'Come to me, all you that are weary and are carrying heavy burdens, and I will give you rest. Take my yoke upon you, and learn from me; for I am gentle and humble in heart, and you will find rest for your souls. For my yoke is easy, and my burden is light' (Matt 11:28–30).

At the most human level, Jesus-Wisdom draws us human beings to himself in the ups and downs of existence, attracting us, even in our resistances, into our own new, not only in our lives but also, and above all, in our deaths. In John's Gospel, we are told explicitly that it is the Father's doing when we are drawn to Jesus (6:43–6) and we find Jesus crying out 'Let anyone who is thirsty come to me, and let the one who believes in me drink' (Jn 7:37–38). Perhaps the deepest theology of Jesus as Attractor is found in the Johannine image of Jesus being lifted up and attracting all to himself as the crucified and risen one: 'And I, when I am lifted up from the earth, will draw all people to myself' (Jn 12:32).

In the light of the many other texts that speak of 'all things' being transfigured in the risen Christ, it is appropriate to see Jesus lifted up in the cross and resurrection as the divine Attractor for the whole universe of creatures in its evolutionary emergence. This theological claim is not warranted by the sciences but by Christian faith in the crucified and risen Christ. It tells a story of hope. In dialogue with evolutionary science, but based on its own sources, it can tell a story of evolutionary emergence as participation in the life of God.

The Costs of Evolution and the Divine Passion of Love

Evolutionary biology has shown us that the emergence of life has costs built into the process. Not only co-operation but also competition, predation, pain and death are intrinsic to evolution. The costs of evolution are not the result of something gone wrong. They are part of the process of the evolutionary development of life. An evolutionary view of the world intensifies the age-old theological problem of evil. In my view, there is no adequate intellectual answer to the problem of evil, but an evolutionary theology of God must address this issue as best it can. I think three fundamental things can be said. The first and most important has already been discussed, that God hears the groaning of creation, embraces it in the incarnation and the cross and, in the resurrection, promises creation's deliverance and fulfilment. The second, taken up here, is that God cares passionately about creation and suffers with it in its groaning. The third, discussed in the next section, is that God humbly respects and waits upon the unfolding of creation according to its own dynamisms.

Does God Suffer with Creatures?

This always difficult question has been unavoidable in theology since the horrors of World War II, above all since the Holocaust. It is also unavoidable in an evolutionary and ecological theology of creation. There is an important Christian tradition that holds to the utter otherness of God and to God's freedom from suffering. In the context of the costs of evolution, it becomes necessary to ask: Is God free from suffering and, if so, in what sense? Does God suffer with suffering creation and, if so, in what sense?

I see the patristic theology of divine impassibility as defending the biblical concept of the radical otherness of the Creator. Paul Gavrilyuk points out that the patristic writers were not advocating an absolute impassibility that would deny 'God-befitting' emotions such as love to God. Rather, they saw impassibility as an apophatic qualifier: 'For the orthodox divine impassibility functioned as a kind an apophatic qualifier of all divine emotions and as the marker of the unmistakably divine identity'.[19] What are ruled out by the 'apophatic qualifier' are characteristics like fickleness, arbitrariness and inconstancy, and all the emotions and passions unworthy of God, the lust, jealousy, vengeance and violence attributed to mythological gods and found in human tyrants.

I am not inclined to follow Jürgen Moltmann and Hans Urs von Balthasar, who in quite different ways push the suffering and the self-emptying of the Word incarnate back into the eternal Trinitarian relations, apparently making suffering and self-emptying essential to Trinitarian life.[20] Is there another way to think about God's suffering with suffering creation? Is there an alternative to the positions of Moltmann and Balthasar, on the one hand, and of those like Thomas Weinandy[21] and Brian Davies,[22] on the other, who oppose the idea of God suffering with creation? I find a helpful resource for different kind of response in the brilliant and influential patristic thinker, Origen of Alexandria (185–254).

The Passion of Love

Origen defends the divine impassibility, and makes it clear that we cannot simply take the Bible literally when it attributes all-too-human emotions to God. But he clearly thinks that we can speak about God suffering for and with creation, in the specific sense that God suffers out of the eternal divine passion of love for creatures. In a beautiful passage from his *Commentary on Ezekiel*, he writes:

> Let me offer a human example; then, if the Holy Spirit grants it, I will move on to Jesus Christ and God the Father. When I speak to a man and plead with him for some matter, that he should have pity on me, if he is a man without pity, he does

---

19. Paul Gavrilyuk, *The Suffering of the Impassible God: The Dialectics of Patristic Thought*. (Oxford: Oxford University Press, Oxford, 2004), 173.
20. Jürgen Moltmann, *The Trinity and the Kingdom of God: The Doctrine of God* (San Francisco: Harper & Row, 1981), 81; Hans Urs von Balthasar, *Theo-Drama: Theological Dramatic Theory*, volume V, *The Last Act* (San Francisco: Ignatius Press, 1998), 268.
21. Thomas Weinandy, *Does God Suffer?* (Edinburgh: T&T Clark, Edinburgh, 2000).
22. Brian Davies, *The Reality of God and the Problem of Evil* (London: Continuum, 2006).

not suffer anything from the things I say. But if he is a man of gentle spirit, and not hardened and rigid in his heart, he hears me and has pity upon me. And his feelings are softened by my requests. Understand something of this kind with regard to the Savior. He came down to earth out of compassion for the human race. Having experienced our sufferings even before he suffered on the cross, he condescended to assume our flesh. For if he had not suffered, he would not have come to live on the level of human life. First, he suffered; then he came down and was seen (cf 1 Tim 3:16). What is this suffering that he suffered for us? It is *the passion of love (caritatis est passio)*. The Father, too, himself, the God of the universe, 'patient and abounding in mercy' (Ps 103:8) and compassionate does he not in some way suffer? Or do you not know that when he directs human affairs he suffers human suffering? For 'the Lord your God bore your ways, as a man bears his son' (Deut 1:31). Therefore God bears our ways, just as the Son of God bears our suffering. The Father himself is not without suffering. When he is prayed to, he has pity and compassion; he suffers *the passion of love (patitur aliquid caritatis)* and comes into those in whom he cannot be, in view of the greatness of his nature, and on account of us he endures human sufferings.[23]

Henri De Lubac highlights this text in his discussion of Origen's view of God, exclaiming that it is 'one of the finest pages, without doubt, one of the most humane and the most Christian pages we have from him . . . An astonishing, wonderful text!'[24] Beginning with a very human example, Origen imagines himself in dire need and asking for help and mercy from another. He describes two responses, the first of a man with no pity. Such a person, Origen tells us, does not *suffer* anything when hearing the sad story. The second is that of a man of gentle spirit, who hears the need of the other and has pity. Origen

---

23. Origen: *Homilies on Ezekiel* 6:3, translation by Thomas P Scheck, *Homilies 1-14 On Ezekiel, Ancient Christian Writers*, 62 (New York: Newman Press, 2010), 92–3. I have modified the translation of the two italicised phrases, highlighting Origen's declaration that the Word suffers 'the passion of love', and his use of an equivalent expression of the Father.
24. Henri De Lubac, *History and Spirit: The Understanding of Scripture according to Origen* (San Francisco: Ignatius Press, 2007), 275.

comments that the first man does not 'suffer' anything when hearing the sad story. This person, Origen seems to be thinking, does not feel the pain of another, and therefore is not moved by it. He does not 'walk in the shoes' of the other. In the second case, we find a person who is capable of empathy, who can imagine being in another's shoes, who has not hardened himself against feeling for the other.

Origen then applies this line of thought to the Saviour. The person who is capable of suffering with another gives us some insight into the Word of God, as one who feels with, who suffers with, suffering creatures. Origen insists that the Word comes to us in the incarnation out of compassion. He makes the point that the Word experiences our sufferings *before* the incarnation. If the Word did not suffer with us, and did not in some way feel our pain, then the Word would not come to us. In his view, then, the motivation for the incarnation is the divine feeling, the divine passion for creatures in their need. The Word comes to us, he tells us, because of the 'the *passion of love*'.

What of the Father, the Creator of the universe? Origen is emphatic that the Father, too, is not impassible but, like the Word, suffers with creatures. I have already pointed out that there is an important sense in which Origen thinks of God as being impassible. But in this text, he shows that there is a real (analogous) sense in which the Father suffers with creatures, out of divine compassion, in the divine passion of love. He tells us that when we approach God in prayer, the Father is moved with compassion, and suffers with us. God the Father, like the Word, suffers *the passion of love*. There is, of course, Jesus's own image of this com-passion in his vivid picture of the father in the parable of the Prodigal Son: 'But while he was still far off, his father saw him and was filled with compassion; he ran and put his arms around him and kissed him' (Lk 15:16).

There is, then, a divine passion of love for needy and suffering creation. This passion is, analogically speaking, a suffering with creatures, a divine feeling for human beings in their need and for the whole creation in its groaning. The passion of love is the overflow of the mutual love of the divine persons in the life of the Trinity. It is the eternal love of the divine Communion turned towards creatures, the dynamic love that is identical with the divine nature—'God is love' (1 Jn 4:8).

Paul tells us that the whole creation is groaning, waiting to be liberated from its bondage to decay and to share in the glorious freedom of the children of God (Rom 8:2). He speaks of us human beings, who already have the Spirit, as groaning while we await our adoption and bodily transformation (Rom 8:23). He then goes deeper, describing the Holy Spirit as groaning with us, expressing the longing that is too deep for words (Rom 8:26).

Origen's theology encourages us to see our universe, and our Earth with all its diverse creatures, and the 'groaning' of these creatures because of the costs of evolution, as held with the divine passionate love of the Trinity. They are held in a love of the Trinity that embraces them, that loves them with a divine passion of love, and that promises them a future where they will share in the transfiguration of all things in Christ. God is involved with the life and death of each creature, holding every single sparrow in the divine creative and life-giving memory.

The idea of a God who suffers with a divine passion for creatures has practical outcomes. It can lead not only to a response of love for the compassionate God but also a deepening of our own feeling for the community of life. If God is a God of passionate love for creation, then it can be said that our, perhaps occasional, human experiences of deep compassion for other creatures, of longing for their healing and liberation, give us a glimpse of the infinite depths of divine compassion for creatures. Elizabeth Johnson points out that speaking of a God who suffers signals that God is in solidarity with those who suffer in our world and it can bring not only consolation but also energy for our own participation in the healing of suffering.[25] It can provide a basis for hope in God's future for the creation, and thus serve as a basis for ecological practice. It challenges us to the work of the kingdom, to our own compassionate engagement in the overcoming and the relief of suffering.

A Humble God who waits upon Creaturely Processes

The costs of evolution raise questions not only about God's suffering with us, but also about divine power. Christians confess in the Creed that God is 'almighty'. They understand God as the one whose immense power and love not only create and sustain the universe but

---

25. Elizabeth A Johnson, *She Who Is: The Mystery of God in Feminist Theological Discourse* (New York: Crossroad, New York, 1992), 266–7.

will bring it to its fulfilment. What needs further discussion is the nature of this divine power. The central source for a Christian theology of divine power can be found only in the life and teaching of Jesus and its culmination in his death and resurrection. The cross reveals divine power as self-emptying, limitless love. The resurrection proclaims that this love is the most powerful thing in the universe, promising life in its fullness to the whole creation. But the God revealed in the cross is a defenceless and humble God.

The Defencelessness of Jesus and the Spirit

The power of the cross is a power-in-love. For Christians, the absolutely vulnerable human being on the cross is the revelation of the nature of this love. It is hard to imagine a more extreme picture of defenceless love than that of a tortured, naked, human being pinned to a cross and left to die. To believe in God as all-powerful is to believe in the omnipotence of divine love and in this love's eschatological victory over sin, violence, brokenness and death. The incarnation and the cross reveal a God of divine vulnerability in love, while resurrection points to the power of this love to heal and save. In the extreme vulnerability of the cross, we do not find the loss of divinity, or the absence of divinity, but the true revelation of God.[26] The vulnerable self-giving love of Christ gives expression in our finite, creaturely world to the divine nature. This love, manifest in Jesus' life and death and culminating in the liberating and transforming power of the resurrection, is the true icon of God.

In his later work, Edward Schillebeeckx wrote of the defencelessness and vulnerability of God in the cross of Jesus. In one of his essays, he outlines divine vulnerability at three different levels: God's defencelessness in creation, God's defencelessness in Jesus Christ, and the defencelessness of the Holy Spirit in the church and in the world.[27] He chooses to speak of the defencelessness of God rather than of divine powerlessness, because powerlessness and power contradict one another, whereas defencelessness and power need not. He says: 'We know from experience that those who make themselves vul-

---

26. Walter Kasper, *The God of Jesus Christ*. (London: SCM, London, 1983), 194.
27. Edward Schillebeeckx, *For the Sake of the Gospel*. (New York: Crossroad, 1990), 88–102.

nerable can sometimes disarm evil!'[28] God was not powerless when Jesus was hung on the cross, but God was 'defenseless and vulnerable as Jesus was vulnerable'.[29]

The Holy Spirit empowers the church community to be the effective sign of Christ to the World. The Spirit breathes through the wider human community drawing it to life, to justice, to peace, to love and to care for the rest of God's creation. But the Spirit of God is present in the world as defenceless love, a love that does not overpower, but depends on human participation. The Christian community at Ephesus is told: 'do not grieve the Holy Spirit of God, with which you were marked with a seal for the day of redemption' (Eph 4:30). It would seem that the Spirit is grieved when the church fails to listen to the signs of the times in the light of the Word, and refuses to be open to the new of God. And the Spirit is grieved when the humanity fails to respond to the needs of the poor and to issues like global climate change and the increasing loss of biodiversity that confront the community of life on Earth.

In God's act of creation, Schillebeeckx sees a kind of divine yielding on God's part, as God makes room for the other. When God creates humans and chooses them as covenant partners, this partnership involves freedom and initiative on both sides. In giving creative space to human beings, God makes God's self vulnerable. Schillebeeckx says of God's act of creation that it is 'an adventure, full of risks'. The creation of human beings is a 'blank cheque which God alone guarantees'. By creating human beings with their finite, free wills, God freely renounces power, and this makes God 'to a high degree "dependent" on human beings and thus vulnerable'.[30]

The Humble God who Waits upon Creation

Athanasius sees God in creation and incarnation as self-humbling. He speaks of divine 'condescension'. This word does not have its contemporary meaning of patronising behaviour, but refers rather to the 'gratuitous descending love of God'.[31] God comes down to us in order

---

28. Edwards Schillebeeckx, *Church: The Human Story of God* (New York: Crossroad, 1993), 90.
29. Schillebeeckx, *Church*, 128.
30. Schillebeeckx, *Church*, 90.
31. Anatolios, *Athanasius*, 55.

to be with creatures. Reflecting on the Christological hymn of Philippians 2:4–8, Athanasius insists that the Word, far from being self-promoting or growing into glory or divinity, is actually self-emptying and self-humbling.[32] Christ is the descending, self-humbling God. This self-humbling is for the sake of our advancement and our deification—'The Son of God humbled himself so that in his humbling we may be able to advance'.[33]

The English adjective 'humble' translates the Latin word *humilis*. This word is derived from the word *humus*, which refers to earth, soil or the ground. In its origin, then, the word 'humble' can mean 'from the earth', 'down to earth' or 'grounded'. In following Philippians 2:8, and Athanasius, in speaking of God as humble, I am referring to God's capacity to overcome the otherness between Creator and creature, to meet us where we are, and to be with the whole creation where it is—in process. God's transcendence is not something that makes God distant. It enables the unthinkable nearness of a grounded, down to earth, God—a God not only of distant quasars, but also a God of this handful of topsoil with its billions of microbes.

The cross reveals that the way divine omnipotence works is in humility. There is every reason to believe the same power-in-love that characterises the incarnation, and the cross and resurrection, also characterises the divine relationship of continuous creation. If this is so, then God can be understood as creating in a way that respects the finite limits and the proper integrity of natural processes and the freedom of human beings. God waits upon the proper unfolding of these processes and upon human freedom

By using the language of waiting upon, I do not mean to suggest that God is passive. There is a waiting upon another that is creative and powerful—but not overpowering—in the active, nurturing way a parent waits upon a child growing into independence, or the way a lover or friend waits upon the other. This kind of waiting upon the other can allow the other over time to flourish and to possess his or her own integrity. The nature of divine love is such that God works with creaturely limits and waits upon them with infinite patience. By creating in love, God freely accepts the limitations of working with finite creatures.

---

32. *C Ar*, 1:40.
33. *C Ar*, 3:52.

God was with Jesus in his cross, holding him in love, and in the Spirit, transforming failure and death into the source of healing and transformation. Based on the true nature of God revealed in Christ, it becomes clear that in creating a universe of creatures, God's love is of a kind that respects and works with the limits of creaturely processes. The power of the triune God is a power-in-love, a divine capacity to respect the proper autonomy and independence of creatures, to work with them patiently, and to bring them to their fulfilment.

God achieves divine purposes, not by over-riding the laws of nature, but by a power-in-love that works in and through natural processes. God's power is of a kind that waits upon the otherness of creatures, which respects the integrity of human freedom and the autopoesis of self-organising natural processes. The triune God accompanies creation, delighting in its beauty and its diversity, suffering with it with the divine passion of love, responding to it creatively, and bringing all to it liberation and transfiguration. God's action, in both creation and salvation, is humble and defenceless, but powerful in the capacity to bring healing and life to the whole creation. This is a God who calls human beings to participation, to share the divine passion of love for the diverse creatures that make up the community of life and to develop a lifestyle and practices that express this passion for Earth and all it creatures.

Sketching an Ecological Theology of the Holy Spirit and the Word of God

Unlike other generations of human beings, unlike Moses, Jesus, Aquinas or Newton, we can see our planet as a whole. We have seen the photographs of Earth-rise from the moon. Astronauts have described what it is like to look at Earth from a great distance and realise that it holds all the wonderfully diverse forms of life we know, all of human history, all of human love. There is a new appreciation of Earth's hospitality to life and of belonging to one global community. We have a new imaginative picture of the interconnections of human beings with all other species and with the life-systems of the planet we share.

At the same time, we are aware of doing irretrievable damage to the forests, the land, the rivers, the seas and the atmosphere of Earth. The use of fossil fuels, along with other human actions, contributes to climate change that accelerates the extinction of many other species and will cause extreme suffering to human beings. We are destroying habitats and losing biodiversity. This betrays not only our responsibility to other forms of life, but also our human intergenerational obligations. If we continue ruthlessly to destroy forests and to exploit the land, the rivers and the seas, we will pass on to coming generations an impoverished planet, depriving our children and grandchildren of much that has brought beauty, joy and wonder to human beings, and nurtured their art and their spirituality.

Clearly this is a profoundly theological issue, and an urgent one for contemporary theology. In some ecological circles, there is an understandable impatience with what is seen as Christianity's anthropocentrism and its preoccupation with individual salvation. This anthropocentrism, it is argued, needs to be replaced by biocentrism, and the one-sided focus on redemption in Christ by a renewed theology of creation. I am convinced, however, that ecological theology, if it is to be truly Christian theology, will be neither anthropocentric nor biocentric, but radically theocentric, centred on the mystery of God revealed in Christ. And if it is to be truly Christian, it will involve not a rejection or bypassing of redemption theology, but a deeper penetration of the mystery of the incarnation and redemption to make manifest their abundant ecological meaning for our own time.

In the light of this, I will sketch three structural elements for an ecological theology that springs from the fullness of the tradition: first, it will be a theology of both Spirit and Word, a theology that is fully pneumatological and radically incarnational; second, it will be a theology of both creation and redemption in Christ; third, this redemption in Christ will involve the deifying transformation of both human beings and other creatures. I will conclude with a very brief reflection on the experience of the Creator Spirit and the Holy Wisdom in an encounter with the natural world.

An Ecological Theology of Both Spirit and Word

In the twentieth century, Yves Congar called the Western church back to a theology in which the Holy Spirit has a proper place. He accepted that there was at least a partial truth in the complaint of Orthodox theologians like Nikos Nissiotis that Western theology has tended towards *Christomonism*—a focus on Christ to the exclusion of the Spirit.[1] After his three-volume work on the Holy Spirit, Congar felt the need to write a further book showing the central importance of restoring to theology the idea of the mutual and reciprocal relationship between Word and Spirit.[2]

What he saw as fundamental to this project was an understanding of the Christ-event as an event not only of the Word but also of the Spirit. And the Spirit's work in this event was not to be restricted to the beginning of Jesus' life. Congar insists that there is a true history of the Spirit in the life and ministry of Jesus, and a true history of his divine identity as beloved Son, in his conception, his baptismal anointing, his ministry as God's servant, his death on the cross, his

---

1. Nikos A Nissiotis, 'The Main Ecclesiological Problem of the Second Vatican Council and Position of the Non-Roman Churches Facing It', in *Journal of Ecumenical Studies*, 6 (1965): 31–62. See Yves Congar, *I Believe in the Holy Spirit* 1 (London: Geoffrey Chapman, 1983), 157.
2. Yves Congar, *The Word and the Spirit* (London: Geoffrey Chapman, 1986).

resurrection and exaltation, and his pouring out of the Spirit on the disciples.[3] This historical perspective on the work of the Spirit in the life of Jesus then sets the stage for a view of the church in which the Spirit acts not only in its foundation but in a concrete and historical way in its life, so that there is always the need to invoke the Spirit anew. In both the Christ-event and in the life of the church, Congar insists, *the Word and the Spirit do God's work together.*[4]

This insight, I believe, is fundamental not just for ecclesiology, but for all Christian theology, including the development of a contemporary ecological theology. I see important resources for such a theology of Word and Spirit in the works of patristic theologians like Irenaeus, Athanasius and Ambrose. Irenaeus (c115–190) was inspired by the biblical notion of the creative power of God's Breath and God's Word: 'He is the creator, who made all things by himself, that is through his Word and his Wisdom—heaven and earth and the seas and all things that are in them'.[5] He wrote often of God acting in creation and redemption through the 'two hands' of Word and Spirit.[6] While Irenaeus holds Word and Spirit together in creation and redemption, he can also differentiate the work of the Three telling us that the Father 'plans and gives commands', the Son 'performs and creates', and the Spirit 'nourishes and increases'.[7]

Athanasius (c 296–377) vigorously affirms the divinity of the Spirit and links the Spirit closely to the one he calls the Word, the Wisdom and the Image: the Spirit is 'not outside the Word, but in the Word', and, being in the Word, the Spirit is in God.[8] Because of his conviction of the unity between the Word and Spirit, Athanasius is able to extend the existing doctrine of the creative Word in the direction of a more clearly articulated theology of the Creator Spirit: 'The Father

---

3. See Congar's *The Word and the Spirit*, 85–100.
4. See Congar's chapter under this title in *The Word and the Spirit*, 21–41.
5. *Against Heresies*, 2, 30, 9. See *The Anti-Nicene Fathers*, volume 1 (Grand Rapids: Eerdmans, 1981) 1:406). Irenaeus, of course, associates Wisdom with the Spirit. Hereafter abbreviated as '*ANF*'.
6. *Against Heresies*, 5, 28, 4 (ANF 1:557). See also *Against Heresies* 4, Pref 4 (ANF 1:463); 4, 20, 1 (ANF 1:487); 5, 6, 1 (ANF 1:531).
7. *Against Heresies*, 4, 38, 3 (ANF 1:521-2).
8. This important principle of Athanasius's pneumatology is found in his third *Letter to Serapion* 3, 5. See *The Letters of Saint Athanasius Concerning the Holy Spirit*, translated by CRB Shapland (London: Epworth Press, 1951) [hence Shapland], 175).

creates all things through the Word in the Spirit; for where the Word is, there is the Spirit also, and the things which are created through the Word have their vital strength out of the Spirit from the Word.'[9] In both creation and new creation in Christ, Athanasius insists, the Three act in one undivided act, yet in distinct ways: The Father 'creates and renews' all things through the Son and in the Holy Spirit.[10] He sees the Spirit as the one who 'joins creation to the Word'.[11] The Spirit is the bond of union between the Word and each creature in God's creative act, and the bond of union between the Word and human beings in the life of grace. It is the Holy Spirit who enables communion between creation and the Word.

Ambrose of Milan, writing in Latin and building on Greek theology, articulates a remarkably clear theology of the Creator Spirit in his *On the Holy Spirit* of 381. He insists that the Spirit is the one who brings life to creatures. With the Father and the Son, the Spirit is the Creator of all things.[12] In a particular way, he sees the grace and beauty of creation as the gift of the Spirit. The Holy Spirit, who brings us to new creation in Christ, is also powerfully at work in the original creation.[13] In a form of Spirit-Christology, Ambrose describes the Spirit as 'the author' of the incarnation. If 'the fruit of the womb is the work of the Spirit',[14] if the Spirit is responsible for the incarnation, then this suggests that there is nothing that the Spirit has not created. The Spirit of God is the *author* of both the creation and the incarnation. Ambrose concludes: 'So we cannot doubt that the Spirit is Creator, whom we know as the author of the Lord's incarnation'.[15]

All things are created through the Wisdom of God, and in the life-giving Spirit, and our redemption occurs through the incarnation of divine Wisdom in the power of the Spirit. It is this kind of understanding of mutual relationships between Spirit and Wisdom/Word that is needed, I am proposing, for an adequate ecological theology

---

9. Athanasius, *Serapion* 3, 5 (Shapland, 174).
10. Athanasius, *Serapion* 1:24 (Shapland, 127).
11. Athanasius, *Serapion* 1:25 (Shapland, 129).
12. Ambrose of Milan, *The Holy Spirit* 2, 5, 32. See *The Fathers of the Church Series*, volume 44 (Washington: The Catholic University of American Press, 1951), 107. Abbreviated hereafter as '*FOC*'.
13. Ambrose, *The Holy Spirit* 2, 5, 33-4 (FOC 44:108).
14. Ambrose, *The Holy Spirit* 2, 5, 38 (FOC 44:108).
15. Ambrose, *The Holy Spirit* 2, 5, 41 (FOC 44:110).

for today. With this in mind, I turn now to dwell explicitly on an equally fundamental structural element in such a theology: the inner relationship between creation and new creation in Christ.

An Ecological Theology of Both Creation and Redemption in Christ

The proposal I will take up in this section, then, is that a truly Christian ecological theology will be found not by contrast to the theology of redemption, but in holding creation and the redemptive Christ-event together in one vision: the God of creation is the God who gives God's very self to us in Jesus of Nazareth and in the Pentecostal Spirit. A Christian theology of creation, then, and a Christian ecological theology, will take its bearings not only from the experience of the natural world, and all that the sciences have to offer in the way of insight into this natural world, and not only from the creation texts of the Old Testament, fundamental as these are, but from what it takes to be the decisive act of God in our human history, the Christ-event.

In this event, God is revealed as self-giving love: A God who bestows God's very self to us in the Word made flesh and in the Spirit poured out. Rahner points out that, because it is truly God's self-revelation, this divine self-bestowal is the authentic expression in our finite history of who God is. Divine self-bestowal can be seen as characterising God's whole action, in creation, grace, incarnation and the final transformation of all things.[16] Creation and redemptive incarnation, creation and new creation in Christ, are united in God's Trinitarian act of self-bestowal. God chooses to give God's self in love to what is not divine and so creation comes to be.

Taking up a theological tradition associated with the Franciscan school, exemplified in Duns Scotus (1266–1308), Rahner sees God as freely choosing, from the beginning, to create a world in which the Word would be made flesh and the Spirit poured out. In this view, the Christ-event is not thought of as an addition to creation, and not understood only as a remedy for sin. Rather, God's self-giving in the incarnation is the very purpose and meaning of creation. The cre-

---

16. Karl Rahner, *Foundations of Christian Faith: An Introduction to the Idea of Christianity* (New York: Seabury Press, 1978), 197.

ation of the universe is an element in the radical decision of God to give God's self in love to that which is not divine.[17]

In the light of the incarnation, then, God's act of creation does not mean only that God creates a finite other, but that God freely communicates God's own reality to the finite other. In this theological vision, the universe emerges, and life evolves on Earth, in the process of God's self-bestowal. God is never absent from this process or from any creature, but always immanent to each in self-giving love. The self-bestowal of the transcendent God is 'the most immanent factor in the creature'.[18] Rahner sees God's saving presence to human beings as more like formal causality than efficient causality: by it we are transformed and fulfilled because God communicates very God's self to us in the Spirit. Without being consumed by the fire of the divine infinity, we are able to receive God's life as our own fulfilment. Rahner further proposes that this divine indwelling by grace is the best analogy we have for the fundamental relationship that God has with all other creatures.[19] In its own specific way, each creature is destined to reach its fulfilment in God. God is creatively present to every entity in such a way that 'the reality of God himself is imparted to the world as its supreme specification'.[20]

It is only in the incarnation that we find what is most specific to the Christian view of God: while God and the world remain eternally distinct, God has so given God's self to the world of creation, that God is 'the very core of the world's reality and world is truly the fate of God'.[21] Through the Spirit, the Word is made flesh and flesh is irrevocably taken to God. The resurrection of the crucified Jesus in the power of the Spirit means that the Word of God is forever flesh,

---

17. 'Resurrection: D Theology', *Encyclopedia of Theology: A Concise Sacramentum Mundi*, edited by Karl Rahner (London: Burns and Oates, 1975), 1442; 'Christology in the Setting of Modern Man's Understanding of Himself and of his World', in *Theological Investigations* 11 (New York: Seabury, 1974), 219.
18. Karl Rahner, 'Immanent and Transcendent Consummation of the World', in *Theological Investigations* 10 (London: Darton, Longman & Todd, 1973), 281.
19. What is true of grace is valid 'in an analogous way for the relationship between God's absolute being and being which originates from him', Karl Rahner, 'Natural Science and Christian Faith', in *Theological Investigations* 21 (New York: Crossroad, 1988), 36.
20. Rahner, 'Christology in the Setting', 225.
21. Karl Rahner, 'The Specific Character of the Christian Concept of God', in *Theological Investigations* 21, 91.

forever matter, forever a creature, forever part of a material universe of creatures. In creation, incarnation and in its culmination in resurrection, God commits God's self to this world, to this universe and its creatures, and does this eternally.

All of this means that an ecological theology must involve both creation and new creation in Christ. New creation is not an escape from original creation, and certainly not its destruction, but its divinely given destiny and fulfilment. In an ecological theology, creation and new creation need to be understood as mutually related and as mutually interdependent. Creation is understood in relationship to new creation and new creation is to be seen as the redemptive fulfilment and transformation of creation.[22]

A Redemption Theology of Deifying Transformation of Both Human Beings and Other Creatures

A third fundamental strategy for a Christian ecological theology is to articulate a theology of redemption, or of new creation in Christ, that is capable of proclaiming the Christ-event in a new time and showing its meaning not only for human beings, but for the whole creation. It would take seriously the range of New Testament texts that speak of the creation and reconciliation of *all things* in Christ (1 Cor 8:6; Rom 8:18–25; Col 1:15–20; Eph 1:9–10; 20–23; Heb 1:2–3; 2 Pet 3:13; Jn 1:1–14; Rev 5:13–14; 21:1–5; 22:13). It would need to offer a viable alternative to theories of satisfaction and substitutionary atonement that no longer communicate the good news of the liberating God of Jesus. It would need to be faithful to the whole of the New Testament, with its diverse images and concepts for what God does for us in Christ.

One of Paul's images is that of transformation: 'And all of us, with unveiled faces, seeing the glory of the Lord as though reflected in a mirror, are being *transformed* into the same image from one degree of glory to another; for this comes from the Lord, the Spirit' (2 Cor 3:18; See Rom 12:2; Phil 3:21). It is by the action of the Spirit that we are transformed into the image of Christ who is the icon of God. Joseph Fitzmyer sees this as 'one of the most sublime' of Paul's descriptions

---

22. On this, see David Wilkinson, *Christian Eschatology and the Physical Universe* (London: T&T Clark, 2010), 86.

of the Christ-event, and notes that from this image the Greek patristic writers derived the idea of deification.[23] Greek theologians, like Maximus the Confessor, link this to the Synoptic tradition of the transfiguration of Christ, with his shining garments seen as representing creation's participation in transfiguration.[24] I find the concept of deifying transformation a viable way of expressing the meaning of redemption today for both human beings and other creatures.

Athanasius is a central theologian in the development of a theology of deification through incarnation. It is important to note that for him the incarnation is not simply about the beginning of Christ's life, but involves his whole life and, absolutely centrally, his death. God enters into bodily existence and death that they might be transformed in God by resurrection. The Word of God become human that humans might be deified.[25] We certainly do not possess the divine nature, but we become 'participants of the divine nature' (2 Pt 1:4) by grace. According to Athanasius, this deifying incarnation of the Word also involves other creatures participating in God in their own way. He says that 'all creation partakes of the Word in the Spirit.'[26] Redemptive deification involves not just human beings, but the whole creation and both occur through being conformed to the Word, in the Spirit. Athanasius writes:

> In him (the Holy Spirit), then, the Logos glorifies creation, and deifying it and adopting it brings it to the Father . . . the Spirit does not belong to the created order, but is proper to the Godhead of the Father, in whom the Logos also deifies created things. And he in whom creation is deified cannot himself be outside the divinity of the Father.[27]

---

23. Wilkinson, *Christian Eschatology and the Physical Universe*, 86.
24. See Andrew Louth, 'Between Creation and Transfiguration: The Environment in the Eastern Orthodox Tradition', in *Ecological Hermeneutics: Biblical, Historical and Theological Perspectives*, edited by David B Horrell, Cherryl Hunt, Christopher Southgate and Francesca Stavrakopoulou (London: T&T Clark, 2010), 211–22.
25. See *Athanasius: Contra Gentes and De Incarnatione*, translated by Robert Thompson (London: Oxford University Press, 1971), 268–9 (modified).
26. Athanasius, *Serapion*, 1.23 (Shapland, 124).
27. Athanasius, *Serapion*, 1.25, translated by Norman Russell in *The Doctrine of Deification in the Greek Patristic Tradition* (Oxford: Oxford University Press, 2004), 175.

Athanasius sees the Spirit as divine precisely because it is in the Spirit that creation is deified by the Word. It is the indwelling Spirit that assimilates creation to the Word. In his thought this applies above all and uniquely to human beings, but it applies, with them, in some real way, to the whole creation. The bodily incarnation of the Word, including the life, death and resurrection of Jesus and the outpouring of the Spirit, transforms flesh, not just the flesh of Jesus, but all flesh. Pope John Paul II has contributed to this line of thought. He writes of the incarnation as the 'greatest work' of the Spirit in the history of creation and salvation and says:

> The Incarnation of God the Son signifies the taking up into unity with God not only of human nature, but in this human nature, in a sense, of everything that is 'flesh': the whole of humanity, the entire visible and material world. The Incarnation, then, also has a cosmic significance, a cosmic dimension. The 'first-born of all creation,' becoming incarnate in the individual humanity of Christ, unites himself in some way with the entire reality of [humanity], which is also 'flesh' and in this reality with all 'flesh', with the whole of creation.[28]

Redemption in Christ, I am suggesting, can be understood as deifying transformation at three levels: 1. At *the human level*, it involves the forgiveness of sin, justification by grace, the indwelling of the Holy Spirit, becoming God's beloved daughter or son, communion in the life of the Trinity, the call to discipleship, and resurrection life; 2. At *the level of matter*, the incarnation, culmination in resurrection, is the beginning of the transfiguration of the universe, with all its processes and entities, 'the embryonically final beginning of the glorification and divinization of the whole of reality',[29] as Rahner says; 3. At *the level of biological life*, although we can have no adequate imaginative

---

28. John Paul II, *Dominum et vivificantem: On the Holy Spirit in the Life of the Church and the World*, 1986, no 50. (English expression modified for inclusivity in square brackets). At <http://www.vatican.va/holy_father/john_paul_ii/encyclicals/documents/hf_jp-ii_enc_18051986_dominum-et-vivificantem_en.html> Accessed 6 January 2010.
29. Rahner, 'Dogmatic Questions on Easter', in *Theological Investigations* 4 (New York: Seabury, 1974), 129. See also Rahner, 'Resurrection', in *Encyclopedia of Theology: A Concise Sacramentum Mundi*, edited by Karl Rahner (London: Burns and Oats, 1975), 1438–42.

picture of creation transformed in God, the biblical promise is for the fulfilment in Christ of 'the creation itself' (Rom 8:19), of 'all things' (Col 1:20), and this includes, in some unforeseeable way, other animals and the whole interconnected world of life on Earth.

God embraces 'flesh' in Jesus of Nazareth, that flesh might be transformed and deified. This flesh, I am arguing, includes each wallaby, dog and dolphin. They are created through the eternal Wisdom of God, and participate in some real way in redemption and reconciliation in Christ through the Spirit of God who dwells in them. In the Word made flesh, God embraces the whole of life on Earth, with all its evolutionary processes, in an event that is both a radical identification in love and an unbreakable promise.

Experience of the Spirit and of Divine Wisdom in Creation

Recently, walking in the Adelaide hills in South Australia, I have been stopped in my tracks by the sheer presence of a great River Red Gum (*Eucalyptus camaldulensis*). It sits at the edge of a creek bed that is nearly dry in summer. What arrested me first was its massive trunk, about four metres in diameter, with its peeling bark ranging in beautiful muted colours from white to grey to reddish brown. It is about thirty-five metres high, and almost lost in the blue-green leaves of its crown were flashes of the brilliant blue, green and orange of Rainbow Lorikeets.

Older River Red Gums drop branches, forming holes that are become home for many creatures. They provide breeding places for fish in times of flood and shelter for crustaceans and insects, and their fallen branches form habitats for many species of wildlife both in creeks and rivers and on their banks. They can live for up to 700 years. The tree I encountered must have been there long before Adelaide was colonised from England in 1836. Much earlier, it would have hosted generations of indigenous Kaurna people, who came to the hills from the Adelaide plains in winter for shelter, firewood and food.

I meet this beautiful old tree in a moment of connection that takes me to stillness before its otherness. I am led into the numinous, to what is beyond the human and beyond words, to the uncontrollable and wild Spirit of God that 'blows where it will' (Jn 3:8). In encountering this great tree, and all that lives in and around it, there is an experience of the Spirit as the ungraspable and unspeakable presence of God, as wonderfully creative fecundity, as the life-giver of the Creed, as the 'dearest freshness deep down things' of Hopkins.[30] But there is another side to this experience. In the Spirit, I can receive this Red River Gum as revelation, as God's self-revelation, as giving expression in its own creaturely way to that same eternal Wisdom of God that becomes flesh and has a human face in Jesus of Nazareth. In its unique, specific and limited way this River Red Gum it is a gift and a presence of divine Wisdom in our world, a revelatory word that speaks quietly and beautifully of the eternal Word.

---

30. Gerald Manly Hopkins, 'God's Grandeur', in *Poems and Prose of Gerard Manly Hopkins*, edited WH Gardner (London: Penguin Books, 1963), 27.

Humans, Chimps and Bonobos: Towards an Inclusive View of the Human as Bearing the Image of God

---

For Elizabeth Johnson, faithful explorer into the mystery of God and the community of creation

In her recent theological anthropology, Celia Deane-Drummond seeks to go beyond the idea of the divine image as associated with unique characteristics of the human, such as reason or freedom. Focus on the uniqueness of such characteristics has often involved marking a sharp separation of humans from other animals, and in some cases of men from women, which can then provide an excuse for oppressive behaviour. She explores, instead, what she calls a liminal theology that celebrates what links humans together with other animals in evolutionary and ecological relationships.

Deane-Drummond seeks to show 'that we have become ourselves and importantly become ourselves in evolutionary terms through navigating boundary relationships with each other, in both a temporal and a spatial sense, including relationships with other species'.[1] These boundaries do not have hard edges, she says, but are somewhat 'fuzzy'.[2] They can show up distinctive marks of the human, but only through communal relationships with others, including other animals. She sees humans as becoming more distinctively and properly themselves, and taking their proper God-given role in the divine theo-drama, through encounters with other species.

It is my hope to contribute to this discussion by focussing particularly on our evolutionary relationship with our nearest living rela-

---

1. Celia Deane-Drummond, *The Wisdom of the Liminal: Evolution and Other Animals in Human Becoming* (Grand Rapids, Michigan: Eerdmans, 2014), 4.
2. Deane-Drummond, *The Wisdom of the Liminal*, 4.

tives, the great apes, and bringing this relationship into dialogue with the early Christian tradition of humans as made in the Image of God. Perhaps it is significant to note that the Judaeo-Christian tradition arose, and particularly in Europe continued to develop, with little or no awareness of other primates. When a chimpanzee and an orangutan were first put on display at the London Zoo in 1835, people were shocked and offended at their likeness to humanity, and Queen Victoria judged the apes to be 'painfully and disagreeably human'.[3]

I will begin by engaging with two scientists, Frans de Waal and Michael Tomasello. Both have contributed to the recent body of work on the evolution of co-operation, and both explore the connections between humans and other apes, particularly chimpanzees and bonobos. Their science is work in progress and controversial, and I will not be able to track all the biological discussion of their work. But I will point to some real differences between them. I have chosen them not only because they are influential figures in the field, but also because they stand in opposing places in some of the controversies.

The aim here is to bring some of their key scientific insights into dialogue with the theological tradition, in the quest to further the theological understanding of the human in relation to other creatures. In particular, I will explore a view of the human as bearing the divine image in a way that is not only distinctive but also inclusive of other animals, rather than exclusive of them. In developing this position, I will take up theological concepts from the Greek patristic tradition, particularly from Athanasius.

Frans De Waal

Frans de Waal is the CH Chandler Professor of Primate Behavior at Emory University and the director of the Living Links Center at the Yerkes Primate Center. In his early work, of the mid-1970s, he discovered and explored reconciliation among primates and pioneered the study of conflict-resolution in animals.[4] Chimpanzees make up after a fight by kissing and embracing. High status male chimps can

---

3. Frans de Waal, *The Bonobo and the Atheist: In Search of Humanism Among the Primates* (New York: Norton, 2013), 101. Charles Darwin saw and felt a connection where the Queen felt a threat (107).
4. Frans de Waal, *Peacemaking among Primates* (Cambridge, MA: Harvard University Press, 1989).

be seen to come between disputing parties to put an end to a confrontation and to the looming violence. Female chimps drag males together to make up after a fight, and remove weapons from their hands. Although de Waal is well aware of how aggressive and violent chimps can be to each other, and to humans, he also sees them as engaging in self-control to avoid confrontation and in peace-making after conflict occurs. He points to the work of Christophe Boesch, who documents ten instances of wild male chimps that have been observed to adopt juveniles who have lost their mothers.[5] De Waal opposes, then, the unrelieved bleak picture of nature 'red in tooth and claw', as well as the behaviourist theory of BF Skinner, and contemporary ideas of genetic determinism.

In his more recent work, he has been exploring what he sees as the basis of human morality in the lives of primates. He fully accepts that humans possess a unique ability to co-operate across large, highly-organised populations, and a complex and well-developed morality. However, based on intensive observation of chimpanzees and bonobos, he argues that these other species can also be highly co-operative, and that they possess an emotional capacity for empathy.[6] He proposes that this capacity for empathy, and the resulting co-operation, shared by various mammal species, is the evolutionary foundation for human morality.[7]

As an example of such empathy, de Waal describes his observation of an elderly female chimpanzee, Peony, who sometimes has trouble walking and climbing because of arthritis. This makes it difficult for her to get up into the climbing frame where other chimps are gathered for a grooming session. When she is struggling to get up to the frame, a younger, unrelated female moves behind her, and puts both hands on her behind to push her up so that Peony can join the rest. Another example is that when Peony is thirsty, and has a long way to

---

5. De Waal, *The Bonobo and the Atheist*, 46.
6. See Frans de Waal, *Our Inner Ape: A Leading Primatologist Explains Why We Are Who We Are* (New York; Riverhead, 2005); *The Age of Empathy: Nature's Lessons for a Kinder Society* (New York: Harmony Books, 2009); Frans BM de Waal and Malini Suchak, 'Prosocial Primates: Selfish and Unselfish Motivations', in *Philosophical Transactions of the Royal Society B* 365/1553 (12 September 2010): 2711–22.
7. Frans de Waal, *The Bonobo and the Atheist*.

walk for water, younger females run ahead to the water source, take up water in their mouths and come to spit it out into Peony's mouth.[8]

De Waal describes an experiment between Peony and an unrelated chimp Rita, which, he claims, first demonstrated that chimpanzees care about each other's welfare.[9] A bucket was filled with green and red tokens. Peony was asked to pick one at a time and hand it to those conducting the experiment. Each time she did this she was rewarded with food. If she chose a green token, Rita was also rewarded, but if she chose a red one, Rita missed out. Peony began to select more green tokens. She made more pro-social choices than choices for herself alone. This was repeated with other pairs of chimps. Sometimes the partner would try to influence the choice by aggressive and intimidating behaviour or by begging. This proved to be counterproductive, resulting in less pro-social choices, as if the one choosing the tokens was punishing the bad behaviour of the partner. Fear was ruled out as an explanation for pro-social choices, because the highest-ranking chimps, with least to fear, proved to be the most generous. It seems that chimpanzees are capable of pro-social choices based upon a feeling for the other.

According to de Waal, recent studies of co-operation among primates have led researchers to three important conclusions: 1. Co-operation does not require family ties – unrelated chimpanzees and bonobos travel together, hunt together, share food and groom one another; 2. Co-operation is often based on mutuality and reciprocity—chimps will share food with another who had earlier groomed them; 3. Co-operation can be motivated by empathy—primates identify with others in distress, arousing emotions that can lead to helping action. De Waal sees empathy as a characteristic of all mammals from rodents to elephants. He suggests that it may have evolved from the maternal care demanded of mammals. Mothers need to respond to the signals of hunger or distress of their young. This sensitivity, along with the neural and hormonal processes that enable it, was then transferred to other relationships, enabling empathy, bonding and co-operation in the wider group.[10]

---

8. De Waal, *The Bonobo and the Atheist*, 4–5.
9. De Waal, *The Bonobo and the Atheist*, 120–1.
10. Frans de Waal, 'One for All: Our ability to cooperate in large societies has deep evolutionary roots in the animal kingdom', in *Scientific American*, 311/3 (September 2014): 54–5.

Rejecting old models of animals as stimulus-response machines, or as instinct-driven, de Waal insists that the animals he studies operate from emotions. He sees no sharp dividing line between human and animal emotions. While our brains are three times larger than those of chimpanzees, they have the same structure and the same parts. A special kind of neuron, known as a spindle cell, thought to be involved in self-awareness, empathy and self-control, is found not only in humans, but also in the brains of other animals, including apes.[11] Scientists from Parma in Italy have explored mirror neurons, which connect humans as well as other animals at a bodily level, as when one's yawn or hand movement causes the same reaction in another. It seems empathy is a bodily characteristic of humans, and other mammals. Emotions can be channelled from one mammal to another in a kind of bodily contagion. Put a needle in a woman's arm and the pain centre in her husband's brain lights up.

As a further example of this kind of bodily channelling of emotion, de Waal describes an observation of the birth of a chimpanzee. May, the delivering mother, stands half upright, with her open hand cupped between her legs ready to catch the baby. Others stand gathered quietly by. An older female, Atlanta, standing next to May, adopts the same position, as if she too were expecting the baby. When May's baby emerges, one chimpanzee screams, others embrace. Atlanta grooms the new mother almost continuously for the next week.[12]

De Waal suggests that it is helpful to think of three levels of empathy in mammals. At the core is what he describes as emotional contagion, the capacity to match another's emotional state. At a second level is the capacity to feel concern for others. This is expressed among chimpanzees and bonobos when consolation is offered to an ape in distress, by hugging, grooming or carefully inspecting an injury. The third level, according to de Waal, found in species such as dolphins, elephants and apes, is the capacity to take the perspective of another and offer targeted help to them.

He describes a test carried out at the Primate Research Institute of Kyoto University. Shina Yamamoto gives a chimpanzee a choice between two ways to obtain orange juice. The chimp can use a rake to bring it closer or suck it up through a straw. But the chimp has no

---

11. De Waal, *The Bonobo and the Atheist*, 80.
12. De Waal, *The Bonobo and the Atheist*, 139.

tools, while a nearby chimp in a separate area has a whole range of tools. This second chimpanzee takes one look at the first one's problem and immediately hands over precisely the right tool. However, if the second chimp is unable to see the first, he simple picks tools at random. De Waal concludes that this experiment indicates not only that chimpanzees readily assist one another, but also that they take the specific needs of the other into account. While he acknowledges that we still know little about the capacities of apes, he insists that 'they are not nearly as selfish as has been assumed'.[13]

De Waal sees human co-operation as grounded in the mutualistic co-operation that is shared by other species. He sees both humans and other animals as highly sensitive to the fair divisions of food and other valued goods. He recognises that humans are the only species to co-operate widely with outsiders. This out-group co-operation, he suggests, can be seen as extension of the in-group co-operation of our evolutionary past. What is truly unique to humans, he proposes, is the highly organised and large-scale nature of their co-operation. Humans also enforce co-operation by punishing freeloaders and advancing the good reputation of co-operators.[14] What sets human morality apart, according to de Waal, is the development of a logically coherent and universal system of moral standards. Because this is lacking in chimps, he is not inclined to call a chimpanzee a 'moral being'.[15]

While de Waal advocates a tolerant stance toward religion, he attempts to develop a bottom-up view of human morality that does not depend upon religious faith. His argument is that morality, in fact, predates religion: 'the moral law is not imposed from above or derived from well-reasoned principles; rather, it arises, from ingrained values that have been there since the beginning of time'.[16]

As a theologian, I am far from convinced that we can do without God, and without a theology of grace and sin. In an earlier work, I have discussed the extremely dangerous other side to our inherited tendency to co-operate with insiders, namely our tendency to make outsiders into scapegoats and enemies, and so to do violence

---

13. De Waal, *The Bonobo and the Atheist*, 147.
14. Frans De Waal, 'One for All', 55.
15. De Waal, *The Bonobo and the Atheist*, 17.
16. De Waal, *The Bonobo and the Atheist*, 228.

to them.[17] I see this tendency as profoundly connected to traditional Christian understandings of original sin and grace. Nevertheless, if de Waal is broadly right in the scientific insights he advances, I can see every reason to embrace the idea that human compassion for others unites us in an evolutionary relationship with the co-operation and empathy found among chimpanzees and bonobos, and more broadly in mammals and other animals. Here, too, grace can be understood to build on nature.

Michael Tomasello

Michael Tomasello is the Co-Director of the Max Planck Institute for Evolutionary Anthropology in Leipzig, Germany. He and his colleagues have been engaged in carefully designed comparative experiments with great apes and with very young children. His experiments are particularly concerned with the evolutionary origins of human co-operation.

He sees humans as the paradigmatically cultural species. He points to two clearly observable characteristics of human culture. The first is its cumulative nature, so that an invention is quickly taken up by others, and improved on in ever new ways. Tomasello calls this the 'ratchet' effect: humans inherit cultural artefacts and practices that accumulate modifications, which then ratchet up in complexity over time. The second observable characteristic is the creation of social institutions, behavioural practices guided by mutually agreed upon rules, which confer rights and responsibilities, and are supported by sanctions. The result is a diverse range of culturally defined entities, including husbands and wives, systems of exchange, money, chiefs and presidents. According to Tomasello, no other species has been observed to possess anything like the cultural ratchet effect or the social institutions found among humans.[18]

Underlying these characteristics is what Tomasello sees as a species-unique level of co-operation. Because of cultural niche construction, and gene-culture co-evolution, humans possess highly

---

17. Denis Edwards, *Partaking of God: Trinity, Evolution and Ecology* (Collegeville, Minnesota: Liturgical Press, 2014), 130–46.
18. Michael Tomasello, with Carol Dweck, Joan Silk, Brian Skyrms and Elizabeth Spelke, *Why We Cooperate* (Cambrdige, Mass: Boston Review, 2009), xii.

developed motivations and skills for co-operation with one another. Borrowing a term from the philosophy of action, Tomasello calls the psychological processes involved in the human level of co-operation 'shared intentionality'.[19] This phrase indicates a capacity to create joint attention and joint commitment with others in co-operative endeavours.

The shared intentionality thesis is central to Tomasello's recent book, which sets out to answer the question: what makes human thinking unique? He begins from two sets of empirical discoveries of recent decades. The first concerns the non-human great apes: There is new evidence for the sophisticated nature of their cognitive abilities, which makes it clear that they think in human-like ways, and can understand causal and intentional connections in their physical and social worlds. This suggests that important aspects of human thinking derive from the same problem-solving abilities that are possessed by great apes. The second concerns very young children who do not yet partake fully of the language and the culture that surrounds them: they are found to operate with some cognitive processes that are not evident in great apes, in the way they engage co-operatively with others in joint attention and in co-operative communication. They possess a joint intentionality.

Based on these and other empirical findings concerning apes and young children, Tomasello sets out to offer a natural history of human knowledge, an evolutionary account of its emergence. His shared intentionality hypothesis structures this account. He describes three components of thinking: cognitive representation, inference and self-monitoring. The shared intentionality thesis proposes that all three components were transformed at least twice in human evolution, as humans were forced to find new ways to co-operate. I will trace, briefly, Tomasello's account of the evolutionary movement from individual intentionality to joint intentionality and from joint intentionality to collective intentionality.

Like de Waal, Tomasello insists that great apes are far from being the stimulus-response machines they were thought to be by many theorists. They not only operate in an intentional way, but also under-

---

19. Tomasello, *Why we Cooperate*, xiii.

stand others as intentional agents.[20] They operate with abstract cognitive representations, to which they assimilate particular experiences. They make causal, intentional and productive inferences from these cognitive representations, and can imagine non-actual situations. And they self-monitor their behavioural decisions-making process. This implies a kind of 'executive' oversight of their own decision-making. Great apes operate in a flexible, intelligent and self-regulating way.[21]

Tomasello assumes that this kind of consciousness existed in the common ancestors of humans and apes, who lived about six million years ago. He puts forward the hypothesis that not only these common ancestors, but also the hominin species of the next four million years, such as the various species of australopithecines, possessed this kind of intelligence, which he names individual intentionality. He calls this intentionality individual because he sees it as intelligence that has evolved mainly in competitive situations within social groups. Although Tomasello acknowledges that great apes co-operate in various ways, in travelling together, foraging in small groups, forming alliances, and in defence against outsiders and predators, he sees them as generally highly competitive rather than co-operative in many facets of life including eating, mating and dominance.

He acknowledges that there is the appearance of a level of co-operation in the way that some bands of chimpanzees hunt for monkeys. But while other researchers like de Waal and Christophe Boesch (colleague of Tomasello's from the Max Planck Institute) interpret this activity as an example of chimpanzees possessing a joint goal and co-ordinated roles, Tomasello interprets the hunt differently.[22] He thinks that each chimp is attempting to capture the monkey for its own benefit, even as it takes into account the behaviour and perhaps the intentions of others. In his view, even in the hunt, chimps operate from an 'I' intentionality rather than from the 'We' of joint intentionality.

By contrast, he finds strong empirical evidence that very young children operate from a 'We' intentionality. Infants from fourteen to

---

20. Michael Tomasello, *A Natural History of Human Thinking* (Cambridge, MA: Harvard University Press, 2014), 20.
21. Tomasello, *A Natural History*, 30.
22. Christophe Boesch, 'Joint Cooperative Hunting among Wild Chimpanzees. Taking Natural Observations Seriously', in *Behavioral and Brain Sciences*, 28 (2005): 692–3. See Tomasello, *A Natural History*, 35.

eighteen months will engage in a joint activity with an adult, such as working together to obtain a toy by each operating one side of an apparatus. He notes that should an adult stop co-operating without explanation, the children regularly attempt to reengage the adult. By the time they are three, children show ongoing commitment to joint activities in the face of distractions. When one child is rewarded half way through an experiment, the lucky child delays the consumption of her rewards until the partner receive hers. No such findings are observed in similar experiments with chimpanzees.[23]

Tomasello relates these experiments with children to evolutionary history, to the emergence of a new cognitive model, which he calls joint intentionality. In Tomasello's account, the move beyond individual intentionality begins when a change in ecology leads to new forms of collaboration. He speculates that it may have begun in an initial, preparatory way soon after the emergence of the species *Homo* around two million years ago. This coincided with an expansion of terrestrial monkeys, like baboons, who may have out-competed hominins for fruits and forced them into a new foraging niche, perhaps into scavenging meat. This may have culminated about 400,000 years ago with *Homo heidelbergensis*.[24] Current evidence suggests that this was the first hominin to engage in a systematic way in collaborative hunting of large game. Thus began a lifestyle in which early humans were interdependent with others in foraging for food, and where there was social selection, where individuals began to evaluate others as collaborative partners. This created selection pressure for the skills and motivations associated with joint intentionality.

The capacity to help one another systematically requires new forms of communication, beginning, Tomasello argues, with informative gestures and iconic gestures—such as warning of a snake with a slithering hand movement. Co-operation in joint intentionality requires new forms of symbolic thinking. Intellectual representation is transformed, since participants must now come to represent each other's perspective on the situation they face. Inference is transformed: it becomes socially recursive, as individuals make inferences about their partner's intentions in relation to their own intentional states. Self-monitoring is transformed as individuals come to imagine

---

23. Tomasello, *A Natural History*, 38–43.
24. Tomasello, *A Natural History*, 48.

the perspective of their partner as well as monitoring their own. This kind of 'I' and 'You' perception involves, simultaneously, jointness and individuality. It is these two characteristics together that define Tomasello's notion of joint intentionality. He sees this kind of joint intentionality as the necessary intermediate step towards the collective intentionality of modern humans.[25]

Collective intentionality, Tomasello argues, appeared when human populations began growing in size and competing with one another. Group life as a whole became one collaborative activity, creating a permanent shared world, a culture, based on collectively known cultural conventions, norms and institutions. Tomasello acknowledges that many species from whales to capuchin monkeys, and above all the great apes, engage in forms of social learning, and possess a form of culture. But human culture is based on a far more developed group way of knowing and acting.

Individuals can now reason from the transpersonal, 'objective', or 'agent-neutral' point of view of the group. It is in this context that co-operative communication begins to operate not only through gesture and pantomime but also in language. Modern humans participate in collective intentionality not just with other individuals, but with the whole social group. This leads to cognitive representation that is conventional and objective; to processes of inference that are reasoned and aimed at truth; to self-monitoring in which individuals adjust their thinking in relation to that of the group.[26]

Tomasello thinks that the step toward collective intentionality probably evolved in a population of modern humans in Africa before they migrated to other parts of the world over 100,000 years ago.[27] As they settled in new local ecological niches, on top of their species-wide cognitive capacity of individual, joint and collective intentionality, they began to develop culturally specific cognitive and linguistic skills, which in a ratchet effect built on one another in cumulative cultural evolution.

Tomasello believes that in the case of human children, ontogeny follows phylogeny—at about their first birthday, they co-operate with others in joint intentionality, and about their third they engage in col-

---

25. Tomasello, *A Natural History*, 78.
26. Tomasello, *A Natural History*, 141.
27. Tomasello, *A Natural History*, 141.

lective intentionality. But these skills emerge only in constant interaction with the social environment. Thus, for Tomasello, the skills of shared intentionality are not simply innate, nor simply learned. They spring from biological adaptations but require, for their flourishing, growing up in a pre-existing cultural collective with its conventions, norms, institutions and language.[28]

Towards an Inclusive Theology of the Divine Image in Creatures

There are some obvious differences between the positions of de Waal and Tomasello. De Waal emphasises what is common to humans and other apes, while Tomasello focuses more sharply on what is distinctive to humans. De Waal is clearly convinced that chimpanzees and bonobos are less selfish and more co-operative than Tomasello's experiments indicate. Tomasello sees de Waal and Christophe Boesch as, at times, 'anthropomorphising apes'.[29] He has challenged experimental results of de Waal and Sarah Brosnan that claim to show that capuchin monkeys possess a 'sense of fairness'.[30]

My theological focus is not on these differences, but on the broader picture that emerges from their work: that human beings can be understood only in terms of evolutionary primate history; that the evolution of large-scale co-operation is fundamental to the emergence of modern humans; that humans have profound similarities to chimpanzees and bonobos, but also have distinct human qualities; that human qualities, including emotions like empathy, the capacity for moral decision-making, large-scale co-operation, intelligence, culture and language, are all related to qualities found in chimps and other apes; that these human qualities can be seen as based on evolutionary adaptations from our common inheritance, but also as requiring a rich social and cultural environment for their development and flourishing.

How might all of this be brought into dialogue with the theological tradition and its understanding of the human being as made in the Image of God? This tradition has often understood the Image of God

---

28. Tomasello, *A Natural History*, 146–7.
29. Garry Stix, 'The "It" Factor', in *Scientific American*, 311/3 (September 2014): 63.
30. See, for example, Juliane Brauer, Josef Call, and Michal Tomasello, 'Are Apes Really Inequity Averse?', in *Proceedings of the Royal Society B*, 273/1605 (2006): 3123–8.

in terms of qualities that seem to separate humans from other animals, as located, for example, in human reason, human freedom, or the human soul. More recently, the International Theological Commission has seen the Image of God in humans as woven from two major strands, communion and stewardship: first, humans are 'persons oriented towards communion' with the triune God and with one another;[31] second, human beings occupy the unique place of 'sharing in the divine governance of visible creation'.[32]

This document of the International Theological Commission contains many rich insights, and in my judgement its vision of humans as persons oriented towards communion is deeply meaningful. The document has important things to say about evolution and also about human responsibility toward other creatures. But when talking about human stewardship of other creatures, it insists on kingly language that I think needs questioning, above all in the context of the ecological crisis of the twenty-first century. It speaks of humans as participating in God's 'governance' and 'lordship' over the universe, of human 'rule' and 'sovereignty' over other creatures, and of humans as 'the summit' of visible creation.[33] Importantly, the document qualifies its kingly language by pointing out that the kingship of Jesus is one of service and of the cross.

In my view, the biblical concept of the human person made in the Image of God needs to be understood in a broader biblical context in which human beings are called to cosmic humility before God and the wonders of God's creation, and in which human beings are called to praise God with other creatures as part of the one community of creation.[34] In the light of the insights of scientists like de Waal and Tomasello, and their findings about what is common to humans and other apes, as well as about what is distinctive to humans, I think we need a more inclusive concept of the Image of God.

---

31. International Theological Commission, *Communion and Stewardship: Human Persons Created in the Image of God*, paragraph 25.
32. *Communion and Stewardship*, paragraph 57.
33. *Communion and Stewardship*, paragraph 57–8.
34. On this, see Richard Bauckham, *Bible and Ecology: Rediscovering the Community of Creation* (London: Darton, Longman & Todd, 2010). This theme is developed by Elizabeth Johnson in her *Ask the Beasts: Darwin and the God of Love* (London: Bloomsbury, 2014), and also in my *Partaking of God*.

Are there resources in the Christian tradition that can help theologian today affirm that humans are made in the Image of God, in a distinctive way, not as over against other creatures, but precisely in our evolutionary inter-relationship and ongoing relations with them? Can these resources help us to affirm that other creatures, such as bonobos, also in their own distinctive way, bear the Image of God? And can resources from the tradition help us see that part of what is distinctive about the way humans bear the image is that they are persons called to communion, not only with one another and the triune God, but also with the community of life on Earth and the wider universe?

I find some such resources in Athanasius. The concept of the Image of God is central to Athanasius's theological anthropology as it was for his predecessor Irenaeus, although Athanasius does not follow Irenaeus's distinction between image and likeness. Athanasius reserves the word 'image' to the eternal Word. Christ, for him, is the Image, the Wisdom, the Radiance, the Word and the Son of the Father. Humanity, then, is 'in the image' of the Image. Athanasius situates humanity in the midst of God's creation, all of which is completely dependent on the creative Word for its existence. Within this wider creation, he has a strong view of humanity's uniqueness. In his 'On the Incarnation' he writes:

> Because he does not begrudge the gift of existence, he made all things from nothing through his proper Word, our Lord Jesus Christ. And among these creatures, of all creatures he was especially merciful towards the human race. Seeing that by the logic of its own generation it would be unable to remain forever, he granted it a further gift, not simply creating humanity like all irrational animals on the earth, but making them in his own image and granting them also a share in the power of his proper Word, so that having as it were, shadows of the Word and being made rational, they might be able to remain in blessedness and live the true life in paradise, which is really that of the saints.[35]

---

35. *On the Incarnation* 3 (Thomson, 138–40).

Held in being, like all other creatures, by the Word of God, humans are granted a 'further gift', a special grace. This special grace is specified as making them in the image of the Word. This grace enables humans to participate in the Logos as creatures of reason (logikos) and thus to 'actively and intentionally' participate in the Word and to rejoice in this participation.[36] Through this grace, human beings were meant from the beginning to share in eternally in the divine communion. The concept of the human made in the Image of God is always for Athanasius, a relational concept, concerned with the uniquely human way of participating in this communion.

Athanasius has a highly developed concept of humans as made in a distinctive way according to the true Image, who is the Word and Wisdom of the Father. He sees humans, at their creation, as given the grace of participating in the Image, and in knowing the Image also knowing the Father. But humans chose to reject God, forfeited the grace of eternal life, and damaged their relationship to the Image. Out of the abundance of divine generosity, the Image of the Father becomes flesh to seek out the lost, to bring forgiveness of sins, abolish the debt to death, and repair and wonderfully renew the Image of God in human beings.

Such an exalted view of the human as bearing the divine image might lead one to suspect that Athanasius's view of being in the image would be an exclusive one. But in fact, in his *Orations Against the Arians*,[37] he defends the concept of other creatures as bearing the imprint of the divine Image. The context is his long treatment of Proverbs 8:22, where Wisdom is found to say: 'The Lord created me as a beginning of his ways for his works'. This was the foundational text for anti-Nicene theology in the fourth century, constantly used as a biblical warrant for claiming that Wisdom had a beginning and is created. Any defence of Nicaea had to deal with this text. Athanasius responds to this challenge by attempting to show that the overall pattern of scriptural language identifies the Wisdom/Word as uncreated and truly divine. With regard to Proverbs 8:22, he argues that it refers not to the divine identity of Wisdom, but to the economy of the Incarnation, where Wisdom is made flesh in the created humanity of Jesus.

---

36. Khaled Anatolios, *Athanasius* (London: Routledge, 2004), 42.
37. My quotations are from the translation by Khaled Anatolios, in *Athanasius*, 110–75.

In this context, he speaks of the created imprint and image of uncreated divine Wisdom in all creatures. As divine Wisdom is the Creator of all things, the whole creation reflects uncreated Wisdom. It is precisely the presence of Wisdom, and the imprint of this divine Wisdom, that enables creatures to exist and to flourish:

> But in order that creatures may not only be but also thrive in well-being, it pleased God to have his own Wisdom condescend to creatures. Therefore he placed in each and every creature and in the totality of creation a certain imprint (*typon*) and reflection of the Image of Wisdom, so that the things that come into being may prove to be works that are wise and worthy of God.[38]

All the creatures we see around us bear the imprint and reflection of the Image of Wisdom. In human beings, Athanasius goes on to say, this imprint of Wisdom is manifest in our human wisdom: 'the wisdom that comes into being within us is an image of his Wisdom'.[39] Because we have this gift of wisdom, Athanasius says, we possess the God-given capacity to recognise the Image of Wisdom in other creatures: 'Thus did the imprint of Wisdom come to be in created things, so that the world, as I have said, may come to know its Creator and Word, and through him, the Father'.[40]

So Athanasius's interpretation of 'the Lord created me' in Proverbs 8:1 is that it is said not of Wisdom, who is Creator, 'but on account of his image that it is in created works'.[41] He notes, too, that in Sirach, Wisdom is said to be 'poured forth' upon on all God's works (Sir 1:9). Again, he interprets this as pointing to the fact that 'his image and his imprint is created in the works, although he himself is not one of the things created'.[42] It is not eternal Wisdom, but Wisdom's created image that is poured out in all creatures. It is through this created wisdom that 'the heavens declare the glory of God, and the stars proclaim the work of his hands' (Ps 19:2).

---

38. *Arians* 2.78.
39. *Arians* 2.78.
40. *Arians* 2.78.
41. *Arians* 2.78.
42. *Arians* 2.78.

Athanasius then offers an image. The son of a king builds a city to fulfil his father's wishes. He inscribes his name on each of the works of the building project, so that each stone may be secured and preserved. And because of the inscription of his name, each inhabitant will be able to remember both him and his Father. For Athanasius, then, animals and plants, mountains and rivers are made according to the Image of Wisdom, and that they all bear Wisdom's imprint: 'For while Wisdom herself is Creator and Maker, her imprint is created in the works and is made according to the image of the Image.'[43]

Athanasius says that the perception of the imprint and Image of Wisdom in creatures is 'the beginning' and 'paradigm', or symbol, of the knowledge of God. When one begins by embarking on this primary path of creation and is guided by wisdom, and 'then ascends by intelligence and understanding and perceives in creation the Creator Wisdom', such a one 'will perceive in her also her Father, as the Lord himself has said, "The one who has seen me has seen the Father"' (Jn 14:9).

However, Athanasius notes, with Paul, that in spite of the imprint of the Wisdom of God being evident in creatures, humans have failed to recognise God's attributes in creatures and have instead made them into false gods (Rom 1:19–25). Nevertheless, God does not abandon what God has created. Out of the abundance of divine generosity, God sends divine Wisdom, through whom all things are created, to be made flesh:

> For God willed to make himself known no longer as in previous times through the image and shadow of wisdom, which is in creatures, but has made the true Wisdom herself take flesh and become a mortal human being and endure the death of the cross, so that henceforth all those who put their faith in him may be saved. But it is the same Wisdom of God, who previously manifested herself, and her Father through herself, by means of her image in creatures—and thus is said to be 'created'—but which later on, being Word, became flesh (Jn 1:14) as John said.[44]

---

43. *Arians* 2.80.
44. *Arians* 2.81.

Thus, in Athanasius we find a theology that sees the eternal Wisdom/Word of God, and this Wisdom/Word made flesh as the one true Image of the Father. He has a profound theology of human beings as distinctively created according to the Image, as having damaged their relationship to the Image, and as through the incarnation of the divine Image, being repaired and renewed in their being according to the Image. But this is not an exclusive view of humans as bearing the divine image. He sees other creatures, through God's creative act, as participating in divine Wisdom, and as created icons of the eternal Image of God. He sees human beings as called to recognise the imprint of Wisdom in the creatures around them, and thus be led to a knowledge of Wisdom, and through Wisdom to her Father.

Conclusion

This dialogue between contemporary science and early theology's insights into the Image of God suggests a more inclusive way of thinking about human beings as made according to the Image of God. It might be summarised in four statements:

1. Humans are made by God according to the Image only in and through their evolutionary relationships with other creatures such as chimpanzees and bonobos. The process of becoming human, and thus being made according to the Image, is not something to be understood as separating humans from other creatures, but as occurring only in relationship with them.
2. Chimps and bonobos, too, can be said to be made according to the Image of God, in their own distinctive ways. They, too, along with other creatures, are created icons of God in our world. With human beings, they form part of the community of life on Earth, a community in which all creatures are united in a communion of praise of their Creator.
3. Essential to what is distinctive about the way that humans bear the Image of God, the International Theological Commission has affirmed, is their communion with one another and with the triune God. The proposal made here is that this communion is to be seen as embracing not only other humans and the triune God of life, but also bonobos and chimpanzees, and the whole community of life on Earth.

4. The concept of stewardship, discussed by the International Theological Commission, can then be understood within such a wider idea of the community of creation (Ps 148; Ps 104), as responsible care for each species, and for the well-being of each living creature.

To be humanly according to the Image is to be committed to the well-being of the community of creatures of Earth, all of which are created icons of the living God. Such an inclusive view suggests an expansion of our love to embrace all our neighbours. As Elizabeth Johnson writes at the end of her Ask the Beasts: 'Inspired by the Spirit who pervades and sustains the community of creation, the human imagination grows to encompass "the other" and the human heart widens to love the neighbors who are uniquely themselves, not humans'.[45] Such an inclusive view does not diminish the human but brings out what it is distinctive to humans in bearing the divine image, as it allows other creatures to take their specific and distinctive identities as icons of holy Wisdom.

---

45. Elizabeth Johnson, *Ask the Beasts*, 284.

'Every Sparrow that Falls to the Ground': The Cost of Evolution and the Christ-Event

In texts found in Matthew and Luke, Jesus speaks of God as involved with every sparrow that falls to the ground (Matt 10:29; Lk 12:6). The focus of these texts is God's provident care for human beings—'the hairs on your head are all counted' (Matt 10:30). But the claim made about humans is based on an assumption that God's care embraces each single sparrow. In this article, I will propose that this Gospel assumption is to be taken at face value.

The saying about every sparrow that falls to the ground reflects the ancient biblical understanding of the Creator's care for all creatures (Ps 84:3; 104:27–28). It is consistent with other passages where Jesus speaks about God's care for birds and flowers as well as human beings (Matt 6:25–34; Lk 12:22–33). It forms a coherent pattern with his use of parables taken from nature, and with his practice of prayer in the hills of Galilee. In his well-known book on Jesus' parables, CH Dodd argues that Jesus understands the natural world as the place of God. He finds that 'the sense of the divineness of the natural order is the major premise of all the parables'.[1] It is because Jesus finds God in the natural world as well as the world of human affairs that he uses parables from both to speak of God's Reign. Jesus looks on sparrows and other creatures with compassionate and loving eyes and sees them as loved by God and as revelatory of God.

Can this claim have meaning today? In the light of our evolutionary history, can we say that God cares for every sparrow that falls to the ground? Loss and death on an unthinkable scale are built into the way things are in an evolutionary world. Whenever theology engages with biology, the issues of pain, death and extinction come to the fore.

---

1. CH Dodd, *The Parables of the Kingdom* (Glasgow: Collins, 1935), 21.

In the context of so much loss in the history of life, can we believe that God really cares for *individual* creatures? In this article, I will answer yes to this question, proposing that it is appropriate to think of God as caring for individual sparrows, wallabies and beetles. This is not intended as a philosophical defence of the goodness of God in the face of so much suffering (a theodicy), found, for example, in the careful argument of Thomas Tracy.[2] Nor am I intending to reflect on the suffering of creation in the light of a general philosophical notion of God. This strategy is employed in much of the discussion on science and theology and it, too, clearly has its own value.

My own approach is to attempt a theology of nature that, from the start, is informed not only by science but also by the Christ-event. Christians see Jesus, in his life, death and resurrection as God's self-communication, as the human face of God. And, in the outpouring of the Spirit, they experience a more mysterious presence of God, one imaged as the Breath of God that gives life to all things and as the wild wind that blows where it will. This two-fold experience of God in Christ and in the Spirit forms the foundation for a Trinitarian theology of creation: the Breath of Life breathes through creation from the beginning, empowering the life-bearing universe at every moment of its evolution; the universe of creatures comes to be in the Word of God, the Word made flesh in Jesus of Nazareth. In this kind of theology, the work of the Creator Spirit is always directed toward the Christ event. With Karl Rahner, I understand the work of creation as having an inner connection to the Christ-event.[3] And with theologians like Irenaeus and Yves Congar, I understand Word and Spirit as acting together in both creation and redemption.[4]

In recent times, a number of scholars involved in the field of science and theology have pointed out that a Christian response to the suffering of creation needs to involve a theology of redemption in Christ. Many have appealed to the idea of divine self-emptying (*kenōsis*) found in Philippians 2:7, and applied this Christological

---

2. Thomas F Tracy, 'Evolution, Divine Action and the Problem of Evil', in *Evolutionary and Molecular Biology: Scientific Perspectives on Divine Action*, edited by Robert J Russell, William R Stoeger, SJ and Francisco J Ayala (Vatican City State: Vatican Observatory; Berkeley, Cal: Center for Theology and the Natural Sciences, 1998): 511–30.
3. Karl Rahner, *Foundations of Christian Faith* (New York: Crossroad, 1978), 197.
4. Yves Congar, *The Word and the Spirit* (London: Geoffrey Chapman, 1986),

concept to creation.⁵ Jürgen Moltmann has developed a theology of Christ as redeemer of the victims of evolution.⁶ Niels Gregersen has proposed a theology of the cross in which God is understood as bearing the costs of natural selection⁷ and Christopher Southgate has argued for a multifaceted approach to evolutionary evil that centres on the Christ event.⁸ In what follows, I will attempt to contribute to this line of thought.

Any Christian reflection on suffering needs, I believe, to acknowledge what Schillebeeckx calls a 'barbarous excess' of suffering and evil in our history.⁹ Schillebeeckx is thinking of the terrible human carnage of the twentieth century, that continues into the twenty-first, the endless stream of human bodies burned and crushed in wars, the hunger and disease that afflict the poorest of the Earth, the women who are women raped and beaten. Alongside this overwhelming tide of human suffering and connected to it, there is the ruthless human abuse of creation and the human induced extinction of uncounted species. This barbarous excess of suffering cannot be rationalised. It confronts us as radically evil.

The costs of evolution that are built into the natural world are of a different order to the sufferings that arise from human sin. But I believe that neither can be brought into a satisfying intellectual system. Neat and tidy theological systems or explanations are neither possible nor helpful. We do know that we are in a world that is in evolutionary process, and that pain and death are part of the process. They are necessary dimension of the kind of evolutionary world in which we find ourselves. We might speculate that they would be necessary for any form of evolutionary process in which sentient life was to appear. But we do not have a God's eye view of the process. A theological response to the suffering of creation will need to be a humble

---

5. John Polkinghorne (ed), *The Work of Love: Creation as Kenosis*, edited by John Polkinghorne (Grand Rapids: Eerdmans, 2001).
6. Jürgen Moltmann, *The Way of Jesus Christ* (London: SCM, 1990).
7. Niels Henrik Gregersen, 'The Cross of Christ in an Evolutionary World', in *Dialog: A Journal of Theology* 40 (2001): 192–207.
8. Christopher Southgate, 'God and Evolutionary Evil: Theodicy in the Light of Darwinism', in *Zygon* 37 (2002): 803–22.
9. Edward Schillebeeckx, Christ: The *Christian Experience in the Modern World* (London: SCM, 1980), 725.

theology, one that is stumbling and tentative, and one that is mindful of the cross of Christ.

In what follows, I will first describe the intensification of the problem of natural evil that arises in the dialogue with contemporary science. Then I will begin a theological response from the idea of God's incarnation in the fleshliness of creaturely life. This will be followed by two brief notes on issues that I see as necessary markers for the rest of this discussion: the redefinition of divine power and the resurrection as promise of the transformation of the natural world. With these in place, I will turn to God's saving love for individual creatures, discussing their embrace in the Spirit here and now and their future redemption in Christ.

The Intensification of Natural Evil in an Evolutionary Worldview

The problem of natural evil has always been complex and difficult. But the issues are greatly intensified for a contemporary theology that is in dialogue with evolutionary biology. Three factors contribute to this intensification. The first is a new understanding of the size and scope of the problem of creaturely loss. Scientists believe that life emerged on Earth more than 3.5 billion years ago in the form of prokaryotes, simple bacterial cells without a nucleus, and eventually evolved into more complex nucleated creatures, the eukaryotes. These provided the foundation for all multi-cellular forms of life. The fossils tell of a wonderful explosion of diverse life-forms in the seas during the Cambrian period (545–495 million years ago). They also tell of a series of terrible extinctions: 248 million years ago, ninety per cent of marine species were lost; 65 million years ago, more than half of the Earth's species, including the dinosaurs, were destroyed. The extinction of the dinosaurs left habitats for mammals to fill and they diversified and flourished. Modern humans appeared only during the last 200,000 years. It has been estimated that ninety-eight per cent of species that have ever existed are now extinct. This presents us with a loss of life on a scale that human beings have never before had to contemplate.

The second factor in the intensification of the theological problem of natural evil is the discrediting of the idea that pain and biological death can be explained as the result of human sin. Evolutionary biology makes it clear that death is deeply structured into the pattern of life. Biological death cannot be attributed to human sin—although it is painfully clear that human sin contributes in a massive way to the suffering of human beings and other creatures. Death and the struggle for existence are built into the life that has emerged over the last three-and-a-half billion years. It is not caused by the actions of modern humans, who are latecomers, arriving on the scene only during the last hundred and fifty thousand years. Nor can it be caused by our predecessors such as *Homo erectus*. Biological death is not something that can be blamed on our human forbears.

The third factor in the intensification of the issue of natural evil is by far the most confronting for theology: suffering, death and extinction are now seen as intrinsic to the process of evolutionary emergence. They are not simply unfortunate side-effects, but are built in to the very process. The clash of tectonic plates gives rise to new habitats that allow new species to emerge, but they also cause deadly earthquakes. Mutations provide novelty for the process of natural selection, but also give rise to terrible damage and hardship. At a more radical level, the whole process of evolutionary emergence depends upon death. Evolution demands a series of generations. Ursula Goodenough points out that while bacteria are not programmed to die, the somatic cells of organisms like ours are programmed to die.[10] It is built into their evolutionary strategy. Death is intrinsic to evolutionary emergence and, without death, there could be no wings, eyes, or brains. Death is part of the price paid for living in a complex world with developed forms of life, including sentient life.

As Niels Gregersen says, the natural world with its beauty and its costs is a 'package deal'.[11] What humans can find brutal in evolutionary history is not accidental to evolution. Gregersen draws the only conclusion possible for one who believes in a God who creates life through evolution. Biological death has to be attributed to the Creator. It has to be affirmed as one of the ways in which 'God creates novelty in evolution'.[12]

Creation is not only exuberant and beautiful, it can also be described as cruciform. This term comes from the work of Holmes

---

10. Ursula Goodenough, *The Sacred Depths of Nature* (Oxford: Oxford University, 1998), 143–51.
11. Niels Henrik Gregersen, 'The Cross of Christ in an Evolutionary World', in *Dialog: A Journal of Theology* 40 (2001): 192–207, 201.
12. Gregersen, 'The Cross of Christ in an Evolutionary World', 198.

Rolston III.[13] For me, it expresses several important things at once. First, it acknowledges honestly the pain and cost of evolving creation. Second, it leads to the thought that, in the cross, God embraces not just suffering humanity but the whole of creation in its travail. Third, it can be taken as raising the question whether all creatures are in some way to be redeemed in Christ. These are themes that I will attempt to explore further.

In his Gifford lectures, Rolston traces the emergence of a world of values. He understands the story of life as the struggle involved in creative advance, as the natural world gives birth to what is new. Suffering is built into the emergence of life that is capable of experience of the world. He points out that pain is not found among plants, but emerges only with zoology: 'Genes do not suffer; organisms with genes need not suffer, but those with neurons do'.[14] He finds life both prolific and pathetic. Most of the sentient young starve, are eaten, abused or abandoned. Suffering is 'the shadow side of sentience, felt experience, consciousness, pleasure, intention, all the excitement of subjectivity waking up so inexplicably from mere objectivity'.[15] The only pathway to consciousness that we know of is through flesh that can *feel its way* through the world. In such a world, pain is eminently useful to survival.

In Rolston's view, the community of life on Earth is wonderfully creative and fruitful. It is continually being regenerated as well as continually being advanced. But creatures from the beginning have given up their lives for others. He insists that the element of struggle in cruciform creation is 'deiform, godly, just because of this element of struggle, not in spite of it'.[16] Ultimately, he sees this struggle of emergence as the work of divine suffering love, as the labour of God.

---

13. Holmes Rolston III, *Genes, Genesis and God: Values and their Origins in Natural and Human History* (Cambridge: Cambridge University Press, 1999), 303-7; Holmes Rolston III, 'Kenosis and Nature', in *The Work of Love: Creation as Kenosis* edited by John Polkinghorne (Grand Rapids: Eerdmans, 2001), 43–65.
14. Rolston III, *Genes, Genesis and God: Values and their Origins in Natural and Human History*, 303.
15. Rolston III, *Genes, Genesis and God: Values and their Origins in Natural and Human History*, 303.
16. Rolston III, *Genes, Genesis and God: Values and their Origins in Natural and Human History*, 306.

Rolston insists that while this is a tragic view of life, it is one in which 'tragedy is the shadow of prolific creativity'.[17]

I think that Rolston's idea that emergence can be seen as the work of divine suffering love is something that theologians need to ponder. At the same time, I believe that the cross of Christ is not to be seen as some kind of necessary outcome of creation, nor as a principle behind creation. The cross is an unpredictable and contingent event. Christian theology needs to insist on the contingency of the cross for two reasons. First, the whole Christ event is to be seen as a totally gratuitous act of God. And, second, the brutal act of crucifying Jesus ought not be seen as simply the following out of a pre-ordained divine plan, but more as God bringing life out of what was in itself a sinful and destructive act. While I do not think the cross of Christ can be reduced to an *a priori* principle of creation, I do think we can look back from the cross with Rolston. Then, in the light of the cross, we can begin to speak of God's identification with the struggling emerging life of a creaturely world.

Talk about creation as cruciform, important as it is in recognising the place of pain and death in evolutionary emergence, does not yet offer a theological response. Such a response needs to talk about the redemption of creation in Christ. The word 'redemption' can be used to refer specifically to the forgiveness of human sin, the atonement. I am using redemption in the wider sense that includes not only forgiveness of human sin, but also liberation from injustice, suffering and death for all of God's creatures as 'all things' are taken up into Christ (Eph 1:10).

Word Made Flesh: The Incarnation of God within the Biotic Community

Christians have long understood the story of Jesus as the story of the Word made flesh (Jn 1:14). Obviously, the flesh that is in mind is first of all the human bodiliness of Jesus. But, as Duncan Reid has pointed out, more than this can be found in the concept of Word made flesh. He argues for an eco-Christology in which the affirmation that God has embraced humanity in Christ is held together with

---

17. Rolston III, *Genes, Genesis and God: Values and their Origins in Natural and Human History*, 307.

the prior claim that the Word of God has become flesh.[18] Flesh not only points beyond the humanity of Jesus to the whole human community embraced by God in the incarnation, but also points beyond human flesh to the whole world of interconnected fleshly life. Flesh embraces the human but also takes us beyond it. It evokes the world of inter-related organisms. It suggests that in becoming flesh, God has embraced the interconnected web of living creatures.

Human beings are part of a three-and-a-half billion-year history of life on Earth. All things are interconnected in this story of life. Jesus of Nazareth, in his humanity, is a product of this evolutionary story. In a biological view of reality, we cannot think of the human without thinking of our evolutionary dependence on the creatures that have gone before us and of our interdependence with the biological systems of our planet. In the Christ-event, God enters into the heart of creation, embracing finite creaturely existence from within. In the Word made flesh, God embraces not only the human but also the evolutionary pattern of life that is intrinsic to and constitutive of human existence. God-with-us in Christ is to be understood as God-with-all-living-things.

Niels Gregersen calls this *deep incarnation*. He argues that, in Jesus, God embraces the whole of biological life. And in the cross of Christ we find a microcosm of God's redemptive presence to cruciform creation. He writes:

> In this context, the incarnation of God in Christ can be understood as a radical or 'deep' incarnation, that is, an incarnation into the very tissue of biological existence, and system of nature. Understood this way, the death of Christ becomes an icon of God's redemptive co-suffering with all sentient life as well as with the victims of social competition. God bears the cost of evolution, the price involved in the hardship of natural selection.[19]

Gregersen's insights that Jesus is God-with-us in the very tissue of biological life and that the cross is an icon of God's redemptive co-

---

18. Duncan Reid, 'Enfleshing the Human', in *Earth Revealing - Earth Healing: Ecology and Christian Theology*, edited by Denis Edwards (Collegeville: Liturgical Press, 2001), 69–83.
19. Gregersen, 'The Cross of Christ in an Evolutionary World', 205.

suffering with all sentient life raise the further question: how does this redemptive work function? It surely must involve more than suffering with creation. In attempting to explore this issue a little further, I will begin by sketching briefly an approach to divine power and an understanding of resurrection life that I find fundamental to this discussion.

Redefining Divine Power in the Light of the Cross and Resurrection

One of the assumptions brought to the table in all discussions of suffering creation is a view of divine power. Assumptions about divine power need to be examined critically. It would seem, for example, that one common concept of divine power is taken from the worst excesses of human tyrants. Tyrants can arbitrarily over-rule anybody and anything. They are not constrained by the demands of justice. They are not limited by respect for the integrity of other people, or by respect for the integrity of the natural world. For them, there are no limits of any kind. If one has been taught to think of God's power in this way, then it is natural to think that God can intervene in any circumstances to change the course of events. Then it is natural to ask in the midst of suffering: Why is God doing this to me?

A radically different view of divine power finds expression in the life, death and resurrection of Jesus. Here power is understood as the power to love. Jesus is certainly a power-filled figure. But the power of Jesus is far from the dominating authority of tyrants and bullies. It is not the lordly authority so often displayed by the rich and the dominant. Dominating authorities achieve their purposes through manipulation, coercion and violence. They crush their opposition, ensuring the promotion of their own causes and the achievement of their own goals. According to the Gospels, Jesus flatly opposes this kind of power and authority:

> You know that among the Gentiles those whom they recognize as their rulers lord it over them, and their great ones are tyrants over them. But it is not so among you; but whoever wishes to become great among you must be your servant, and whoever wishes to be first among you must be slave of all (Mk 10:42–44).[20]

---

20. Here, as elsewhere, I am using the translation of the New Revised Standard Version (Oxford: Oxford University Press, 1989).

Jesus is remembered as forbidding the use of dominating power in his community. There is to be no overpowering of others, no bullying, no coercion. This Gospel rejection of domination is not a rejection of power. On the contrary, the Gospels see the power of God at work in Jesus. He speaks and acts with amazing authority (Mk 1:22–27). He is anointed with the power of the Spirit of God, so that he can go about doing good, bringing healing and hope (Acts 10:38). The power of God at work in Jesus finds its ultimate expression in resurrection life. The New Testament is a message of divine saving power—God has raised Jesus from the dead and through the life, death and resurrection of Jesus there is healing and hope for our world. This Spirit-endowed power is understood not as tyrannical power but as the power to love.

In First Corinthians, Paul reflects on the startling truth that God's action to save was accomplished not through human achievement or success but through the cross. God's powerful work of healing and new creation occurs in and through the apparent failure of Jesus' mission and the absolute vulnerability and shame of his death: 'We proclaim Christ crucified, a stumbling block to Jews and foolishness to Gentiles, but to those who are called, both Jews and Greeks, Christ the power of God and the wisdom of God' (1 Cor 1:23–24). According to Paul, all ordinary notions of wisdom and power are overturned in the cross of Christ.

In Philippians, we are told that what is needed in the Christian community is 'the mind' of Christ, who did not regard equality with God as something to be exploited but 'emptied himself', taking the form of a slave, and 'became obedient to the point of death—even death on a cross'. Self-emptying (*kenōsis*) is transformed into life. It leads to Jesus' exaltation and the achievement of the divine purposes (Phil 2:5–11). In these texts and many others, it is clear that the cross of Christ is meant to shape the Christian concept of power and authority. Christian authority is a vulnerable authority. It cannot coerce but can only seek to speak the truth in love (Eph 4:15). It seeks to persuade, to invite and constantly bears witness to the truth.

The cross of Christ redefines divine power. In the light of the cross, power is to be seen in terms of the unthinkable capacity to embrace the vulnerability of loving. This divine capacity to love can be understood involving a supreme respect for the integrity of the other. When such a notion of divine power is brought to the theology of creation, it suggests that since creation is a free act of love, God may be self-limited in love in creating a universe that has its own integrity.

Ted Peters and other theologians have rightly pointed out that a powerless God is no answer. Rightly, he sees the Spirit as the power of God at work in creation and in new creation, bringing us to our eschatological future.[21] But the power of God revealed in the resurrection is not a power that preserves Jesus of Nazareth from brutality and death. It is a power of the Spirit, by which the brutal ugliness of the cross is transformed into an event of life for the world. God's power is revealed to be of a specific kind. It does not destroy human integrity or natural processes, but brings life in and through them.

In this section, I have been proposing that the Christ-event calls for a revised notion of divine power. God is thought of as committed to respecting the limitations imposed in creating a finite world that enjoys its own integrity. This would mean that God may not, for example, be free to arbitrarily decide that the pattern of death that is part of the natural world could be set aside in my own case. God may not be able to do this because it may not be true to who God is. God may have freely and lovingly engaged in an evolving world and freely accepted the limitations that this involves. In this context, it would not make sense for me to pray that I will never die. It makes perfect sense for me to pray that God's Spirit be with me in my life and death and bring me to new life in Christ.

The Risen Christ: The Beginning of the Transformation of the Universe

In his letter to the Romans, Paul talks of creation waiting and longing to share in redemption in Christ (Rom: 8:19–22). In Colossians, we hear not only of all things being created in Christ, but also of all things, everything in the universe, being reconciled in him (Col 1:15–20). A similar theme appears in Ephesians: All things, absolutely everything in the universe, will be gathered up and transformed in the risen Christ (Eph 1:9–10, 20–3). In Revelation, there is the promise of 'a new heaven and a new earth'. In this work of new creation, the risen Christ is the Alpha and the Omega, the first and the last, the beginning and the end (Rev 22:13). Christians who celebrate the

---

21. Ted Peters, *God—the World's Future* (Minneapolis: Fortress, 1992), 314.

great Easter Vigil use these words as they light the Easter candle, the sign of the risen Christ. Then, illuminated by the light of the Easter candle, they listen to readings from Scripture beginning with the first Genesis account of the creation of all things. Every Easter, and in some way every Eucharist, is a celebration of the whole of creation transformed in the light of the risen Christ.

The understanding of the resurrection that I am advocating takes this Christian promise seriously. It sees it as involving a transformed bodily and personal existence for human beings in a transformed universe. It understands the resurrection of Jesus as not only the promise but also the beginning of the communion of all creation with God. Teilhard de Chardin expresses this with the concept of the risen Christ as the Omega of evolution. He sees the risen one as already existing and operating at the heart of the natural world. Christ the Omega radiates the love that empowers the process of the unfolding of the universe, enabling evolutionary emergence from within and drawing the universe to its future in God.[22]

Like Teilhard, Karl Rahner sees the risen Christ as already at work in the transformation of the universe. He says of Jesus: 'When his body was shattered in death, Christ was poured out over the cosmos.'[23] The eternal Word of God has been involved with creation from the beginning. But now, not only in his divinity, but also in his humanity, Christ the risen one is at the heart of the whole universe as the beginning of its transfiguration. Rahner sees the risen Christ as the 'pledge and beginning of the perfect fulfilment of the world', the 'representative of the new cosmos' and the 'irreversible and embryonically final beginning of the glorification and divinization of the *whole* reality'.[24] This means, Rahner insists, that Christians who believe in incarnation and resurrection ought to be more committed to matter than those who call themselves materialist. Christians are, or ought be, the most radical of materialists. We are 'sublime' materialists because we cannot think of a future for ourselves in God without thinking of the future of God's creation.[25]

---

22. Teilhard de Chardin, *The Phenomenon of Man* (London: Collins, 1995), 319–22.
23. Karl Rahner, *On the Theology of Death* (New York: Herder and Herder, 1961), 66.
24. Karl Rahner, 'Resurrection', in *Sacramentum Mundi* 5, edited by Karl Rahner (New York: Herder and Herder, 1970), 331–3, 333; Karl Rahner, 'Dogmatic Questions on Easter', in *Theological Investigations* 4 (New York: Seabury, 1966), 121–33, 129.
25. Karl Rahner, 'The Festival of the Future of the World', in *Theological Investigations* 7 (New York: Herder and Herder, 1971), 181–5, 183.

As Robert John Russell has pointed out in a number of articles, this objective position on eschatology brings theology into a real confrontation with science.[26] As is well known, the scientific picture of the future involves either the universe collapsing back on itself in a fiery end or, as seems more likely at present, endlessly expanding and cooling in bleak dissipation. Neither scenario is easy to reconcile with a realistic understanding of the Easter promise. As Russell insists, this calls for serious work in the interface between science and theology. I cannot take up this issue here, except to point to Russell's work. As part of a more complex argument, he suggests that we might need to think of the Easter event as having a transforming effect on the laws of nature themselves. This would mean that 'the 'freeze or fry' predictions for the cosmological future might have been applicable 'had God not acted at Easter and if God were not to continue to act to bring forth the ongoing eschatological transformation of the universe'.[27]

The focus of my work in this article is on the participation of individual non-human creatures in redemption in Christ. I am assuming rather than arguing for the transformation of all things in Christ and the promise of personal and bodily resurrection life for human beings. In this context, my central question is about other organisms: Do individual sparrows and kangaroos participate in their own way in redemption in Christ?

Individual Creatures—Embraced in the Spirit

In a Trinitarian theology of creation, the Holy Spirit can be seen as the Breath of Life that is creatively present to each creature, enabling it to exist and empowering it towards the new—'When you send forth your spirit they are created; and you renew the face of the ground' (Ps 104:30). As the Nicean-Constantinopolitan Creed puts it, the

---

26. Robert John Russell, 'Bodily Resurrection, Eschatology, and Scientific Cosmology: The Mutual Interaction of Christian Theology and Science', in *Resurrection: Theological and Scientific Assessments,* edited by Ted Peters, Robert John Russell and Michael Welker (Grand Rapids: Eerdmans, 2002), 3–30; Robert John Russell, 'Eschatology and Physical Cosmology: A Preliminary Reflection', in *The Far Future Universe: Eschatology from a Cosmic Perspective,* edited by George FR Ellis (Philadelphia: Templeton Foundation, 2002), 266–315.
27. Russell, 'Bodily Resurrection, Eschatology, and Scientific Cosmology: The Mutual Interaction of Christian Theology and Science', 19.

Holy Spirit is *Lord and Giver of Life*. In the Christian tradition, the Spirit is the Life-Giver in two inter-related senses—as the giver of existence and biological life on the one hand, and as the giver of new life in Christ on the other.

In such a theology, Word and Spirit are inter-related in the works of creation and salvation. For this reason, Karl Rahner speaks of an *entelechy*, or inner orientation, of the Spirit to the Christ event.[28] The Creator Spirit can be seen as the dynamic presence of God in the events of the first second, in the formation of atoms, in the evolution of the first galaxies and stars, in the shaping of our solar system and in the emergence of the enormous variety of living things on Earth. The Spirit is the power that enables the universe to unfold and evolve. When, after fourteen billion years, human beings emerge, the Spirit is present to them as the mysterious closeness of God, surrounding them in gracious self-offering love. In both ongoing creation and in grace, the Spirit is the presence of God that brings life. And in creation and grace, the Spirit is always the Spirit of Christ—the Christ-directed Spirit.

God is present, in the Spirit, to each creature here and now, loving it into existence and promising its future. Creation is always an act of love. This means that in some way salvation begins in and with creation. I agree, then, with important insights of Ruth Page. She responds to the suffering of creation with a theology of God's saving love for each individual creature. She argues that God's presence to creatures involves both creation and redemption as God *companions* each creature with love.[29] She insists on God's care for individual creatures here and now. She sees God as both 'letting the world be' and 'companioning' the world and all its creatures. I am much in agreement in her theology of companioning, but differ from her in stressing not only the presence of the Spirit companioning each creature here and now and also the promise of redemptive fulfilment in Christ.

This divine companioning establishes each creature's own identity, possibilities and proper autonomy. The presence of the Spirit is the immanent divine power of ongoing creation (*creation continua*). This is not some abstract power, but the personal presence of divine love. If God is understood as embracing each creature with love, this has

---

28. Karl Rahner, *Foundations of Christian Faith* (New York: Crossroad, 1978), 317–18.
29. Ruth Page, *God and the Web of Creation* (London: SCM, 1996).

immediate ecological consequences. As Page points out, it means that God knows and cares about each creature's habitat.[30] This can only mean that the Spirit is grieved (Eph 4:30) when human beings abuse and destroy habitats.

The Breath of God is the immanent divine power that enables creation itself, in its own integrity and through the functioning of its own laws, to break through to what is new. The Spirit of God is present with every creature in the universe as its faithful companion, accompanying it with love, valuing it, bringing it into an interrelated world of creatures, holding it creatively in the dynamic life of the divine Communion. This divine Companion delights in creatures in their beauty, their inter-related diversity and their fecundity as they already exist as self-expressions of the divine Wisdom (Prov 8:30).

But the Spirit is also a faithful Companion to creation in it struggle and pain. In this context, I think it is helpful to build on a line of thought, which is implicit in Paul, to see the Creator Spirit as the midwife to the birth of the new. The Spirit is with creation as it groans in labour, enabling the emergence of new life. Creation waits with 'eager longing' for its liberation from 'bondage to decay' and for 'the freedom associated with the glory of the children of God' (Rom 8:19–23). Something new is to be born: 'For we know that the entire creation has been groaning together in the pangs of childbirth up till now' (8:22). The Spirit, then, can be understood as the faithful companion of creation in its travail and as the midwife of new creation. Paul sees the Christian experience of the Spirit as the 'down-payment and guarantee' (2 Cor 1:22; 5:5; Eph 1:13–15), the 'first-fruits' of God's harvest (Rom 8:23). If the Spirit is the midwife to new creation, this points to the unimaginable: the participation of all creatures in the dynamism of the divine life.

The Creator Spirit is with creatures in their finitude, death and incompletion, holding each in redemptive love, and is in some way already drawing each into an unforeseeable eschatological future in the divine life. This promise points to an unimaginable participation of all creatures in the dynamism of the divine life. The Spirit is with each creature now, with every wild predator and its prey and with every dying creature, as midwife to the unforeseeable birth in which all things will be made new.

---

30. Page, *God and the Web of Creation*, 71.

Individual Creatures—Redeemed in Christ

In this final section, I will explore the idea that the death and resurrection of Jesus is to be seen as a promise, not only for human beings, but also for other living creatures as well. I will propose that *individual* animals and birds will be taken up into God.

Holmes Rolston III has pointed to the example of the 'backup' pelican chick. White pelicans have developed a highly successful evolutionary strategy that involves hatching an extra disposable chick, which functions as an insurance against the loss of the primary chick. Often this chick is pushed out of the nest and left to die or to become prey for other creatures.[31] Jay McDaniel asks about the redemption of all such chicks. May we hope, he asks, that a 'backup' pelican chick, abandoned in favour of its stronger sibling, continues in some way beyond death and finds its fulfilment and redemption in some kind of 'pelican heaven'? He makes the important point that if there is fulfilment for creatures beyond their death, it will be one that is appropriate to their own interest and needs: 'If there is a pelican heaven, it is a *pelican* heaven'.[32]

Based upon the promise of resurrection, I will argue that we can expect some kind of fulfilment beyond death for pelican chicks and sparrows that fall to the ground. The character of God revealed in the Christ-event is, I believe, that of a God who cares about individual sparrows and in some way takes them into the divine life. How might this be envisaged? In what follows, I will outline three responses to this issue, and then develop my own approach.

1. *Universal Resurrection.* Jürgen Moltmann sees evolution as producing countless victims. He criticises the evolutionary theologies of Teilhard de Chardin and Karl Rahner for failing to see evolution from the perspective of its victims. He sees Jesus Christ as the redeemer of evolution. Moltmann envisages God's eschatological action as involving the raising of the dead, the gathering of the victims and the seeking of the lost. This will bring a redemption of the world that evolution could never achieve. He

---

31. Holmes Rolston III, *Science and Religion: A Critical Survey* (New York: Random House, 1987), 138.
32. Jay McDaniel, *Of God and Pelicans: A Theology of Reverence for Life* (Louisville, Kentucky: Westminster/ John Knox, 1989), 41–9, 45.

sees God's new creation as a literal waking and a gathering of every creature of every time. This is not the outcome of evolutionary history but an act of God at the end of history. It is the coming of Christ in glory to all creatures of all times simultaneously, in a single instant.[33] Some find a tension between Moltmann's view of the Spirit at work in creation and his insistence on the need for evolution to be redeemed. In a subsequent work, Moltmann seems more inclined towards a concept of transformation of this present creation in Christ. He takes the words from Revelation, 'Behold I make all things new' (21:5), to mean that nothing is lost. All is brought back in a new form: 'The *creatio ex nihilo*, the creation out of nothing, is completed in the eschatological *creatio ex vetere*, the creation out of the old'.[34]

2. *Objective Immortality.* Alfred North Whitehead, the founding figure of process philosophy, has developed the notion of objective immortality. This refers to the impact of creatures on God. He sees creatures as participating in eternal life through the effect they have on God.[35] Whitehead distinguishes between the primordial nature of God and the consequent nature. The consequent nature represents the responsive nature of God by which God receives, sustains and saves creation. Every event in creation finds its permanent fulfilment in God's consequent nature. Such an event becomes immortal by being received into God. It can then never be effaced. It has 'objective immortality'. Alongside this objective view, some process thinkers also defend a form of subjective immortality in which the individual self continues as a centre of experience.[36] Jay McDaniel adopts objective immortality, while also hoping for the individual pelican chick's renewal after death.[37] In a recent book, John Haught describes objective immortality as the salvation that occurs when creation is taken up into the divine experience: 'all the suffering and tragedy as well as the emergence

---

33. Jürgen Moltmann, *The Way of Jesus Christ* (London: SCM, 1990), 303.
34. Jürgen Moltmann, *The Coming of God: Christian Eschatology* (London: SCM, 1996), 265.
35. Alfred North Whitehead (1929, 1957), *Process and Reality: An Essay in Cosmology* (New York, Harper and Row,1929), 526-33.
36. Ian Barbour, 'God's Power: A Process View', in *The Work of Love: Creation as Kenosis* edited by John Polkinghorne (Grand Rapids: Eerdmans, 2001), 1–20.
37. McDaniel, *Of God and Pelicans: A Theology of Reverence for Life,* 47–8.

of new life and intense beauty' is being saved by 'being taken eternally into God's feeling for the world'.[38]

3. *Material Inscription.* Ernst Conradie seeks a view of divine transcendence that respects the otherness of God but does not detract from ecological commitment.[39] He suggests the metaphor of multiple dimensions as a way of approaching the transcendent realm. He proposes that eternity be conceived of as a 'depth' dimension beyond the space-time continuum. This dimension of eternity includes space and time but transcends them. In this eternal dimension, past and present events may be experienced simultaneously. Conradie proposes a further metaphor of 'material inscription'.[40] This refers to the whole history of the cosmos being not only held in the mind of God but also inscribed or fixated in the dimensions of space and time. With this inscription, the goodness of the material creation is affirmed forever. This means that how we act towards creation has eternal significance. Conradie insists that creation needs to be healed. He suggests that the 'many rooms' of the Father's house may mean that it will be possible to heal the brokenness of the past and to celebrate the joy of forgiveness. Because they are materially inscribed, the events of the past will be as real and concrete as the original experiences, but all these retrieved events will need to pass through God's judgment and mercy.

The three approaches described above each clearly have their own value. Moltmann rightly affirms the need for the redemption of individual non-human creatures. But in my view his heavy emphasis on a radically new creation overturning the old tends to undermine the goodness of creation and ecological commitment. And I am not so sure that it is appropriate to claim that every creature that ever lived will have its own individual existence again in resurrection life. The Whiteheadian concept of 'objective immortality' is a positive contri-

---

38. John Haught, *God After Darwin: A Theology of Evolution* (Boulder, Colo.: Westview. 2000), 43.
39. EM Conradie, *Hope for the Earth* (Bellville: University of Western Cape Publications, 2000).
40. EM Conradie, 'Resurrection, Finitude and Ecology', in *Resurrection: Theological and Scientific Assessments*, edited by Ted Peters, Robert John Russell and Michael Welker (Grand Rapids: Eerdmans, 2002), 277–96, 292.

bution, but I find it something of a minimalist one. I think we need a more Christological, redemptive and relational concept. Ernst Conradie's metaphor of 'material inscription' is an imaginative approach that promotes ecological commitment while insisting on the need for the healing of creation. My own tendency is to locate this inscription in the life-giving Spirit of God. I will outline this approach in four points.

1. *The future of creation remains obscure and shrouded in mystery.* The future of the universe is radically mysterious to us because it is caught up in the abiding mystery of the incomprehensible God. The future of creation is not something about which we have information. What we have in the resurrection of Jesus Christ is a promise. The promise does not give a clear view of the future. All claims about the afterlife necessarily involve a large element of negative theology. I believe that it is important to preface all attempts to make sense of Christian eschatological claims with the acknowledgment that future life in God is beyond our comprehension. Our ideas about life beyond death can only be based upon our view of God as a God who promises to bring life. They are based upon trust in the God of resurrection. As Elizabeth Johnson says, in the end, 'everything depends on the character of God'.[41]

2. *Individual creatures are inscribed in the eternal divine life through the Holy Spirit.* The life-giving Spirit of God embraces every creature in our evolutionary history, enabling it to exist within an inter-related universe. In the proposal being made here, this embrace of the Spirit is seen as a promise that each creature 'will be set free from its bondage to decay and will attain the freedom of the glory of the children of God' (Rom 8:21). Paul sees the Spirit as the one who brings resurrection life: 'If the Spirit who raised Jesus from the dead dwells in you, he who raised Jesus from the dead will give life to your mortal bodies also through his Spirit that dwells in you' (Rom 8:11). I think it can be argued that this Spirit of God can be seen as the life-giving presence of God immanent to all of bodily creation, the power of resurrection life not only for human

---

41. Elizabeth Johnson, *Friends of God and Prophets: A Feminist Theological Reading of the Communion of Saints* (London: SCM, 1998), 201.

bodies, as Paul emphasises here, but for all creatures. Although this Breath of God is never contained in any one body, the Spirit is very much to do with bodies, breathing life into all bodies. The Spirit of God 'operates through and within embodiment'.[42]

Because the Holy Spirit is the immanent one, the life-giving one, the one who comes close to each creature in love, and the one who mediates the power of resurrection life, I think it can be said that it is through the Spirit that creatures are inscribed in the divine life. In Luke's Gospel, Jesus tells the disciples to rejoice that their names are written in heaven (10:20). The idea of a written record kept by God, and the image of the 'Book of Life' are widespread in the biblical tradition (Ex 32:32; Ps 56:8, 69:28, 139:16; Job 19:23; Mal 3:16–18; Phil 4:3; Rev 20:12–14, 21:27). What is being suggested here is that, as human beings are inscribed in the Book of Life, so, in their own distinctive ways, all creatures are eternally inscribed in the life of God through the life-giving Spirit. The Spirit does not abandon the sparrow that falls to the ground, but gathers it up, inscribing it eternally in life of the Trinity. It is the Spirit of God that brings the fallen sparrow into the realm of redemptive life in Christ.

3. *Individual Creatures find Healing and Fulfilment in Christ.* In the risen Christ, the wounded find healing and the poor and the oppressed are lifted up. The biblical and Christian tradition has used the concept of the last judgment to express this final act of salvation in Christ. As Dirk Evers points out, the often misused concept of the final judgment needs to be rehabilitated and renewed. It is the crucified who determines what is eternally valid, and what is set right. It is the crucified who heals by revealing and responding to both the wounds of the victim and the shame of the perpetrator.[43] The concept of the last judgment has fallen from favour because it has been used to instil terror. It needs to be

---

42. Gunter Thomas, 'Resurrection to New Life: Pneumatological Implications of the Eschatological Transition', in *Resurrection: Theological and Scientific Assessments,* edited by Ted Peters, Robert John Russell and Michael Welker (Grand Rapids: Eerdmans, 2002), 255–76, 268.
43. Dirk Evers, 'Memory in the Flow of Time and the Concept of Resurrection', in *Resurrection: Theological and Scientific Assessments,* edited by Ted Peters, Robert John Russell and Michael Welker (Grand Rapids: Eerdmans, 2002), 239–54, 253.

rediscovered as something that assures us that not only will evil be acknowledged and rejected, but also that nothing good will ever be lost. All will be taken up into Christ. In particular, I believe it needs to be rediscovered as expressing hope for the healing of the whole of creation in Christ. It is the risen Christ in whom 'all things will be reconciled' (Col 1:20). It is the risen Christ who says, 'Behold I make all things new' (Rev 21:5). But the question remains: How is this to be envisaged?

4. *Redemption in Christ will be specific to each kind of creature.* God's redemption of any creature is always a relational event. Based upon God's wisdom and justice, I believe that it can be taken as a fundamental principle that redemptive fulfilment of any creature will be specific to the creature involved. God relates to each creature on its own terms. The proposal I am making is that the diverse range of creatures that springs from the abundance of this divine Communion will find fulfilment in being taken up eternally into this Communion. But it is fundamental to this proposal to insist that such a fulfilment will be one that fits the nature of each creature. While I think it can be argued that the fulfilment of a human being will necessarily be personal one, the fulfilment of a mosquito may be of a different order, one that in God's wisdom is fully appropriate to a mosquito.

5. *Some individual creatures may find redemption in the living memory and the eternal life of the Trinity and the Communion of Saints.* It may be, then, that while it is appropriate for some creatures to share in resurrection with a transformed individual existence in God, it is at least possible that God may find it appropriate for other creatures to be taken up into divine life in another way— in the living memory of the divine Communion. This idea draws upon the Trinitarian theology of God as Communion, the concept of the Communion of Saints and the liturgical theology of memory (*anamnesis*). I have already indicated that I number myself among those who hope for a transformation of the whole of creation in Christ, and for a fully personal and bodily participation in resurrection life for human beings. It is important to note that resurrection refers to a radically transformed and unimaginable bodiliness. Many would think that this promise holds for their beloved dog and, in my view, they may well be right. But I think it is at least a question whether bodily resurrection is necessarily

the most appropriate fulfilment for bacteria or a dinosaur. It seems possible that in the wisdom of God it may be more appropriate for an individual dinosaur to reach its fulfilment by being treasured in the divine life of the Three and celebrated for ever in the Communion of Saints.

I believe that we can proclaim that the dynamic shared life of God will involve the holding and treasuring of every creature of every time in the living present of the Trinity. The Christian tradition gives a central place to sacred memory (anamnesis). When Christians gather for the Eucharist, they remember what God has done in the life, death and resurrection of Jesus. But this is far from being simply a memory of the past. It functions powerfully and realistically in the present. It both promises and anticipates the divine Communion. It brings those gathered into living communion with Jesus Christ and makes them participants in divine Trinitarian Communion.

This experience may provide an analogy for an approach to God's redemptive and living memory of a dinosaur. It offers a hint that God may have a way of being with an individual dinosaur in its lifetime, inscribing it eternally in the Spirit, bringing it to redemptive fulfilment in Christ, and celebrating it eternally in the living memory and experience of the divine persons. In the Communion of Saints, human beings may come to share something of the delight that the divine Persons experience in celebrating and treasuring the individual existence of each creature. The Communion of Saints would then be thought of as opening up to the communion of all creation.

In a discussion of some of these ideas recently, one participant pointed to the way children and their parents have rediscovered dinosaurs in the last twenty years. Of course, this has been partly a matter of effective media packaging and commercial exploitation. But there has also been a genuine delight in dinosaurs on the part of many children and adults around the world. We have come to see them as a part of our living heritage. This kind of memory gives us a tiny hint, perhaps, of the treasuring that goes on eternally in the life of the divine Communion, a treasuring that will be shared by all those who are called to share this life. In this view, individual creatures are taken up into the living experience of Trinitarian God. They abide permanently within the everlasting compassionate love of the Three. They are celebrated, respected and honoured in the Communion of Saints.

I have been arguing that the resurrection promise means a future for individual sparrows and kookaburras. As I finish this work, I can see a sparrow sitting on a low branch outside my window. What I have been arguing is that this sparrow is known and loved by God, that the life-giving Spirit surrounds it with love and accompanies it in its life and death, that the Spirit inscribes it eternally in the life of God, that this sparrow participates in redemption in Christ, and that it is eternally treasured and celebrated in the Communion of the Trinity and the Communion of Saints. According to the line of thought developed here, what cannot be known for certain is whether, in God's wisdom this sparrow is appropriately fulfilled in the living memory of the Trinity, which is surely more powerful and more liberating than anything we can envisage, or whether God also finds it appropriate to raise this sparrow up in some other way. What I think can be said with confidence is that it will find its fulfilment in Christ.

Christopher Southgate rightly points out that a theology of salvation will need to involve not only the claim I have made here, that 'God does not abandon the victims of evolution,' but also the idea that 'humans have a calling, stemming from the transformative power of Christ's action on the Cross, to participate in the healing of the world'.[44] He insists that we human beings have an important role in the redemption of creation. We are responsible to do what we can to heal the harm we have done and to ensure the flourishing of the biodiversity of our planet. Southgate sees the future of humans and the rest of creation as radically inter-related. He suggests that it is only by being humbly involved in the healing of nature that we human beings can become fully alive.

I believe that this is the very meaning of what we do in the Eucharist. Every Eucharist is a living memory of Christ that is also an anticipation of the transformation of all things in Christ. The Eucharist, then, is also an *anamnesis* of the whole of creation. Gathered at the table, we celebrate the three-and-a-half billion-year history of life that finds its radical yes to God in the paschal event of Christ. The Eucharist is an event of praise and thanksgiving on behalf of the whole of creation – 'All creation rightly gives you praise'. It is a living, participatory memory of all that God has done for us in creation

---

44. Christopher Southgate, 'God and Evolutionary Evil: Theodicy in the Light of Darwinism', in *Zygon* 37 (2002): 803–22, 817.

and redemption. It is also an experience of the divine eschatological Communion. All creatures are embraced and loved in this divine Communion. To participate in God is to participate in God's feeling for individual creatures. It is to remember every sparrow that falls to the ground and to know that it has its place in God.

'Sublime Communion': The Theology of the Natural World in *Laudato Si'*

To read, or re-read, *Laudato Si'* is to discover fresh insights into the relationship between God and the planetary community of life on Earth, our common home. Those who spend time with this encyclical find themselves renewed in hope, taken by joy at the beauty of Francis's vision, sobered by the challenges he puts before us, and summoned again to see their lives as an ecological vocation, radically committed to Earth and all its creatures.

There is much to be grateful for in this encyclical: that it is grounded so clearly in the major issues we face, global climate change, loss of biodiversity, and our abuse of the gift of water; that it reflects on these issues from a profound theology of the communion of creation; that it seeks to go to the human roots of the problems we face in its critique of technocratic and anthropocentric worldviews; that its central vision of integral ecology holds together the protection of God's creation with commitment to our human brothers and sisters, above all the poor and excluded; that it invites dialogue about international and national solutions to the issues we face; and that it calls all of us to a profound ecological conversion. At every point, it models a dialogical stance. The whole document is developed under the sign and inspiration of St Francis of Assisi, and his commitment both to poor and needy human beings and to God's other creatures, who are also in their own way our sisters and brothers.

Pope Francis makes explicit his intention that *Laudato Si'* is now 'added to the body of the Church's social teaching' (paragraph 15). As he notes, his work builds on that of Paul VI, John Paul II, and Benedict XVI (paragraph 4–6). But with this more developed document, Francis makes it clear he now means to bring the protection of God's creation formally, and permanently, into the centre of Catholic social teaching, along with its long-standing commitment to inter-human justice and peace.

In the theological world, Catholic Social Teaching is usually linked to social ethics and moral theology, rather than directly to other areas of theology such as biblical studies, spirituality, or the discipline of this article, systematic theology. But I think it is obvious that *Laudato Si'* sets an agenda for the church and the world that is of such importance that it must also be a dialogue partner for systematic theologians now and into the future. In seeking to engage with *Laudato Si'* from this perspective, I will begin with some reflections on the encyclical in the light of recent contributions to ecological theology by systematic theologians.

It is notable that some priorities evident in the work of ecological theologians are not well represented in the encyclical. One of these priorities is the incarnation. In reaction to the almost exclusive emphasis on the redemption of human beings by Christian churches in recent centuries, some early attempts at ecological theology and spirituality focussed almost exclusively on creation theology. One of the ways that this focus on creation has found expression is in the blending of creation spirituality and popular science, as in the 'new story' of the universe, or in the emergence of 'evolutionary consciousness'. Many people have found genuine inspiration in a wide variety of recent creation spiritualities. In some of them, however, there is little connection with Christology and, at times at the popular level, there is no place for Jesus of Nazareth, for the theology of the incarnation, or for salvation in Christ.

In this context, some theologians have thought it a priority to construct an ecological theology that clearly shows the profound connection between God's creative act and God's saving act in Jesus Christ.[1] In particular, they have sought to show the radical meaning of the incarnation for the whole of creaturely reality, some of them

---

1. Ernst Conradie led an international and ecumenical project on this issue, that has found expression in the two volumes he edited, *Creation and Salvation*, volume 1, A Mosaic of Selected Classic Christian Theologies (Zurich: LIT, 2012), *Creation and Salvation*, volume 2, A Companion on Recent Theological Movements (Zurich: LIT VERLAG, 2012), and also in *Christian Faith and the Earth: Current Paths and Emerging Horizons in Ecotheology*, edited by Ernst M Conardie, Sigurd Bergmann, Celia Deane-Drummond and Denis Edwards (London: Bloomsbury, 2014).

through the concept of 'deep incarnation'.[2] And they have attempted to see divine action in both creation and in the saving incarnation as a fully Trinitarian act of God through the eternal Word and in the Holy Spirit. Perhaps because of its attempt to speak to those who are not Christian, in its important second chapter, *Laudato Si'* is focussed mainly on creation theology, and does not explore in any detail the interconnection between creation and incarnation. There are, however, important brief comments on Jesus Christ at the end of chapter two, and also throughout the encyclical, and on the Trinity in three paragraphs at its end, which I will highlight in this essay.

A second priority in the recent work of some ecological theologians has been the attempt to deal responsibly with a century and a half of evolutionary science. Two things in particular confront theology. The first is that the evolution of life on Earth has been determined by contingent events, such as a meteorite hitting Earth, and that it depends upon the randomness of genetic mutations as well as on the ordering process of natural selection. Our theology of the natural world has to be robust enough to deal with randomness and contingency. Far more demanding for theology, however, is a second issue, that of the costs of evolution, costs built into the process: the loss, the pain, the predation, the deaths, the extinctions of most species that ever lived over the 3.8 billion year history of life.[3] *Laudato Si'* has some acknowledgment of evolution (par. 79–81), and speaks of God's self-limitation in creating a world that develops with its own proper autonomy (paragraph 80), but in my judgment it too often portrays God's creation as a harmonious ordered cosmos without

---

2. See *Incarnation: On the Scope and Depth of Christology*, edited by Neils Henrik Gregersen (Minneapolis, MN: Fortress, 2015); Celia Deane-Drummond, *Christ and Evolution: Wonder and Wisdom* (Minneapolis: Fortress, 2009); Denis Edwards, *Partaking of God, Trinity, Evolution and Ecology* (Collegeville: Liturgical Press, 2014); Elizabeth Johnson, *Ask the Beasts: Darwin and the God of Love* (London: Bloomsbury, 2014).
3. On these costs, see particularly *Physics and Cosmology: Scientific Perspectives on the Problem of Natural Evil*, edited by Nancy Murphy, Robert John Russell and William R Stoeger (Vatican City State: Vatican Observatory, 2007), and Christopher Southgate, *The Groaning of Creation: God, Evolution, and the Problem of Evil* (Louisville: Westminster John Knox, 2008). For examples of recent responses from ecological theologians, see Deane-Drummond, *Christ and Evolution*, 159–93; Denis Edwards, *How God Acts: Creation, Redemption and Special Divine Action* (Minneapolis: Fortress Press, 2010); and Johnson, *Ask the Beasts*, 181–235.

acknowledging the violence, pain and death of the natural world. In my view, a theology of the cross, a theology of God with suffering creation, is needed to speak in some way to this violence. *Laudato Si'* is already a large document, and it is entirely understandable that it could not do everything. But I think it is important to note that it does not deal with the dark side of nature or with the theology of the cross.

While the encyclical does not contribute greatly to the development of ecological theology on the issues of the incarnation and evolution and its costs, it provides a major stimulus and inspiration to contemporary theology with its vision of the natural world in relation to God. It offers an illuminating, inspiring and, at least in Catholic Church teaching, new theological view of the natural world, of animals, plants, mountains, rivers, seas, and of human beings interconnected with nature and part of nature. In what follows, I offer an analysis of *Laudato Si*'s theology of nature according to three threads that can be found running through the encyclical: 1. The value of non-human creatures in themselves before God; 2. The concept of other creatures as revelatory of God; and 3. The theology of the sublime communion of creation.

The Value of Non-Human Creatures in Themselves

One of the crucial questions for any ecological theology concerns the meaning and value of non-human creatures. Do they receive their meaning and value only from their usefulness to human beings? Or do they have meaning and value in themselves? The Catholic tradition has tended to see the rest of the creation as ordered to the human and as existing simply for human use. Even the Second Vatican Council, in its *Pastoral Constitution on the Church in the Modern World*, strikes a clearly anthropocentric note.[4] But does not more need to be said, above all in the age of the Anthropocene?[5] *Laudato Si'* does say far

---

4. *Gaudium et Spes*, 12, 24.
5. According to the International Union of Geological Sciences, our geological period is the Holocene, which began after the last major ice age, 11,700 years ago. Atmospheric chemist and Nobel laureate Paul Crutzen has been a leading advocate for naming our current time period the Anthropocene, in recognition of the way human activity is changing Earth's atmosphere, geology, hydrology and biology. The term has been taken up by other scientists, although not by all, and by the Pontifical Council of Sciences, of which Paul Crutzen is a member, in for example, its publication 'Sustainable Humanity, Sustainable Nature, Our Responsibility' at <http://www.pas.va/content/accademia/en/publications/extraseries/sustainable.html> Accessed XXX.

more, and in doing so offers a new development in Catholic teaching in the clarity of its claim that non-human creatures have value in themselves. This teaching, of course, is not new to ecological theology, but its incorporation into Catholic Social Teaching is an important new development.

This new position makes its first appearance in the opening chapter of *Laudato Si'*, where Pope Francis discusses the loss of biodiversity. He points out that the current extinction of species which is due to human actions may mean the loss of valuable resources for human beings in food and medicines, now and far into the future. But he goes on to say that it is not enough to think of these species as resources for human beings, 'while overlooking the fact that they have value in themselves' (paragraph 33). Clearly Francis recognises that species of plants and animals, and also reptiles, insects and microorganisms, may have enormous value to humans, but he insists that we must also recognise that they have intrinsic value. They have value before God their Creator, and they give glory to God by being what they are. Francis laments that because of human actions, 'thousands of species will no longer give glory to God by their very existence, nor convey their message to us' (paragraph 33).

In his reflection on the biblical accounts of creation, Francis completely opposes the interpretation of the 'dominion' text (Gen 1:28) as supporting unbridled exploitation. He recognises that Christians may have contributed to such a false view by incorrectly interpreting the Scriptures, and he insists that 'nowadays we must forcefully reject the notion that our being created in God's image and being given dominion over the earth justifies absolute domination over other creatures' (paragraph 67). The dominion text needs to be read, he says, in its context and with an appropriate hermeneutic, which includes reading it in the context of Genesis 2:15, where we are told to 'till and keep' the garden of the world. Francis proposes that tilling and keeping can be understood as involving a mutual relationship between human beings and other creatures, where humans receive from other creatures what they need for their sustenance, and humans in turn protect and care for their fellow creatures. Francis points to biblical texts that speak of our responsibilities to a donkey, an ox, or a bird's nest (Ex 23:13; Deut 22:4–6), and insist that 'the Bible has no place for a tyrannical anthropocentrism unconcerned for other creatures' (paragraph 68).

In this biblical context, Francis returns to the notion of intrinsic value: 'we are called to recognize that other living beings have a value of their own in God's eyes' (paragraph 69). He goes on immediately to quote the *Catholic Catechism*, which says of other creatures that 'by their existence they bless him and give him glory',[6] and Psalm 104 which sings: 'the Lord rejoices in all his works'.[7] Building on the Scriptures and on the *Catechism*, Francis seems to acknowledge that he is saying something new with his emphasis on creatures having value in themselves: 'In our time, the Church does not simply state that other creatures are completely subordinate to the good of human beings as if they had no worth in themselves and can be treated as we wish. The German bishops have taught that, where other creatures are concerned, "we can speak of the priority of being over being useful"' (paragraph 69).

Other creatures have value, then, because they are God's creatures and give praise to God by their very existence. Francis comes back to the idea of creatures having value in themselves and, in this instance, speaks explicitly of their 'intrinsic value', when he considers the way we are called to respect and protect ecosystems: 'We take these systems into account not only to determine how best to use them, but also because they have an intrinsic value independent of their usefulness. Each organism, as a creature of God, is good and admirable in itself; the same is true of the harmonious ensemble of organisms existing in a defined space and functioning as a system' (paragraph 140). The traditional idea of human use of other creatures is not denied in *Laudato Si'* but embraced within a theology that sees them as having their own God-given meaning and value, and so as demanding respect, protection and, as I will show below, love, from human beings.

What is the basis for this claim that other creatures have intrinsic value? A careful reading reveals that Francis sees three reasons as supporting this claim. The first is the traditional theological concept that other creatures are 'the locus' of divine presence (paragraph 88). In these creatures, Francis points out, we encounter God's Holy Spirit. He says that 'the Spirit of life dwells in them', and in our encounter with them we are invited into relationship with this indwelling

---

6. *Catechism of the Catholic Church*, 2416.
7. Ps 104:31.

and life-giving Spirit of God (paragraph 88). Later in the encyclical, Francis writes: 'The universe unfolds in God, who fills it completely. Hence, there is a mystical meaning to be found in a leaf, in a mountain trail, in a dewdrop, in a poor person's face' (paragraph 233). This means, Francis says, that we are called to find God in all things, to be open to discover the divine presence in all the creatures we encounter. At this point Francis quotes from Bonaventure, who says that 'contemplation deepens the more we feel the working of God's grace within our hearts, and the better we learn to encounter God in creatures outside ourselves' (paragraph 233).

A second reason offered to support the claim that other creatures have value in themselves, a reason that seems characteristic of Francis, and one that is not often expressed in theology or church teaching, is that God loves each of them. Francis speaks of creation as springing from 'God's loving plan in which every creature has its own value and significance' and as 'a reality illuminated by the love which calls us together into universal communion' (paragraph 76). In a particularly rich section of the encyclical, Francis points out that the creation springs not from arbitrary omnipotence or self-assertion but from the divine freedom, as an act of love:

> Creation is in the order of love. God's love is the fundamental moving force in all created things: 'For you love all things that exist, and detest none of the things that you have made; for you would not have made anything if you had hated it' (Wis 11:24). Every creature is thus the object of the Father's tenderness, who gives it its place in the world. Even the fleeting life of the least of beings is the object of his love, and in its few seconds of existence, God enfolds it with his affection (paragraph 77).

Every sparrow, every frog, the members of every threatened species—each is 'the object of the Father's tenderness', and each is enfolded with God's affection. It is this divine love for each creature that teaches our hearts to be open to love these same creatures, to be moved by their plight, to feel for them and where needed to act on their behalf. In the 'prayer for our earth' at the end of encyclical Francis brings together these two themes, the presence of God and God's tender love for all creatures, which can be seen as foundational for the theology of intrinsic value that appears throughout the encyclical:

> All powerful God,
> you are present in the whole universe,
> and in the smallest of your creatures.
> You embrace with tenderness all that exists.
> Pour out upon us the power of your love,
> that we might protect life and beauty.

Francis presents a third argument for this intrinsic value in the Christian vision of the risen Christ. He sees the whole creation as destined to participate in the fullness of God already attained by the risen Jesus. This means that 'the ultimate purpose of other creatures is not to be found in us'. Rather, Francis writes, 'all other creatures are moving forward with us and through us towards a common point of arrival, which is God, in that transcendent fullness where the risen Christ embraces and illumines all things' (paragraph 83). Francis's eschatology involves the idea that all other creatures will, in their own way, participate in the transformation of all things in Christ. This theology of hope for other creatures takes us beyond the medieval picture that could embrace the resurrection of humans and the transformation of the universe, but which saw no real future for animal and plant life. Of course, we have no adequate imaginative picture of our own future in God, let alone that of the wider creation. What we have is the promise of God in the resurrection. Francis argues from the idea that all creatures have a future in God to their value in themselves. Both of these ideas involve a change from positions that have long been taken for granted in much general Catholic theology.

Other Creatures as Revelatory of God

The unambiguous clarity of Francis's teaching on the intrinsic value of other creatures, while based on insights found in the Scriptures, the Christian tradition, and at times in the *Catholic Catechism*, and in agreement with aspects of recent ecological theology, is to be seen, in my view, as a real development in church teaching. What I take up now, the idea that other creatures can be revelatory of God, that they can be said to constitute a book of nature alongside the book of the Bible, is not so much a development, as a return to a traditional view, one that has often been ignored. It is a view found, among others, in Augustine, Aquinas, and particularly in Bonaventure. In this second theological thread of *Laudato Si'*, the emphasis is no longer on the meaning of creatures in themselves, but on their revelatory meaning for human beings. Francis sees the whole universe of creatures as speaking words of love to us:

> The entire material universe speaks of God's love, his boundless affection for us. Soil, water, mountains: everything is, as it were, a caress of God. The history of our friendship with God is always linked to particular places which take on an intensely personal meaning; we all remember places, and revisiting those memories does us much good. Anyone who has grown up in the hills or used to sit by the spring to drink, or played outdoors in the neighbourhood square; going back to these places is a chance to recover something of their true selves (paragraph 84).

Francis insists that each creature has its own particular word to speak. None is superfluous. Each can become a caress of God for us. Taking up words of Pope John Paul II, Francis says of the book of creation: 'God has written a precious book, "whose letters are the multitude of created things present in the universe"' (paragraph 8:5).[8] He then turns to the Canadian bishops who, he says, rightly point out that 'no creature is excluded from this manifestation of God' (paragraph 85). He quotes their words: 'From panoramic visions to the tiniest living form, nature is a constant source of wonder and awe. It is also a continuing revelation of the divine'.[9]

Building on this picture of creation as a book of God, Francis says that the contemplation of creation allows us to discover in each thing 'a teaching' which God wishes to give to us. Again, he refers to words of John Paul II, with two separate quotations: 'for the believer, to contemplate creation is to hear a message, to listen to a paradoxical, silent voice'[10]; 'alongside revelation properly so-called, contained in Scripture, there is a divine manifestation in the blaze of the sun and the fall of night'.[11]

---

8. John Paul II, *Catechesis* (30 January 2002), 6: *Insegnamenti* 25/1 (2002): 140.
9. Canadian Conference of Catholic Bishops, Social Affairs Commission, Pastoral Letter, *You Love All That Exists . . . All Things are Yours, God, Love of Life* (4 October 2003), 1.
10. John Paul II, *Catechesis* (26 January 2000), 5: *Insegnamenti* 23/1 (2002), 123.
11. John Paul II, *Catechesis* (2 August 2000), 3: *Insegnamenti* 23/2 (2000), 112.

It is worth noting the words used by Francis of our encounters with other creatures, and the words of others whom he quotes with approval: other creatures 'speak' to us of God's love, are 'a caress' of God, a 'precious book' whose letters are the multitude of created things, a 'manifestation' of God, a 'continuing revelation' of the divine, a 'teaching' that God wishes to give us, a 'message' from God, and a 'divine manifestation'. No doubt Francis agrees with Pope John Paul II, in the quotation above, in making a distinction between revelation properly so-called, in the Scriptures, and the manifestation of God in the natural world around us. Holding to this distinction, however, does not compromise the clear teaching that there is a fundamental revelation of God at work in creation itself.

The encyclical turns to an important text in Thomas Aquinas to point out that the manifestation of God in the natural world requires a multitude of diverse creatures (paragraph 86). Aquinas sees the diversity of creatures as springing directly from the divine intention, because divine goodness necessarily transcends the limits of any one creature. For this reason, 'what was wanting to one in the representation of the divine goodness might be supplied by another'.[12] It is the diversity of creatures, including great soaring trees, eagles, kangaroos, ants and humans, that represent the abundance of divine goodness better than any one kind of creature might.

Francis returns to the theme of the book of creation in his brief treatment of the Trinity. He refers to Bonaventure's conviction that originally the reflection of God the Trinity was easily recognisable in the creation, 'when that book was open' to us human beings and our eyes had not yet been darkened. Bonaventure, Francis points out, teaches that '*each creature bears in itself a specifically Trinitarian structure*'.[13] We would readily be able to contemplate the Trinity in the creatures around us if our human gaze was not so partial, dark and fragile (paragraph 239). We would find reflected in each of them the power, the wisdom and the goodness of God.

The teaching of *Laudato Si'* on the book of creation is summed up succinctly by Francis when he writes that 'nature is filled with words of love' (paragraph 225). But he insists, if we are to hear the words of love addressed to us, in birds, trees, flowers, mountains, beaches and

---

12. Thomas Aquinas, *Summa Theologiae*, I, q 47, art 1.
13. Bonaventure, *Quaest. Disp. de Myst. Trinitatis*, 1, 2 concl.

deserts, we need to cultivate a contemplative stance before God's creation. He asks: How can we listen to the words spoken in the creatures around us if our lives are dominated by 'constant noise, interminable and nerve-wracking distractions, and the cult of appearances?' (paragraph 225). We need to free ourselves from constant busyness, from always being in a hurry, we need to slow down and take time, if we are to find our Creator speaking a word of love in the creature before us.

The Sublime Communion of Creation

In this analysis, it has been proposed that two threads of the theology of nature developed in *Laudato Si'* are first, that non-human creatures have value in themselves and, second, that they can reveal something of God to us. Important as these two threads are, they do not yet represent what I see as the integrating centre of the encyclical, Francis's theology of the communion of creation.

This theme appears in various ways throughout the encyclical, and is developed explicitly in chapter two. Even without the theological language of communion, it appears in the constant emphasis on relationships with other human beings, with other creatures, and with God. An example is when Francis says of the biblical creation texts: 'They suggest that human life is grounded in three fundamental and closely intertwined relationships: with God, with our neighbour, and with the earth itself' (paragraph 66). This stance is already a challenge to much Christian literature and preaching which speak only of relating to God and our fellow human beings.

Over and over again in *Laudato Si'* we are told that everything is connected. I will highlight just two examples. Francis writes of our relationship with other living creatures: 'Because all creatures are connected, each must be cherished with love and respect, for all of us as living creatures are dependent on one another' (paragraph 42). Here the interconnection of creatures leads to an ecological stance. In the second example, Francis is concerned to show that care for creation and care for our fellow human beings belong together in a stance that he calls integral ecology: 'Everything is connected. Concern for the environment thus needs to be joined to a sincere love for our fellow human beings and an unwavering commitment to resolving the problems of society' (paragraph 91).

At one point in the encyclical, Francis makes the fundamental point that we humans do not relate to nature as if we were separate from it. We inter-relate with other creatures in the natural world because we ourselves are a part of nature: 'Nature cannot be regarded as something separate from ourselves or as a mere setting in which we live. We are part of nature, included in it and thus in constant interaction with it' (paragraph 139). From the scientific point of view, of course, we know that we are completely dependent on the 13.8 billion-year history of the universe, since all the atoms that make up our bodies have been produced in the stars, and on the 3.7 billion-year history of evolution on Earth. For our continued existence, we depend not only on the climate, the atmosphere, the seas, the rivers, and the land itself, but also on the birds, the bees, the insects, the worms and the millions of microbes that are at work in each of our bodies.

These interconnections are grounded for Francis in theological reality. When we think of nature as God's creation, he says, we can see it as 'a reality illuminated by the love that calls us together into universal communion' (paragraph 76). In theological discussions, the word communion usually points, first, to the divine life of the Trinity and, second, to what the Spirit brings about in the life of the church. Francis extends its use to embrace the whole creation drawn by divine love. The networks of relationships that science discovers at every level, from that of the atom, to molecules, cells, organisms, ecosystems, the planetary community, the Milky Way Galaxy, and the universe, can now be seen in a new light, as creaturely participation in the divine communion that is the life of the triune God. *Laudato Si'* links this concept of universal communion with Francis of Assisi's theological conviction that we form one family with other creatures, that they are our kin, as common creatures before their Creator:

> This is the basis for our conviction that, as part of the universe, called into being by the one Father, all of us are linked by unseen bonds and together form a kind of universal family, a sublime communion which fills us with a sacred, affectionate and humble respect. Here I would reiterate that 'God has joined us so closely to the world around us that we can feel the desertification of the soil almost as a physical ailment, and the extinction of species almost as a painful disfigurement' (paragraph 89).

Before continuing to explore Francis's theology of sublime communion, it is worth noting the place of human feelings in the above quotation. Here, and elsewhere in his writing, Francis gives a priority to feelings that is far from common in church teaching, and in theology, no doubt reflecting something of his own Ignatian tradition. The sense that we belong to one universal family, to one sublime communion, he says, fills us with a 'sacred, affectionate, and humble respect'. Francis is clearly aware that such feelings can inspire an ecological lifestyle. The last sentence of the above quotation, taken from *Evangelii Gaudium* (paragraph 215), makes a profound link between our bond with other creatures, and the strong feelings that can be invoked in us by their destruction and loss, feelings that can lead to a renewed ecological praxis.

Francis goes on to insist that authentic communion with the natural world also necessarily involves us in feeling with suffering human beings: 'A deep communion with the rest of nature cannot be real if our hearts lack tenderness, compassion and concern for our fellow human beings' (paragraph 91). As he says, again, in this context, 'everything is connected' (paragraph 91). Or, as he said earlier, in *Laudato Si'*, we need to realise that 'an ecological approach *always* becomes a social approach' (paragraph 49).[14] In words that were used earlier by Leonardo Boff, Francis insists on the integration of the issues of justice and the environment 'so as to hear *both the cry of the earth and the cry of the poor*' (paragraph 49).[15] This integration is a central idea of the encyclical that is taken up explicitly in its fourth chapter on 'Integral Ecology'.[16]

When our hearts are open to universal communion, Francis says, the sense of family 'excludes nothing and no one' (paragraph 92). We 'have only one heart' that feels for our fellow human beings and for other creatures who are brother and sister to us: 'Everything is related

---

14. Italics in the original.
15. Italics in the original. See Leonardo Boff, *Cry of the Earth, Cry of the Poor* (Maryknoll, NY: Orbis, 1997).
16. While I am not focussing on the concept of integral ecology in this article, it may be worth noticing that this is a term that may not appeal to all scientists. I see it not so much as a scientific term, as an ethical one, an important attempt by Pope Francis to communicate to both the church and the general public, the idea that commitment to other human beings, above all the poor, and commitment to the wider natural world, are not to be played off against each other, but belong together as aspects of the one moral and spiritual stance before God.

and we human beings are united as brothers and sisters on a wonderful pilgrimage, woven together by the love God has for each of his creatures and which also unites us in fond affection with brother sun, sister moon, brother river and mother earth' (paragraph 92).

The concept of universal communion appears again in the final chapter of *Laudato Si'* when Francis discusses the ecological conversion to which we are called. He sees this conversion as including a number of attitudes which together foster a 'spirit of generous care, full of tenderness' (paragraph 220). Ecological conversion involves, he says, 'a loving awareness that we are not disconnected from the rest of creatures, but joined in a splendid universal communion' (paragraph 220). He calls upon all Christians to make the grace they have received evident in their relationships with other creatures: 'In this way, we will help nurture that sublime fraternity with all creation which Saint Francis of Assisi so radiantly embodied' (paragraph 221). It is clear that the 'sublime fraternity' of this text, which we might add 'divine sorority', echoes and reinforces the 'sublime communion' of paragraph 89, discussed above.

I have been proposing that the theology of the natural world that Francis offers us involves three threads: other creatures have intrinsic value, they are revelatory of God, and we and they form a sublime communion in God. What is it, theologically, that makes the interrelated creation a *sublime* communion? Clearly, fundamental to the answer of *Laudato Si'* is the creation theology already discussed, that God loves each of God's creatures in themselves, that each creature and the whole creation manifests the Creator, and that the love of the Creator draws all creatures into a communion of love. But Francis also points, briefly, to the Christological and Trinitarian depths of this communion.

The encyclical sees all creatures as bound up with the mystery of Christ—'All things have been created through him and for him' (Col 1:16). It speaks of the Word of God who became flesh, who 'entered into the created cosmos, throwing in his lot with it, even to the cross' (paragraph 99). From the beginning, but above all in the incarnation, the mystery of Christ is at work in a hidden manner in the natural world. Several times, *Laudato Si'* focusses on the risen Christ at work in the whole creation. In one example, after referring to Collosians 1:19–20 and 1 Corinthians 15:28, Francis writes: 'Thus the creatures of this world no longer appear to us under merely natural guise because the risen One is mysteriously holding them to himself and directing them towards fullness as their end. The very flowers of the field and the birds which his human eyes contemplated and admired are now imbued with his radiant presence' (paragraph 100).

As I have noted earlier, Francis understands the whole creation as being drawn to its fulfilment through the risen Christ, and he sees Christ as already present to all things, holding them in love, and in some mysterious way already filling them with his light. Later in the encyclical we read that 'Christ has taken unto himself this material world and now, risen, is intimately present to each being, surrounding it with his affection and penetrating it with his light' (paragraph 221).

In discussing the sacraments, Francis offers a brief theology of incarnation in relation to ecology: 'For Christians, all the creatures of the material universe find their true meaning in the incarnate Word, for the Son of God has incorporated in his person part of the material world, planting in it a seed of definitive transformation' (paragraph 235). In discussing the Eucharist, Francis writes that, when we gather to celebrate, this definitive transformation is already present in anticipation: 'fullness is already achieved . . . Joined to the incarnate Son, present in the Eucharist, the whole cosmos gives thanks to God' (paragraph 236). In reflecting on the Sabbath, Francis points to Sunday as a time of rest, a time to be mindful of resurrection and new creation, when we are led to recognise that the risen humanity of Christ is already 'the pledge of the final transfiguration of all created reality' (paragraph 237).

Francis takes the notion of universal communion to its most sublime level in his brief words on the Trinity. Building on Aquinas's theology of the divine persons as subsistent relations, he sees the world of creatures as 'a web of relationships' which is 'created according to the divine model' (paragraph 240). He notes that here we human beings can see a key to our fulfilment: 'The human person grows more, matures more and is sanctified more to the extent that he or she enters into relationships, going out from themselves to live in communion with God, with others, and with all creatures' (paragraph 240). In relating to God, to other humans, and with God's other creatures, we live the Trinitarian dynamism imprinted on us in our creation—we are created to be relational beings in a universe of creatures in which everything is interconnected.

In his paragraph on Mary, Francis sees her as profoundly connected to the communion of creation. As she once mourned the death of Jesus, 'so now she grieves for the sufferings of the crucified poor and for the creatures of this world laid waste by human power' (paragraph 241). But now she is completely transfigured, living with Jesus, as a sign of the promise to all creatures: 'In her glorified body, together with the Risen Christ, part of creation has reached the fullness of its beauty' (paragraph 241). At the end of the encyclical Francis says that we can hope we will come to share in this transfigured existence with the risen Christ, with Mary, and with all of God's other creatures. Then we will be able to 'read the mystery of the universe' which will be brought to its fullness in God (paragraph 243). He tells us that 'eternal life will be a shared experience of awe, in which each creature, resplendently transfigured, will take its rightful place and will have something to give those poor men and women who will have been liberated once and for all' (paragraph 243).

This vision of the communion of creation, immensely deepened by a theology of incarnation and resurrection, impels us to give ourselves to the care of our common home. God has taken Earth and its creatures to God's self irrevocably in the incarnation. In words that echo Karl Rahner, Francis writes: 'In the heart of this world, the Lord of life who loves us so much, is always present. He does not abandon us, he does not leave us alone, for he has united himself definitively to our earth, and his love constantly impels us to find new ways forward' (paragraph 245).[17]

Conclusion

I have pointed out how Francis uses the word sublime of the communion of creation, and of the fraternity of all creatures. He uses it a third time in the encyclical and I think this usage gives a clue to the way he understands the word. It appears in a quotation from John of the Cross's commentary on his poem *The Spiritual Canticle*. The verse on which John of the Cross is commenting is part of his description of the profound union of the human person with the Word of God, the Beloved. John of the Cross writes of this Beloved:

---

17. See Karl Rahner, 'A Faith that Loves the Earth', in *The Mystical Way in Everyday Life*, translated by Annemarie Kidder (Maryknoll, NY: Orbis Books, 2010), 55.

> My Beloved is the mountains,
> And lonely wooded valley,
> Strange islands,
> And resounding rivers,
> The whistling of love-stirring breezes.[18]

Francis does not quote the verse, but simply refers to the commentary on these lines, where John of the Cross says of the mountain, valleys, islands, rivers, and breezes that 'in each of these sublime realities is God' (paragraph 234). The word 'sublime' here indicates the experience of the natural world as suffused with the presence of God. In the poem, John of the Cross says that the Beloved *is* the mountain while in the commentary he says that *in* each of these sublime realities, such as the mountain, is God. Francis comments: 'This is not because the finite things of this world are really divine, but because the mystic experiences the intimate connection between God and all beings, and thus feels that "all things are God"' (paragraph 234). He says that when a person stands awestruck before a mountain, he or she cannot separate this experience from God, and comes to see that the interior awe being lived is to be entrusted to God. He points to the words of John of the Cross on lonely wooded valleys: 'Lonely valleys are quiet, pleasant, cool, shady and flowing with fresh water; in the variety of their groves and in the sweet song of the birds, they afford abundant recreation and delight to the senses, and in their solitude and silence, they refresh and give rest. These valleys are what my Beloved is to me' (paragraph 234). Mountains, valleys, islands, flowing streams, breezes, are sublime realities, because in them we can encounter the Beloved, because they give expression to the Beloved, and because they are, meaning they symbolise what the Beloved is to the human lover.

In *Laudato Si'*, then, there is a rich concept of sublime communion that points to the mystical experience of finding God in all creatures. But there is a further resonance to this word that I find important in this context. In philosophical aesthetics, the word "sublime" is often understood in relation to the word 'beautiful'. Often the word beauti-

---

18. John of the Cross, *The Spiritual Canticle*, 14, in *The Collected Works of St. John of the Cross*, translated by Kieran Kavanagh and Otilio Rodriguez (Washington DC: Institute of Carmelite Studies, 1979), 462.

ful is used of something that fits with our notions of what is reasonable, what is rightly ordered, and what is pleasingly proportioned. Something can be spoken of as sublime when it throws our notions of reason, order, and proportion into utter confusion, when it points to what is totally beyond us, to the incomprehensible. The sublime can be shocking and disorienting.

This line of thought suggests that 'sublime communion' could be developed to embrace what is not taken up in *Laudato Si'*, the pain, the deaths, the chaos, the randomness, the ugliness of so much of the natural world. It could include what cosmology tells us of the 13.8 billion-year history of the observable universe, the more than a hundred billion galaxies that make it up, and the possibility of multiverses. A theology of the sublime communion of creation could engage with the strange otherness and counter-intuitive nature of what we have discovered about our world at the quantum level of reality. And it could embrace the costs of evolution as well as the beauty and rich diversity of life around us.

A theology of the natural world as sublime communion could recognise and accept aspects of our world that are not pleasant or beautiful to human eyes. It could recognise that without faith the world might seem highly ambiguous to us, as both beautiful and violent. A theology of the sublime communion of creation would be based not simply on observation of the natural world, but on the revelation given in Christ that, in spite of appearances, in spite of what can seem like the violent and dark side of nature, the emergent and evolving creation is the work of unthinkable and incomprehensible love.

A theology of the natural world as sublime communion necessarily involves, then, the recognition of our finitude and incomprehension. It would need to take seriously the words of God to Job from the whirlwind that begin: 'Where were you when I laid the foundations of the earth?' (Job 38:2). Above all, it would need to ponder the incarnation and the cross as God's radical and deep identification with creation in its groaning. With Paul it would see Christ crucified as the power of God and the wisdom of God (1Cor 1:24). But it would also recognise, with him, that God's foolishness is wiser than human wisdom, and God's weakness is stronger than human strength (1 Cor 1: 25). And so, along with proclaiming the incarnation and the cross as God's identification with suffering creation, it would proclaim the resurrection of the crucified Jesus as the unbreakable promise of God to the whole creation.

This analysis of *Laudato Si'* has proposed that the encyclical offers us the basis for a systematic theology of the natural world, in which other creatures have value in themselves, in which they can be seen as revealing God, and in which they, with us, form a sublime communion of creation in God. While the theology builds on the Scriptures and church teaching it offers us something new, a church teaching and a theology that demands of us a radically different way of thinking, feeling and acting with regard to other creatures. It is a summons to ecological conversion for each person, for the church, and for theology.

'Everything is Interconnected': The Trinity and the Natural World in *Laudato Si'*

All those who read *Laudato Si'* are struck by the way Pope Francis says over and over again that everything is interconnected, or that everything is interrelated. In this article, I will seek to explore the significance of this theme. In particular, I will ask about its theological meaning, attempting to bring out two aspects of Pope Francis's thought: 1. The insight that interrelationships of the natural world can be seen as a pale reflection of the dynamic relations of Trinitarian life; and 2. The conviction that ecological conversion, learning to relate to the natural world, as well as to other humans and to God, is essential to the very nature of the human made in the image of the dynamically relational God.

When Cardinal Peter Turkson, president of the Pontifical Justice and Peace council, launched *Laudato Si'* on 18 June 2015, he was accompanied by three other speakers. One was German climate scientist and member of the Pontifical Academy of Sciences, Professor Hans Joachim Schellnhuber. With him were Italian educator, historian and member of the Sant'Egidio community, Valeria Martano, and from the United States, head of Catholic Relief Services and former Dean of Notre Dame Business School, Dr Carolyn Woo. Sitting alongside Cardinal Turkson, representing Ecumenical Patriarch Bartholomew, was well-known Orthodox theologian Metropolitan John Zizioulas of Pergamon. The two women and two men, the variety of disciplines, and the presence of the Orthodox Metropolitan, reflected something of the inclusive scope of *Laudato Si'*.

In his presentation, Metropolitan John expresses the Ecumenical Patriarch's personal joy and satisfaction in the issuing of the encyclical. He notes how *Laudato Si'* insists on the biblical truth that 'human life is grounded in three fundamental and closely intertwined relationships with God, with our neighbour and with the earth itself' (paragraph 66). He points out that Christian theology has consistently ignored this third relationship. But, he continues, when theology leaves out the rest of creation it contradicts two fundamental aspects of Christian faith. The first is the incarnation. In assuming human nature, Metropolitan John says, 'the Son of God took over material creation in its entirety'.[1] Christ came in the flesh, he insists, 'to save the whole creation through the Incarnation, not only humanity'.[2] The second aspect of faith that he sees as contradicted when Christians ignore the natural world is the Eucharist. In the Eucharist, the church offers to God the whole creation in the form of bread and wine, and human beings learn that instead of being proprietors of creation, they are its priests. In the whole of life, they are called to lift up the creation to God in thanksgiving and praise.

The focus of Metropolitan John on the great Christian themes of Incarnation and Eucharist is deeply meaningful. My intention here is to focus on a third, closely related theme, the most fundamental theme of all, the nature of God. This will mean seeking to uncover the relation between what the encyclical has to say about the communion of creation and what it says explicitly about God the Trinity. Early in the encyclical, Pope Francis acknowledges the leadership of Ecumenical Patriarch Bartholomew in the development of a Christian theology and ethics of care for the whole creation. He highlights key ideas in the works of the Ecumenical Patriarch: Bartholomew's insistence on the need to repent for our crimes against the planet, which he declares to be sin against God; his analysis of the ethical and spiritual roots of environmental problems; and his challenge to a new way of life, replacing greed with generosity, rediscovering asceticism, and finding liberation from fear and compulsion. In this context, Francis includes an important quotation from the Patriarch that sets the scene for *Laudato Si'* with the idea of creation as a sacrament of communion:

---

1. http://www.lastampa.it/2015/06/18/vaticaninsider/eng/the-vatican/metropolitan-zizioulas-laudato-si-is-an-occasion-of-great-joy-and-satisfaction-for-the-orthodox-9OC5q2xdD2pJqXY3ArkqzI/pagina.html
2. http://www.lastampa.it/2015/06/18/vaticaninsider/eng/the-vatican/metropolitan-zizioulas-laudato-si-is-an-occasion-of-great-joy-and-satisfaction-for-the-orthodox-9OC5q2xdD2pJqXY3ArkqzI/pagina.html

As Christians, we are also called "to accept the world as a sacrament of communion, as a way of sharing with God and our neighbours on a global scale. It is our humble conviction that the divine and the human meet in the slightest detail in the seamless garment of God's creation, in the last speck of dust of our planet (paragraph 9).

The concept of the world of creatures as a sacrament of communion, and of each creature as the place where divine and human meet, has many resonances in *Laudato Si'*. I will explore these resonances, and the theological basis for the claim that all things are interconnected, in three steps. In the first, I will discuss Pope Francis's understanding of creation as a universal and sublime communion. Then I will take up his explicit comments on God the Trinity. In the third step, I will reflect on what *Laudato Si'* suggests concerning the Trinitarian basis for ecological conversion.

The Universal Communion of Creation

One of the key contributions of *Laudato Si'* to contemporary theology, and to Christian ecological practice, is its theology of the natural world. Nature has been largely missing from Western theology and preaching since medieval times. And when the natural world was discussed, it was often seen in anthropocentric terms as existing simply for human use. For much of this time, the focus has been almost exclusively on the salvation of the individual human being. Pope Francis has done much to restore nature to its rightful place, so that once more, theology has to deal with not two, but with three interrelated realities, with human beings, the rest of the natural world, and God. I will explore his theology of the natural world in three steps: the conviction that other creatures have intrinsic value; the idea that other creatures are a word of God to human beings; and the view that we and the rest of God's creatures form a universal communion of creation.

The intrinsic value of other creatures

In a great deal of Christian teaching, other creatures exist only for human use. Pope Francis challenges this view, insisting that other creatures have meaning and value not simply because of their *use* to human beings, but *in themselves*. He says, for example: 'Together with our obligation to use the earth's goods responsibly, we are called to recognize that other living beings have a value of their own in God's eyes'. He goes on to say that by their very existence, these creatures give glory to God. Like the Psalmist, he sees God as taking delight in all God's creatures: 'the Lord rejoices in all his works (Ps 104:31)' (paragraph 69). Pope Francis insists that it is *not* the case that other creatures are created simply for human use. Of course, he recognises that we do constantly use other creatures, but he insists that they have their own meaning, dignity and value, and when we use them we must use them with respect and care for them. God delights in each of them, and by their very being they praise God. Writing about the integrity of ecosystems, Francis speaks explicitly of the intrinsic value of both the individual creature and the system:

> We take these systems into account not only to determine how best to use them, but also because they have an intrinsic value independent of their usefulness. Each organism, as a creature of God, is good and admirable in itself; the same is true of the harmonious ensemble of organisms existing in a defined space and functioning as a system (paragraph 140).

Three theological reasons for the intrinsic value of other creatures can be found in intrinsic value in *Laudato Si'*. The first is that each creature is the place of God's dwelling. So Francis writes that nature as a whole is the 'locus of his presence' and that 'the Spirit of life dwells in every living creature and calls us to enter into relationship with him' (paragraph 88). The second reason is that God loves each creature. Francis states: 'God's love is the fundamental moving force in all created things'. He goes on to say: 'Every creature is thus the object of the Father's tenderness, who gives it its place in the world. Even the fleeting life of the least of beings is the object of his love, and in its few seconds of existence, God enfolds it with his affection' (paragraph 77).

The third reason is that our eternal life involves other creatures. Our final salvation, of course, is in God, and necessarily beyond our concepts and our imagining, but Francis insists that what we Christians hope for is a transformed life that we will share with other creatures:

The ultimate destiny of the universe is in the fullness of God, which has already been attained by the risen Christ, the measure of the maturity of all things. Here we can add yet another argument for rejecting every tyrannical and irresponsible domination of human beings over other creatures. The ultimate purpose of other creatures is not to be found in us. Rather all creatures are moving forward with us, and through us, towards a common point of arrival, which is God in that transcendent fullness where the risen Christ embraces and illumines all things (paragraph 83).

Later in the encyclical, Pope Francis writes: 'Eternal life will be a shared experience of awe, in which each creature, resplendently transfigured, will take its rightful place and have something to give those poor men and women who will have been liberated once and for all' (paragraph 243). He makes it clear that in his theological vision, eternal life involves not just the matter of the universe, but also biological life, the life of plants, animals as well as humans. For Pope Francis, other creatures are not simply for human use, but have their own intrinsic value, since they are the place of divine presence, they are loved by God, and God has a future for them, with us, in Christ.

Other creatures as words of God to us

Alongside his insistence on the meaning of other creatures in themselves, Francis also points to their meaning for us humans. He highlights the ancient theological conviction that alongside the explicit revelation of God in Jesus Christ, creation itself is already a kind of revelation. Other creatures speak to us of God. Each creature is a word of God. Anthony Kelly explains: 'The universe, created in the Word (*Logos*) is a world of endlessly differentiated "words" (*logoi*) or meanings'.[3] In an evocative statement, Pope Francis speaks of the experience of the natural world as a caress of God: The entire material universe speaks of God's love, his boundless affection for us.

---

3. Anthony J Kelly, *Laudato Si': An Integral Ecology and the Catholic Tradition* (Adelaide: ATF Theology, 2016), 92.

> Soil, water, mountains: everything is, as it were, a caress of God. The history of our friendship with God is always linked to particular places which take on an intensely personal meaning; we all remember places, and revisiting those memories does us much good. Anyone who has grown up in the hills or used to sit by the spring to drink, or played outdoors in the neighbourhood square; going back to these places is a chance to recover something of their true selves (paragraph 84).

Francis goes on to say that God has written a precious book, 'whose letters are the multitude of created things present in the universe' (paragraph 85). From vast, panoramic vistas to the tiniest living form, the natural world is 'a continuing revelation of the divine' (paragraph 85). Much later in the letter, Francis writes: 'Nature is filled with words of love, but how can we listen to them amid constant noise, interminable and nerve-wracking distractions, or the cult of appearances?' (paragraph 225) We need to find freedom from the noise of life in order to relate to the natural world and to hear the words of love it speaks to us.

The Sublime Communion of Creation

Francis goes beyond teaching that other creatures have their own intrinsic value, and that they speak of God to us, two ideas that are profoundly important in ecological theology, to offer a vision of human beings united with other creatures in one community of creation. He speaks of this community as a sublime communion of creatures in God.

The word *communion* has deep resonances in Christian theology. It is used of the church itself, when the church is understood in Eucharistic terms as the communion of all those who participate in Christ and are made one in him. At a far deeper level, it is used of the Trinity, where God is understood, not in individualistic terms, but as a divine communion of persons, in dynamic mutual relations of love, profoundly one-in-being. By using the concept of 'sublime communion' of human beings and other creatures, Francis undermines the paradigm of human domination over other creatures, and replaces it with a radically relational paradigm, one in which everything is interconnected:

> This is the reason for our conviction that, as part of the universe, called into being by the one Father, all of us are linked by unseen bonds and together form a kind of universal family, a sublime communion which fills us with a sacred, affectionate and humble respect. Here I would reiterate that 'God has joined us so closely to the world around us that we can feel the desertification of the soil almost as a physical ailment, and the extinction of a species as a painful disfigurement' (paragraph 89).

The theme of the sublime universal communion of all creatures is closely related to St Francis of Assisi's idea that other creatures are family to us, our sisters and brothers, and that Earth is our mother. So Pope Francis, in the above quotation, speaks of the 'universal family' as well as the 'sublime communion' of creatures. And a little later, he writes in words that echo St Francis: 'Everything is related, and we human beings are united as brothers and sisters on a wonderful pilgrimage, woven together by the love God has for each of his creatures and which also unites us in affection with brother son, sister moon, brother river and mother earth' (paragraph 92).

Authentic communion with the natural world, in Francis's view, is deeply interconnected with our sense of communion with other humans, above all with those who are suffering: 'A deep communion with the rest of nature cannot be real if our hearts lack tenderness, compassion and concern for our fellow human beings' (paragraph 91). As he says, again, in this context, 'everything is connected'. In words that echo Leonardo Boff, Francis insists that we need to integrate the issues of justice and the environment 'so as to hear *both the cry of the earth and the cry of the poor*' (paragraph 49).[4] This integration is a central idea of the encyclical that is taken up explicitly in its fourth chapter on Integral Ecology. When our hearts are open to universal communion, Francis says, the sense of family 'excludes nothing and no one'. He goes on to say that we 'have only one heart' that feels for our fellow human beings and for other creatures, our brothers and sisters before God (*LW* 92).

---

4. Italics in the original. See Leonardo Boff, *Cry of the Earth, Cry of the Poor* (Maryknoll, NY: Orbis, 1997).

Laudato Si' on God the Trinity

Near the end of *Laudato Si'* Pope Francis offers some brief comments that are explicitly focused on the Trinity and the relationships between creatures. Before turning to them directly, it is worth noting the way in which the creative role of the divine persons appears in the body of the encyclical. Pope Francis pictures the Source of All as the Father who, out of radical love, stretches out the divine hand to give creation its being. The whole creation is a gift from this person, the love from which all things spring and the one who draws all things into communion: 'creation can only be understood as a gift from the outstretched hand of the Father of all, and as a reality illuminated by the love which calls us together into universal communion' (paragraph 68). Every single creature, Pope Francis tells us, is 'the object of the Father's tenderness' (paragraph 77).

With regard to the Word of God, Pope Francis sees the destiny of the whole creation is bound up with the mystery of Christ. Referring to Colossians 1:15, he speaks of this mystery of Christ as present in creation from the beginning: 'All things have been created through him and for him' (paragraph 99). In the incarnation, the divine Word of creation (Jn 1:1–14) 'entered into the cosmos, throwing in his lot with it, even to the cross' (paragraph 99). Through the incarnation, the mystery of Christ, present from the beginning, is 'at work in a hidden manner in the natural world as a whole, without thereby impinging on its autonomy' (paragraph 99). Francis speaks of the risen and glorious Christ as present throughout creation, holding creatures to himself and directing them to their fullness in God (Col 1:19-20; 1 Cor 15:28), so that 'the very flowers of the field and the birds which his human eyes contemplated and admired are now imbued with his radiant presence' (paragraph 100). Noting the connection of this line of thought with Teilhard de Chardin (*LS*, footnote 53), Francis states says that the ultimate destiny of the whole universe is the fullness of God already attained by the risen Christ (paragraph 83).

The Holy Spirit, according to Pope Francis, quoting Pope John Paul II, possesses 'infinite creativity' (paragraph 80).[5] When discussing God's self-limitation in creating a world that needs to develop, and that possesses its own rightful autonomy, Francis speaks of the Spirit of God as the one who enables the appearance of the new in

---

5. John Paul II, *Catechesis* (24 April 1991), *Insegnamenti* 14 (1991), 856.

creation: 'The Spirit of God has filled the universe with possibilities and therefore, from the very heart of things, something new can always emerge' (paragraph 80). Because the Creator Spirit is deeply present in each creature, enabling its existence and its flourishing, each tree, each bird, is the locus of the Holy Spirit: 'The Spirit of life dwells in every living creature and calls us to enter into relationship' (paragraph 88).

How are we to understand the relationship between the work of the three persons in the creation of a universe of creatures? Pope Francis answers this question in the first of his paragraphs specifically devoted to the Trinity. His answer is the classical theological one, that the three act as one, as a single divine principle, but that they perform the one work of creation in accordance with the personal property of each person. So Francis writes of the first person of the Trinity as the 'ultimate source of everything, the loving and self-communicating foundation of all that exists' (paragraph 238). The Son, or the eternal Word, is the reflection of the first person, the 'reflection through whom all things are created', and who 'united himself to this earth when he was formed in the womb of Mary' (paragraph 238). The Spirit, the 'infinite bond of love', is 'intimately present at the very heart of the universe, inspiring and bringing new pathways' (paragraph 238).

Pope Francis explores the way the Trinity leaves its mark on creation. He points to Saint Bonaventure's teaching that before our eyes had been darkened by sin, humans would have been able to read the book of nature, and find there the reflection of the Trinity. Because of sin we now the book of the Bible to rightly interpret the book of nature. Even now, Bonaventure teaches, each creature bears within itself a Trinitarian structure: each creature in its very existence represents the Source of All, as the cause of its being; in its identity, each represents the Word of God as its exemplar; in its goodness, each represents the Spirit, who brings it to its final fulfilment.

Pope Francis goes further, pointing out how the complex inter-relationships of creatures found in the natural world are an echo of the Trinitarian life. Earlier, he had already referred to an important text where Aquinas insists that the goodness of God is better represented by the wonderful variety of inter-related creatures around us than by any individual creature:

> The universe as a whole, in all its manifold relationships, shows forth the inexhaustible riches of God. Saint Thomas Aquinas wisely noted that multiplicity and variety 'come from the intention of the first agent' who willed that 'what was wanting to one in the representation of divine goodness might be supplied by another', in as much as God's goodness 'could not be represented fittingly by any one creature'. Hence we need to grasp the variety of things in their multiple relationships (paragraph 86).

In his explicit treatment on the Trinity towards the end of *Laudato Si'*, Francis refers to Aquinas's theology of the Trinity as subsistent relations.[6] This fundamental insight means that the relations in God are what God is. The Word of God is always from the Source of All, and the Spirit is always from the Source of All and the Word. Anthony Kelly points to the connection between these eternal divine 'processions', and the created 'process' of an evolutionary universe of creatures: 'The relational vitality occurring within the eternal depth of God is named in theology as the "divine processions" of the Word and the Spirit, creating the universe in its dynamic image. From the divine processions within God flows the 'process' of the universe unfolding through the ages. This is to say that the divine processions are imaged forth in the unfolding of the cosmic process'.[7]

The divine persons exist only in being dynamically related to one another. There is real distinction of the persons, but always fully equality and mutual love in the divine unity. There is no fourth in God, only the three persons in dynamic mutual relationships. God is radically and essentially relational. Pope Francis sees the relationships of the created world as reflecting the dynamic relations of the divine life of the Trinity:

> The divine Persons are subsistent relations, and the world, created according to the divine model, is a web of relationships. Creatures tend towards God, and in turn it is proper to every living being to tend towards other things, so that throughout the universe we can find any number of constant and secretly interwoven relationships (paragraph 240).

---

6. Thomas Aquinas, *Summa theologiae*, 1a 40.2.
7. Kelly, *Laudato Si'*, 91.

It seems clear that Pope Francis is here suggesting that we can think of the relationships we find in the natural world, including those we find revealed by the natural sciences, as representing, however distantly, their model in the dynamic mutual relations of the Trinity. I think it is helpful here to ponder some of the interrelationships revealed in the sciences. Jesuit cosmologist, William Stoeger, points out that the sciences reveal that all entities, at every level, are constituted by their relationships.[8] If one thinks of an atom, a molecule or a cell, we find entities constituted by patterns of relationship that are nested upon one another. There is a series of levels of organisation of matter and of life, in which each member is a new whole, but is constituted of parts that precede it. Each entity is constituted by more fundamental entities. Each is interrelated with others, forming a larger system.

Stoeger names these patterns that are discovered by the sciences 'constitutive relationships'. He describes these constitutive relationships as 'those interactions among components and with a larger context which jointly effect the composition of a given system and establish its functional characteristics within the larger whole of which it is a part, and thereby enable it to manifest the particular properties and behaviour it does'.[9] It is the relationship between constituents and the interrelationships with its environment, that make an entity what it is.

Each entity, then, is constituted by more fundamental entities, and each is related to others as part of a larger system. Arthur Peacocke has pointed to an incomplete example of a series of wholes that are constituted by parts preceding it in the series: 'atom—molecule—macromolecule—subcellular organelle—cell—multicellular functioning organ—whole living organism—populations of living organisms—ecosystems—the biosphere'.[10] One might go on and think of the way the community of life on Earth is interrelated with, and dependent

---

8. William R Stoeger, 'The Mind-Brain Problem, the Laws of Nature and Constitutive Relationships', in *Neuroscience and the Person: Scientific Perspectives on Divine Action*, edited by Robert John Russell, Nancey Murphy, Theo C Meyering and Michael Arbib (Vatican City State: Vatican Observatory Publications, 1995, 1997).
9. Stoeger, 'The Mind-Brain Problem, the Laws of Nature and Constitutive Relationships', 136–7.
10. Arthur Peacocke, *Theology for a Scientific Age: Being and Becoming–Natural, Divine and Human* (Minneapolis: Fortress Press, 1993), 38.

upon, the Sun and its solar system, the Milky Way Galaxy, our Local Group of Galaxies, the Virgo Supercluster, and the Universe.

Constitutive relationships involve all those relationships that make something what it is. They may be physical, biological or social relationships. We human beings depend upon relationships of all kinds for our existence and our flourishing. Atoms in the neurons of our brains and in the blood flowing in our brains have come from the process of nucleosynthesis in long dead stars. We are made from stardust. We could not be who we are without the 3.8 billion-year evolutionary history of life on our planet. We could not be who we are without all the life systems of our planet. We become who we are in relationship to families, friends, communities, and the land to which we belong, with its bacteria, insects, plants, birds and animals.

At the deepest level, we can move beyond science to theology, to describe that unique relationship that constitutes us in being, a relationship that functions at a far deeper level than all the others, the relationship of creation itself. This is the relationship by which the Creator Spirit is radically interior to each of us, and to every other creature, enabling our existence in an interrelated world of creatures. While science suggests a world of entities that exist as constituted by constitutive relationships, a Christian theology can locate this world of entities in relation to a God who is a Trinity, a God of dynamic mutual relations. It sees God as Communion. While it recognises the infinite difference between the interrelationships of creaturely existence and God the Trinity, it sees every goanna, river red gum and wallaby, every star in the Milky Way galaxy, every human being as existing only from the divine Communion.

The Foundation of Ecological Conversion in the Trinity

Pondering the web of relationships we find in the natural world and the Trinity as the ultimate model for the relational universe leads Pope Francis to a further, wonderfully insightful line of thought with regard to the human. He proposes that human fulfilment is radically relational, and that it involves a three-fold relationship, with other humans, with other creatures, and with God:

> This leads us not only to marvel at the manifold connections existing among creatures, but also to discover a key to our

own fulfilment. The human person grows more, matures more and is sanctified more to the extent that he or she enters into relationships, going out from themselves to live in communion with God, with others and with all creatures. In this way, they make their own that Trinitarian dynamism which God imprinted in them when they were created (paragraph 240).

What is it that truly fulfils us as human beings? What is that enables us to grow and mature? What is that makes us holy? Pope Francis makes the claim that the answer to all of these questions is found in going from ourselves to enter into relationships. This is the one path to fulfilment, maturity and holiness. This is a very large claim, but it is a claim that is substantiated by everything the encyclical has to say about the communion of creation of which we are a part and the Communion of the Trinity in which we and all other creatures participate. As Francis puts it: 'Everything is interconnected, and this invites us to develop a spirituality of that global solidarity which flows from the mystery of the Trinity' (paragraph 240).

This spirituality of global solidarity involves a three-fold communion, and Francis points out that when we enter into this three-fold communion we are true to ourselves, to the deepest part of ourselves. We are faithful to the Trinitarian image imprinted on us from the very beginning as creatures made in the divine image. The three-fold communion then, is that to which our very nature direct us, as humans bearing the imprint of the Trinity. A consequence of this is that when human beings close themselves off from the natural world around them, or the human world, or the living God, then they distort their own being and live in a state of alienation. Anthony Kelly makes this point:

> Since our being is fundamentally relational, the fulfilment of such relational existence consists in living out our manifold relationships to the Other, namely to God, to our neighbour, and to the neighbourhood of 'our common home'. The implication is that, if any of these levels of relationship is denied, existence is distorted.[11]

---

11. Kelly, *Laudato Si'*, 98.

It becomes clear, then, how closely this insight connects to what Pope Francis has to say in the rest of the encyclical about ecological conversion. The need for this conversion is already evident in the emptiness many people experience in their lives. Taking up words of Pope Benedict, Francis writes about the way our alienation from the natural world leads to the experience of an inner desert: 'The external deserts in the world are growing, because the internal deserts have become so vast' (paragraph 217). Learning to relate to nature, to birds and trees and animals, is part of coming to ourselves. It is part of an interior conversion. It is also the discovery of who we are, in relation to Earth and its creatures, our human brothers and sisters and God.

And, as Pope Francis insists, ecological conversion involves us in what he calls integral ecology, a holistic spirituality, that hears both the cry of the earth and the cry of the poor (paragraph 49). It involves the discovery that we each have an ecological vocation: 'Living our vocation to be protectors of God's handiwork is essential to a life of virtue; it is not an optional or a secondary aspect of our Christian experience' (paragraph 217). Fidelity to this ecological vocation is not an add-on to Christian life, but of its very essence. It is also essential to our humanity. Pope Francis points to Francis of Assisi as the example of integral ecology and of true conversion: 'In calling to mind the figure of Saint Francis of Assisi, we come to realize that a healthy relationship with creation is one dimension of overall personal conversion' (paragraph 218). Describing this ecological dimension of conversion, Pope Francis writes:

> This conversion calls for a number of attitudes which together foster a spirit of generous care, full of tenderness. First, it entails gratitude and gratitude and gratuitousness, a recognition that the world is God's loving gift, and that we are called quietly to imitate his generosity in self-sacrifice and good works . . . It also entails a loving awareness that we are not disconnected from the rest of creatures, but joined in a splendid universal communion (paragraph 220).

Ecological conversion is simply about learning to live as part of this 'splendid universal communion'. Of course, this necessarily involves us in a transformation in the way we see the natural world, and in the way we feel for it. It involves us in changes in lifestyle, in a new asceticism, in new priorities, and in personal and communal action to protect other creatures and to enable their flourishing. But a deeply theological foundation for all of this is offered in Pope Francis's Trinitarian conviction that we human beings grow into ourselves, mature and participate in the holiness to which we are called, in so far as we learn to go out of ourselves to live in communion with other human beings, with plants, animals, rivers, seas and mountains, and with the living God.

B. Creation, Eucharist and Spirituality

Eucharist and Ecology:
Keeping Memorial of Creation

Everyday there are further reports and predictions about global climate change. While scientific experts disagree about details, there is a broad consensus that it is occurring and that on all available models it will get far worse. It seems clear that human use of fossil fuels is a major cause. A little reflection on the disappearance of the glaciers that are the sources for great rivers, or on the way that even a small rise in sea levels will impact on the low-lying rice fields of Asia, suggests that climate change may be the most important issue facing the human community of the twenty-first century. It is interconnected with all other ecological issues, such as the need to do all we can to safeguard the biodiversity of our planet and to maintain the integrity of wetlands, rivers, lakes and seas. Ecological issues are deeply intertwined with and cannot be separated from issues of global justice and peace.

The danger is that the size and complexity of the ecological issues we face can lead to a feeling of powerlessness and hopelessness. I am convinced that the Christian gospel of hope has something fundamental to offer here. In a common statement in 2002, Pope John Paul 11 and Ecumenical Patriarch Bartholomew offered a hope-filled challenge to this generation:

> It is not too late. God's world has incredible healing powers. Within a single generation we could steer the earth towards our children's future. Let that generation start now, with God's help and blessing.[1]

---

1. *Joint Declaration on Articulating a Code of Environmental Ethics,* 10 June 2002. In *Origins* 32: No 6 (20 June 2002), 81–4, at 84.

This is the kind of leadership needed from church authorities in our time. In another statement, John Paul II has said that we human beings have failed God in devastating forests, waterways, habitats and the atmosphere of our planet, but this makes it all the more important for us to build up the sense that the human community of this generation is called to an *'ecological conversion'*.[2] Such an ecological conversion involves a new way of seeing, thinking, feeling and acting. It seems clear that, for Christians of this generation, this conversion will need to be a central dimension of their life of faith. It seems obvious, too, that their central acts as a Christian community, the celebration of Eucharist, will need to be a source for and an expression of their ongoing ecological conversion. This line of thought raises important questions: Are there authentic and intrinsic links between the Eucharist and the way we think, feel and act with regard to the natural world? Are there ways in which our eucharistic celebrations can better enable the ecological conversion that John Paul II has advocated? How is Eucharist related to ecological action and lifestyles?

I will attempt a partial response to these questions by reflecting first on the fundamental sign of the Eucharist, the giving and receiving of fruits of the Earth at a shared table. Then I will explore the eucharistic *anamnesis* as a memorial of creation as well as redemption. This will lead to a consideration of the Eastern theme of the Eucharist as the 'lifting up' of creation to God. Finally, I will reflect on the Eucharist as an invocation of the eschatological Spirit, who brings us into a Trinitarian Communion that embraces the whole creation.

The Eucharistic Symbols: Fruits of the Earth at a Shared Table

In a recent article, David Power describes the central sign of the Eucharist as 'the communion of the diverse members of the church in the elements of bread and wine, around a common table, sharing in the things of earth'.[3] His focus is on what it means in terms of commitment to justice that Christ gives himself to the church in this way. The question I am exploring is similar and related: What does it

---

2. Pope John Paul II, *General Audience Address*, 17 January 2001. In *L'Osservatore Romano* 4 (24 January 2001), 11.
3. David N Power, 'Eucharistic Justice', in *Theological Studies* 67 (December 2006): 856–79, at 860.

mean in terms of ecological conversion that Christ gives himself to us at a common table in bread and wine, fruits of the Earth and work of human hands?

In *The Eucharistic Mystery*, Power suggests that the symbolic act of Eucharist can be considered at four levels of significance: 1. As bread and wine shared at a common table; 2. As related to social, economic and cultural realities; 3. As celebrated by a community of mutual service that overcomes social distinctions; 4. As proclaiming and representing Christ's saving death and abiding presence. He insists that nothing of the meaning of the first level, the innate meaning of food and drink, is abolished in accommodating the deepest meaning of representing Christ.[4] An ecological theology of the Eucharist can begin at this first level, asking: How does partaking in bread and wine at a common table express our relationship to the community of life on Earth?

Xavier Léon-Dufour offers some helpful reflections on the meaning of bread and wine for the biblical world. Bread stands for basic food, the food that enables survival, the food that no one can be without.[5] It is used as a metaphor for food in general (Amos 4:6; Mk 3:20. 11:5; 15:17). As the food which sustains and nourishes life, it is always seen as the gift of the Creator. It is a sign of God's constant care and presence (Ex 23:25; Ps 78:20; 132:15; 146:7; Matt 6:11). As the gift of God, bread is meant to be shared, above all with the hungry (Isa 58:7; Ez 18:7).

Because bread is the necessary food of everyday life, it can also become the sign of God's promise. For the people of the Exodus, wheat is the first among the crops of the promised land (Deut 8:8; 11:14). Bread becomes a symbol of the eschatological banquet (Ps 78:23–25; Rev 2:17). This is why in Luke we find the man sitting with Jesus at table exclaiming in response to the words of Jesus: 'Blessed is anyone who will eat bread in the kingdom of God!' (Lk 14:15) The bread of the Eucharist is always ordinary bread, the bread of daily life, but precisely as such it is the bread of the kingdom.

---

4. David N Power, *The Eucharistic Mystery: Revitalizing the Tradition* (New York: Crossroad, 1992), 294–6.
5. Xavier Léon-Dufour, *Sharing the Eucharistic Bread: The Witness of the New Testament* (New York: Paulist Press, 1987), 58–9. In the next few paragraphs I am following Léon-Dufour.

It is important to note, that the bread of biblical faith is not an individualistic portion, but the one loaf that is broken and shared. It is the one loaf of Paul: 'Because there is one bread, we who are many are one body, for we all partake of the one bread' (1 Cor 10:17). It is the bread broken in chapter 9 of the *Didache*: 'As this broken bread was scattered over the mountains, and when brought together became one, so may your church be brought together from the ends of the earth into your kingdom'.[6]

If bread represents everyday nourishment and sustenance, wine represents the God-given abundance of life. It is associated with life (Sir 31:27), friendship (Sir 9:10), love (Cant 1:2; 4:10), joy (Eccl 10:19; Zech 10:7) and music (Sir 32:6; 40:20; Is 5:12). While wine can express the divine wrath (Ps 60:5; Rev 16:19), it normally represents the generous bounty of the gifts of creation that come from the hand of God. It is a sign of heavenly joy (Amos 9:14; Hos 2:4; Jer 31:12). It is a drink of festival, a drink to 'cheer peoples' hearts' (Ps 104:15).

Wine is a sign of blessing, a sign of the abundance of creation and the blessing of God. In the accounts of the last supper, Jesus speaks of the 'fruit of the vine' that he will not drink again until he will drink it new with his community in the Reign of God (Mk 14:25; Matt 26:29; Lk 22:18). It is to be noted that the word used to describe what Jesus takes up and prays over is not 'wine', but the 'cup'. In First Corinthians, for example, Paul writes:

> In the same way he took the cup also, after supper, saying, 'This cup is the new covenant in my blood. Do this as often as you drink it in remembrance of me.' For as often as eat this bread and drink this cup, you proclaim the Lord's death until he comes (1 Cor 11: 25–26).

The word 'cup' has its own special resonance. It recalls the communal sharing of the various cups of a Jewish festive meal. It reminds us of the way the metaphor of the cup functions in the psalms. In response to God's bounty, the psalmist gives thanks: 'I will lift up the cup of salvation and call on the name of the Lord' (Ps 116:13). There is the 'overflowing cup' provided at the table of the Shepherd (Ps 23:6). At the deepest level, the true cup for the faithful people of the covenant

---

6. RCD Jasper and GJ Cuming, *Prayers of the Eucharist: Early and Reformed*, third edition (New York: Pueblo, 1987), 23.

is nothing else but the God of Israel: 'my chosen portion and my cup' (Ps 16:5).

The one loaf and the one cup shared at the eucharistic table are gifts of God's good creation that both sustain life and make community. The sharing of the loaf and the cup is always an event grounded in the Earth and its fruits. It is this sharing of the fruits of the Earth that becomes the memorial event of Christ's self-giving. The world of crops and vineyards, of sunshine and rain, of Earth's bounty and its many forms of life, are represented in the loaf and the cup and are forever linked to Christ as the signs through which he bestows himself. Alexander Schmemann writes:

> That is why it is not 'simply' bread that lies on the *diskos*. On it all of God's creation is presented, manifested in Christ as the new creation, the fulfillment of the glory of God. And it is not 'simply' people who are gathered in this assembly, but the new humanity, recreated in the 'ineffable glory' of its Creator.[7]

Eating and drinking bread and wine together remind us of our grounding in the whole interconnected pattern of fleshly life, of hunger and thirst, nourishment and refreshment. The bread we share brings to mind the grain sown by farmers, the cycles of ploughing, sowing and reaping, and families that depend on the land and what it yields, and the fruitfulness and generous bounty of the Earth. We are led to remember those who bake bread, and the lovely smell of bread rising. The wine calls to mind fruitful vineyards set in rolling hills, the celebrations of vintage, the skill of wine-making, the pleasures of smell and taste, drinks shared, and the joy of memorable moments of celebration.

David Power writes: 'It is important that a community of Christian people receive food from a common and blessed loaf made from the soil of their land and from the toil of its inhabitants, and from a cup radiant indeed with the sun but pressed out by tired feet.'[8] While the pressing of grapes by tired feet may be metaphorical, Power's focus on the local community is fundamental for an ecological theology of Eucharist. To break bread in the Eucharist is always a local event, an

---

7. Alexander Schmemann, *The Eucharist: Sacrament of the Kingdom* (Crestwood, New York: St Vladimir's Seminary Press, 1988), 118.
8. Power, 'Eucharistic Justice', 867.

event of a local church. It represents not only the local people, but the land that forms and nourishes them. Wherever possible, the bread of the Eucharist should be made locally from grain grown locally, and the wine, radiant with sunshine, should come from local vineyards, representing the fruits of the land in the place and all human work that grows, creates, builds, supports and heals.

Bread and wine present challenges to Christians gathered for the Eucharist. They raise questions about the ecological, economic and political realities they represent. The way we grow and process our food and drink can come at an unbearable cost to other human beings and to other creatures of our planet. Ruthless land-clearing, irrigation and fishing practices, lack of commitment to biodiversity and neglect of the rights of animals can cause terrible suffering. The bread and wine of the Eucharist call us to be mindful of those who suffer economic exploitation and ecological devastation. They call us to solidarity with those whose lands are already being flooded and with those who depend on rice produced in low-lying areas for their daily 'bread'.

Participating at a common table set with bread and wine calls us to thanksgiving and to conversion. The bread and wine lead us to praise and thanksgiving for the daily gift of food and for the joy of God's abundant blessings in creation. This is already by its nature the beginning of an ecological conversion, a turning towards a love for our planet and all its creatures as the gift of God. When the name of Christ is invoked over the bread and wine, the liberating and creative Spirit leads us towards a new way of feeling, living and acting as responsible inhabitant of a global community of life.

The *Anamnesis* of Creation and Redemption

It matters a great deal for an ecological theology that what is commemorated in the Eucharist involves both creation and redemption. Louis Bouyer has pointed out how that what is commemorated in both Jewish and Christian prayers of thanksgiving involves the whole action of the one God who creates and saves. *Anamnesis* embraces all that God has done for us in a single view.[9] It embraces not only what God has already done but the promise of God that all things will be

---

9. Louis Bouyer, *Life and Liturgy* (London: Sheed and Ward, 1956), 116, 130.

transformed in Christ. In this section, I use the word *anamnesis* or commemoration to refer to the whole eucharistic prayer, rather than simply to the prayer that follows the narrative of the last supper.[10] I will point to examples from the tradition where the *anamnesis* of creation is made explicit, with the intention of suggesting that the eucharistic prayer is intrinsically a memorial of creation and that this has ecological significance.

Since the time of Gregory Dix and his 1945 classic *The Shape of the Liturgy*, there has been discussion of his proposal that, at the end of his final meal with his disciples, Jesus would naturally have used the tripartite Jewish prayer of blessing over a cup of wine, the *birkat ha-mazon*. Liturgical scholars have attempted to trace a trajectory from the *birkat ha-mazon* to the earliest extant Christian eucharistic prayers, such as the *Didache*, the liturgy called *Addai and Mari* and the *Apostolic Tradition* and beyond them into the later tradition. More recently, this approach has been challenged. For one thing, the earliest manuscript available for the *birkat ha-mazon* is the tenth century *Siddur Rav Saadya Gaon*. We cannot be sure what form of prayer Jesus would have used at meals and historians are not confident that there is any one clear line of liturgical development. As Paul Bradshaw says, we now 'know much less about the liturgical practices of the first three centuries of Christianity than we once thought we did'.[11] The picture is one of diversity rather than of one uniform pattern.

Of course, Louis Bouyer had long ago insisted on the significance for Christian liturgy of synagogue prayers and the wider context of Jewish prayers of praise even as he focused on meal *berakah*.[12] More recently, Cesare Giraudo has argued that the background for Christian Eucharist needs to be located in the broader *todah* (proclamatory prayers of praise) tradition of Jewish prayer.[13] Maxwell Johnson has pointed to the variety of possible sources that include the meal practices of the Greco-Roman symposium, the annual Passover meal,

---

10. See Power, *The Eucharistic Mystery*, 90, note 20.
11. Paul Bradshaw, *The Search for the Origins of Christian Worship: Sources and Methods for the Study of Early Liturgy*, second edition (Oxford: Oxford University Press, 2002), x.
12. Louis Bouyer, *Eucharist: Theology and Spirituality of the Eucharistic Prayer* (Notre Dame: University of Notre Dame Press, 1968).
13. Cesare Giraudo, *La struttura letteraria della preghiera eucaristica: Saggio sulla genesi letteraria di una forma* (Rome: Biblical Institute Press, 1981).

and the whole variety of diverse Jewish prayer forms, including the *birkat ha-mazon*, oral forms of which would have existed from an early stage.[14] He insists that it cannot be assumed that early Christian eucharistic practice followed any one pattern or structure.

My purpose here is not to enter into this discussion but, having noted the complexity of the historical issues, to bring into focus the way early Christian eucharistic prayers remember, praise and thank God for creation as well as for redemption. I begin with the *birhat ha-mazon*, not only because an early form of it may have influenced Christian eucharistic practice, but also because it faithfully represents the broader Jewish prayer and faith that certainly did influence Christian liturgy. This prayer, said over the cup of wine at the end of the meal, has a tripartite structure: it involves first a blessing of God for creation, then a thanksgiving for the gift of the land, followed by intercession for the people of God. The blessing for creation reads:

> *Blessing of him who nourishes*
> Blessed are you, Lord our God, King of the universe, for you nourish us and the whole world with your goodness, grace, kindness and mercy.
> Blessed are you, Lord, for you nourish the universe.[15]

One of the things to notice about this prayer is that its focus is not on a primordial act of God in the beginning, and not on the creation accounts of Genesis, but on God's continuous and faithful nourishment of human beings and of the whole universe of creatures. This nourishing role of God can be understood, I believe, in relation to what we now call *creatio continua*, the action by which God enables the whole universe and all its creatures to exist, to act and to evolve. The word 'nourish' brings the action of God very close. It suggests the kind of creation theology found in Psalm 104, praise for the God who sustains and provides for each creature, breathing into each the breath of life. It suggests that the food and drink on the table are the gift of the Creator who continually creates and sustains all things.

---

14. Maxwell E Johnson, 'The Apostolic Tradition', in *The Oxford History of Christian Worship*, edited by Geoffrey Wainwright and Karen B Westerfield Tucker (Oxford: Oxford University Press, 2006), 32–75, at 44–7.
15. Jasper and Cuming, *Prayers*, 10.

The *Didache* is the earliest known example of a Christian church order. It seems to have its origin in Syria, perhaps in the second half of the first century. In chapter 10, we find a series of three prayers that parallel the *birkat-ha-mazon*: a prayer of blessing for God's holy name, a prayer that after recalling God's creation of all things, including food and drink, gives thanks for the nourishment given to us in Christ, and a prayer of intercession for the church that ends in a doxology. The first two prayers are these:

> *And after you have had your fill, give thanks thus:*
> We give thanks to you, holy Father, for your holy Name which you have enshrined in our hearts, and for the knowledge of the faith and immortality which you have made known through your child Jesus; glory to you for evermore.
>
> You, almighty Master, created all things for the sake of your Name, and gave food and drink to humankind for their enjoyment, that they might give you thanks; but to us you have granted spiritual food and drink and eternal life through your child Jesus. Above all we give you thanks because you are mighty; glory to you for evermore. Amen.[16]

As David Power notes, the first prayer echoes the Jewish theology of the divine Name, a theology closely linked to creation. The glory of the Name is made manifest in creation as well as in God's saving acts.[17] In the second prayer, the link between creation and the divine name is made explicit: God is praised for creating all things for the sake of the Name. The prayer moves from God giving food and drink for human enjoyment to become a thanksgiving for the nourishment of eternal life given to us in Jesus.

Also from East Syria is the eucharistic prayer that goes by the name of *Addai and Mari*. It offers praise to God for creation and thanksgiving for the work of redemption and then continues with a prayer for the church that includes an invocation over the bread and wine. In its present form, there is an *epiclesis* of the Spirit, but as the earliest manuscripts we have date from as late as the tenth century, there are doubts about its original form. Like the *Didache*, this prayer

---

16. Jasper and Cuming, *Prayers*, 23 (slightly adapted).
17. Power, *The Eucharistic Mystery*, 84.

is based upon a Syriac theology of the name of God, as its opening makes clear:

> Worthy of glory from every mouth and thanksgiving from every tongue is the adorable and glorious name of the Father and of the Son and of the Holy Spirit. He created the world through his grace and its inhabitants in his compassion; he saved men through his mercy, and gave great grace to mortals.[18]

The prayer continues by joining in praise with all the angels 'who glorify your name', and then leads into the Sanctus. There is a lovely balance in this opening prayer between on the one hand, God's creation of the world and its inhabitants out of compassion and, on the other, God's salvation and grace given to us out of divine mercy.

Justin Martyr provides important descriptions of early Christian worship in his *Dialogue with Trypho*, written in Ephesus about 135, and his *First Apology*, written in Rome about 150. In the *Apology*, he offers an account of baptism that culminates in Eucharist and an outline of a normal Sunday celebration. In the *Dialogue with Trypho*, he makes it clear that the eucharistic prayer is not only a memorial of the passion, but also a thanksgiving for creation:

> The offering of fine flour . . . which was handed down to be offered for those who were cleansed of leprosy, was a type of the bread of thanksgiving, which our Lord Jesus Christ handed down to us to do for a remembrance of the suffering which he suffered for those who are cleansed in their souls from all wickedness of human beings, so that we might give thanks to God, both for creating the world with all things that are in it for the sake of humanity, and for freeing us from the evil in which we were born, and for accomplishing a complete destruction of the principalities and powers through him who suffered according to his will.[19]

Three elements are united in Justin's notion of the Eucharist as a memorial of the cross: it is a thanksgiving for creation, for

---

18. Jasper and Cuming, *Prayers*, 41.
19. Jasper and Cuming, *Prayers*, 27 (slightly adapted).

redemption from sin, and for cosmic redemption. The other possible source of information about eucharistic practice in Rome is the *Apostolic Tradition*, often ascribed to Hippolytus of Rome (c170—c 236), but much is unclear both about its original form and the extent to which it represents the usage of the Roman church. This prayer moves from a thanksgiving for creation, which is very brief, and for the redemptive work of Christ, which is more extensive, to intercession. The thanksgiving for creation appears in this form:

> We render thanks to you, O God, through your beloved child Jesus Christ, whom in the last times you sent to us as a saviour and redeemer and angel of your will; who is your inseparable Word, through whom you made all things, and in whom you were well pleased.[20]

The Word of creation is identified with the Word of redemption. David Power points to the similarity with the thought of Irenaeus, who battled Gnostic dualism by affirming the one mediation of the Word through whom God creates and redeems all things. For Irenaeus, the offering of bread and wine with thanksgiving and the invocation of the name of Christ shows that the work of creation and its restoration are central to Christian redemption. Power points out that there is an echo of this kind of creation theology in the blessing of fruit, cheese, olives and oil that the *Apostolic Tradition* inserts at the end of the eucharistic prayer.[21] Irenaeus sees the Eucharist as confirming the incarnation, the goodness of creation and the resurrection of the flesh: 'Our manner of thinking is conformed to the Eucharist, and Eucharist conforms to our manner of thinking.'[22] The Eucharist expresses gratitude for creation, in the offering of the fruits of the earth, as well as for God's work of redemption and it does this by invoking the name of Christ over the gifts. It thus confirms the

---

20. Jasper and Cuming, *Prayers*, 35.
21. Power, *The Eucharistic Mystery*, 93.
22. *Adversus Haereses* IV, 18.5. See David N Power, editor, *Iraneus of Lyons on Baptism and the Eucharist: Selected Texts with Introduction, Translation and Annotation*, Alcuin/GROW Liturgical Study 18 (Bramcote, Nottingham: Grove Books, 1991), 21.

doctrine of the one God creating and redeeming the world through the one Word.[23]

The church order of the *Apostolic Constitutions* probably had its origin in the second half of the fourth century, during the doctrinal controversies with Eunomius. Book 8 contains a eucharistic prayer with an extremely long preface, which begins from a celebration of God the source of all. It speaks of God as bringing 'all things from non-existence to existence'. It then goes on with a highly detailed celebration of creation, a small part of which is given here:

> You girded the world that was made by you through Christ with rivers and flooded it with torrents, you watered it with everflowing springs and bound it round with mountains as an unshakeable and most safe seat for the earth.
>
> For you filled the world and adorned it with sweet-smelling and healing herbs, with many different living things, strong and weak, for food and for work, tame and wild, with hissing of reptiles, with the cries of variegated birds, the cycles of the years, the numbers of months and days, the order of the seasons, the course of rain-bearing clouds for the production of fruits and the creation of living things, a stable for the winds that blow at your command, the multitude of plants and herbs.[24]

Reading this detailed thanksgiving for creation today leads one to long for eucharistic prayers shaped in the light of contemporary cosmology, evolutionary biology and ecological consciousness.

The anophora of St Basil praises the God of all creation, and that of St John Chysostom praises God who brings us out of non-existence into existence. There is little of creation in the Roman canon. In Eucharistic Prayer II of the revised Roman Catholic liturgy, creation and redemption are held together in Christ: 'He is the Word through whom you made the universe, the Saviour you sent to redeem us'. Eucharistic Prayer III begins: 'Father you are holy indeed, and all creation rightly gives you praise. All life, all holiness comes from you through your Son Jesus Christ Our Lord by the working of the Holy

---

23. See Power, *The Eucharistic Mystery*, 109–10
24. Jasper and Cuming, *Prayers*, 106.

Spirit'. And in Eucharistic Prayer IV, God is addressed: 'Source of life and goodness, you have created all things, to fill your creatures with every blessing, and lead all people to the joyful vision of your light.'

This brief survey of liturgical sources suggests that the memorial of the Eucharist is traditionally understood as an act of praise and thanksgiving for God's creation. I think it can be argued theologically that the Eucharist is intrinsically a memorial of creation and redemption together. This is supported in the classical theology of Irenaeus who sees creation and redemption united in the one Word. It finds support today in a theology like that of Karl Rahner, who sees creation, redemption and final fulfilment as distinct aspects of God's one act of self-bestowal in love.[25]

This concept of the Eucharist as keeping memorial of creation is of fundamental importance in a time when human action is radically altering the climate with disastrous effects for human beings and for other creatures on Earth. We keep memorial of God's good creation, that embraces the fourteen billion-year history of the universe, the 3.7 billion-year history of Earth and the emergence of life on our planet in all its diversity and beauty. Remembering creation involves a critical mindfulness. As David Power says, we include suffering in the remembrance of Christ, and this needs to include the suffering of the whole creation.[26] We remember the vulnerable state of the community of life on Earth today and bring this to God. We are called to a solidarity that involves all the human victims of ecological destruction as well as the animals and plants that are destroyed or threatened. We remember those already displaced from the homes and their heritage. We cannot but be painfully aware of the threat to many millions of other people.

We pray in solidarity with the global community, that the Eucharist which brings us into peace and communion with God may 'advance the peace and salvation of all the world' (Third Eucharistic

---

25. See for example Karl Rahner, 'Christology in the Setting of Modern Man's Understanding of Himself and of his World', in *Theological Investigations* 11 (New York: Seabury, 1974), 215–29, particularly at 225.
26. Power, *The Eucharistic Mystery*, 314–15. In his reflections at this point, Power argues that the creation story and the story of redemption cannot be given a similar historical footing. While this is undoubtedly true, I think what needs emphasis in our liturgies is God's *creatio continua*, and the one differentiated act of the God who creates and saves.

Prayer). When we come to the Eucharist, we bring the creatures of Earth with us. We remember the God who loves each one of them. We grieve for the damage done to them. We feel with them. We hope for their future in God. We commit ourselves to their wellbeing.

The Lifting Up of All Creation to God

The eucharistic memorial is not only an act of thanksgiving and praise for creation and redemption, it is a lifting up of the whole creation to God. In exploring the ecological meaning of the eucharistic memorial, I find helpful insights in the work of two Orthodox theologians, Alexander Schmemann and John Zizioulas, now Metropolitan John of Pergamon. Schmemann explores the biblical meaning of memory, and finds it grounded in a theology of God's creative memory:

> Here we should recall that in the biblical, Old Testamental teaching on God, the term memory refers to the attentiveness of God to his creation, the power of divine providential love through which God 'holds' the world and *gives it life*, so that life itself can be termed abiding in the memory of God, and death the falling out of this memory. In other words, memory, like everything else in God, is *real*, it is that life that he grants, that God '*remembers*'; it *is* the eternal overcoming of the "nothing" out of which God called us into 'his wonderful light'.[27]

Memory is a gift given by God to human beings. In us, memory becomes our responding love to God, 'the encounter and communion with God, with the life of life itself'.[28] It is given to the human, out of all creation, to remember God and through this remembrance to truly live. Schmemann says that if every creature in our world witnesses to God and declares the glory of God, it is only the human being who remembers God, 'and through this living knowledge of God, comprehends the world as God's world, receives it from God, and raises it up to God'.[29]

---

27. Schmemann, *The Eucharist*, 125.
28. Schmemann, *The Eucharist*, 125.
29. Schmemann, *The Eucharist*, 125-6.

Salvation is the restoration of memory as a life-giving power. Christ is the incarnation and the gift to humankind of God's memory in its fullness, as love directed to each human being, towards the world and all its creatures.[30] In liturgy, we recall what has already been given to us, the creation of the world, its salvation in Christ and the coming of the kingdom of God. This kind of remembering involves the past and the future in the present: 'We recall, in other words, both the past and the future as living in us, as given to us, as transformed into our life and making it life in God.'[31]

This memory is an act of thanksgiving and blessing. As the world is created by the word of God through blessing, so it is saved and restored to us by thanksgiving and blessing. In thanksgiving and blessing, 'we recognise and comprehend the world as icon, as communion, as sanctification'. According to Schmemann, when in the Eucharist we remember Christ who 'took bread', this bread means the matter of creation, the whole world of creatures, transformed as new creation in Christ.[32]

John Zizioulas has spelled out his ecological theology in a series of lectures given at Kings College London.[33] He argues that the ecological crisis cannot be met simply by arguments based on reason. What is required, if we hope to change priorities and life-styles, is a different *culture* and a different *ethos*. Zizioulas is convinced that what is needed above all is a *liturgical* ethos. Like many Othodox theologians, he sees human beings as called by God to be 'priests of creation'. He distinguishes this priestly task sharply from the notions of sacrificial priesthood that he associates with medieval and Roman Catholic theology.

For Zizoulas, the concept of being a priest of creation is linked to the idea of being fully personal. He sees each baptised person as called to be, like Christ, a fully *personal* being. This involves being relational rather than self-enclosed, being able to go out of self to the other, in what he calls *ek-stasis*. Persons are always ecstatic, in the sense that they achieve personhood only in communion with others. Humans are relational beings. Their vocation is to relate in a fully personal way to God, to other humans and to other creatures of God.

---

30. Schmemann, *The Eucharist*, 128.
31. Schmemann, *The Eucharist*, 130.
32. Schmemann, *The Eucharist*, 176.
33. John Zizioulas, 'Preserving God's Creation: Three Lectures on Ecology and Theology', in *King's Theological Review* 12 (1989): 1–5, 41–5 and 13 (1990): 1–5.

According to Zizioulas, humanity and the rest of creation comes to their completion in the life of God through each other.

When humans come to the Eucharist, they bring the fruits of creation, and in some way the whole creation, to the eucharistic table. In the East, the central eucharistic prayer is known as the anaphora, a word which means the lifting-up. In the Eucharist, creation is *lifted up* to God in offering and thanksgiving. The gifts of creation are lifted up to God and the Spirit is invoked to transform the gifts of creation, and the assembled community, into the Body of Christ.

An important element in Zizoulas's thought is his insistence that this priesthood is not confined to the ordained but is the God-given role of all the faithful. Equally important is the conviction that this 'lifting up' is not restricted to liturgical celebrations but is meant to happen in the whole of life. It is meant to involve all human interactions with the rest of creation. The 'lifting up' of creation is meant to be played out around the planet continually by every human being. Fundamentally this priestly task seems to involve an authentic personal love for other creatures in all their specificity and uniqueness. It involves a fully human feeling for them and celebration of them in God. Our stance towards the rest of creation, our personal engagement with it as fully relational beings, is a central dimension of our life before God and salvation in Christ.

The ecological crisis requires the deepest resources of the human community. With Zizioulas, I believe that in the Eucharist Christians have the source for an authentically ecological ethos and culture.[34] It does not provide answers to all the practical questions that confront us, but it does offer a motivation and a genuinely ecological ethos.[35] We lift up creation to God and praise God on behalf of all of Earth's creatures: 'All creation rightly gives you praise' (Third Eucharistic Prayer); 'In the name of every creature under heaven, we too praise your glory' (Fourth Eucharistic Prayer). I have long been struck by Yves Congar's remark that whenever he prays the great doxology at the end of the eucharistic prayer he is conscious of the whole cre-

---

34. See Partricia A Fox, *God as Communion: John Zizioulas, Elizabeth Johnson, and the Retrieval of the Symbol of God* (Collegeville: Liturgical Press, 2001), 70.
35. Zizioulas says: 'All this involves an *ethos* that the world needs badly in our time. Not an ethic, but an *ethos*. Not a programme, but an attitude and a mentality. Not legislation, but a culture.' See his 'Preserving God's Creation', in *King's Theological Review* 13 (1990), 5.

ation. At this moment, we lift up the whole creation through, with and in Christ, 'in the unity of the Holy Spirit' to the eternal praise and glory of God.[36]

The liturgical stance makes clear how human beings are related to other creatures. On the one hand, we are closely interconnected with them in a kinship of creation. On the other hand we are unique as personal creatures called to remember and praise God on behalf of the whole creation. This calls us into a relational stance before the whole of creation. Christian eucharistic practice, when understood and lived in all its depth, is capable of sustaining an ongoing conversion to a personal and loving stance before the rest of creation.

Invoking the Eschatological Spirit

As the eucharistic prayer is always a memorial that involves praise and thanksgiving to God for both creation and redemption, and as it is always a lifting up of creation to God, so it is also always an invocation of the eschatological Spirit. Even when there is no explicit *epiclesis*, the Spirit of God is invoked over the gifts of bread and wine and over the assembly that they might become the body of Christ. It is always the eschatological Spirit who creates an event of communion. The Spirit makes the assembly an eschatological event that anticipates the future when all will things will be taken up and find their fulfilment in divine Communion.

Communion with each other in Christ is a participation in and a tasting of the divine Communion, in which the whole creation will be transfigured and all creatures will find their eternal meaning and their true home. This Communion, of the 'Source of Life and Goodness' with the eternal Word and the life-giving Spirit, is both the origin of all things and the fulfilment of all things. It is this dynamic Communion of the Three that creates, sustains and empowers all the diverse forms of life on our planet. It is what enables a community of life to emerge and to evolve. In ways beyond imagination, this Trinitarian life will be the fulfilment of all the creatures of our planet, and all the wonders of our universe. As we participate in the Eucharist, we know our own kinship with all the creatures sustained and nourished

---

36. See Yves Congar's remarks on the doxology in his *I Believe in the Holy Spirit*, Volume II (New York: Seabury Press, 1983), 224.

by the presence and action of the triune God in whom 'we live and move and have our being' (Acts 17:28) and we taste in anticipation the final communion of all things in the shared life of God.

The Spirit at work in the Eucharist is the Creator Spirit, the Breath of Life who empowers the unfolding of the universe from the beginning and enables the evolution of all the diverse creatures of our planet. It is this Spirit who will bring the universe and its creatures to their final fulfilment in Christ. The Christ we encounter in the Eucharist is the risen one, the one in whom all things were created and in whom all are reconciled (Col 1:15–20). Even when we focus our attention in the eucharistic memorial on Christ's death and resurrection, this is not a memory that takes us away from creation. It involves us directly with creation, with Earth and all its creatures. When we remember Christ's death, we remember a creature of our universe, a product of our evolutionary history, freely handing his whole bodily and personal existence into the mystery of a loving God. When we remember the resurrection, we remember part of our universe and part of our evolutionary history being taken up in the Spirit into God. As Rahner says, the resurrection of Jesus is not only the *promise* but the *beginning* of the glorification and divinisation of the whole of reality.[37] The Eucharist is the symbol and the sacrament of the risen Christ who is the beginning of the transfiguration of all creatures in God. Eucharist is both sign and agent of the transforming work of the risen Christ in the whole of creation. The Eucharist points towards and anticipates the divinisation of the universe in Christ.

At the end of 2 Corinthians, Paul prays: 'The grace of the Lord Jesus Christ, the love of God and the communion (*koinōnia*) of the Holy Spirit be with all of you' (2 Cor 13:13). The communion of the Holy Spirit not only unites us with Christ and with all those who partake of the one bread and the one cup, but also takes us beyond the local assembly and beyond the wider church to a communion of all God's creatures. Jürgen Moltmann says that the experience of the Spirit 'leads of itself beyond the limits of the church to the rediscovery of this same Spirit in nature, in plants, in animals, and in the ecosystems of the earth.'[38] The experience that we are a part of an

---

37. Karl Rahner, 'Dogmatic Questions on Easter', in *Theological Investigations* IV (New York, Seabury Press, 1974), 129.
38. Jürgen Moltmann, *The Spirit of Life: A Universal Affirmation* (Minneapolis, Fortress, 1992), 10.

inter-related community of creation, that we are in some ways kin with other creatures before God, this too is part of the *koinōnia* of the Holy Spirit.

Because our eucharistic communion involves us with the Word in whom all things are created and with the Spirit who breathes life into all creatures, it is a communion that involves us with the whole community of life on Earth. This means, as Tony Kelly says, that the 'most intense moment of our communion with God is at the same time an intense moment of our communion with the earth'.[39] By being taken up into God, we are caught up into God's loving engagement with the creatures of our planetary community. This begins to shape our ecological imagination: 'The Eucharist educates the imagination, the mind, and the heart to apprehend the universe as one of communion and connectedness in Christ'. In this eucharistic imagination, a distinctive ecological vision and commitment can take shape.[40]

With this kind of imagination at work in us, we can see the other creatures of Earth as our kin, as radically interconnected with us in one Earth community of life before God. We can begin to see critically—to see more clearly what is happening to the Earth. We are led to participate in God's feeling for the life-forms of our planet. An authentic eucharistic imagination leads to an ecological ethos, culture and praxis.

Conclusion

The argument I have been making is that when Christians gather for Eucharist they bring creation with them. The one loaf of bread and the one cup of wine, fruits of the Earth, work of human hands, given and received at a common table, are the signs in which Christ gives himself to us. Eating and drinking this bread and this cup together continually points to our inter-relationship with all the living creatures of Earth, and with the land, the atmosphere, the rivers and the seas that support life. At the heart of the Eucharist is the memorial of praise and thanksgiving. It is fundamental to an ecological

---

39. Tony Kelly, *The Bread of God: Nurturing a Eucharistic Imagination* (Melbourne: HarperCollins, 2001), 92. See also his *Eschatology and Hope* (Maryknoll, NY: Orbis, 2006), 181–200.
40. Kelly, *The Bread of God*, 100–1.

theology to understand this as memorial of God's marvellous deeds that include creation as well as redemption and the promise of final transformation. The eucharistic memorial is always a lifting up of the whole creation, a lifting up that takes place not in the Eucharist, but one that is lived in the whole of life in an ecological ethos and an in ecological vocation. Every Eucharist is an invocation of the Spirit who makes us one with each other in Christ, and makes us one with the whole creation in the eschatological communion of the Trinity.

These considerations raise further questions: How can our celebrations better manifest and highlight the ecological meaning already inherent in the eucharistic symbols? How might our celebrations better reveal the liturgical and theological truth that in the Eucharist we keep memorial of God's work of creation as well as God's work of redemption, and better bring out its ecological consequences? What might help us rediscover the deeply Christian idea that we lift up creation to God in praise and thanksgiving in every Eucharist and in the whole of life? How might we make more explicit the idea that in the Eucharist the Spirit of God brings us into an eschatological communion with the Trinity that involves all the creatures of God? How can we further unpack and explore the all the symbols, words, actions, gestures as well as the ritual logic of the Eucharist to bring out its ecological meaning?

What I think becomes clear in these reflections is that human action, which is an expression of love and respect for the living creatures, the atmosphere, the seas and the land of our planet, can be seen as not only in continuity with, but also as in some way part of the work of the eucharistic Christ. On the other hand, knowing and wilful acts that contribute to global climate change and to the destruction of habitats and species can be seen as a denial of Christ. They deny the meaning of what we celebrate when we gather for Eucharist.

Participating at a common table set with bread and wine calls us to a memorial thanksgiving that is already the beginning of an ecological conversion, a turning towards a love for our planet and all its creatures as the gift of God. When the name of Christ is invoked over the bread and wine, the Creator Spirit leads us toward a way of feeling, living and acting as part of a global community of life. These signs are intrinsically rich in ecological meaning. They point us to the whole of creation. They locate us within a sacramental approach to the whole of life.

Celebrating Eucharist in a Time of Global Climate Change

While I was re-working this article, *The Australian* newspaper carried a story of a lecture given by Tim Flannery, director of the Museum of South Australia. The headline was 'Climate calamity forecast by end of century'. In the article, Flannery is reported as saying that by the end of the century, temperatures will have risen by 3° C. The cause of this, he says, is simply human beings using fossil fuels. Australia burns more fossil fuel per capita and exports more coal than any other nation. A three degree rise in temperature would mean the loss of world heritage areas, the destruction of our coral reefs and our cities under increasing water stress. The Murray could dry up or be seriously damaged. Even a temperature rise of two degrees would mean the loss of Kakadu and our mountain rainforests, with their fauna.[1]

This news report is one among many. It seems that every day there are new media reports about global climate change. There is a growing sense of urgency about the issue. While scientific experts disagree about the details of their predictions, few now dispute that global warming is happening, that it will get far worse, and that our use of fossil fuels is a major cause. It seems clear that this will be the most important issue that the human community will face in the twenty-first century. For a Christian believer, committed to love for God's creation and to respect for the dignity of every person, responding to this issue will be necessarily a central dimension of the life of faith.

I will explore this issue in relation to the celebration of the Eucharist, which I take to be central to the life of the Christian community. What does global climate change mean for the Christian community

---

1. Verity Edwards, 'Climate Calamity Forecast by End of Century', *The Australian* (18 August 2005), 4.

that gathers each Sunday in the name of Jesus to listen to the Word of God and break the bread? This article begins with some brief ideas from science, first on long-term climate change and then on human-induced climate change. Then it gathers insights on creation in relation to the Eucharist from the West (Teilhard de Chardin) and from the East (John Zizioulas). Finally, it builds on these ideas with the theme of the Eucharist as the *living memory* of all God's creatures.

Long-Term Climate Change

It has long been clear that our planet goes through a pattern of ice-ages followed by warmer interglacial periods. Since the 1970s, this pattern has been better understood by scientists. They have been able to show that three regular variations of the orbit of the Earth cause predictable cycles of long-term climate change.

The most frequent of these variations is a wobble in the Earth's rotational axis, called precession, which occurs about every 22,000 years. The second is a variation to the tilt in the Earth's axis, and it occurs every 41,000 years. The third is caused by the shape of the orbit of the Earth around the Sun, and it occurs every 100,000 years. These three variations do not have much effect on the amount of solar energy hitting the Earth, but they effect its distribution. They cause substantial change to both the regional and the seasonal distribution of the heat that comes from the Sun. The result is a predictable cycle of ice ages followed by warmer periods.

The last ice age was about 20,000 years ago. The present interglacial period (the Holocene) is about 12,000 years old and well advanced. Ice cores taken from Antarctica and Greenland and transported to laboratories provide a record of climate change over the last 400,000 years. They provide a record of temperature variation and, in addition, the gases trapped in tiny air bubbles in the ice reveal the level of carbon dioxide and methane in the atmosphere in different periods. Scientists have also been able to map the distribution of the ice sheets during these different periods.

All of this has shown the close relationship between three factors: the variations in solar radiation hitting the Earth, the size of the ice sheets, and the levels of carbon dioxide and methane in the atmosphere. While long-term climate change is driven by variations in the Earth's orbit, it *takes effect* by altering the cycles of carbon dioxide and methane and the size of the ice sheets. What has changed is that it is human activity that is now impacting on the levels of carbon dioxide and methane in the atmosphere and causing the ice sheets to melt. Human beings are changing the planetary energy balance in a substantial way.[2]

Human-Induced Climate Change

An appropriate level of trace gases in the atmosphere is essential for life as we know it. These gases include carbon dioxide, methane, nitrous acid, as well as water vapour. When the Sun's energy reaches Earth, part of it is reflected back by the atmosphere, the clouds and the surface of the planet. Trace gases absorb some of this heat and prevent it escaping into space. This is 'greenhouse effect'. It means that the average temperature of the Earth over the last 700 million years has ranged between 5°C and 25°C, allowing life to evolve and flourish on Earth.

Humans force the climate by increasing levels of carbon dioxide and methane in the atmosphere. They do this by burning fossil fuels (coal, oil and gas), by land clearing and by various agricultural practices. In 1992, many governments of the world, including that of Australia, signed the United Nations Framework Convention on Climate Change. Under this convention, the research of thousands of scientists from many different countries was co-ordinated and gathered in the work of the Intergovernmental Panel on Climate Change. This Panel's fourth report is due in 2006. In its third report (2001), it states: 'there is new and stronger evidence that most of the warming observed over the last fifty years is attributable to human activities'. It says that human activities will continue to change atmospheric conditions during the twenty-first century. Global average temperatures and sea levels will rise under all IPPC scenarios. The report projects an increase in global average surface temperature of between 1.4°C and 5.8°C.[3]

---

2. On these issues see: James Hansen, 'Defusing the Global Warming Time Bomb', in *Scientific American* (March 2004): 40–9.
3. The Intergovernmental Panel on Climate Change, *Climate Change 2001: The Scientific Basis* at <http:www.girda.no/climate/ipcc_tar/wgl/467.htm> Accessed 5 May 2005.

The global average temperature increased 0.75°C during the period of extensive measurement beginning in late 1800s. About 0.5° has occurred after 1950. A recently released report commissioned by the Australian Government accepts that further climate change is now inevitable and will need to be adapted to in all decisions made by Australian governments and industry. It points out that some regions are highly vulnerable to climate change: Cairns and the Great Barrier Reef, the Murray Darling Basin and south west Western Australia.[4] The climate modeling by CSIRO's Division of Atmospheric Research predicts that average temperatures across Australia will increase somewhere between 0.4° and 2°C by 2030 and between 1° and 7°C by 2070. They predict a rise in sea level and an increase in cyclonic wind intensity.[5]

It is clear that the danger of melting the ice sheets and the need to preserve coastlines puts a very low limit on human interference with climate. The oceans are already storing an excessive amount of heat and this will have long-term term consequences even if the climate is stabilised. Those in low-lying areas like Kiribati, Tuvalu and Bangladesh are not only under threat, but already experiencing enormous problems. A one-metre rise in sea levels would flood rice fields in Bangladesh, Vietnam, Thailand, India and China, and force many millions from their homes. The Christian community that assembles Sunday after Sunday in Australia cannot but bring this issue to the centre of consciousness, prayer and action. It raises the theological question: How is climate change related to our Christian experience of the Eucharist? I will begin to explore a response to this question with some key ideas from Teilhard de Chardin and John Zizioulas.

Learning From the West: Teilhard de Chardon (1881–1955)

There appears to be a revival of interest in Teilhard de Chardin with conferences and collections of scholarly articles being published on his work.[6] Among recent books on various aspects of his work is a

---

4. *Climate Change: Risk and Vulnerability: Promoting an efficient adaptation response in Australia* (Canberra: The Australian Greenhouse Office, 2005), vii.
5. *Climate Change*, vii.
6. See for example, Arthur Fabel and Donald St John (editors), *Teilhard in the 21st Century: The Emerging Spirit of Earth* (Maryknoll, NY: Orbis, 2003).

new study by Thomas King of Teilhard's *The Mass on the World*.⁷ At the beginning of his book, King notes that Teilhard's *Mass* has been embraced recently by both Pope John Paul II and the then Joseph Cardinal Ratzinger. This is notable because Teilhard was never allowed to publish his beloved *Mass*, or any other religious or theological writings, during his lifetime. In *Gift and Mystery*, Pope John Paul II wrote that the Eucharist 'is celebrated in order to offer "on the altar of the whole earth the world's work and suffering" in the beautiful words of Teilhard de Chardin'.⁸ Then in his final encyclical on the Eucharist, he proposes a cosmic theology of the Eucharist:

> This varied scenario of celebrations of the Eucharist has given me a powerful experience of its universal and, so to speak, cosmic character. Yes cosmic! Because even when it is celebrated on the humble altar of a country church, the Eucharist is always in some way celebrated *on the altar of the world*. It unites heaven and earth. It embraces and permeates all of creation. The Son of Man became man in order to restore all creation, in one supreme act of praise, to the One who made it from nothing. He, the Eternal High Priest, who by the blood of his Cross entered the eternal sanctuary, thus gives back to the Creator and Father all creation redeemed. He does so through the priestly ministry of the Church, to the glory of the most Holy Trinity. Truly this is the *mysterium fidei* which is accomplished by the Eucharist: the world which came forth from the hands of God the Creator now returns to him redeemed by Christ.⁹

I have quoted this text at length because it not only refers to, and builds on, Teilhard's *Mass* but because it partially anticipates the work of this article, in offering a theology of the Eucharist that is radically connected to the redemption of the whole of creation in Christ. In *The Spirit of the Liturgy*, Cardinal Ratzinger also brings out the inner

---

7. Thomas M King, *Teilhard's Mass: Approaches to 'The Mass on the World'* (New York: Paulist, 2005).
8. John Paul II, *Gift and Mystery: On the Fiftieth Anniversary of My Priesthood* (New York: Doubleday, 1996), 73.
9. John Paul II, *Ecclesia de Eucharistia: On the Eucharist in its Relationship to the Church* (Strathfield, NSW: St Pauls, 2003), paragraph 8.

connection between creation and the Eucharist and refers positively to Teilhard's *Mass*. He sums it up: 'The transubstantiated Host is the anticipation of the transformation and divinization of matter in the christological "fullness"'. The Eucharist 'provides the movement of the cosmos with its direction; it anticipates its goal and at the same time urges it on'.[10] In a recent book on the Eucharist, Walter Cardinal Kasper also takes up Teilhard's thought on the Eucharist. He sees it as a rediscovery of the ancient cosmic doctrine of the Eucharist and describes its role as anticipating and contributing to the divinisation of creation.[11]

All his life, Teilhard longed for this kind of recognition by the wider church of the deep theological interconnection between creation and the Eucharist. He was born in Auvergne in southern France and, from his early days, was shaped by his passion for rocks and fossils, and by Ignatian spirituality, with its focus on radical commitment to Jesus Christ and to finding God in all things. While serving as a stretcher bearer on the front line during World War I, Teilhard wrote his first important essay, on 'Cosmic Life'. Already *communion* had become his central theme, communion with the Earth, and communion with God in creation. To this, he would add the deeply held conviction that *union differentiates*.

Unable to celebrate the Eucharist, he wrote an essay called *The Priest* near the Aisne River in 1918. A short time later, in 1923, he wrote *The Mass on the World* in the Ordos Desert, while on a scientific expedition in Western Mongolia. Teilhard's *Mass* is not to be thought of as a kind of devotional extra alongside his more substantial works like *The Human Phenomenon*. His *Mass* is a carefully worked and reworked text that reveals what is at the centre of Teilhard's thought.[12]

---

10. Joseph Cardinal Ratzinger, *The Spirit of the Liturgy* (San Francisco: Ignatius Press, 2000), 29.
11. 'In an ecclesiastical situation in which a one-sidedly individualistic understanding had veiled the much more comprehensive doctrine put forward by the tradition, he discovered anew the cosmic dimension and irradiation of the Eucharist. He did not confuse the transubstantiation in the strict sense of this word with the universal presence of the Logos; but he saw that the Eucharist indicates the direction to be taken by the cosmic movement, namely the divinization of the world, which it anticipates.' Walter Cardinal Kasper, *Sacrament of Unity: The Eucharist and the Church* (New York: Crossroad, 2004), 127.
12. See King, *Teilhard's Mass*, 59–95.

He begins by saying that since he has neither bread, nor wine, nor altar, he will lift himself to the 'majesty of the real' and 'make the whole Earth' his altar.[13] On this altar, he will offer all the labours and all the sufferings of creation:

> All the things in the world to which this day will bring increase; all those that will diminish; all those too that will die: all of them, Lord, I try to gather into my arms, so as to hold them out to you in offering. This is the material of my sacrifice; the only material you desire.[14]

> Over every living thing which is to spring up, to grow, to flower, to ripen during this day say again the words: This is my Body. And over every death-force which waits in readiness to corrode, to wither, to cut down, speak again your commanding words which express the supreme mystery of faith: This is my Blood.[15]

As his prayer unfolds, he sees the power of God at work in Christ and present in the Eucharist as transforming the Earth from within: 'It is done. Once again the Fire has penetrated the earth . . . Without earthquake or thunderclap: the flame has lit up the whole world from within'.[16] Because the Word is made flesh, no part of the physical universe is untouched. All matter is the place of God. All is being divinised. All is being transformed in Christ: 'Through your own incarnation, my God, all matter is henceforth incarnate'.[17] Because of this, Earth, the solar system and the whole universe become the place for encounter with the risen Christ.

> Now, Lord, through the consecration of the world the luminosity and fragrance which suffuse the universe take on for me the lineaments of a body and a face—in you . . . As for me, if I could not believe that your real Presence animates

---

13. Teilhard de Chardin, 'The Mass on the World', in *Hymn of the Universe* (London: Collins, 1965), 19.
14. Teilhard, *The Mass on the World*, 20.
15. Teilhard, *The Mass on the World*, 23.
16. Teilhard, *The Mass on the World*, 23.
17. Teilhard, *The Mass on the World*, 24.

> and makes tractable and enkindles even the very least of the energies that invade me or brush past me, would I not die of cold?[18]
>
> So, my God, I prostrate myself before your presence in the universe which has now become living flame: beneath the lineaments of all that I shall encounter this day, all that happens to me, all that I achieve it is you I desire, you I await.[19]

Teilhard sees the risen Christ as united to the immanent God who is creatively present to all creatures, enabling them to exist and to evolve. The incarnation is extended and prolonged in the Eucharist. The unique presence of Christ in the Eucharist is extended in the divinizing presence of Christ at work in the whole of creation. The Eucharist is an effective prayer for the transformation of the universe in Christ. It points towards and anticipates the divinization of the whole world in Christ.

Learning from the East—John Zizioulas (1931–)

John Zizioulas, a distinguished lay theologian and ecumenist, was ordained Metropolitan of Pergamon in 1986 and called to serve in the Ecumenical Patriarchate of the Orthodox Church. At the heart of his theology is the Trinitarian theology of God as communion. Since he understands God's being as communion, Zizioulas sees communion as the deepest reality. It is the very being of things. Being is communion. Zizioulas says that 'it is communion that makes beings "be": nothing exists without it, not even God'.[20]

Because his view of God is radically Trinitarian it is also fully personal and interpersonal. And in the light of this relational view of divine life, he understands the human person not as an individual but as someone who goes out of self to others. These others include not only the Trinitarian God and other human beings, but also the other creatures of Earth and of the universe. Zizioulas spells out his ecological theology particularly in a series of lectures given at Kings

---

18. Teilhard, *The Mass on the World*, 25.
19. Teilhard, *The Mass on the World*, 29.
20. John Zizioulas, *Being as Communion: Studies in Personhood and the Church* (New York: St Vladimir's Press, 1985), 17.

College London in 1989.[21] Since 1994, he has been actively involved in a series of summer seminars on environmental issues sponsored by the Ecumenical Patriarchate and the World Wide Fund for Nature. These seminars have gathered people from around the world, including environmentalists, educators, scientists and theologians, to discuss the ecological issues confronting our global community.

At the heart of Zizioulas's ecological theology is his conviction that the ecological crisis cannot be met simply by arguments based on reason or ethical arguments. While these clearly have their place, far more is required. Zizioulas insists that if we hope to change priorities and life-styles, we will need a different *culture* and a different *ethos*. As a Christian theologian, Zizioulas is convinced that what is needed above all is a *liturgical* ethos. Of course, he recognises that ecological conversion can be inspired by many other sources as well as Christianity, but he sees the Christian community as possessing a unique foundation for a radically ecological ethos in its Eucharistic spirituality.

Zizioulas understands human beings to be called by God to be 'priests of creation'. He distinguishes this priestly task that he finds in the early church from the medieval and particularly the Roman Catholic notion of the sacrificial priesthood. He sees each baptised person as called to be, like Christ, a fully *personal* being. This involves being relational rather than self-enclosed, able to go out of self to the other, in what Zizioulas calls *ek-stasis*. Persons are always ecstatic, in the sense that they achieve personhood only in communion with others. Human beings are called to relate in a fully personal way to God, to other humans and to other creatures of God. In God's plan, humanity and the rest of creation will come to completion in Christ through each other. Humanity comes to its completion and creation comes to participate fully in the life of God, by humans relating in a fully personal and loving way with creation.

When humans come to the Eucharist, they offer to God the fruits of creation. In the Eucharist, creation is *lifted up* to God in offering and thanksgiving. In the East, the Eucharistic Prayer is known as the Anaphora, a word which means the lifting-up. From the human side, the Eucharist is the lifting-up of creation to God. The Holy Spirit is

---

21. John Zizioulas, 'Preserving God's Creation: Three Lectures on Ecology and Theology', in *King's Theological Review* 12 (1989): 1–5, 41–5 and 13 (1990), 1–5.

invoked to transform the gifts of creation, and the community assembled, into the Body of Christ. In Zizioulas's theology, the exercise of this priesthood involves all the baptised faithful. He points out that early Christian liturgical texts followed Jewish prayers in beginning from a blessing of the gifts of creation. All ancient Eucharistic liturgies began with thanksgiving for *creation* and then continued with thanksgiving for *redemption* in Christ. All of them were centred on the lifting up of the bread and wine to the Creator rather than on the consecration of the elements.[22]

Just as, for Zizioulas, this 'lifting up' of creation is not confined to the ordained but is the God-given role of all the faithful, so it is not restricted to liturgical celebrations but is meant to happen in the whole of life. It involves all human interactions with the rest of creation. The 'lifting up' of creation is meant to be played out around the planet continually by every human being. Fundamentally this priestly task is nothing other than an authentic love for other creatures in all their specificity, a fully human and personal love of them in God. Our stance toward the rest of creation, our personal engagement with it as fully relational beings, is a central dimension of our life before God and fundamental to our salvation in Christ.

The ecological crisis requires the deepest resources of the human community. What Zizioulas points out is that in the Eucharist there is a profound and radical source for an authentically ecological ethos and culture. As Patricia Fox says, Zizioulas's view is that it is 'the culture created through the living ethos of a vibrant Christian community, centred on the Eucharist' that offers the most powerful long-term resource for ecological commitment. She says: 'the liturgy is the key formative source of initiation into a way of being that can shape and transform humanity's relationships and behaviour towards every other entity'.[23]

In Zizioulas's view, it is Christian Eucharistic practice that is capable of sustaining an ongoing conversion to a personal and loving stance before the rest of creation. It does not provide answers to the practical questions that confront us, but it does provide a profound motivation and a genuinely ecological ethos: 'All this involves

---

22. Zizioulas, 'Preserving God's Creation', in *King's Theological Review* 12 (1989): 4.
23. Partricia A Fox, *God as Communion: John Zizioulas, Elizabeth Johnson, and the Retrieval of the Symbol of God* (Collegeville, Minnesota: Liturgical Press, 2001), 70.

an *ethos* that the world needs badly in our time. Not an ethic, but an *ethos*. Not a programme, but an attitude and a mentality. Not legislation, but a culture'.[24]

Eucharist as the Living Memory of all God's Creatures

In what follows, I will gather insights from Teilhard and Zizioulas into a theology of the Eucharist as the *living memory* of the whole of creation. Because of the urgency of the issue of global climate change, my focus will be on the Eucharist as the living memory of the community of life on Earth. This includes, of course, not only the diverse living things that inhabit our planet, but also the atmosphere, the seas and the land. I will develop this theme by working through four steps: the Eucharist as the living memory of creation as well as redemption, as sacrament of the transformation of all creation in Christ, as anticipation of the participation of all God's creatures in the life of the Trinity and as solidarity with the victims of climate change.

The memory of creation as well as redemption

The concept of *anamnesis* is central to Eucharistic theology. The word can be translated as a memorial or simply as memory, but I think it is best translated as living memory. In every Eucharist, we remember the events of our salvation in Christ, in such a way that they are made present to us powerfully here and now and that they already anticipate the future transformation of all things in Christ. This kind of memory not only recalls the past but acts in the present and opens out toward God's future. It is natural and appropriate for the Christian community to focus its attention in the Eucharist on the central events of Christ's death and resurrection. But it is also appropriate to remember, with Zizioulas, that every Eucharist is a thanksgiving memorial for God at work in creation as well as in redemption.

This is something that was long ago explored by liturgical scholar Louis Bouyer. In his treatment of the *anamnesis* of the Eucharist, Bouyer points out that the early Eucharistic prayers were closely connected to their origins in the Jewish prayer forms used in syn-

---

24. Zizioulas, 'Preserving God's Creation', in *King's Theological Review* 13 (1990): 5.

agogues and especially in homes, above all in the Passover meal.²⁵ These prayers were always based on memory and thanksgiving. They begin with a blessing of the gifts of creation. What is called to mind is God's work that involves both creation and salvation. The anamnesis of both Jewish prayer forms, and the older Christian Eucharistic prayers, involve an *anamnesis* of both creation and redemption.²⁶

In my view, this is of fundamental importance in a time when human action is radically altering the climate with disastrous effects for human beings and for other creatures on Earth. When we come to the Eucharist, we bring the creatures of Earth with us. We remember the God who loves each one of them. We grieve for the damage done to them. We feel with them. We cannot but learn the kind of ethos that Zizioulas speaks of, an ethos that leads to a different way of acting.

This ancient theology can be found at work in our current liturgical texts. In every Eucharist, we begin by bringing creation to the table, bread and wine, 'fruit of the Earth and the work of human hands'.²⁷ Our everyday Eucharistic prayers bring out the radical inner relationship between God's action in creation and redemption: 'He is the Word through whom you made the universe, the Saviour you sent to redeem us' (Second Eucharist Prayer). They make it clear that when we come to the Eucharist we bring creation with us. As Zizioulas says, we lift the whole of creation to God. We praise God on behalf of all of Earth's creatures: 'All creation rightly gives you praise' (Third Eucharistic Prayer); 'In the name of every creature under heaven, we too praise your glory' (Fourth Eucharistic Prayer).

In every Eucharist, we remember the events of Christ's life, death and resurrection and experience their power to bring healing and salvation. We also remember God's good creation, the fourteen billion-year history of the universe, the 4.5 billion-year history of Earth and the emergence of life on Earth in all its diversity and beauty. We remember the vulnerable state of the community of life on Earth today and bring this to God. All of this is caught up in the mystery of Christ celebrated in each of our Eucharists. In the great doxology at the end of the Eucharistic prayer, we lift up the whole creation

---

25. Louis Bouyer, *Life and Liturgy* (London: Sheed and Ward, 1956), 15–28.
26. Bouyer, *Life and Liturgy*, 132.
27. For the sake of brevity, I will restrict my examples to current Roman Catholic liturgical texts. Further examples could be found in the liturgical texts and hymns of other Christian communities.

through, with and in Christ, 'in the unity of the Holy Spirit' to the eternal praise and glory of God.[28]

Sacrament of the transformation of creation in Christ

A second inner connection between what is happening to the community of life on Earth and our Eucharistic gatherings is found in the idea that the Christ we encounter in the Eucharist is the risen one, the one in whom all things were created and in whom all are reconciled (Col 1:15–20). The risen Christ is the one in whom creation is renewed and transformed: God's eternal wisdom and plan for the fullness of time is 'to gather up all things in him, things in heaven and things on earth' (Eph 1:10).

Even when, in the Eucharist, the focus of the memorial is on Christ's death and resurrection, this is not a memory that takes us away from creation. On the contrary, it involves us directly with creation. It connects us to Earth and all its creatures. When we remember Christ's death, we remember a creature of our universe, part of the interconnected evolutionary history of our planet, freely handing his whole bodily and personal existence into the mystery of a loving God. When we remember the resurrection, we remember part of our universe and part of our evolutionary history being taken up in the Spirit into God. This is the beginning of the transformation of the whole creation in Christ. As Karl Rahner says, this resurrection of Jesus is not only the *promise* but the *beginning* of the glorification and divinisation of the whole of reality.[29]

All of this supports Teilhard's claim that there is a connection between the Eucharist we celebrate and the transformation of the universe in the risen Christ. I think this relationship is best understood as a *sacramental* one. The traditional teaching has always been that in eating and drinking we participate in the risen Christ (1 Cor 10:16–17). Bread and wine become sacramentally the body and blood of the risen one. In participating at the Eucharistic table, we participate sacramentally in Christ, but this Christ is the one in whom the

---

28. See Yves Congar's remarks on the doxology in his *I Believe in the Holy Spirit*, Volume II (New York: Seabury Press, 1983), 224.
29. Karl Rahner, 'Dogmatic Questions on Easter', in *Theological Investigations* IV (New York, Seabury Press, 1974), 129.

universe is being transformed in the power of the Spirit. The bread and wine are the sacrament of the Christ who is at work in creation. What is symbolised is wonderfully made present. What is made present is Christ in the power of resurrection, not only the promise but also the beginning of the transformation of all things. Every Eucharist is both sign and agent of the transforming work of the risen Christ in the whole of creation

The one we encounter sacramentally in the Eucharist is the one in whom all things were created and in whom all will be transfigured. This means that human action, which is an expression of love and respect for the living creatures, the atmosphere, the seas and the land of our planet, can be seen as not only in continuity with, but also as in some way part of the work of the Eucharistic Christ. Wilfully pumping up more and more carbon dioxide into the atmosphere, with all its known effects on the living systems of our planet, cannot but be seen as a denial of Christ. It is a denial of the meaning of all that we celebrate when we gather for Eucharist.

Anticipating the participation with all creatures in the divine communion

One of the things that can be learnt from the East, and from the theology of John Zizioulas, is that every Eucharist is an eschatological event. It is an event of the Spirit that anticipates the future when all will be taken up into God. The Eucharist is profoundly Trinitarian. Our Eucharistic communion, our communion with each other in Christ, is always a sharing in and a tasting of the divine Communion of the Trinity. And it is always an anticipatory experience of the future when all things will be taken up into the dynamic shared life of the triune God. Eucharistic communion is a participation here and now in the divine Communion of the Trinity in which all things will be transfigured and find their eternal meaning and their true home.

In the Eucharist, we are taken up into God. We participate in the divine Communion. It is this Communion that is source of all the life on Earth. It is this Communion that enables a community of life to emerge and evolve. And, in ways that are beyond our imagination and comprehension, it is this Communion that will be the fulfilment of all the creatures of our planet, and all the wonders of our universe.

As we participate in the Eucharist, we taste in anticipation the fulfilment of all things taken up into the divine life of the Trinity.

As Tony Kelly has said, 'The most intense moment of our communion with God is at the same time an intense moment of our communion with the earth'.[30] We are caught up into God and into God's love for the creatures of our planetary community. Kelly points to the way that the Eucharist shapes our ecological imagination: 'The Eucharist educates the imagination, the mind, and the heart to apprehend the universe as one of communion and connectedness in Christ'. It is in and through this Eucharistic imagination that a distinctive ecological vision and commitment can take shape.[31] With this kind of imagination at work in us, we can see the other creatures of Earth as our kin, as radically interconnected with us in one Earth community of life before God. We can begin to see critically—to see more clearly what is happening to the Earth. We are led to participate in God's feeling for the life-forms of our planet. A Eucharistic imagination leads to an ecological ethos, culture and praxis.

Solidarity with the victims of climate change

The Eucharist always involves the memory of the cross. The theologian Johannes Metz writes of the memory of the passion as a 'dangerous' memory.[32] He sees the cross of Jesus as an abiding challenge to any complacency we might have before the suffering of others. It brings those who suffer to the very centre of Christian faith. It constantly challenges ideological justifications of the misery of the poor and the victims of war, oppression and natural disasters. The resurrection certainly offers a dynamic vision of hope for the suffering of the world, but it does not dull the memory of the suffering ones. They are always present, forever imaged in the wounds of the risen Christ.

This dangerous and critical memory provides an alternative way of seeing. It leads to solidarity, to alternative life-styles and to personal and political action. The World Council of Churches, in its reflections on solidarity with victims of climate change, points to the

---

30. Tony Kelly, *The Bread of God: Nurturing a Eucharistic Imagination* (Melbourne: HarperCollins, 2001), 92.
31. Kelly, *The Bread of God*, 100–1.
32. Johann Baptist Metz, *Faith in History and Society: Towards a Practical Fundamental Theology* (London: Burns and Oates, 1980), 109.

many communities of people, especially in the Southern hemisphere, who are particularly vulnerable to climate change: 'Though their per capita contribution to the causes of climate change is negligible, the will suffer from the consequences to a much larger degree'.[33] Climate change aggravates the social and economic injustice between rich and poor in our global community. To contribute to this destruction of lives, of homes, of livelihoods and of communities 'is not only a sin against the weak and unprotected but also against the earth—God's gift of life'.[34]

The Eucharist, as a living memory of all those who suffer, calls the Christian community to a new solidarity that involves all the human victims of climate change and includes the animals and plants that are destroyed or threatened. Solidarity involves personal and political commitment to both of the two strategies that have been identified as responses to climate change, those of *mitigation* and *adaptation*. Adaptation will mean re-ordering society, budgeting in readiness for climate disasters, training personnel and allocating resources. In a particular way, it will involve, as a matter of justice, hospitality to environmental refugees.

When we Australian Christians gather for Eucharistic celebrations, we gather in solidarity with Christians who assemble for Eucharist in Kiribati, in Tuvalu, in Bangladesh. We gather in solidarity with those who share other forms of religious faith in the Pacific, in South-East Asia, in Africa, and in all parts of our global community. We remember those already displaced from the homes and their heritage. We are painfully aware of the threat to many millions of other people. We are mindful of Australia's contribution to greenhouse, of our wealth created by coal, of our use of motor vehicles. We pray in solidarity with the global community, that the Eucharist that brings us into peace and communion with God, may 'advance the peace and salvation of all the world' (Third Eucharistic Prayer). We commit ourselves again to discipleship, to an ecological ethos, lifestyle, politics and praxis, as people of Easter hope.

---

33. *Solidarity with Victims of Climate Change: Reflections on the World Council of Churches' Response to Climate Change* (Geneva: World Council of Churches, 2002), 10.
34. *Solidarity with Victims*, 10.

Planetary Spirituality: Exploring a Christian Ecological Approach

The twentieth century has left us some important legacies. One of the positive legacies is a wonderfully enriched understanding of the universe of which we are a part. Based originally on Albert Einstein's work on general relativity and the astronomical observations of Edwin Hubble, twentieth century science took us from the idea that we inhabit one galaxy, to the view that our galaxy, the Milky Way, is one of billions of galaxies in the observable universe, and that this universe is not static but expanding dynamically. We now know that our universe began from an unthinkably small, dense and hot state 13.7 billion years ago, and that it has been expanding and cooling ever since. It is made up of something like a hundred billion galaxies, and our Milky Way Galaxy is estimated to contain about two hundred billion stars.

One of these stars is the Sun, with our beautiful home, Earth, set just at the right distance from the Sun to nourish and sustain life. Part of our legacy is the picture we now have of Earth as a blue-green planet set against the inter-stellar darkness of space. Unlike other generations of human beings, unlike Moses, Jesus, or Newton, we can see Earth as a whole. We have a picture of what it is like to observe Earth-rise from the moon. We have a new appreciation of Earth's hospitality to life. We can see human beings as a global community. We have an imaginative picture of the interconnections of human beings with all other species on our planet and with the life-systems, the seas, the atmosphere, the land, the forests and the rivers. Astronaut Rusty Schweigert says, that from the moon Earth appears so small that you could block it out with your thumb, but then, he continues: 'Then you realize that on this beautiful, warm, blue and white circle, is everything that means anything to you', all of nature and history, birth and love, and then you are changed forever'.[1] I am convinced that this vision of Earth as one interconnected planetary community represents a precious new moment in cultural history.

At the same time, we are doing terrible, irretrievable damage to the forests, the rivers, the seas, the soil and the atmosphere of Earth. Our use of fossil fuels is contributing to climate change that accelerates the extinction of many other species and will cause great suffering to human beings. We are destroying habitats all over our planet. If we continue on this path, if we continue to destroy forests and to exploit the land, the rivers and the seas ruthlessly, we will pass on to coming generations an impoverished planet. Many wonderful forms of life will be gone forever. These forms of life, I believe, have their own integrity, their own right to exist. When we destroy them recklessly, we do something that is terribly wrong in itself. But it is also wrong because it betrays our intergenerational obligations. We deprive our children and our grandchildren of what has always nurtured humanity, its spirituality, its art, its joy-in-life. We do them a very great wrong.

Planetary Spirituality

In this context, something is emerging that I think can be called a planetary spirituality. People around the globe have begun to recognise that we are called to a new way of being on Earth. There is a growing movement of people who are connected in a common love of Earth and its creatures, a movement of farmers, artists, school children, scientists, industrialists, politicians and religious leaders, people living in villages as well as in great cities. Many have undergone, and are still undergoing, a process of conversion as they commit themselves to a lifestyle and a politics that involves respecting and protecting other species and enabling them to flourish, conserving the forests, the rivers, the seas and land, and handing on to future generations the bounty of our planet.

I am convinced that this movement, for all its obvious human limitations and sinfulness, can be understood as a new form of

---

1. In Elizabeth A Johnson, *Quest for the Living God: Mapping Frontiers in the Theology of God* (New York: Continuum, 2007), 181.

global spirituality, in Christian terms as a work of the Holy Spirit. The Spirit who breathed life into the whole creation from the beginning, the Holy Spirit who is the very Breath of Life, now breathes through our human community calling us to a new respect for life, for each and every human being in all their unique dignity, and for the other creatures who share this planet, for great ancient trees in old-growth forests, for unknown insects in rain forests, for threatened species of birds and fish, for the great whales of the Southern Ocean.

Many of us find a sense of mystery, wonder and transcendence in our experience of the natural world: looking up at the Milky Way through clear skies and pondering the unthinkable size and wonder of our galaxy and its part in the universe; walking in a rainforest and being caught up in amazement at the extravagant exuberance of so many forms of life; quietly contemplating a great, old River Red Gum in a dry creek bed; being overwhelmed by the beauty and abundance of marine life on the Great Barrier Reef; simply attending to one flower before us and truly appreciating its fragility and its beauty. In these and many other experiences, we are taken beyond ourselves into mystery and awe. All of this, I think, is part of an ecological and planetary spirituality.

Human spirituality and human aesthetics are nurtured by such experiences. They have always been available, even when we have failed to attend to them. What is new is the sense that we form one global community of human beings beyond all barriers of race and class and nation, that we need each other, and that we are deeply interconnected with all the other creatures, with the Milky Way Galaxy, with rainforests, with the marine life of the reefs, with this ancient tree, with the flowering plant before us. Planetary spirituality involves not only a real receptivity and respect for the natural world, but a deep sense of global solidarity, and a radical, life-long commitment to act for the good of the whole Earth community.

At the heart of this planetary spirituality is the sense that all is given. Life in all its diversity and beauty is a most beautiful and precious gift. It is not to be abused or squandered. It is a gift given by a generous and bountiful God. The creatures we encounter are the expressions of divine self-giving. This is not to suggest a romantic or idealised view of the natural world, but a clear-eyed view of its evolutionary dynamics, of the costs of evolution as well as its fruitful outcomes, of predation and extinctions as well as mutual interdependence and cooperation. A planetary spirituality will need to see the universe of creatures of which we are a part in all its finitude, well aware of the 'groaning' of creation (Rom 8:22), yet also rejoicing in its beauty, fecundity and diversity and standing before it as a most amazing gift.

In attempting to describe this new experience of planetary spirituality, I am very conscious that here in this land we have the precious heritage of a very ancient, indigenous spirituality, with its sense of the land as a nurturing mother, with the natural world understood as sacred, and with human beings understood as called to be custodians of the land. I think that a Christian spirituality for the twenty-first century has a great deal to learn from this indigenous spirituality. It also has much to learn from the spirituality of other religious traditions. One of the signs of the times in Australia, and in many other places, is not only the growing pluralism of religions, but also the pluralism of spiritualities. There is a growing experience of meeting others beyond the borders of traditions in forms of meditation and prayer, and the emergence of interfaith experiences of spirituality. There are also those no longer in contact with particular religious traditions, who still see themselves as engaged in a spiritual quest. In recent times, researchers like David Tacey[2] in Australia and Ursula King[3] in the United Kingdom have pointed to the growing phenomenon of the emergence of spirituality that is not closely linked to the great religious traditions.

What I am suggesting is that there is a new, emerging experience of ecological spirituality, a planetary spirituality shared by people of various religious traditions and by people not committed to any religion. We have a new sense of ourselves as a human community within a global community of life, where every form of life has its own intrinsic value. This emerging spirituality involves a respect for the dignity of each human being and for the gift and potential of the intellectual, artistic, ethical and spiritual life of the human community. It involves a sense of belonging with, and of interdependence with, the other creatures of our planet, and a commit-

---

2. David Tacey, *The Spirituality Revolution: The Emergence of Contemporary Spirituality* (Hove, UK: Brunner-Routledge, 2004).
3. Ursula King, *The Search for Spirituality: Our Global Quest for a Spiritual Life* (New York: BlueBridge, 2008).

ment to their wellbeing. There is a new awareness of accountability to the future of life. We know that we are responsible for the flourishing of life in all its abundance in the future. And we know that we are responsible to future generations of human beings. We are called to do all we can to ensure that the beauty and bounty of Earth can be the heritage of our children, grandchildren and great grandchildren.

We are part of the abundant and diverse history of life that has emerged on this blue-green planet over the last 3.7 billion years. We now know that we are deeply connected to the emergence of the universe, that we are children of the universe. But along with this cosmic sense, we know that we are grounded here, that Earth is our home, that we are deeply rooted in the life-systems of our planet, in the interconnected web of life. Alongside the sense of the cosmic, we know that the local and the particular matters, this place, this bioregion, this river, this species, this animal, this tree.

Christian Spirituality

This transformation to an ecological consciousness is already underway, but it needs the co-operation, the commitment and the best efforts of the whole human community. I believe that the role of the religions of the world is crucial. For many people, their faith tradition is at the centre of who they are. Whether they are Jewish, Muslim, Buddhist, Hindu, Christian or belong to another tradition, it is religious faith that can provide the deepest, strongest and most enduring ground for their commitment to Earth and its creatures. This means, I believe, that those of us who belong to such traditions have to do our best to bring out the ecological meaning of our spiritual traditions. And we need to do this in such a way as to build a new consensus between us about care for the planet as central to spirituality.

Here, I will point very briefly to some of the ways that Christian tradition can support an ecological spirituality for today. It is important to acknowledge that biblical faith can be, and has been, co-opted as a basis for ruthless exploitation of Earth and its resources, and that it has often been presented in a damaging, other-worldly way. I am convinced that this is a fundamentally flawed reading of the Scriptures as a whole and of Christian faith.[4] It is important to acknowledge, as well, that many Christian communities have not been in the forefront of the ecological movement. I see this as all the more reason to point to the interconnection between what is central to Christianity and an ecological spirituality for our time.

What is specific to Christian spirituality and to the Christian view of God is its concept of God as Trinity. Christianity finds the deepest truth about God, the God who embraces and enables the emergence and existence of every creature on our planet, in the conviction that God is Communion. God is a Trinity of endlessly dynamic mutual love. We find this God revealed to us in Jesus, his preaching and practice of the kingdom, his death and resurrection and in the Pentecostal outpouring of the Spirit. God gives God's very self to us in the Word made flesh and in the Spirit poured out in grace. In what follows, I will focus on three ways in which this Triune God is understood as acting for us, in creation, incarnation and in the resurrection of the crucified Jesus.

Creation is an absolutely free gift. In the life of the Trinity, there is an endless generativity of the Word and a breathing forth of the Spirit, in an eternal, dynamic communion of love that involves radical equality and total mutuality. Creation occurs because this God freely chooses to give God's self to a community of creatures. Creation springs forth from within the divine life. God creates through the Word and in the Holy Spirit. The universe and all its creatures

---

4. On this, see the volumes of the Earth Bible Project: *Readings from the Perspective of Earth: The Earth Bible 1,* edited by Norm C Habel (Sheffield/Cleveland: Sheffield Academic Press/Pilgrim Press, 2000); *The Earth Story in Genesis: The Earth Bible 2,* edited by NC Habel and S Wurst (Sheffield/Cleveland: Sheffield Academic Press/Pilgrim Press, 2000); *The Earth Story in Wisdom Traditions: The Earth Bible 3,* edited by NC Habel and S Wurst (Sheffield/Cleveland: Sheffield Academic Press/Pilgrim Press, 2001); *The Earth Story in the Psalms and the Prophets: The Earth Bible 4,* edited by NC Habel (Sheffield/Cleveland: Sheffield Academic Press/Pilgrim Press, 2001); *The Earth Story in the New Testament: The Earth Bible 5,* edited by NC Habel and V Balabanski (Sheffield/Cleveland: Sheffield Academic Press/Pilgrim Press, 2002); *Exploring Ecological Hermeneutics,* edited by NC Habel and P Trudinger (Atlanta: Society of Biblical Literature, 2008). For another perspective, see *Ecological Hermeneutics: Biblical, Historical and Theological Perspectives,* edited by David Horrell, Cherryl Hunt, Christopher Southgate and Francesca Stavrakopoulou (London: T&T Clark, 2010). See also Ernst Conradie, *Christianity and Ecological Theology: Resources for Further Research* (Stellenbosch: Sun Press, 2006).

exist out of nothing, as God holds all things in being through the Word and in the Spirit, enabling them to exist, to interact and to evolve into what is new. Every creature is a word that reflects the eternal Word and Wisdom of God. A great rainforest, a threatened species, this flower before me, is an icon of divine Wisdom. Each has its own integrity before God.

In every creature, the Creator Spirit dwells, closer to it that it is to itself, breathing it into existence and life. It is in this triune God that we, and all other creatures with us, 'live and move and have our being' (Acts 17:28). Elizabeth Johnson writes:

> In our day we discover that the great, incomprehensible mystery of God, utterly transcendent and beyond the world, is also the dynamic power at the heart of the natural world and its evolution. Groaning with the world, delighting in its advance, keeping faith with its failures, energizing it graciously from within, the Creator Spirit is with all creatures in their finitude and death, holding them in redemptive love and drawing them into an unforeseeable future in the divine life of communion. Rather than being simply stages on the way to *Homo sapiens*, the whole rich tapestry of the created order has its own intrinsic value, being the place where God creatively dwells.[5]

By the action of this same Creator Spirit, the Word through whom all things come into being is made flesh and lived among us (Jn 1:14). What is at the heart of Christianity is the conviction that the God of creation, the utterly transcendent God, gives God's self to creatures out of love in the incarnation. In Jesus of Nazareth, a living, breathing, fragile creature of our planet, like us the product of 3.7 billion years of evolutionary history, God takes matter and biology to God's very self. In the life, death and resurrection of Jesus, God forgives human sin, restores the image of God in us, adopts us as God's beloved children, and deifies us, transforming us by grace so that we might participate in the Trinitarian life of God.

In Jesus of Nazareth, God has embraced not just the human creatures of our planet, but the whole emergent world of biological life,

---

5. Johnson, *Quest for the Living God*, 198.

rainforests and insects, wallabies and whales, and the land, the seas and the atmosphere that support life. God has become an Earth creature, one of us, part of the interconnected web of life, so that all of Earth's creatures might be transformed in God, each in its own distinctive way. This means that a Christian view of creation, and a Christian ecological spirituality, will be incarnational and Christological. It will also be grounded in the Christian conviction of the bodily resurrection of the crucified Jesus.

As Paul said long ago, it is Christ crucified who is the true Wisdom and the Power of God (1 Cor 1:24, 30). Because of the resurrection, divine Wisdom is forever the crucified one, Jesus of Nazareth, the flesh and blood member of the biological community of Earth. God is forever human. God is forever biological. God is forever matter. And this constitutes an unbreakable divine promise not just to human beings but to the whole creation, a hope 'that the creation itself will be set free from its bondage to decay and will obtain the freedom of the glory of the children of God' (Rom 8:21). It is important to note that we have no good imaginative picture of God's future for ourselves or for other creatures. As Paul says, 'we hope for what we do not see' (Rom 8:25). And we Christians need to admit that we have often made this hope into something Platonic and otherworldly. But the true biblical hope at the heart of Christianity is a hope for this world, based on a divine promise that this world will be transformed in Christ, when all things reach their own fulfilment (Col 1:15–20). And in this process, our own participation, our loving acts, our ecological commitments and actions, will have lasting significance. Nothing will be lost. All will be transformed in Christ and brought to its proper fulfilment by the Spirit of God.

A Christian ecological spirituality will be shaped, I believe, by these central Christian truths, of creation, incarnation and the resurrection of the crucified. These Christian doctrines cannot be separated one from the other. They are deeply interconnected in what Christianity sees as the divine economy of self-bestowing love. All of them involve not just human beings but, with them, the whole creation. The Word in whom all things were created is the Word made flesh, that all flesh, and all creation, might be transformed by the Spirit and brought to its fulfillment in the dynamic life of the Trinity.

The Way of Wisdom

In the biblical book of *Proverbs*, we are told that Wisdom is a cosmic principle, involved with God in the whole of creation, delighting in the creation of all things. Yet she comes to be with us: 'Wisdom has built her house' in our midst, she has set her table and invited all to her feast (Prov 8:22–9:1). In the book of *Sirach*, we hear how cosmic Wisdom has pitched her tent among us (Sir 24:8). In the *Wisdom of Solomon*, we find that Wisdom is the 'fashioner of all things' (Wis 7:22) who comes to those who love her: 'She hastens to make herself known to those who desire her. One who rises early to seek her will have no difficulty, for she will be found sitting at the gate . . . she goes about seeking those worthy of her, and she graciously appears to them in their paths, and meets them in every thought' (Wis 6:12–16).

Jesus was a Wisdom teacher, in the tradition of the sages of Israel, who taught in parables taken from nature and from human affairs. He found God at work in the world around him. He is reported to have insisted on the importance of seeing things properly: 'The eye is the lamp of the body. So, if your eye is healthy, your whole body will be full of light; but if your eye is unhealthy, your whole body will be full of darkness' (Matt 6: 22–23). Jesus himself must have keenly observed the world around him, the birds of the air and the wildflowers of Galilee, the way the tiniest seeds produce great shrubs in which the birds can nest, the way a woman mixes a little yeast in the dough and the result is the marvellous sight, smell and taste of newly baked bread. Jesus lived the way of Wisdom. He taught that 'not one sparrow will fall to the ground without your Father' (Matt 10:29).

For Christians, following Jesus means following the way of Wisdom, seeing *all things* as loved by God, and as revelatory of God. Christians see Jesus as divine Wisdom, Wisdom made flesh.[6] Paul tells us that Christ crucified is the true Wisdom of God (1 Cor 1:24, 30). In the light of his resurrection, Jesus was celebrated by the first Christians as the cosmic Wisdom of God, the one in whom all things are created and all things are reconciled: 'He is the image of the invis-

---

6. On this see my *Jesus the Wisdom of God: An Ecological Theology* (Maryknoll, NY: Orbis, 1995) and *Ecology at the Heart of Faith* (Maryknoll, NY: Orbis, 2006). See also Celia Deane-Drummond, *Eco-Theology* (London: Darton, Longman & Todd, 2008) and *Christ and Evolution: Wonder and Wisdom* (Minneapolis: Fortress, 2009).

ible God, the firstborn of all creation; for in him all things in heaven and earth were created . . . and through him God was pleased to reconcile all things to himself' (Col 1:15–20).

Following the way of Wisdom today involves a paschal experience of the cross and resurrection, an experience of vulnerability and grace, of letting go of self and finding abundance. To follow Jesus-Wisdom is to see every sparrow as held and loved by God. It is also to see every sparrow and every great soaring tree as created in the Wisdom of God that is made flesh in Jesus of Nazareth. To live in wisdom, in the full Christian sense, means seeing the whole of creation as coming forth from the dynamic abundance of the Trinity, as evolving within the dynamism of the life of the Three, and as destined to find fulfilment in this shared life.

But I think a spirituality of Wisdom is shared in different ways by many religious traditions. Perhaps from all our different religious backgrounds we can co-operate to build a wise way of living on our planet, a Wisdom way of life for a global community. Such a way of Wisdom would involve us all in an ongoing conversion to a new, ecological way of feeling, thinking and acting in our world. It clearly would demand a new lifestyle and politics.

The way of Wisdom is the way of loving knowledge, through love. If it is to be an authentic ecological spirituality I think it will involve a rediscovery of asceticism and true mysticism. It will be a mysticism that finds the incomprehensible mystery of God in the boundless beauty of the natural world as well as in its strangeness and otherness. It will be a mysticism that involves an enduring, life-long, indeed eternal, commitment to the good of Earth. It will respect and love Earth and all its diverse forms of life and act to preserve Earth's bounty and beauty for present and future generations. Conversion to the Earth, to solidarity with the creatures that make up our planetary community, must involve action. It is not only a radical reorientation of thought, and it is not only the discovery of a new capacity for feeling for non-human creation. It is both of these issuing forth in personal, political and ecclesial action.

The way of Wisdom involves both enlightenment and action together. To act wisely is not only to act in accord with all the available empirical evidence, but also to act in a way that is at one with the gift of the Spirit breathing through creation and breathing love in us. Loving knowledge is the kind of knowing we have of a beloved friend.

It is not a love that claims to comprehend or to control the other, but recognises the other, even in the intimacy of deep friendship, as an abiding mystery. I think this kind of loving knowledge is an important foundation for ecological practice. It is a knowing that recognises the limits of what we can claim to know, that accepts the mystery of the other in humility.

A sound eye, seeing things rightly, is of the essence of the way of Wisdom. Sallie McFague contrasts the 'arrogant eye' with the 'loving eye'. The arrogant eye is characteristic of the typical Western attitude to the natural world. It objectifies, manipulates, uses and exploits. The loving eye does not come automatically to us. It requires training and discipline to see things with a loving eye. McFague points out that the loving eye requires detachment in order to see the difference, distinctiveness and the uniqueness of the other. Too often we imagine we know who or what the other is, instead of taking the trouble to find out. McFague writes:

> This is the eye trained in detachment in order that its attachment will be objective, based on the reality of the other and not on its own wishes or fantasies. This is the eye bound to the other as is an apprentice to a skilled worker, listening to the other as does a foreigner in a new country. This is the eye that pays attention to the other so that the connections between knower and known, like the bond of friendship, will be on the real subject in its real world.[7]

What is required is that we learn to love others, human and non-human, with a love that involves both distance and intimacy. This involves cultivating a loving eye that respects difference. This is the way of Wisdom, a way of seeing each creature in relation to God, in Christian terms as a unique manifestation of divine Wisdom, as embraced by God in the incarnation and destined to share in the redemption of all things in Christ. Wisdom finds expression in us in conversion from the model of individualism and consumption to the simplicity of what McFague calls 'life abundant': where what matters are the basic necessities of food, clothes and shelter, medical care, educational opportunities, loving relationships, meaningful work, an

---

7. Sallie McFague, *Super, Natural Christians: How We Should Love NNature* (Minneapolis: Fortress Press, 1997), 116.

enriching imaginative and spiritual life, time with friends, and time spent with the natural world around us.[8]

What I think we need for the twenty-first century is what might be called a mysticism of ecological praxis. Liberation and political theologians have recognised that those committed to the cause of liberation need to be both political and mystical, and the same is true of those committed to the good of the community of life on Earth. The mystical can enable us to hope against hope, to act with integrity and love in the political and the personal spheres in times of adversity and failure, up to and including death. Edward Schillebeeckx says that the mystical seems in modern times 'to be nurtured above all in and through the praxis of liberation'. Those committed to a new way of being on Earth discover the same need for repentance and conversion, the same asceticism, the same dark nights, as is the case in contemplative mysticism. He says: 'Without prayer or mysticism politics soon becomes cruel and barbaric. Without political love, prayer or mysticism soon becomes sentimental or uncommitted interiority'.[9]

Commitment to the poor and commitment to the wellbeing of life on this planet must go together as two interrelated dimensions of the one Christian vocation. Ecological conversion is not opposed to, but intimately involved with, conversion to the side of the poor. Ecological conversion, like conversion to the side of the poor, will need to involve both the political and the mystical, and the discovery of the mystical precisely in the political.

What then would a mysticism of ecological praxis, the way of Wisdom, look like? I would suggest that it might embrace some of these kinds of experiences:

- The experience of being caught up in the utter beauty of the natural world, when this leads to a wonder and a joy that seem boundless.
- The experience of learning to see what is before us with a loving eye.
- The experience that all is gift.
- The experience of seeing ourselves as born of and dependent upon the 13.7 billion-year history of the evolving and expanding

---

8. Sallie McFague, *Life Abundant: Rethinking Theology and Economy for a Planet in Peril* (Minneapolis: Fortress Press, 2001), 209–10.
9. Edward Schillebeeckx, *Jesus in Our Western Culture: Mysticism, Ethics and Politics* (London: SCM, 1987), 75.

universe, and the product of the 3.7 billion-year history of the evolution of life on Earth.
- The experience of the natural world as *other*, of being overwhelmed by natural forces, by the size and age of the universe, and of being taken far beyond human comfort zones into a mystery that is beyond us.
- The experience of being called to ecological conversion, of coming to know other creatures of Earth as kin, of coming to know that each has its own value and its own integrity.
- The experience of being overwhelmed by the complexity of the ecological crisis, of perhaps being near despair, but still living and acting in hope.
- The experience of conversion from the model of individualism and consumption to the simplicity of 'life abundant' and knowing in this the truth of God.
- The experience of commitment to the good of the whole Earth community, and to the conserving of the natural world for future generations, that has the character of a life-long commitment, which we can recognise as sheer grace.

Experience of Word and Spirit in the Natural World

Do we experience God in our encounters with birds, animals, trees, forests, mountains, deserts and beaches? Or, to focus the question of this paper a little more precisely, does the Christian theological tradition offer support for the idea that we can experience the triune God in the natural world? Behind this question I think there are two further questions: Is God the Trinity to be understood as really present in the natural world? If God is understood as present, is this presence of God something we can properly be said to experience?

I will take up these two questions with the help of two theologians of the tradition, Athanasius of Alexandria from the fourth century and Karl Rahner from the twentieth. In the first section of the essay, I will explore a theology of God's triune presence in creatures, in dialogue with Athanasius. In the second, I will seek to show that we can truly be said to experience this presence of God, building on Karl Rahner. The third section simply offers three examples of the experience of God the Trinity in the natural world.

The Presence of God in Creatures

Is God truly present in the natural world around us? When I walk on a quiet beach, can I see this beach as a place of divine presence? Can I think of a rainforest, with all its interconnected, exuberant forms of life, as filled with the presence of God? Some theologians, conscious of the costs of evolution, and the pain of many creatures, speak of the absence of God from the natural world. But I remain convinced we need to think of God as radically present, even in the loss and pain evident in biological life and in the costs of evolutionary emergence.

The Christian theological tradition has long been committed to the idea that God is radically present to all creatures, conferring on them their existence and their capacity to act within a community of creation. I will illustrate this statement by reference to Athanasius, a key figure in the full articulation of the theology of the Trinity. Reading him, there is the sense of a theology that is still young and vibrant. His view of the Trinity is radically scriptural. It is never abstract, but a theology of a God engaged with creatures, a God who acts, who creates and saves. I will focus first on his view of God's presence to creatures, and then on his idea that creatures bear an imprint or image of holy Wisdom.

The Immediacy of God to Each Creature

Athanasius sees creation from the perspective of Jesus Christ and his life-giving cross. He sees the Word who is made flesh, the Word of the cross, as the very Word of creation. What John 1:3 says of the Word is foundational for all of his work: 'All things came into being through him, and without him not one thing came into being'. The Word through whom all entities in the universe exist, is the very same Word who is made flesh (Jn 1:14) to bring creation to its healing and transformation. The Word of creation is the Word of salvation.

Like others in the fourth century, Athanasius sees Christ not only as the Word of God but also as the Wisdom of God. He uses these expressions interchangeably, and interprets biblical references to the Word and the Wisdom of God intertextually. Athanasius is like many others in his own time in seeing God as creating through God's Wisdom/Word. Where Athanasius differs from many of his contemporaries is in his conviction of the full divinity of both the Wisdom/Word and the Spirit. In fourth century philosophical and theological culture, permeated as it was by Platonic thought, it was natural to suppose that there is a vast distance between finite creatures and the infinite God, and that some kind of intermediary is needed to bridge this distance. The tendency was to think of creatures as participating in an intermediary, and of the intermediary as participating in the all holy God. For the Christian community this intermediary was the Wisdom/Word. Behind this tendency there was a conviction of God's complete otherness from creatures. There was an assumption that the all-holy God is not to be contaminated or demeaned by immediate contact with creatures. In any case, finite and vulnerable creatures might not be able to withstand exposure to the fire of the divinity. Some kind of buffer was needed.[1]

It is understandable, then, that the Alexandrian priest Arius was convinced not only that the Word is an intermediary between God and creatures, but also that the Word is not to be identified with the all-holy God. In his view, there was a time when the Word was not. This means that the Word is ultimately a creature and that the true and eternal God is beyond the Word. Such a view was shared by many Christians, including influential bishop-theologians. The transcendent otherness of God seemed to rule out an immediate relationship between God and created entities.

Basing himself on his reading of the Scriptures and the Christian tradition, Athanasius completely rejects the notion of a created intermediary between God and creatures. For him there is no buffer. God is immediately present to the creatures that God creates. Athanasius shares fully in his opponents' conviction of the radical otherness of the Creator. He has a highly developed theology of creation *ex nihilo*. Creatures have in themselves no reason for their existence. They exist only because the Creator confers existence on them at every point. For Athanasius, too, there is an infinite difference, an ontological gulf, between creatures and their Creator.

How is this gulf bridged? Not, for him, by a hierarchical chain of being linking Creator and creatures; and not, for him, by a created intermediary. He insists that the gulf is bridged only by the fully divine Word coming down to be present to creatures in the fully divine Spirit. Only God can bridge the gap. For Athanasius, the eternally divine Word of God is 'present in all things' and 'gives life and protection to everything, everywhere, to each individually and to all together'.[2] From the creaturely side, creation is an ongoing relation of participation, by which creatures exist securely only because they partake of this Word of God so profoundly present to them in the

---

1. See Peter J Leithart, *Athanasius* (Grand Rapids, Michigan: Baker Academic, 2011), 91.
2. Athanasius, 'Against the Greeks', in *Athanasius: Contra Gentes and De Incarnatione,* in RW Thompson, editor and translator (Oxford: Clarendon Press, 2004), 41.

Spirit. Athanasius speaks of the Word of God as 'governing', 'establishing', 'leading', 'providing for' and 'ordering' creation.[3]

Athanasius writes of divine Wisdom as enabling all the diverse creatures and the elements of the natural world to work together in balance and harmony. Like a gifted musician, divine Wisdom brings the whole universe into a beautiful interrelationship: 'The Wisdom of God, holding the universe like a lyre', draws together the variety of created things, 'thus producing in beauty and harmony a single world and a single order within it'.[4] Because of the Wisdom/Word of God, all the elements of creation work together in kinship:

> Through him and his power fire does not fight with cold, nor the moist with the dry, but things which of themselves are opposites come together like friends and kin, animating the visible world, and becoming the principles of existence of bodies. By obedience to the Word of God things on earth receive life and things in heaven subsist. Through him all the sea and the great ocean limit their movements to their proper boundaries, and all the dry land is covered with all kinds of different plants, as I said above.[5]

It is through participating in divine Wisdom, interiorly present to all creatures, that these creatures not only exist, but are brought into productive relationships with one another. The Holy Spirit is the bond that unites creatures to Wisdom, so that it is only in the Spirit that each creature participates in divine Wisdom. For Athanasius, then, each creature exists from the Source of All, the Father, through the Wisdom/Word present to each of them in the Spirit.

The ontological gap between Creator and creatures is overcome because the triune God comes down, or 'condescends', to engage with creatures on their level, in the ongoing relationship of creation. God is immediately present to each entity through the Word and in the Spirit. In the act of continuous creation, the Spirit enables each creature to be open to, and to receive, the creative Word. By partaking of the Word in the Spirit, individual creatures exist and interact in the community of creation. For Athanasius, both creation and new cre-

---

3. Athanasius, *Against the Greeks*, 41.
4. Athanasius, *Against the Greeks*, 42.
5. Athanasius, *Against the Greeks*, 42.

ation occur through this structure of participation of the Word in the Spirit: 'The Father creates and renews all things through the Word in the Holy Spirit'.[6]

The God who comes down to be with creatures is a God of humble love. God comes to be with creatures in humility out of the abundance of divine, generous and compassionate love. Athanasius scholar, Khaled Anatolios, points out that Athanasius radically transforms the idea of divine transcendence by means of the biblical categories of divine mercy and loving kindness. God's transcendence does not distance God from creatures. It is a transcendence of unthinkable mercy and generosity. Because of these biblical attributes, God can transcend God's own transcendence.[7] God can be intimately present to finite creatures.

It is precisely because the Word and Spirit are fully divine, and possess the divine capacity for mercy and loving kindness, that they can be intimately and interiorly close to creatures in the relationship of continuous creation. Because of this divine capacity, no creaturely mediation is needed. The Creator is deeply present in humility and self-giving love to the creature. The character of God in creating thus accords with the kenotic character of God revealed in the incarnation.[8] In both creation and incarnation, the Word of God is a self-humbling God.[9]

So the distinction between God and all creatures is not bridged by a created intermediary, but solely from God's side, in a loving generosity that is itself fully divine. Because Word and Spirit are one with the Father's essence, the Word's creative presence in the Spirit means, of course, that the Father, the Source of All, is also immediately present to each creature.[10] As Athanasius puts it, using again a favourite image, the one who experiences the Radiance is enlightened by the Sun itself and not by any intermediary.[11]

---

6. Athanasius, *Letters to Serapion*, 1:24.6.
7. Khaled Anatolios, *Retrieving Nicaea: The Development and Meaning of Trinitarian Doctrine* (Grand Rapids, Michigan: Baker Academic, 2011), 104.
8. Anatolios, *Retrieving Nicaea*, 104.
9. Athanasius, *Against the Arians*, 1.39; 3.52.
10. Khaled Anatolios, *Athanasius: The Coherence of his Thought* (New York: Routledge, 1998), 113.
11. Athanasius, *Against the Arians*, 3.14.

In Athanasius, as in other major theologians of the tradition, there is absolutely no opposition between God's transcendence and God's immediate presence to creatures.[12] On the contrary, it is divine transcendence that enables God's immanence to created entities. It is a disastrous distortion of the Christian tradition to see God's transcendence as opposed to God's immanent presence. Divine transcendence enables God to be more interiorly present to creatures that they could ever be to one another. It is precisely God's transcendence, understood in terms of divine capacity for self-humbling love, that enables God to be immediately and intimately with creatures in the relationship of creation. Every creature on Earth, every whale, every kangaroo, every sparrow, exists by participation in the Father through the Word in the Spirit—'not one of them is forgotten in God's sight' (Lk 12:6).

One of the attractive elements in Athanasius's theology is that he sees the wonderful diversity and abundance of creation as springing from the absolute generativity of divine life. He brings out this generativity in the beautiful biblical images he uses for the Trinity: God is a Spring, ever pouring forth a River from which we drink in the Spirit; God is a Light with its eternal Radiance that enlightens us in the Spirit; God is the Father, eternally begetting the Son in whom we participate by adoption as God's children in the Spirit; God is the Font of Wisdom, bringing forth the Wisdom of God, which we receive through the Spirit of Wisdom.[13]

The triune God that Athanasius defends is a God of endless life, a God who is fruitful by nature. He argues that those who reject the eternity of the Word and the Spirit are also denying the dynamic generativity of divine life. He insists that the fruitfulness of the natural world has its source in the generativity of the eternally dynamic triune God.[14] The stars of the night sky, rainforests with their uncounted life forms, this bird I can see in a nearby tree, all spring from the divine generativity of the God who is a Spring, eternally pouring forth a River of Living Water, from which all creatures drink in the Spirit.

---

12. Anatolios, *Athanasius*, 40.
13. Athanasius, *Letters to Serapion* in Mark DelCogliano, Andrew Radde-Gallwitz and Lewis Ayres (trans), *Works on the Spirit: Athanasius and Didymus: Athanasius's Letters to Serapion on the Holy Spirit and Didymus's On the Holy Spirit* (New York: St Vladimir's Seminary Press, 2011), 1.19.1–7.
14. Athanasius, *Against the Arians*, 2:2.

Each Creature Bears the Imprint of the Image of Wisdom

Athanasius sees Jesus Christ as the true Image of God. He speaks often of Christ not only as Word of God, Wisdom of God, Son of God, and Radiance of God, but also as Image of God. He sees humans as made according to the Image who is Christ. This being made according to the Image is distorted by sin, and it is restored through the saving and deifying work of Christ, in the grace of the Holy Spirit. It is worth noting today, when Christian theology is in search of a more inclusive notion of the human in relation to other creatures, that Athanasius employs the concept of the Image of Wisdom in relation not only to humans but also to other creatures.

In his *Orations against the Arians*, after describing Wisdom as coming down to be with creatures so that they might exist and flourish, he goes on to speak of each creature as bearing the created imprint or reflection of divine Wisdom:

> But in order that creatures may not only be but also thrive in well-being, it pleased God to have his own Wisdom condescend to creatures. Therefore he placed in each and every creature and in the totality of creation a certain imprint (*typon*) and reflection of the Image of Wisdom, so that the things that come into being may prove to be works that are wise and worthy of God.[15]

All the creatures around us, in his view, bear this reflection of the Image of Wisdom. This can only mean that, for Athanasius, all creatures are in their own way made according to the Image of Wisdom. Each of them is a creaturely reflection of uncreated Wisdom. Each of them is a created image, an icon, of the eternal Image and Wisdom of God.

In human beings, according to Athanasius, the imprint and reflection of divine Wisdom is found in their human wisdom: 'the wisdom that comes to be within us is an image of his Wisdom'.[16] Because humans possess this gift of wisdom, they have the capacity to recognise the image of Wisdom in other creatures—'Thus did the imprint of Wisdom come to be in created things, so that the world, as I have

---

15. Athanasius, *Against the Arians*, 2.78.
16. Athanasius, *Against the Arians*, 2.78.

said, may come to know its Creator and Word, and through him, the Father'.[17] The imprint of divine Wisdom in humans enables them, in their encounters with other creatures, to come to know the Wisdom who made them. And in knowing this Wisdom, they can also know the Source of All, the Father. They can come to know the triune God through the imprint of Wisdom found in the creatures around them.

In Sirach, Wisdom is said to be 'poured forth' (Sir 1:9) upon on all God's works. Athanasius sees this text as referring not to Wisdom's divine being, but to Wisdom's created image poured out upon all creatures.[18] He distinguishes between divine Wisdom and her image in creatures: 'For while Wisdom herself is Creator and Maker, her imprint is created in the works and is made according to the image of the Image'.[19] Athanasius notes, with Paul, that in spite of God's attributes being evident in the creation since the beginning, human beings have over and over failed to recognise God and have instead worshipped false gods (Rom 1:19–21). Nevertheless, God does not abandon humanity, but out of extravagant divine generosity, sends divine Wisdom to be with us in the flesh:

> For God willed to make himself known no longer as in previous times through the image and shadow of wisdom, which is in creatures, but has made the true Wisdom herself take flesh and become a mortal human being and endure the death of the cross, so that henceforth all those who put their faith in him may be saved. But it is the same Wisdom of God, who previously manifested herself, and her Father through herself, by means of her image in creatures—and thus is said to be 'created'—but which later on, being Word, became flesh (Jn 1:14) as John said.[20]

The Wisdom of God who is beyond all creaturely limits becomes flesh in Jesus Christ. This same divine Wisdom is intimately present to all creatures in the act of continuous creation. They exist because they participate in this Wisdom, and in their specific, creaturely way, they

---

17. Athanasius, *Against the Arians*, 2.78.
18. Athanasius *Against the Arians*, 2.79.
19. Athanasius, *Against the Arians*, 2.80.
20. Athanasius, *Against the Arians*, 2.81.

bear the created imprint of Wisdom, and in this sense are images of the Image.

Human Experience of the Spirit

Do we human beings actually experience the Spirit of God? Do we encounter the living God in our day-to-day lives? As in an earlier discussion of this question,[21] I will propose that the Christian answer to these questions can only be yes, but that it is necessary to qualify this answer from the beginning in two ways. First, the experience of the Spirit is not of the same order as the experience of particular objects in the world, such as a tree, a dog or a human being—the experience of the Spirit, it will be suggested, is a far more mysterious and global experience, one that occurs in and through these ordinary experiences of life. Second, language, culture, and psychological factors play a fundamental role in all our experiences. The fact that all experience is mediated by language, culture and the psychology of the experiencer, suggests a critical and cautious approach to claims about the experience of the Holy Spirit. Pre-existing understandings and language always enter into experience and are necessary aspects of its interpretation. Experience is, by necessity, filtered through the psychological history and imaginative life of the individual subject.

Granted these fundamental cautions, I believe with Karl Rahner, that we can say that we do experience the Holy Spirit. The experience of God is a central theme of Rahner's theological work,[22] and I find him a particularly helpful guide on this fundamental issue. He is often thought of as a highly philosophical thinker, but at the end of his life he insisted that all of his theology grew from the profound conviction at the heart of St. Ignatius's *Spiritual Exercises* that we really do expe-

---

21. Denis Edwards, *Human Experience of God* (New York: Paulist, 1983).
22. Karl Rahner, 'Experience of the Holy Spirit', in *Theological Investigations* 18 (New York: Crossroad, 1983), 189–210; Karl Rahner, 'Reflections on the Experience of Grace', in *Theological Investigations* 3 (New York: Seabury, 1974), 86–90; Karl Rahner, 'The Experience of God Today', in *Theological Investigations* 11 (New York: Seabury, 1974), 149–65; Karl Rahner, 'Experience of Self and Experience of God', in *Theological Investigations* 13 (New York: Seabury, 1975), 122–32; Karl Rahner, 'Experience of the Spirit and Existential Commitment', *Theological Investigations* 16 (New York: Seabury, 1979), 24–51; Karl Rahner, *Foundations of Christian Faith: An Introduction to the Idea of Christianity* (New York: Crossroad, 1978), 137.

rience the living God.[23] Rahner was an advocate for what he called the 'mysticism of everyday life': not only the great saints, he insisted, but also ordinary Christians are called to the mystical. In the light of increasing secularisation, Rahner insisted that in the future Christian faith would have to spring from an interior conviction, and that it would need to involve personal experience of God. He expressed this in his saying that the Christian of the future will be a mystic, or he or she will be nothing.[24]

Because he was convinced that ordinary people do experience the Spirit, but also that this can be an obscure and unnoticed experience, Rahner believed that the proclamation of the gospel of Jesus should begin from the place where the Spirit is already at work in a person's life, and is already experienced, at least in an obscure way.[25] He saw it as fundamental for pastoral practice to evoke such experiences of the Spirit, to bring them to consciousness. He named the pastoral process of evoking where a person or a community experiences mystery and transcendence as the practice of 'mystagogy'.

What insights does Rahner offer into this experience of God? I think it is helpful to see his thought on this issue as moving in three steps. The first step is his analysis of our everyday knowing and loving of other creatures, by which he seeks to show that this everyday knowing and loving is always accompanied by an experience of mystery, whether this be consciously attended to or not. By mystery, he means the experience of what is boundless and incomprehensible, beyond all our everyday concepts and language. Mystery points to the inexhaustible depths of the reality that we encounter in the everyday. In our knowing of another creature, we form a concept of the specific person or object, and as we focus on the specific person or object, we always do this within a wider context or horizon. Although we do not always notice it, this wider context involves all possible objects of knowledge. We situate specific objects of knowledge against an

---

23. Karl Rahner, *Ignatius of Loyola Speaks*. (South Bend, Ind: St Augustine's Press, 2013), 6–23; Harvey D Egan, *Karl Rahner: Mystic of Everyday Life* (New York: Crossroad, 1998), 28–54.
24. Karl Rahner, 'The Spirituality of the Church of the Future', in *Theological Investigations* 20 (New York: Crossroad, 1981), 149.
25. Karl Rahner, 'Faith 1. The Way to Faith', in *Encyclopedia of Theology: A Concise Sacramentum Mundi*, edited by Karl Rahner (London: Burns and Oates, 1975), 496–500.

unlimited range of possible knowing. There is always an openness to more. When we ask questions, they always open us up to further questions. Our minds are never satisfied. The horizon of our everyday knowing is boundless, reaching out towards the infinite.

We experience mystery not only in our knowing, but also in our loving. Particular acts of love for another can contain an implicit invitation to a love that is unconditioned and that has no boundaries. The partial fulfilment we experience in our love and commitment to others can open out towards a love that has no limits. There is a restless yearning that is not met, and which cannot be loaded onto the limited human objects of our love, without doing great damage. There is a boundless expanse to the human mind and heart, and this boundless expanse is always there as the context of ordinary knowledge and love.

Having evoked this experience of mystery that accompanies everyday knowing and loving, Rahner's second step is to appeal to Christian revelation and particularly to a Christian theology of Grace. In his theology, the saving Grace of Christ is offered to all human beings of every time and place. Grace is then God present in self-offering love, an offer that each person is free to accept or reject. God is always present in the Spirit, offering God's self in love. Because of God's gracious presence to each person in the Spirit, the openness to mystery we experience can be understood as openness to the Spirit.[26] The dynamic openness of the human person is Spirit-filled. In the light of revelation, the experience of mystery can then be known to be experience of Grace, or experience of the Spirit, or as Rahner often says, the experience of Holy Mystery.

Rahner's third step is to propose that there are moments of special grace in our lives, where the created object we encounter may itself become a pointer to the Spirit, so that the experience of the Spirit is brought to the forefront of consciousness. Rahner offers many examples of such experiences, usually negative experiences,[27] where the limits of the everyday break down, and we are lead beyond ourselves into the incomprehensible mystery of God. He speaks of someone attempting to forgive, even when there is no reward for it, and the forgiveness is taken for granted; of someone trying to love God, even

---

26. Rahner, 'Experience of the Holy Spirit', 198.
27. Karl Rahner, 'The Ignatian Mysticism of Joy in the World', in *Theological Investigations* 3 (New York: Seabury, 1974), 277–93.

when there seems no obvious response; of someone who makes a decision to follow conscience even though this cannot be explained to others.[28] In such moments, what at first seems like emptiness and darkness can be found to be the place where Love is with us, where we are held in Love.

The three examples I will offer in the next section differ from Rahner's in two ways. Following Athanasius, I will articulate the experiences in a more fully Trinitarian way, as experiences of the Word and the Spirit. And I will focus on positive experiences, particularly on those that occur in our encounters with the natural world. It is essential to keep in mind, however, the dark and painful experiences of nature, when to us human beings it can seem harsh and cold. We cannot forget the pain, loss, death and extinction that is intrinsic to evolutionary history. We need to acknowledge, I believe, the real ambiguity in our experience of nature. The natural world is both unspeakably beautiful and also a place of competition and violence. In this ambiguity, I believe it is the good news of Jesus that is decisive for Christians. In Wisdom made flesh, God is revealed as Love that embraces suffering creation, transforming it from within, promising liberation and fulfilment. It is in the light of Wisdom made flesh that we may dare to think that in spite of all the violence and death, the glimpses we have of the presence of the God of love in the natural world can be trusted. It is in Christ that we can find the courage to say in spite of the ambiguity, Love is the meaning of the whole creation.

Brachina Gorge

On a recent Catholic Earthcare pilgrimage to the Flinders Ranges, a group of us were led into unforgettable experiences of Adnyamathanha country and culture. Sharpy Coultard guided us on a journey to Chambers Gorge and walking with him up the gorge, we came to a place where it opens out into a space like a natural theatre, perfectly shaped for ceremonial events, with ancient carvings on its rock walls. Sharpy shared with us his great love for this sacred place, and his feeling for it as a place of deep meaning. I had a sense of holy ground, and of quiet presence. Sharpy then led us over the low hills to a point where we could look out to Mount Chambers as he told the

---

28. Rahner, 'Experience of the Holy Spirit', 200–3.

traditional story of its creation. On our way back, we came across a large male emu, leading eight small chicks across the nearby hillside.

As we travelled the next day to Wilpena Pound, and then to a special place for me, Brachina Gorge, I reflected that while the Flinders Ranges had always been a place of spiritual connection, this sense had been heightened in me. There had been something lacking in my earlier experiences, which was no longer lacking, because of the chance to relate with Sharpy and other members of the Adnyamathanha people, and to learn from them of their culture and spirituality. As we moved through Brachina Gorge, we pondered its origins 800 million years ago, from a low-lying basin filled by the sea. We wondered at the Ediacara fossils found in and near Brachina Gorge, soft-bodied, highly developed creatures, preserved in impressions in the quartzite, creatures that lived 600 million years ago, and whose discovery gave rise to the naming of a new period of life. As we travelled through the gorge, the late-afternoon light lit up the ranges that towered above us in brilliant ochre-reds. Moving along quietly, we came across dozens of shy, beautiful, yellow-footed rock wallabies come down from the hills to the creek bed.

I thought of the times I had camped in Brachina Gorge, watching the evening light on the ranges, being woken by birdsong, and finding peace, quiet joy, and inner freedom. I remembered how even on the long drive up from Adelaide, I would feel the pressures of everyday life begin to lift and something inexpressible, a sense of wholeness, begin to come to the fore. The healing and peace found in this place can be seen as the quiet, almost unspeakable, experience of the Spirit of God. And the emu with his young, the yellow-footed rock wallabies, the tree full of cockatoos, the smooth rounded rocks of the creek bed, and the brilliant colours of the cliffs above us, can all be seen as creaturely icons of Holy Wisdom.

Willunga Hills

When doing theological work, I am often sitting at the kitchen table of a little house south of Adelaide. I look out over a rolling landscape toward the Willunga Hills.[29] These hills are folded into one another

---

29. This section is a revised version of Edwards, *Partaking of God: Trinity, Evolution and Ecology* (Collegeville, Minnesota: Liturgical Press, 2014), 152-3.

in beautiful rounded shapes that draw the eye and quieten the spirit. They run right across the horizon down to the sea on my far right. In between my window and the hills is a wide undulating plain. There are waves of late summer golden paddocks, green vineyards, olive plantations, and stands of eucalyptus.

Much closer, in the many greens of the indigenous shrubs that make up the front garden, beautiful little black and white birds with gold on their wings, New Holland Honeyeaters, flit between the branches looking for nectar, while magpies scratch around in the ground for grubs. This place leads me toward stillness. It offers liberation from the busyness of life, from the multiplicities of demands, and the noise that fills so much of contemporary existence.

There is an invitation to be quiet before the mystery it mediates. It is an invitation all too easy to resist, but to say yes, to dwell even for a short time in the mystery, is to find healing and peace. It is to be open to all that is in this place as a gift. It is to sense the presence of unspeakable Love, of the Spirit of God, at the heart of the natural world. It is to know Holy Wisdom revealed in honeyeaters, paddocks, vineyards, gum trees and the Willunga Hills.

The River Red Gum

Walking at Morialta, in the foothills near Adelaide, I have been stopped in my tracks by the sheer presence of a great River Red Gum (*Eucalyptus camaldulensis*).[30] This tree sits near a creek bed that is now often dry in summer. What arrested me first was its massive trunk, more than four metres in diameter. The cracked, peeling bark displays a beautiful range of muted colours: blacks, greys, browns, reds and creamy whites. The tree must be about forty metres high. Almost lost in the blue-green leaves of its crown are flashes of the brilliant blues, greens and oranges of dozens of rainbow lorikeets. On the ground, Rosellas, orange-red, with bright blue wings, forage in the undergrowth for seeds.

Older River Red Gums, like this one, drop branches, forming holes that become home for birds and many creatures. They provide shelter

---

30. Revised version of Edwards, *Jesus and the Natural World* (Melbourne: Garratt, 2012), 47, and 'Sketching an Ecological Theology of the Holy Spirit and the Word of God', in *Concilium*, 4 (2011): 13–31.

for insects, and some offer breeding places for fish in times of flood. Their fallen branches form habitats for many species of wildlife. River Red Gums can live for up to 700 years. The tree that I encounter was here long before Adelaide was colonised by England in 1836. It would have hosted generation after generation of indigenous Kaurna people, who in winter would move up to the foothills from the Adelaide plains for shelter, firewood and food.

I meet this beautiful old tree in a moment of connection that takes me to stillness before its otherness. I am led into a sense of presence, to what is beyond the human and beyond words, to the uncontrollable and wild Spirit of God that 'blows where it will' (Jn 3:8). In encountering this great tree, and all that lives in and around it, there is an experience of the Spirit as the unspeakable presence of God, as wonderfully creative fruitfulness, as the Life-Giver of the Creed, as the 'dearest freshness deep down things' of Hopkins.

There is another dimension to this experience. In the Spirit, I can receive this river red gum as revelation, as God's self-revelation, as giving expression in its own creaturely way to that same eternal Wisdom of God that becomes flesh and has a human face in Jesus of Nazareth. In its unique, specific and limited way, this River Red Gum is a gift and a presence of divine Wisdom in our world, a revelatory word that speaks quietly and beautifully of the eternal Word. It is the gift of the Wellspring of all creation, the generous and generative Lover, who is Origin and Source of All.

C. Divine Action

Exploring How God Acts

Events like the South Asian tsunami of 26 December 2004, Hurricane Katrina, or the recent bushfires of South Eastern Australia, raise fundamental theological questions about God's action: If God is a God of love, why is this happening? How do we think about God at work in the natural world? Does God send tsunamis, floods, and bush fires? Evolutionary biology reveals not only the abundance and diversity of life, but also the costs of the process of evolutionary emergence, the predation, the competition for resources, the death and the extinctions. We now know as no generation before us that the costs are built into the process. How do we think about God at work in this costly process? Do we think of God as sending suffering? Is it God that causes the cancer that kills my friend? What is the meaning of the classical Christian teaching of God's providence? Does God intervene in our lives? Does God overturn or bypass the laws of nature?

These questions are all raise the issue of divine action. How do we think about God acting in the word, in creation, grace and in the Christ-event? My intention here is simply to sketch the beginning of one theological approach to this issue. It is fundamental to acknowledge at the beginning of such a discussion that our knowledge of divine action is analogical and very limited. What we know is based on the Christ-event. It is also based in part upon the empirical reality of the universe we observe around us, which is the fruit of divine creative action. My proposal is that these two sources suggest seven characteristics of divine action, which I will sketch below. After outlining these characteristics, I will explore the issue of divine action further by reflecting on special divine acts, considering three types of such acts, God's action in the history of the universe, in the life of grace and in the history of salvation.

Some Characteristics of Divine Action

Divine Action has a specific and historical character

Jesus' call to discipleship, his healing of Bartimaeus and his death on a Roman cross were concrete, historical and limited. If the Christ-event can be taken by Christians as revealing something about the way God acts in other contexts, then it is significant that in this event God's action always has this particular and historical character. In many discussions of divine action, God's creative act, the act by which God enables all things to exist and to act, is called general divine action. The question is then put: On top of this general divine action, are there also special divine acts in the history of the universe, in salvation history and in our own lives? Recently, Niels Gregersen has challenged this way of thinking.[1] He points to the sciences of complexity and to the example of a cell that emerges as a self-organizing and self-producing (autopoietic) system. In such a system, there is a 'rewiring' that goes on from moment to moment, as a result of the system in relationship to it environment. This involves an enormous number of steps which are not covered by any one scientific law, but require a variety of interacting scientific explanations. This suggests a theological conclusion: If God is engaged with every aspect of ongoing creation, then God's engagement must be with the particulars: 'For if God is not in the particulars, God is not in the whole of reality either.'[2] I think that Gregersen is right to insist that in the evolution of the universe and in the emergence of life on Earth, divine action involves the historical, the unpredictable and the specific. I will propose that divine action with regard to creation and grace is intrinsically particular.

God's action in creation and redemption can be seen as one act of self-bestowing love

Karl Rahner sees the Christ-event as revealing the true nature of God's action. What is revealed is a God who bestows God's self to

---

1. Niels Henrik Gregersen, 'Laws of Physics, Principles of Self-Organization, and Natural Capacities: On Explaining a Self-Organizing World' in *Creation: Law and Probability*, edited by Fraser Watts (Aldershot, Hampshire: Ashgate, 2008), 97.
2. Gregersen, 'Laws of Physics', 98.

creation in the Word and in the Spirit. With Scotus, Rahner sees creation as always directed towards the self-giving of the incarnation. Rahner sees God's action in creation, redemptions and final fulfillment as fundamentally one act of divine self-bestowal although this one act is an intrinsically differentiated process.[3] In this theological vision, the universe emerges, and life evolves on Earth, in the process of God's self-bestowal. God is never absent from this process, but always immanent to the world in self-giving love. The self-bestowal of the transcendent God is "the most immanent factor in the creature."[4] I believe with Rahner that God's act is one act of self-bestowal, and with Gregersen that is one act as it takes effect in creation is always particular and historical. I find a useful analogy in human acts, such as life-long commitment in love to a partner, which can be seen as one act that finds expression only in many particular acts. In this view, every galaxy, every insect in a rain forest, and in a unique way every human person, is a particular location where God is present in bestowing love.

God's creative presence in self-bestowing love empowers and enables the evolutionary emergence of creatures.

A second fundamental concept in Rahner's theology of creation is that of creaturely self-transcendence. This is worked out in Rahner's anthropology and in his evolutionary Christology, but it functions throughout many aspects of his work.[5] The two concepts of divine self-bestowal and creaturely self-transcendence are inter-related: it is God's self-bestowal that enables and empowers creaturely self-transcendence. I think that this act of God that enables evolutionary emergence can be understood, in relational and Trinitarian terms, as the interior, dynamic relationship of all things in the evolving

---

3. Karl Rahner, *Foundations of Christian Faith: An Introduction to the Idea of Christianity* (New York: Seabury Press, 1978), 197.
4. Karl Rahner, 'Immanent and Transcendent Consummation of the World', in *Theological Investigations,* 10 (London: Darton, Longmann & Todd, 1973), 281.
5. Karl Rahner, *Hominisation: The Evolutionary Origin of Man as a Theological Problem* (London: Burns and Oates, 1965), 98–101; 'Christology within an Evolutionary View of the World', in *Theological Investigations,* 5 (Baltimore: Helicon, 1966), 157–92; *Foundations,* 178–203.

universe to their Creator through the indwelling, life-giving Spirit.[6] Rahner proposes a large pattern of evolutionary self-transcendence, one that brings out the inner connection between evolution and christology. The material universe transcends itself in the emergence of life, and life transcends itself in the human. In human beings, the universe becomes open to self-consciousness and freedom, and to a fully personal response to God's self-bestowal in grace. Within this context of an emergent and self-transcending universe, the Christ-event is the radical self-transcendence of the created universe into God. With Rahner, I believe that both divine self-bestowal and creaturely self-transcendence can be understood to characterize not only creation, but also grace, incarnation, and the final consummation of all things in Christ.

God's action is not interventionist, but works consistently in and through the laws of nature, rather than by violating or bypassing them

God is interiorly present to the whole creation and to every part it, nearer to it than it is to itself, as the very ground and source of its existence, enabling and empowering it at every moment. Divine transcendence does not make God distant. It enables God to be more interior to things than any creature could ever be. God never breaks in upon creation because God is already there. As Brian Davies says, it is 'the whole of God', not just a bit of God, who is actively present in all that exists.[7] In the theological tradition associated with Aquinas, God has been called the primary cause, the one who confers existence on all things. Everything we see around us in the universe, every bit of empirical data, is created. It belongs to the world of interacting creaturely causes, which Aquinas sees as secondary causes. God is never found as a cause amongst other causes in the universe. Aquinas sees miracles as an exception, because in a miracle God replaces the created cause, but on this I respectfully disagree. The proposal that I am making is that even in miracles God acts *consistently* through second-

---

6. I discuss this in some detail in *Breath of Life: A Theology of the Creator Spirit* (Maryknoll, NY: Orbis, 2004).
7. Brian Davies, *The Reality of God and the Problem of Evil* (New York: Continuum, 2006), 233.

ary causes. This world of secondary causes involves not only what science has already mapped with its laws and theories, but also aspects of the natural world that are not yet well-modeled by the sciences.

God's action enables creaturely autonomy to flourish

The divine act of creation is a relationship whereby God establishes the creature in genuine difference from God's self. Because of God's love and respect for creatures, this difference means that the creature has its own otherness, integrity and proper autonomy. A fundamental principle of the God-world relationship, one that is grounded in the tradition of Aquinas, and one that Rahner often repeats, is expressed in the axiom: Radical dependence on God and the genuine autonomy of the creature are directly and not inversely related.[8] The closer we creatures are to God, the more we can be truly themselves. Creaturely integrity is not diminished because a creature's existence is dependent on God, but flourishes precisely in this dependence. In discussing this issue, Herbert McCabe points out that creation is an act of love that enables the other to be itself. It is not an interference with things: 'Unless we grasp the truth that creation means leaving the world to be itself, to run itself by its own scientific laws so that things behave in accordance with their own natures and not at the arbitrary behest of some god, we shall never begin to understand that the Lord we worship is not a god, but the unknown reason why there is anything instead of nothing.'[9] God's creative act enables the creaturely world to flourish in its own integrity and proper autonomy

In acting through creaturely processes, God accepts the limits of these processes and works creatively with them

It makes an enormous difference whether one thinks of God as able to do absolutely anything or as acting in a way that respects and accepts the limits of finite entities and processes. Based on what we know of God in Christ, I think it can be said that in the incarnation God lovingly accepts the limits of matter and flesh and the specificity of time and place. In a similar way, it can be argued that when God creates

---

8. See for example, Rahner, *Foundations*, 78-9.
9. Herbert McCabe, *God Still Matters* (London: Continuum, 2002), 11-12.

through creaturely processes, such as the emergence of hydrogen and helium in the Big Bang, the synthesis of further elements in stars, and the combination of random mutation and natural selection in the evolution of life on Earth, God engages creatively with creaturely processes in all their specificity, concreteness and their limits. By creating in love, God freely accepts limitations. God's freedom is not that of an arbitrary despot, but freedom that expresses itself in love. God acts only in love, respecting the process. If one thinks, as Christians do, that the divine purposes include the emergence of human beings, then the divine purposes are achieved with extraordinary patience, as God waits upon, empowers and enables the 3.7 billion year history of life on Earth, with modern human beings appearing only in the last 200,000 years. This is not a passive waiting, but the waiting upon another of a loving parent with a child, or a lover with the beloved, an active nurturing engagement that enables the other to flourish in all her freedom and integrity. God's nature, as lovingly respectful of both human freedom and the finite limits and autonomy of natural processes, may set limits on what God can do in particular circumstances. God will achieve the divine purposes, but not in ways that over-ride the proper autonomy of creaturely processes. The love that defines the divine nature is a love that works with limitations, that lives with the process, a love that accompanies creation, and promise to bring all to liberation and healing in Christ.

God acts in creation through processes that involve chance and lawfulness

Evolutionary biology has taught us that random mutations function as a source of novelty for natural selection in the evolution of life. In theological terms, this can be seen as part of the way God creates. Arthur Peacocke has pointed out that randomness at the molecular level seems essential if the Creator is to explore the full gamut of potentialities of life. It is chance and law together that allow for the thorough exploration of living and non-living forms of organisation.[10] DJ Bartholomew writes that chance offers a way of creating a richer environment that would otherwise be possible: 'chance

---

10. See Arthur Peacocke, *Theology for a Scientific Age: Being and Becoming—Natural, Divine and Human* (Minneapolis: Fortress Press, 1993), 115–121.

offers the potential Creator many advantages which it is difficult to envisage being obtained in any other way.'[11] Although Aquinas never had a chance to consider the place of random mutation in biological evolution, he had already integrated contingency and chance into his thought: 'Contingency is not incompatible with providence, nor are chance or fortune or voluntary action.'[12] For Aquinas, contingency, chance and human freedom are secondary causes through which God acts. Chance can be thought of as an expression of divine creativity. God acts through random events as God works through the laws of nature. The Creator, then, is to be seen as less like a monarch who controls every aspect of the history of the universe according to some pre-existing blue-print and more like an artist exploring in creation, responding in spontaneity and in freedom to what is given.[13] God acts dynamically, responsively, respectfully, and lovingly in and through a whole variety of secondary causes, including the chance and the lawfulness of the natural world.

Special Divine Acts

I have proposed that God's action with regard to creation is both one and diverse. It is one act of self-giving love. But God's acts with regard to creation are plural because they take effect in specific circumstances and in particular times and places, in a range of particular creaturely processes and entities. Christian theology sees some acts of God, such as the call of a prophet or the Christ-event as *special*. In the approach I am taking, special divine acts are intrinsic to the way God acts. I am not, then, doing what is often done, starting from an assumption of general divine action in the ongoing creation of all things, and then asking whether there are also special divine acts on top of this general notion. The proposal here is that divine acts are always specific to a particular entity or process. In this sense they are

---

11. DJ Bartholomew, *God of Chance* (London: SCM, 1984), 97. See also the series of essays in *Creation: Law and Probability,* edited by Fraser Watts (Aldershot, Hampshire: Ashgate, 2008).
12. Thomas Aquinas, *Summa contra gentiles,* 3.75.2. Translated by Vernon Bourke in *Summa contra gentiles Book Three: Providence Part 1* (Notre Dame: University of Notre Dame, 1956, 1975), 249.
13. See Elizabeth A Johnson, 'Does God Play Dice? Divine Providence and Chance', in *Theological Studies,* 57 (1996): 15.

always special. I understand these acts as *objectively* special, in the sense that they have objective effects in the created world, and that these are God-given. I will begin by focusing on God's acts in the providential guidance of creation, then turn to grace at work in the life of human persons and finally consider special divine acts in the history of salvation.

Special Acts in the Providential Guidance of Creation

Approaches to Special Divine Acts

Not all theologians support the idea that there are special divine acts. Maurice Wiles, for example, argues that divine action is to be understood simply as the one act of continuous creation: he sees "the whole continuing creation of the world as God's one act." In this view, what traditionally have been understood as specific divine acts are subsumed within this one creative act.[14] My approach differs from his in two fundamental respects. First, Wiles' theology of divine action begins from a theology of creation and then interprets everything else, including the incarnation and redemption, as aspects of creation. The approach I am taking begins from the Christ-event as the act of divine self-bestowal, and then seeks to understand creation in terms of Christ. Second, unlike Wiles, I defend the idea that God does act in specific and special ways.

Keith Ward takes a very different approach. He sees God as acting in special ways in the lives of human beings and in the evolution of the physical universe as well as in the history of salvation.[15] God's special providential acts, he suggests, account for the bias in evolution towards complex and sentient life-forms.[16] In his further reflection on Darwinian evolution, Ward gives the impression that he is placing the scientific theory of natural selection and the causal influence of the God as explanations *at the same level*. He argues, against Richard Dawkins, that natural selection is insufficient as an explanation for the purposive nature of evolution, insisting that the additional explanation of God's action is required.[17] I have reservations about this

---

14. Maurice Wiles, *God's Action in the World* (London: SCM, 1986), 93.
15. Keith Ward, *Divine Action* (London: Collins, 1990), 74–102, 127.
16. Keith Ward, *God, Chance and Necessity* (Oxford: One World, 1996), 83.
17. Ward, *God, Chance and Necessity*, 93.

strategy. Of course, in the approach I am taking, God's creative act is needed as an explanation at the metaphysical level. But I think it is important for theology to recognize the integrity of scientific explanation at its own level, that of empirical reality.

I am arguing for a theology of special divine acts that fully respects the integrity of secondary causes, including all the processes that drive biological evolution. In such a theology, these processes are seen as the proper domain of science. In recent years, divine action has been studied by philosophers, theologians and scientists working together in a collaborative and intensive way. During the 1990s, the Center for Theology and the Natural Sciences at Berkeley and the Vatican Observatory co-sponsored a series of research conferences and publications on the theme of divine action, exploring it in relation to quantum cosmology, chaos and complexity, evolutionary and molecular biology, neuroscience and the person, and quantum mechanics.[18] There was broad agreement on a concept of divine action that includes not only God's continuous creative act, but also special and objective divine acts. Over the series of conferences, a consensus emerged around an approach to divine action that was special and objective, but non-interventionist.[19] A nonintervention-

---

18. Robert J Russell, Nancey C Murphy and Chris J Isham, editors, *Quantum Cosmology and the Laws of Nature: Scientific Perspectives on Divine Action*, second edition (Vatican City State; Berkeley, Calif: Vatican Observatory; Center for Theology and the Natural Sciences, 1996); Robert J Russell, Nancey C Murphy and Arthur Peacocke, editors, *Chaos and Complexity: Scientific Perspectives on Divine Action* (Vatican City State; Berkeley, Calif: Vatican Observatory; Center for Theology and the Natural Sciences, 1995); Robert J Russell, William R Stoeger, SJ, and Francisco J Ayala, editors., *Evolutionary and Molecular Biology: Scientific Perspectives on Divine Action* (Vatican City State; Berkeley, Calif: Vatican Observatory; Center for Theology and the Natural Sciences, 1998); Robert J Russell, Nancey C Murphy, Theo C Meyering and Michael A Arbib, editors, *Neuroscience and the Person: Scientific Perspectives on Divine Action* (Vatican City State; Berkeley, Calif: Vatican Observatory; Center for Theology and the Natural Sciences, 1999); Robert John Russell, Philip Clayton, Kirk Wegter-McNelly and John Polkinghorne, editors, *Quantum Mechanics: Scientific Perspectives on Divine Action* (Vatican City State; Berkeley, Calif: Vatican Observatory; Center for Theology and the Natural Sciences, 2001).
19. See Robert J Russell, 'Introduction', in *Chaos and Complexity*, 6–13; 'Introduction', *Quantum Mechanics*, ii–iv. Russell has provided a full account of his own view and that of others in three chapters of his recent book *Cosmology: From Alpha to Omega: The creative mutual interaction of theology and science* (Minneapolis: Fortress Press, 2008), 110–225.

ist view of divine action was taken to mean that God acts in nature *without breaking or suspending the laws of nature.*

Within this consensus, five different approaches emerged. First, Ian Barbour (with Charles Birch and John Haught on occasions), represented the perspective of Process Theology, understanding divine action as the inviting lure of God, which is operative in every actual occasion, but which does not determine the outcome in an exclusive way. Second, a significant group, including Robert John Russell, Nancey Murphy, George Ellis and Thomas Tracy, explored the idea that God acts in the indeterminacy of quantum events to bring about particular outcomes.[20] Third, John Polkinghorne saw God as acting in the openness of nature, which he finds represented in chaotic and complex systems, to bring about outcomes through the top-down imparting of information. Fourth, Arthur Peacocke saw God as acting in and through and under every aspect of nature, acting on the system as a whole, by way of analogy with a 'top-down' or 'whole-part' cause in nature. Finally, William Stoeger and Stephen Happel worked consistently with Aquinas' distinction between primary and secondary causality, and understood God as acting in the world through a whole range of secondary causes. While owing a debt of gratitude to various of the positions outlined above, it is the last of them that I am attempting to explore further. Stoeger's position is that God acts in the whole of the natural world, by God's immanent and differentiated presence to all things, not only through the laws of nature of which we have a partial understanding, but also through those processes and regularities of nature that are still unknown to us. I see myself as attempting to build on this approach, in a theology of special divine action that takes effect through a variety of created causes.

---

20. Murphy sees God as acting in all quantum events, not as the sole determiner of events, but in a mediated action, in the sense that God always acts together with nature at the quantum level. Tracy suggests seeing God as acting in some rather than all quantum events, in order to bring about the effects of God's providence. Russell proposes that God acts in all quantum events until the appearance of life and consciousness, and then God increasingly refrains from determining outcomes, leaving room for top-down causality in conscious creatures, particularly in humans. For a summary of these views see Russell, 'Divine Action and Quantum Mechanics: A Fresh Assessment', in *Quantum Mechanics*, 293–328.

Divine action through secondary causes

I opt for the approach to divine action in which God is thought of as acting through secondary causes because it represents a foundational metaphysical understanding of the God-world relationship, which is at the heart of the Christian tradition and which I find intellectually coherent and religiously meaningful. At its centre is the idea that the Creator is present to all creatures, closer to them than they are to themselves, conferring existence and the capacity to act on every entity and every process. There are three reasons why I choose to give primary place to this way of understanding special divine acts. First, it upholds the absolute mystery and transcendence of the Creator, and resists any tendency to see God as one cause among others in the world. Second, it is a view that gives proper autonomy and independence to creaturely causes and processes, and fully respects the integrity of the natural sciences. Third, it is an approach that is less likely than some other options to exacerbate the theological problem of suffering. At least in the way I am proposing it, the approach to divine action through secondary causes involves the idea of God accepting and working with the creaturely limits of these secondary causes.[21]

A common objection to the idea that God acts through secondary causes is that it does not tell us *how* God acts through them. In response, I think that it is important to say that from a theological perspective, we do not know *how* God's creative act works. What we know is the result of this act but not the act itself. There is a very good reason for an apophatic stance in relation to God's creative act. God's creative act *is* God. Whatever we see, whatever science studies, is not God. We have no direct access to God's creative act, only to its effects, the universe of creatures we find around us, with the relationships between them and the laws that govern them. We never find any particular point of intersection (the 'causal joint') between God and creatures, because we have no empirical access to God. In a sense, of course, every creature in the universe is this point of intersection, but what we have empirical access to is simply the creature. So a theology of divine action not only should not spell out how God

---

21. On this see Russell, *Cosmology: From Alpha to Omega*, 189–190, and 249–72, particularly 252.

acts, but should insist that this is something we cannot know.[22] What we know about the nature of God comes from the Christ-event and, on this basis, we can say important things about divine action, but we can no more comprehend the nature of God's act any more than we can comprehend the divine essence.

God's special action in the emergence of life

How, then, might we speak about God's action in, for example, the emergence of life on our planet 3.7 billion years ago? In the approach I am advocating, this can be seen as a special act of God in the sense that God chooses, eternally, that the universe would bring forth biological life on our Earth by means of emergence and increasing complexity. What makes this act special is that 1. this action of God has a specific effect in creaturely history, the emergence of life in the universe, and 2. this specific effect is intended by God. Through the creative act of God in the eternal Word and through the immanent Spirit inert matter becomes something new. God's one act of self-bestowing love is expressed in the specific and special act of the emergence of life on Earth.

This act of God takes effect in and through all the regularities and constraints of nature, including chance events occurring within the structure provided by the laws of nature. It involves a whole series of events in the 13.7 billion year history of the universe, particular the formation of stars, in which elements like carbon, so necessary for life on Earth, can be synthesized. It involves particular features of our planet, including its placement at the right distance from the Sun, its formation from the molecules that are the raw materials of life from the matter surrounding the Sun, the continual bombardment of the young Earth by ice-bearing comets, the formation of a first atmosphere, and many other factors studied in the sciences. In all of these events, God is acting in specific and special ways. And in all of this, and a great deal more, is part of that special act by which God brings life to the Earth.

---

22. In his recent work, Russell makes it very clear that his own approach to noninterventionist divine action respects the mystery and otherness of God, and is not meant as an explanation of how God acts, let alone a description or explanation of a 'causal join'. See, for example, *Cosmology: From Alpha to Omega*, 126.

As is well-known, science cannot yet offer anything like a full explanation of the origin of life. What I am proposing is that in principle it is the role of science to explain everything possible about this event. There are no gaps in the causal explanation that theology should fill. In the divine act that brings forth life on Earth, God acts in and through secondary causes, through the natural world, and the regularities, contingencies, processes and laws studied by the sciences. These are the expression of God's creative act. God acts powerfully, creatively and dynamically, not in a way that over-rides the processes of nature, but precisely in and through them.

The dynamism and the creaturely limits of special divine acts

This conception of special divine action involves a dynamic understanding of God's engagement with every aspect of the expanding and evolving universe, and with the whole process of the evolution of life in all its complexity, including that of human beings. God wants a world of diverse living creatures to evolve on our planet and acts in all the regularities and contingencies of the natural world to bring this about. God is always present, in the Word and in the Spirit, always breathing life into the process, always engaged, always responsive, and always achieving the divine purpose of creating a world of creatures to which God will give God's self in love.

But this dynamic presence of God in the Word and in the creative Spirit to all things is precisely a presence in love. It is the love exemplified in a staggering way in the cross of Jesus. Creation is an act of self-giving love. And divine love involves divine respect for the independence and integrity of the creature and the creaturely processes involved in the emergence of life on Earth. God does not over-ride the process, nor by-pass the laws of nature. God embraces creatures in their limitations and allows things to unfold in a fully creaturely way that involves enormous lengths of time. God works with the process.

I have already pointed out that in order to have human beings and koalas you need to have carbon. Carbon exists only because of the formation of galaxies and stars in the expanding universe. The production of the carbon, and the other elements that make us up, takes billions of years of star-burning. God creates with infinite patience and with a divine capacity not only to empower, but also loving to wait upon the emergence of all that is needed for the evolution of life.

These processes involve false starts and set-backs and the exploring of new directions. God works creatively, dynamically, and responsively, loving the process, delighting in the emergence of a world of creatures with their own independence and integrity.

Special Divine Acts in the Life of Grace

How do we think of God acting in our own personal lives? According to the long tradition of Christian faith, there are times when we can experience the Holy Spirit in moments of grace. And according to this same tradition, God acts providentially and personally in lives. I will consider each of these briefly as instances of special divine action.

Experiences of the Holy Spirit

Do we experience the Spirit of God? Does God break in upon our day to day lives, addressing us, calling us, challenging us, inviting us, loving us? I am convinced that the answer to these questions can only be yes.[23] Of course, cultural and psychological factors play a role in the interpretation of all of our experiences and this suggests a cautious and critical approach to claims about the experience of the Holy Spirit. What is claimed to come from the Spirit will *always* be, at least in part, the product of a human imagination. It will always be interpreted with the aid of pre-existing images, language and concepts.

Granted this, I believe that we can claim with thinkers like Rahner that we do experience the Spirit and that this occurs in ordinary human experience of the world.[24] Rahner points to the boundless openness of the human mind and heart. This boundless expanse is always there as the context of ordinary knowledge and love. On the basis of Christian revelation, which tells us that 'God's love has been

---

23. I have dealt with this in some detail in *Human Experience of God* (New York: Paulist Press, 1983).
24. Karl Rahner, 'Experience of the Holy Spirit', in *Theological Investigations*, 18 (New York: Crossroad, 1983), 196-7. See also his *Foundations of Christian Faith*, 137; 'Reflections on the Experience of Grace', in *Theological Investigations*, 3: 86-90; 'The Experience of God Today', *Theological Investigations*, 11: 149-65; 'Experience of Self and Experience of God', *Theological Investigations*, 13: 122-32; 'Experience of the Spirit and Existential Commitment', in *Theological Investigations*, 16: 24-51.

poured into our hearts through the Holy Spirit that has been given to us' (Rom 5:5), Rahner argues that this dynamic openness of the human person can be understood as an openness towards the Spirit of God present to us by grace in self-offering love.

There are also moments of special grace in our lives, where the experience of the Spirit is brought more clearly to the forefront of conscious experience. These can be positive experiences: when we are caught up in the exuberance of life in a rain forest, when we ponder and are deeply touched by the absolute gift of mutual friendship, when the birth of a child fills us with awe. There are also negative and extremely painful moments that lead us into mystery: when loneliness takes hold in our hearts, when we face failure in our projects, when grief seems unendurable, and yet we come to know that we have been held in what seemed hopelessness, emptiness and pain.

Grace can come to us in any moment. We are challenged by an encounter with a homeless person, and forced to ask hard questions about our use of wealth and our collusion in systems that damage people. We are entranced by the song of a single bird and led beyond it for a moment to the Source of all music. In a quiet moment in the celebration of the Eucharist we are led to stillness before God. The experience of the Spirit can be an experience of radical intimacy or disruption, but in either case it is an experience mediated by our engagement with created words, events and persons. Experiences of grace are mediated by secondary causes: we encounter others in our world, and find in these encounters an openness to a Holy Other, present in a mysterious way beyond concepts and words.

Personal providence

What of God's day-to-day care of us? Are we right to find God at work providentially in the small as well as the large events of our lives? With many others in the Christian tradition, I am convinced that personal providence is a central dimension of Christian faith and fundamental to a gospel way of life: 'Look at the birds of the air; they neither sow nor reap nor gather into barns, and yet your heavenly Father feeds them. Are you not of more value than they?' (Matt 6: 26). Jesus tells his disciples that there is no need to worry. They are to set their hearts on the kingdom of God and what they need will be provided (Matt 6:23).

Two ideas seem linked in this Christian notion of personal providence: 1. the conviction that God does things for us, and 2. the understanding that God's doing of things for us is personal. God does things for us as persons. Providence involves the idea that we are being cared for. Events occur that we take as a gift. Taking life in this way does not necessarily involve the idea of God acting in an interventionist way. It can also be understood within a noninterventionist theology of God acting through secondary causes. It is possible to hold a strong notion of providence together with the idea of a God who does not over-rule creaturely cause and effect, but acts in and through them. In this view, God really comes to us, responds to us, and provides for us, through secondary causes.

Karl Rahner offers a simple everyday example of a special providential act.[25] I have a good idea that proves to be effective and important and I think of it as a gift of God. Is it appropriate to think this way? Can this good idea be understood as providential? There may be natural explanations for this good idea that has come upon me, but this does not rule out the interpretation of it as an act of God. If in fact I do experience the good idea as a place of encounter with the living God, then I am surely right to think that the God who is present as Source of All in every aspect of creation is now truly mediated to me in this event of a good idea. It is appropriate, then, to see this good idea, which may well have a natural explanation, as willed by God, as given by God, and thus as a genuine experience of God's special providence. There are many such experiences in all that makes up our daily life. As saints like Ignatius of Loyola have taught us, the spiritual journey is a continual learning to find God in all things and this is based on the conviction that God is there *for us* in all things.

The claim that God cares for us, and that we experience God's providence in a personal way does not mean that our lives will be without pain, failure, grief and death. The Christian assertion of a God who cares for us can be made with integrity only when the hunger, cruelty and violence of our world are fully acknowledged. The kind of theology of providence I am advocating does not mean that God is thought of as intervening in the order of nature to make my life pain-free. It proposes rather, that the God who provides for me through secondary causes respects the limits and the proper auton-

---

25. Rahner, *Foundations of Christian Faith*, 88.

omy of the created order. This means that while God can be seen as acting in secondary causes for my well-being, God may not be free to intervene in the functioning of secondary causes in a way that overturns the laws of nature in order to preserve me from suffering. In his life and ministry, Jesus found God in all things and he had a profound believe in divine providence. But God did not respond to Jesus' cry 'Abba, Father, for you all things are possible; remove this cup from me' (Mk 14:36) by intervening miraculously to save Jesus from suffering and death. The divine response was to be with Jesus in suffering and death, transforming it in the power of the Spirit into resurrection life and salvation for the world.

We can and do experience God's providential care, but we also experience life as painful and, for some of us, as unbearably cruel. The sense of providence in some aspects of life can be accompanied by experiences of suffering. Providence does not mean that I will not suffer cancer. It clearly does not mean that I will not die. But it means that God will be with me in my illness and that when I die I die in Christ. In this view of providence, then, it is appropriate to think of God as doing things for me. It is appropriate to think of some events as a gift given to me. But it does *not* follow, as it may seem to at first sight, that when I am diagnosed with a serious illness, I am to see this as something God is sending to me. When tragedy strikes me or someone I love, it is not God who is doing it to me, except in the broad sense that God is creating and sustaining a world that unfolds according to its own patterns, and these patterns involve illness and death. God wants our life. God does not want out suffering. God does not send us suffering and grief.

Great suffering can befall us. Providence means that even here, especially here, God is not absent but radically with us. God does not send us suffering, but the cross reveals that suffering *is* the place of God. Even when we cry out like Jesus, 'My God, my God, why have you forsaken me?' (Mk 15:34) we are not abandoned. God is the faithful companion in our suffering, profoundly with us in love, feeling with us with divine capacity to be with others in their pain, and taking us into life. There are times, even in great suffering, when we can come to know, perhaps only in retrospect, that we held and loved even in what seems utterly unbearable.

Suffering and grief are built into the kind of world in which we live, a world of natural process and human freedom. God is made flesh in this world in Jesus of Nazareth, embracing the flesh that is subject to suffering and death and the humanity distorted by human sin. Suffering flesh is taken into God, forever. Providence does not take suffering from our world. It assures us of a God who is with us as the faithful companion of our lives and deaths, with us in it all, leading us into resurrection life.

Special Divine Acts in the History of Salvation

Christian faith sees God acting freely in special ways that include Israel's experience of the Mosaic Covenant, the words of the prophet Isaiah, the life, death and resurrection of Jesus of Nazareth and the Spirit poured out at Pentecost. A little reflection makes it clear that in each of these cases, God is not becoming present where God was formerly absent. God was *totally* with Israel before the Covenant. God was fully present to every part of the universe, including all flesh, before the incarnation. How, then, can we think about special divine acts such as the incarnation in relationship to God's abiding, enabling, interior presence with all things?

The Incarnation

I have been proposing that in a special divine act, a creaturely reality expresses and mediates God's self-giving love. We encounter God in and through the mediations of the natural world. In a particular event or person, God freely brings to particular and historical expression the act of self-giving love by which God has been immanent to creation from the beginning. A created reality expresses and mediates the immanent presence and action of God. In something of a similar way, cooking a meal for a human beloved can be a special act that embodies and brings to concrete expression the life-long act of committed love.

In what Christians see as God's most uniquely special act in our history, God acts in and through the mediation of the humanity of Jesus. He is the unique historical expression of the love that is already interior to all the entities, processes and persons that make up our universe. As Rahner has noted, traditional theology tended to see events like the incarnation according to a model of divine intervention. In Christian history, this interventionist model has coexisted with a more universal view of God as the "deepest energy of the world."[26] The universal and interventionist models of divine action were never completely reconciled. What is needed today, Rahner says, is the emergence of a "universalist basic model in which God in his free grace, from the very beginning and always and everywhere, has communicated himself to his creation as its innermost energy and works in the world from the inside out."[27] It is, of course, precisely this model that I am seeking to advance in these pages.

In a theology of divine action understood as self-bestowal, the incarnation governs creation from the beginning. Jesus in his created humanity makes God's self-bestowing love and promise of fulfillment historically accessible and tangible. His is the human face of divine love in our history. The divine self-bestowal always and everywhere at work in particular ways in all things finds its radical expression in our history in the words and deeds, the death and resurrection of Jesus of Nazareth.[28]

The sacramental structure of special divine acts

In Christian theology, a sacrament is a visible sign and agent of divine self-bestowal. The prime instances of this in the life of the Christian community are sacramental celebrations, like Baptism and Eucharist. But, as a great deal of twentieth century theology and church teaching has made clear, these sacraments reflect the fact that the church itself has a sacramental nature. It is a sign and agent of communion with God and of human community, called to be the universal sacrament

---

26. Karl Rahner, and Karl-Heinz Weger, *Our Christian Faith* (London: Burns and Oates, 1980), 77.
27. Rahner and Weger, 'Our Christian Faith', 78–9.
28. 'The event of God's promise of himself in Jesus makes that deepest promise by God of himself to the world historically accessible and irreversible. It is always and everywhere the fundamental energy and force of the world and its history. It is therefore perfectly possible to understand the event of Jesus without the aid of images of an intervention in the world from outside. In doing without such an image, however, we must let history really be history and clearly realize that this deepest energy and power of the world and its history is God in his sovereign freedom, who, by his free promise of himself, has made himself this deepest energy and force of the world.' Rahner and Weger, *Our Christian Faith*, 103–4.

of salvation.[29] At a more fundamental level still, Jesus of Nazareth is the fundamental and primary sacrament of God in the world.[30] He is the radical expression of, and mediation of, divine self-bestowal. As the incarnate Word and Wisdom of God, he is the sacrament of divine self-bestowal in the world. He is the real symbol of God, in which God is manifested and acts in a world of matter and flesh.

It is fundamental to note that Jesus' humanity is created and part of the network of secondary causes that make up creation. Like us, Jesus is part of evolutionary history, dependent on the hydrogen that formed in the beginning of the universe, on the carbon and the other elements synthesized in stars, and on the long history of evolutionary emergence on Earth. Precisely as created, and as interconnected with evolutionary history, with all flesh, Jesus is the irreversible historical expression of God's self-bestowal and the sacrament of salvation for out world. In Jesus Christ, and in the life of the church, we find that the economy of God, the structure of revelation and salvation, has a sacramental structure. This, of course, is another way of saying that God acts in our world through the mediation of creatures, through secondary causes.

This leads to a further proposal: that divine action as such has a sacramental nature. The sacramental character of divine action is not limited to Jesus as the fundamental sacrament of God, or to the communion of the church and its sacramental celebrations. Every experience of divine action, each in its own different way, has a sacramental structure: God's one act that embraces creation, salvation and final fulfillment finds sacramental expression in our history in particular events, words and persons. A diverse range of creatures become mediations of the divine, sacraments of divine action. Such sacramental mediations are differentiated in the way they participate in and mediate the one act of divine self-bestowal. Their variety comes from the various created realities that mediate the divine in our history. Based on revelation in Christ, and led by the Spirit, Christians discern what is truly of God. For them the various sacramental mediations of the

---

29. See *The Dogmatic Constitution on the Church* of the Second Vatican Council, paragraphs 1 and 48.
30. See, for example, Henri De Lubac, *Catholicism: A Study of the Corporate Destiny of Mankind* (New York: Sheed and Ward, 1950); Edward Schillebeeckx, *Christ the Sacrament of Encounter with God* (New York: Sheed and Ward, 1963); Karl Rahner, *The Church and the Sacraments* (New York: Herder and Herder, 1963).

one divine act find their central focus and basis for interpretation in the Word made flesh.

I have proposed that there are special acts of God, and that these include God's creative and providential action in evolutionary emergence, God's personal action in the life of grace and in the experience of personal providence, and God's action in the history of salvation, particularly the Christ-event. These special acts are not interventions that overturn of bypass the laws of nature, but are acts of God in and through the mediation of the natural world, its regularities and contingencies. These special acts of God are intrinsic to divine action because God's one act of self-giving takes effect in the created order in ways that are limited, specific and historical. They are not uniform but wonderfully diverse. Some are certainly more central than others, and God's act in Christ is what is most central and most special to any Christian theology of special divine acts.

Conclusion

I have been attempting to respond to the suffering built into evolutionary emergence, not by attempting a theodicy, but by contributing to a renewed theology of divine action. This strategy is based on the analysis that a particular theology of divine action in Christianity, a theology that sees God in highly interventionist ways, has contributed to the problem we have in dealing with suffering. A renewed theology of divine action will not remove or explain the intractable theological problem of suffering, in my view, but it may remove something that exacerbates the problem.

In response to the costs built into evolution, I think that a theology of divine action has to be able to offer a view of God working creatively and redemptively in and through the natural world to bring it to healing and wholeness. I see at least three requirements for such a theology of divine action. First, it would need to be *noninterventionist* theology that sees God as working in and through the natural world rather than as arbitrarily intervening to send suffering to some and not to others. Second, it would need to be a theology in the light of the cross, whereby God's action is understood as embracing the limits of created entities and processes, waiting upon creation in love, living with its processes, accompanying each creature, rejoicing in every emergence, suffering with every suffering creature, and promising to bring all to healing and fullness of life. Third, God's action in creating an emergent universe would need to be understood in the light of the resurrection and its promise that all things will be transformed and redeemed in Christ (Rom 8:19–23; Col 1:20; Eph 1:10; Rev 21:5). In this paper I have attempted the beginning of a response to the first two of these requirements.

My proposal is that while a Christian theological notion of divine action cannot offer a full explanation of suffering, it can remove common misunderstandings that spring from traditional Christian notions of divine action. It can offer an alternative to the popular view of an interventionist and arbitrary God, in a view of God who acts in and through all the interactions of creatures, always respecting their integrity, their proper autonomy and their creaturely limits, enabling and empowering them to exist, to interact, and to evolve and promising to bring them to fulfillment. It also needs to do more that I have attempted here, to offer an eschatological vision that sees suffering in the context of hope based on the resurrection. Such a theology would need to be eschatological from the ground up. It would need to offer hope not just human beings but the whole of creation.

Why Is God Doing This? Suffering, the Universe and Christian Eschatology

The South Asian tsunami of 26 December 2004 brought intense suffering to the peoples of Indonesia, Sri Lanka, India and Thailand. It left more than 221,000 dead, and many more injured. Millions more had their homes and livelihoods destroyed and were caught up in long-term trauma and grief. In Australia, as in other parts of the international community, the tsunami called forth an immediate response of compassion and generosity. It also raised theological questions: If God is a God of love, why is this happening? Why is God doing this? Newspapers responded to these questions with a number of articles from various religious leaders. In the face of such devastating loss, the answers offered seemed inadequate. Some failed to respect the pain of the victims and their families and others distorted the Christian gospel.

Scientists explained the cause of the tsunami, pointing to the dynamic movement of the thirteen tectonic plates that make up the crust of the Earth and to the earthquakes that occur when these plates collide with one other. The South Asian tsunami was the result of an earthquake near the meeting point of the Australian, Indian and Burmese plates. The Australian plate is rotating into the Indian plate creating a region of seismic activity in the Indian Ocean. It appears that what happened in December 2004 was a subduction earthquake, where one plate passes under the edge of another. The Indian plate slipped past the Burmese plate, causing the vertical displacement of water that became the destructive tsunami.

There is a close relationship between the movement of plates and the evolutionary history of life on Earth. The constantly-changing dynamic system of tectonic plates allows for the emergence of mountain ranges, rivers, rainforests and fertile plains, providing habitats that allow life to evolve in new ways. There is an inner connection between the physical processes that drive the geology of Earth and the diversity of life. The evolution of life, with its abundance and beauty, is accompanied by terrible costs to human beings and to other species. Here, as elsewhere in the natural world, the costs are built into the system. They are built into the geology and the underlying physics of a dynamic life-bearing planet.

The Issue: A Universe with Suffering Built-In

This brings into focus the specific issue of this book. The emergence of life on Earth over the last 3.8 billion years can be understood only in the context of the geological dynamics of our planet; Earth can be understood only as part of the planetary system that formed around the young Sun in the Milky Way Galaxy about 4.5 billion years ago; our galaxy can be understood only within the context of the expanding universe that began from an extremely dense and hot state fourteen billion years ago. The laws and constants that govern the universe allow it to be life-bearing, but the costs of emergence are built-in at the level of these same laws and constants.

In the intense questioning of God that followed the tsunami, my own theological instinct was to say nothing in the public discussion. It seemed a time for grief, for lament and for human solidarity. Theological comment ran the risk of trivialising the ongoing pain. In the context of a local Christian community, however, there was no choice but to say something about the religious issues that were being discussed so widely. It seemed important to ask whether it is appropriate to think of God as sending disasters to some people and as saving others from them. This, of course, is to call into question the widespread Christian assumption of an interventionist view of divine action. It seemed necessary to offer an alternative view of God working in and through the natural world. And in this natural world, tsunamis, with all their costs, are deeply connected to what brings life to the Earth and its creatures. The Christian sources do not offer any kind of adequate intellectual answer to the question that asks *why* God creates in such a way. What Christianity offers, based on the Christ-event, is a God who embraces the pain of the world and promises that all things will be healed and transformed in the power of resurrection. Christians live as people of the promise. Only in trusting in the promise do they have any kind of response to offer to suffering.

These inadequate reflections are recalled here, because implicit in them is the agenda that faces Christian theology in the light of the suffering built into the universe. The theological task is to respond, however inadequately, to the idea that so much that is beautiful and good arises by way of increasing complexity through emergent processes that involve tragic loss. The costs are evident in the 3.8 billion year history of life with its patterns of predation, death and extinction. We know, as no generation has known before us, that these costs are intrinsic to the processes that give rise to life on Earth in all its wonderful diversity.

My proposal is that while a Christian theological notion of divine action cannot offer a full explanation of suffering, it can remove common misunderstandings that spring from traditional Christian notions of divine action, and it can offer an eschatological vision that sees suffering in the context of hope based on the resurrection. Such a theology would need to be eschatological from the ground up. It would need to be in creative dialogue with sciences such as cosmology and biological evolution. It can be argued that it ought to bear some relation to key ideas that emerged from the extensive dialogue on divine action that took place in the 1990s. Robert John Russell describes the consensus that emerged from this work in notion of divine action that is not only *general* but *special*, that is *non-interventionist*, and that is not only *subjective* but also *objective*.[1] A helpful notion of divine action would need to offer some alternative to the popular view of an interventionist and arbitrary God. It would need to offer hope to not just human beings but the whole of creation.

I believe that a number of theologians might offer a 'thick' Christological, Trinitarian and eschatological re-thinking of divine action. They include Wolfhart Pannenberg, Jürgen Moltmann, and the one I have chosen to work with, Karl Rahner. Before turning to Rahner, I will attempt to clear the ground by discussing the way a Christ-centred theology might locate itself vis-à-vis scientific cosmology and the way it might see itself in relation to the limits of what it ought to say about suffering and about God.

---

1. Robert John Russell, 'Introduction', in *Quantum Mechanics: Scientific Perspectives on Divine Action*, edited by Robert John Russell, Philip Clayton, Kirk Wegter-McNelly and John Polkinghorne (Vatican City State; Berkeley, Calif: Vatican Observatory; Center for Theology and the Natural Sciences, 2001), ii–iv.

Theology's Location in Relation to Scientific Cosmology

The kind of Christian theology I have in mind is committed to certain ideas about the universe: that God creates *ex nihilo*; that God is present and engaged in every aspect of the universe in *creatio continua*; that God has purposes in creating the universe that include not only the emergence of life and of human beings but also the Christ-event and the eschatological fulfilment of all things. On the basis of its own sources, it does not possess special information about the origin or emergence of the universe. It does not compete with science, but engages with what scientific cosmology has to offer, because it sees this as the best information currently available about the way God's creative act takes effect in our world. When science puts forward a view of the universe as expanding from a compressed hot state over the last fourteen billion years, theology can dialogue with this worldview, recognising that theology done in the light of science will always have a tentative and revisable character because it is always open to further scientific developments.

Over the last few years, astronomers like Martin Rees have popularised the idea that the observable universe may be part of a much larger 'multiverse', or ensemble of universes.[2] As Stoeger, Ellis and Kirchner point out in a recent article, there are two distinct reasons why the idea of a multiverse has received increasing attention: on the one hand it has been seen by some scientists as intrinsic to the originating process that generated out own universe; on the other, it has been offered as an explanation of why our universe seems to be fine-tuned for life and consciousness.[3] I will consider these separately.

The Multi-Domain Universe

A number of research programs in early universe cosmology, such as the chaotic inflation associated with Andrei Linde, suggest that the processes that would have brought our universe into existence from a primordial quantum configuration would also have generated other universes or universe regions. I follow Stoeger, Ellis and Kirchner in

---

2. Martin Rees, *Before the Beginning: Our Universe and Others* (London: Touchstone, 1997), 177–86.
3. WR Stoeger, GFR Ellis and U Kirchner, 'Multiverses and Cosmology: Philosophical Issues', in *ArXiv: astroph/0407329*, 2.

calling this kind of situation a multi-domain universe as distinct from a multiverse in the strict sense, which refers to a collection of causally disconnected universes. How does theology relate to the idea of a multi-domain universe? In my view, Christian theology has nothing to say from its own resources about whether the universe as a whole consists simply of the observable universe or of a universe of many domains, as some cosmological models suggest. This is a question for further research in cosmology, and Christian theology can live happily with either outcome.

The Fine-Tuned Universe

The second reason for the popularity of the multiverse is that it provides a way of avoiding the theological issue raised by the fine-tuning of the universe. If any of the parameters that govern our universe, including its constants and initial conditions, were even slightly different, then life and human consciousness could not have emerged. The universe is made in such a way that it is ordered to complexity, to life and to humanity. It is a life-bearing universe. This leads to the question: Why is our universe so fine-tuned to the emergence of life? Of course, one possible answer to this question is the existence of a creator. Some scientific thinkers avoid the theological implications of fine-tuning by invoking the idea of the existence of range of diverse universes, covering all possible parameters. In this case, they argue, it is not surprising that one universe, ours, turns out to be congenial to the emergence of life.

While this argument appears in scientific texts, it is not strictly a scientific argument. Martin Rees, for example, writes in support of the multiverse proposal: 'If one does not believe in providential design, but still thinks the fine-tuning needs some explanation, there is another perspective—a highly speculative one, so I should reiterate my health warning at this stage. It is the one I much prefer, however, even though in our present state of knowledge any such preference can be no more than a hunch'.[4] Rees is rightly cautious about the lack of evidence for this form of multiverse proposal, and acknowledges that it seems in tension with 'Ockam's Razor', but says that he still prefers the idea of the multiverse to providential design. Clearly this

---

4. Martin Rees, *Our Cosmic Habitat* (London: Phoenix, 2002), 164.

is, at least in part, a *theological* argument. It is an argument based on avoiding the idea that fine-tuning could be caused by a creative providence. Of course, theological convictions have often motivated scientific research in the past and there is no reason why they should not do so in the future. But Christian theology has no need to oppose the idea of providential design. It sees the fine-tuning of the universe as expressing the will and action of the Creator. It is not inclined to embrace the multiverse concept simply in order to avoid the theological implications of fine-tuning.

Christian theology, however, does not have any special information about how God brings about this fine-tuning. There is every reason to assume that it occurs through secondary causes that are open to scientific exploration. And if a case were to be made for a multiverse on scientific grounds, then Christian theology would need to be open to this massively enlarged picture of the creation. While theology can and should reflect on the inter-relationship between fine-tuning and the emergence of life, mind and spirituality, I am not inclined to attempt to make a case for the existence of God dependent on fine-tuning. Such an argument could make sense only if the observable universe is all that there is. It is important for Christianity to keep an open mind on further scientific developments that may support the idea of a multi-domain universe and even the possibility of some form of multiverse. The biblical God is a God of boundless fecundity, endless creativity and infinite mystery. There is no theological reason to limit such a God's creative action to the observable universe.

The Limits of Theology in Relation to Suffering and to God

Theologians who are committed to thinking from the perspective of the living memory of Jesus of Nazareth, his life, death and resurrection, find that there are limits to what they can say about both suffering and God: suffering does not find any kind of full explanation in the Christian tradition, but is understood as a critical memory that calls for liberating and healing praxis and that opens in hope to a future in God is not subject to our limited human concepts but confronts us as incomprehensible and uncontrollable Mystery.

The critical memory of suffering

The theologian Edward Schillebeeckx recognises that certain kinds of suffering can be transformative. But he finds what he calls a 'barbarous excess' of suffering and evil in our history: 'There is too much *unmerited* and *senseless* suffering for us to be able to give an ethical, hermeneutical and ontological analysis of our disaster'.[5] Auschwitz cannot be rationalised. Nor, he says, can the quiet suffering of a grieving parent in one's own neighbourhood. This excess of suffering provokes protest and resistance. The appropriate human response to suffering is action that brings liberation and healing. But death sets a radical limit to all human responses and shows that far more is needed. Schillebeeckx speaks of suffering as a 'negative experience of contrast'. The human 'no' to the excess of suffering opens out in hope to a better world that can claim our 'yes'. This 'open yes' becomes the basis for healing and liberating action. And from time to time there are experiences of meaning and happiness that sustain and nourish this 'open yes'. Schillebeeckx sees this human experience of longing for liberation as finding transcendent depth in the various religious traditions. He understands Christians as finding in Jesus the human face of this transcendence and the one in whom the yearning of humanity becomes a well-founded hope.[6]

Christianity contains both a challenge to respond to suffering and a vision of a God who is with creation in its travail and who promises to bring it to its transfigured fulfilment (Rom 8:19–22). The cross of Jesus stands as an abiding challenge to complacency before the suffering of others and to ideological justification of the misery of the poor. It brings the suffering of the poor to the centre of Christian faith. The resurrection offers a dynamic vision of hope for the suffering of the world, but it does not dull the memory of the suffering ones. They are always present, forever imaged in the wounds of the risen one.

Johannes Metz speaks of the *memoria passionis* as 'the dangerous memory of freedom in the social systems of our technological civilization'.[7] This dangerous and critical memory provides an alter-

---

5. Edward Schillebeeckx, *Christ: The Christian Experience in the Modern World* (London: SCM, 1980), 725.
6. Schillebeeckx, *Church*, 6.
7. Johann Baptist Metz, *Faith in History and Society: Towards a Practical Fundamental Theology* (London: Burns and Oates, 1980), 109.

native way of seeing. It breaks through ideological commitments. It can lead to solidarity, to alternative lifestyles and to personal and political action. The Christian gospel does not explain suffering, but presents it as a constant challenge to liberating praxis.

The critical memory of the shattering otherness of God

In one of his essays, David Tracy speaks of the 'shattering otherness' of God.[8] The Christian theological and mystical traditions carry a sense of God's otherness that is far more radical, far more 'shattering' than is assumed in everyday discourse both inside and outside the church. The Greek patristic theologians developed the idea of an apophatic or negative theology, based upon the infinite distance between God and any human concept of God. The great medieval theologians acknowledged the analogical nature of all language about God and carefully incorporated a negative moment in all their positive affirmations. The Fourth Lateran Council (1215) declared something that theology takes as foundational: 'No similarity can be said to hold between Creator and creature which does not imply a greater dissimilarity between the two.' The fourteenth century English mystical classic speaks of meeting God in the 'Cloud of Unknowing'. John of the Cross's beautiful poem images the union of love with the Beloved as a 'Dark Night'. The radical incomprehensibility of God is the beginning point and end of all theology. What we can comprehend is not God. All of our concepts and all of our words come from our everyday experiences of things in this world. They cannot be used of God in any univocal way. We speak truly of God only in stumbling ways and only within the limits of analogies and metaphors from everyday experience.

As Rahner has often pointed out, God is *abiding* mystery to us. God is precisely what we cannot comprehend. While Christians believe that this uncontrollable and incomprehensible mystery has come close to us and is revealed to us in Jesus of Nazareth and in the outpouring of the Holy Spirit, this does not do away with the mystery.[9] In Christ and the Spirit God is revealed an unthinkable love,

---

8. David Tracy, 'The Hidden God: The Divine Other of Liberation', in *Cross Currents* 46/1 (1996): 5–16.
9. Karl Rahner, *Foundations of Christian Faith: An Introduction to the Idea of Christianity* (New York: Seabury Press, 1978), 44–89.

love beyond all comprehension, a love that is closer to us than we are to ourselves. And in the light of this revelation, God is understood as a dynamic Trinitarian Communion, as shared life in which otherness is embraced. But the otherness of this Mystery is not something theology can comprehend or control.

In this section, I have pointing to what might be seen as limits or parameters for a theology based on the Christ-event that attempts to respond to the issue of suffering. From within its own tradition, such a theology has no resources to explain suffering. It is called to memory, solidarity, liberating practice and hope. And its deepest tradition keeps it in full recognition of God's shattering otherness. God is a God before whom, like Job, we finally fall silent. These two parameters suggest that theology on its own resources will never be able to offer a full rational explanation for suffering in relationship to God, but this is not to argue that nothing can be said. Important things can be said within these parameters, and one of them concerns the way theology and the church understand and image God acting in the world.

Rahner's Theology of Divine Action

With these limits in mind, I will explore Rahner's concept of divine action, asking whether it has anything to offer at both the pastoral level and the level of the theology-science dialogue, in response to the suffering that is built into creation. Much of Rahner's work is found in short, often topical, papers in the twenty-three volumes of his *Theological Investigations*. While he nowhere offers an extended treatment of divine action as such, I will attempt to show that he has a theology of divine action, that this forms a systematic whole, and that it has something to offer in reflection on the suffering that is built-in to the universe. I will gather his work into a short synthesis, built up around six characteristics of his view of divine action, and will argue that the first two, God's self-bestowal and creation's self-transcendence, form the twin systematic foundations for the rest.

God's self-bestowal

According to Rahner, the central insight of Christian revelation is that *God gives God's self to us* in the Word made flesh and in the Spirit poured out in grace. The self-giving of God defines every aspect of

God's action. Because of this, the story of the universe, and everything that science can tell us about its long history, is part of a *larger* story, the story of divine self-bestowal. The creation of the universe is an element in the radical decision of God to give God's self in love to that which in not divine.[10] This means that the story of salvation is the real ground of the history of nature, and not simply something unfolding against the background of nature.[11] The story of the universe exists *within* a larger vision of the divine purpose.

God creates in order to give God's self to creation as its final eschatological fulfilment. This fulfilment will be the salvation not only of human beings but also of the whole creation. God wills to bestow God's very self in love, and creation comes to be as the addressee of this self-bestowal. Creation, incarnation and final fulfilment are united in one great act of divine self-communication. The incarnation is not thought of as add-ons to creation. It is not an afterthought. It is not a corrective for a creation that went wrong. It does not come about simply as a remedy for sin, although it is this. With the Franciscan school of theology, exemplified in Duns Scotus (1266–1308), Rahner holds that God freely choses, from the beginning, to create a world in which the Word would be made flesh and the Spirit poured out.[12] The Christ-event is the irreversible beginning of God's self-giving to creation that will find its fulfilment only when the whole of creation is transformed in Christ.

Rahner insists that what is most specific to the Christian view of God is the idea of a God who bestows God's very self to creation.[13] This is a God who creates creatures that are *capax infiniti*, who without being consumed in the fire of divinity, are able to receive God's life as their own fulfilment. Christianity's insistence, against pantheism, on the difference between God and the world does not mean

---

10. Rahner, 'Christology in the Setting', in *Theological Investigations* 5, 219. I am building here on an article that forthcoming in *Philosophy and Theology*, 'Resurrection of the Body and Transformation of the Universe in the Theology of Karl Rahner'.
11. Karl Rahner, 'Resurrection: D Theology', in *Encyclopedia of Theology: A Concise Sacramentum Mundi* (London: Burns and Oats, 1975), 1442.
12. This means that creation and incarnation are 'two moments and two phases of the *one* process of God's self-giving and self-expression, although it is an intrinsically differentiated process'. *Foundations of Christian Faith*, 197.
13. Rahner, 'The Specific Character of the Christian Concept of God', in *Theological Investigations* 21, 185–95.

that there is a distance between God and the creature. Rather, God in God's being *is* this difference.[14] What is truly Christian is a theology, which while maintaining the radical distinction between God and the world, understands God's self-giving in such a way that God is the very core of the world's reality and the world is truly the fate of God. The history of the universe attains its ultimate meaning from the fact that this history is directed to the self-bestowal of God, which will be the final fulfilment not just of human beings but the whole universe in God, and this future in not only promised but already begun in the life, death and resurrection of Jesus Christ.[15]

How is God's creative presence to creatures to be understood? Rahner rejects the notion that the divine immanence can be understood simply on the model of efficient causality. This model is based on the relationship between finite beings that are distinct from one another prior to the causal relationship. This is an inadequate model for a God who creates in a process of self-bestowal. Rahner finds a better model in the theology of grace, and its final fulfilment in glory. This cannot be understood simply as efficient causality whereby one finite entity achieves an effect in another. It is better understood as a kind of formal causality, by which the indwelling God, while remaining radically transcendent, really determines a creature's being. In formal causality a principle of being becomes a constitutive element in another being by communicating itself to the other.[16] God communicates God's self to us and we are transformed in God. In grace, and in glory, God freely gives God's self to us as our fulfilment and we are divinised. Because God is God and not a created cause, neither divine transcendence nor creaturely freedom is compromised.

---

14. 'God is not merely the one who as creator establishes a world distant from himself as something different, but rather he is the one who gives himself away to this world and who has his own fate in and with this world. God is not only himself the giver, but he is also the gift.' Rahner, 'The Specific Character of the Christian Concept of God', 191. See also his 'Christology in the Setting of Modern Man's Understanding of Himself and of his World', in *Theological Investigations* 11, 224.
15. Rahner, 'Book of God—Book of Human Beings', in *Theological Investigations*, 22, 223.
16. Rahner, *Foundations of Christian Faith*, 121. In some earlier works, Rahner calls this *quasi*-formal causality, with the *quasi* indicating the uniqueness of this kind of formal causality, in which both divine transcendence and creaturely integrity are fully maintained.

On the basis that creation is one, and that the one history of the *whole* creation is directed to divine self-bestowal, Rahner proposes that the divine indwelling characteristic of grace is an appropriate analogy for the fundamental relationship that God has with the whole universe and all its creatures.[17] This means that Rahner can say that the creative immanence of God to the world is of such a kind that 'the reality of God himself is imparted to the world as its supreme specification.'[18] Creation is intrinsically directed towards self-bestowal. It is not simply that God creates something other over against God's self, but that God freely communicates God's own reality to the other. The universe emerges in the process of God's self-bestowal. God is always immanent to the world in self-giving love. Rahner sees this self-bestowal of God, as the absolutely transcendent, as 'the most immanent factor in the creature.'[19] This concept of creation is eschatological from the ground up.

Creation's self-transcendence

The concept of divine self-bestowal looks at creation from the side of God, from the perspective of the divine purposes. A second fundamental concept looks at this same divine action from a creaturely perspective. It points to the effect of God's immanent presence: *creation has the capacity for self-transcendence.* This concept is worked out in Rahner's anthropology[20] and in his evolutionary Christology,[21] but it functions throughout many aspects of his work. Along with the concept of divine self-bestowal, it provides a way of grasping the radical unity of God's one and undivided act, an act that involves creation, redemption and final fulfilment.

---

17. What is true of grace is always valid 'in an analogous way for the relationship between God's absolute being and being which originates from him.' Karl Rahner, 'Natural Science and Christian Faith', in *Theological Investigations* 21, 36.
18. Rahner, 'Christology in the Setting', 225.
19. Karl Rahner, 'Immanent and Transcendent Consummation', in *Theological Investigations* 10, 273–89, 281.
20. Karl Rahner, *Hominisation: The Evolutionary Origin of Man as a Theological Problem* (London: Burns & Oates, 1965), 98–101.
21. Karl Rahner, 'Christology within an Evolutionary View', in *Theological Investigations* 5, 157–92; *Foundations of Christian Faith*, 178–203.

The theological tradition has understood continuous creation as God sustaining creatures in being (*conservatio*) and enabling them to act (*concursus*). Rahner transforms this into a theology of becoming, a theology of self-transcendence. In his evolutionary Christology, he begins from the fundamental *unity* he finds in creation. All of creation is united in its one origin in God, in its self-realisation as one united world, and in its one future in God. In this context, he reflects on the transitions to the *new* in the history of the universe, particularly when matter becomes life, and when life becomes self-conscious spirit. The emergence of the new requires explanation, not only at the level of science, but also at the level of theology, which needs to understand God's creative act as enabling the universe to become. Rahner argues for a theology of the active self-transcendence of creation, by which he means a dynamism that is truly intrinsic to creation, but which occurs through the creative power of the immanent God. He sees it as the constant 'pressure' of the divine being that enables creation to become more than it is in itself.[22] This 'pressure' does not belong to the essence of the finite being and it cannot be discerned by the natural sciences. It is understood as the interior, dynamic relationship of all things in the evolving universe to their Creator.

The material universe transcends itself in the emergence of life, and life transcends itself in the human. In human beings, the universe becomes open to self-consciousness, freedom and a truly personal response to God in grace. Within this context, Rahner sees the Christ-event as the definitive self-transcendence of the created universe into God.[23] Jesus in his humanity is a part of evolutionary history, a part that is radically open to the divine bestowal. If the Christ-event is considered from below, it can be seen as the self-transcendence of the evolving universe into God. If it is considered from above, it can be seen as God's irreversible self-bestowal to creation. In this one person, we find the irreversible self-communication of God to creatures and the definitive human acceptance of this communication. This is what makes Jesus the saviour.[24]

---

22. Karl Rahner, 'Natural Science and Christian Faith', in *Theological Investigations* 21, 16–55, 37.
23. In Jesus, we find the 'initial beginning and definitive triumph of the movement of the world's self-transcendence into absolute closeness to the mystery of God'. Rahner, *Foundations of Christian Faith*, 181.
24. Rahner, *Foundations of Christian Faith*, 193.

In one of his essays, Rahner writes of the *two* ways in which the theology of God's immanence needs to be developed for our time. What he points to are the two aspects of divine action discussed in these first two sections, God's self-bestowal and creation's self-transcendence.[25] I think it can be concluded that, for Rahner, these are *two consistent and fundamental characteristics of divine action*. These two aspects of the one divine action are mutually inter-related: It is God present in self-bestowal who enables creaturely self-transcendence. Divine self-bestowal and creaturely self-transcendence characterise not only creation, grace and incarnation, but also the final consummation of all things in Christ.

Enabling creaturely autonomy to flourish

Rahner sees creation as an absolutely unique relationship. It is not an extrapolation from, or an intensification of, causal or functional relationships between things in the world.[26] Creation is a relationship in which the world is always totally from God and always dependent on God. In this relationship, God establishes the creature and its genuine *difference* from God's self. The creature has its own otherness, integrity and autonomy.

A fundamental principle in Rahner's theology of the God-world relation, one that he often repeats, is expressed in the axiom: *The radical dependence and the genuine reality of the existent coming from God vary in direct and not in inverse proportion.*[27] In ordinary experiences of causality, the more an entity depends upon something else, the less it possesses its own reality and autonomy. There is an *inverse* relationship between dependence and autonomy. But the relationship of creation is radically different. It is an incomparable relationship, one that does not suppose a pre-existing other, but creates the other as other, constantly maintaining it as creation while setting it free in its own autonomy. In this relationship, dependence on God and creaturely freedom and autonomy exist in *direct* relationship to one another.

This claim is finally grounded for Rahner in the human experience of grace. The person who has experienced freedom and responsibility in the depth of their being, and has known this before God and

---

25. Rahner, 'Christology in the Setting', 223–6.
26. Rahner, *Foundations of Christian Faith*, 77.
27. Rahner, *Foundations of Christian Faith*, 79.

as grounded in God, is in a position to understand something of this relationship between God and creature. In this kind of experience, a created person experiences his or her own freedom as a reality. It is experienced as 'a freedom coming from God and a freedom for God'.[28] The more we are grounded in God, the more free we are. This leads to Rahner's conviction that, in relation to God, 'radical dependence grounds autonomy'.[29] This provides a glimpse of the nature of all genuine creaturely autonomy vis-à-vis the Creator. Creaturely integrity is not diminished because of the creature's existence is radically dependent on God, but flourishes precisely in this dependence.

It is clear, in this view, that divine action is understood as entirely compatible with creaturely integrity. It is important to note, however, that one who holds this view may take one of two possible further positions: either that God acts in creation with absolutely unlimited power or that God's power is a power-in-love that waits upon human freedom and the integrity of natural processes. Rahner's view of the compatibility between divine action and creaturely autonomy is best seen in conjunction with a view of divine power as power-in-love. Walter Kasper, among others, makes this view of divine power explicit. He points out that the cross and resurrection of Jesus reveal that divine omnipotence is the transcendent power to give oneself in love. It is radically power-in-love. It is not that God strips God's self of power to reveal God's love on the cross: 'On the contrary, it requires omnipotence to be able to surrender oneself and give oneself away'.[30] The cross and resurrection *redefine* divine power. It is redefined as the infinite capacity for self-giving love, and for enabling the integrity of the other.

It has always been understood that God can only act in accordance with the divine nature. This nature is revealed in the Christ-event as radical love. The divine nature is revealed as transcendently vulnerable in love. The God revealed on the cross is a God whose nature it is to respect the integrity of creatures, to wait on them patiently, to work through them and to bring them to fulfilment. The power of God revealed in the cross and resurrection is a *cruciform* power, not the despotic power of a tyrant. This means that while God's creative and

---

28. Rahner, *Foundations of Christian Faith*, 79.
29. Rahner, *Foundations of Christian Faith*, 79.
30. Walter Kasper, *The God of Jesus Christ* (London: SCM Press, 1983), 195.

redeeming action is compatible with human and creaturely integrity, and enables them to flourish; there may be times when *God's nature*, as lovingly respectful of both human freedom and the finite limits of creation, sets limits on what God can do at any one stage in the history of the universe. The love that defines the divine nature is a love that lives with the process, a love that accompanies creation, sometimes suffering with it, promising healing and liberation.

Rahner sees the resurrection of Jesus as *ontologically* the beginning of the divinisation of the universe.[31] In it, the final destiny of the world is decided and already begun. This is the most powerful thing imaginable. But it will occur only in and through all the creativity and all the finitude, all the set-backs and all the failures of creaturely processes. Nothing will undo the divine promise. But this promise will be realised in and through God working patiently and lovingly with human beings and with the whole creation and bringing it through the process to its divinising fulfilment.

Immanent rather than interventionist

While Rahner's early work does not explicitly address the issue of whether God acts in an interventionist way, his theology is based from the beginning on the idea of a God who acts from *within* creation in a way that cannot be thought of as interventionist. I will mention three examples. First, he sees *revelation* as occurring universally as human beings experience the always present mystery of God in grace and struggle to articulate this experience explicitly in concepts, words and symbols. All of this culminates in Christ. A second example is in his *Christology*, where Jesus is seen as the self-transcendence of creation into God and as God's irrevocable self-giving to creation. In his *anthropology*, Rahner works with the Roman Catholic teaching of the immediate creation of the human soul, and interprets this in terms of God's one act of continuous creation that, by means of a process of self-transcendence from within creation, enables the emergence of unique and diverse spiritual beings made in the image of God. In

---

31. The resurrection is 'the embryonically final beginning of the glorification and divinization of the whole of reality'. Karl Rahner, 'Dogmatic Questions on Easter', in *Theological Investigations* 4 (London/New York: Darton, Longman and Todd/Seabury Press, 1974), 121–33, 129.

each case the self-bestowal of God and the self-transcendence of the creature are not interventions from without, but the deepest meaning of God's one creative and redeeming act.

Rahner discusses the issue of divine 'intervention' briefly in his *Foundations of Christian Faith*, first published in German in 1976. He argues that if we are to experience God in the world, then it cannot be simply as one element in the world, but as the ground of the world. If we are to find God in the openness to mystery that occurs in our experience of created realities, God must be 'embedded' in this world to begin with.[32] What is sometimes seen as a special 'intervention' of God is to be understood as the historical expression of God's self-communicating presence that it intrinsic to the world. Every so-called 'intervention', although it is free and unpredictable, is a becoming concrete and historical of that one intervention by which God has embedded God's self in the world from the beginning as its 'self-communicating ground'.[33] This means, of course, that God never becomes a cause amongst other causes within the world. God acts from within creation in the form of primary causality. This primary causality finds expression in, and is mediated through, a range of secondary, created causes.

Rahner holds for *special* acts of God, seeing them as 'objectifications' of God's one self-bestowing action. This occurs when a created reality mediates and expresses the immanent presence and love of God. A created reality has the role of giving expression to the divine action. Because this role really does belong to the created events themselves, Rahner is among those who speak of *objective*, special divine action. He holds that such events are capable of being recognised as special only within the context of subjective experience of grace.[34]

This means that God's one act of self-bestowing love (primary causality), an act that embraces both creation and salvation, can find expression in a variety of created, secondary causes, and these can be seen as objective and special divine acts. Included amongst these would be the graced experience of meeting God in prayer, the Jewish experience of knowing and responding to God in the events of Exodus and Covenant and the Christian experience of meeting God in

---

32. Rahner, *Foundations of Christian Faith*, 87.
33. Rahner, *Foundations of Christian Faith*, 87.
34. Rahner, *Foundations of Christian Faith*, 88.

the created humanity of Jesus of Nazareth. In such divine acts, the one self-bestowing act of God finds objective expression in and through a range of created secondary causes. These include words, persons and events. To those with eyes to see, these become symbolic mediations of the divine. In this way, Christians understand Jesus of Nazareth as the radical symbol, or sacrament, of God. They see him as the radical expression of, and mediation of, the divine self-bestowal.

Rahner offers a 'modest' example of a special divine act. A person has a 'good idea' that proves effective and is experienced as a gift from God. Can this be understood as genuinely inspired by God? There may well be a natural explanation for the good idea, in psychological or neurological terms. But this does not mean that it cannot be seen as an act of God—in the sense that in this experience one encounters the God who is present in every dimension of creation and is really mediated in this event of a good idea. When a good idea is experienced subjectively by one who sees the event as the objectification and place of encounter with the ground of all reality, it can be understood as willed by God, as God-given and hence inspired. It becomes, in Rahner's view, a genuine experience of God's special providence.

In a later (1980) book, co-authored with Karl-Heinz Weger, a book that sets out to deal honestly with difficult questions of the day, Rahner makes his most developed and explicit comments on interventionist and non-interventionist approaches to divine action. He speaks of a 'fundamental change' in the move away from an interventionist view of God.[35] He insists that, even for traditional theology, God was not one object amongst others in the world, nor a being outside the world who intervenes from time to time, but the immediately present, immanent, all-embracing and ultimate ground of being. But he acknowledges that this traditional theology also envisaged, as a matter of course, interventions of God that could be located at certain points of space and time. The traditional idea of the history of salvation was 'based mainly on the model of interventions by God'. This interventionist model coexisted with a more universal view of God as the 'deepest energy of the world'.[36] The universal and interventionist models of divine action were never completely reconciled in Christian theology.

---

35. Rahner and Weger, *Our Christian Faith*, 57.
36. Rahner and Weger, *Our Christian Faith*, 77.

Rahner does not condemn the older approach, because he too holds for a genuine history of salvation and for a particular and special revelation, above all in Jesus Christ. But he argues for the emergence of a 'universalist basic model in which God in his free grace, from the very beginning and always and everywhere, has communicated himself to his creation as its innermost energy and works in the world from the inside out'.[37] He wants to show is that it is possible 'with all due caution and modesty, to do without a particularist model of external intervention by God into his world at particular points of space and time, without having to interpret Christianity "naturalistically"'.[38]

Within this context, Rahner sees Jesus as the one who makes God's deepest promise historically accessible and irreversible. This promise is already the fundamental energy at work in all things in the universe, and because of this Rahner believes that it is possible to understand the event of Jesus without the image of intervention.[39] It is the resurrection of Jesus that gives expression to this promise. The resurrection is an event of revelation, but not one coming from 'outside'.[40] This important claim is simply stated by Rahner. In my view, it is one that needs further development in contemporary theology.

The hiddenness of the future

Rahner's insistence on the promise of the resurrection is accompanied by an insistence that we cannot picture its content. To think we might picture our final and definitive state 'would be still more absurd than to suppose that the caterpillar could imagine what it would be like

---

37. Rahner and Weger, *Our Christian Faith*, 78–9.
38. Rahner and Weger, *Our Christian Faith*, 84.
39. 'The event of God's promise of himself in Jesus makes that deepest promise by God of himself to the world historically accessible and irreversible. It is always and everywhere the fundamental energy and force of the world and its history. It is therefore perfectly possible to understand the event of Jesus without the aid of images of an intervention in the world from outside. In doing without such an image, however, we must let history really be history and clearly realise that this deepest energy and power of the world and its history is God in his sovereign freedom, who, by his free promise of himself, has made himself this deepest energy and force of the world.' Rahner and Weger, *Our Christian Faith*, 103–4.
40. Rahner and Weger, *Our Christian Faith*, 111.

to be a butterfly'.⁴¹ He takes up this theme in a systematic way in his essay on the hermeneutics of eschatological statements.⁴² At the centre of his approach to the interpretation of the biblical and traditional depictions of the future, as, for example the great wedding feast, or Christ judging between sheep and goats, is the thesis that *the future of the world in God remains radically hidden to us.*

This future is the coming of the incomprehensible God. It is announced and revealed in Christ, but it is revealed only as 'the dawn and the approach of mystery as such'.⁴³ This conviction provides Rahner with a basis for distinguishing between genuine interpretations and false interpretations of eschatological predictions and images. A genuine interpretation will preserve the mystery, while a false one will present the future as if it were the literal report of a spectator. This criterion is based on Rahner's conviction that the future is known as an inner moment of the present. Genuine knowledge of the future in God is knowledge of the eschatological present. It is a projection based on what is already experienced of God. The future will be the fulfilment of the salvation already given in God's self-communication through grace, in the Spirit, and through Jesus Christ, the Word made flesh.

What we encounter in the experience of grace is the God whom Rahner calls *absolute future*. He distinguishes *absolute* future from all *this-worldly* futures.⁴⁴ The absolute future is God's self-bestowal: it is the consummation of creation and redemption already promised and initiated in the life, death and resurrection of Jesus. By contrast, all 'this-worldly' futures occur in the ordinary dimensions of time and space as particular events or states of this world. Each of them, by definition, remains open to a further future. The Christian claim is that the evolution of the universe will end, not in emptiness, but in the divine self-bestowal. This absolute future is already a constitu-

---

41. Karl Rahner, 'Hidden Victory', *Theological Investigations* 7, 151–8, 156.
42. Rahner, 'The Hermeneutics of Eschatological Assertions', in *Theological Investigations* 4, 323–46. He incorporates much of this into his *Foundations of Christian Faith*, 431–7.
43. Rahner, 'The Hermeneutics of Eschatological Assertions', 330.
44. Karl Rahner, 'Marxist Utopia and the Christian Future of Man', in *Theological Investigations* 6, 59–88; 'A Fragmentary Aspect of a Theological Evaluation of the Concept of the Future', in *Theological Investigations* 10, 235–42, 235–41; 'The Question of the Future', in *Theological Investigations* 12, 181–201.

tive element of the unfolding of the universe. It has already found irrevocable expression and been made visible in Jesus Christ. His resurrection is the promise and the beginning of the absolute future, the transformation of all things in Christ. Absolute future is another name for God. It not only comes towards us but is also the sustaining ground of the movement towards the future.[45]

God, then, is known not as one object among others that we might plan for the future, but as the ground of this whole projection towards the future. This absolute future has definitively promised itself to us in Jesus Christ.[46] The absolute future comes to each person in grace. It is offered to each and its acceptance is the ultimate task for each. The content of Christian preaching consists of the question of the absolute future and, properly speaking, *of nothing else*.[47] Because of this, it is essential to the church and a fundamental task of theology to act as the guardian of the '*docta ignorantia future*'.[48] Rahner uses the language of learned ignorance, associated with Nicholas of Cusa (1401–64), to point to theology's critical role of resisting closure with regard to the future. Keeping open the question of the future is theology's most basic task. Rahner holds that even in final blessedness, God will remain the eternal mystery to which human beings commit themselves in the ecstasy of love. Christianity in its essence is openness to the question of the absolute future.

New creation: self-transcendence of the history of this universe

What is the relationship between the coming of God as our absolute future and the world that we attempt to construct? Rahner's response is in terms of his fundamental principles of divine self-bestowal and creaturely self-transcendence.[49] The coming Reign of God will not simply be the outcome of the history planned and accomplished by humans. Nor will it simply come upon us from outside. It will be the deed of God. It will be the self-bestowal of God. But it will also be the *self*-transcendence of history.

---

45. Rahner, 'Marxist Utopia and the Christian Future of Man', 62.
46. Rahner, 'The Question of the Future', 190.
47. Rahner, 'The Question of the Future', 188–9.
48. Rahner, 'The Question of the Future', 181, 198.
49. Karl Rahner, 'The Theological Problems Entailed', in *Theological Investigations* 10, 260–72.

Rahner argues that there is a dialectical tension between the two statements that *history will endure* and that *history will be radically transformed*. This tension maintains an openness to the future while still giving a radical importance to the present. He makes the strong claim that 'history itself constructs its own final and definitive state'. What endures, he says, is the *work* of love, as it is expressed in the concrete in human history. It is not merely some distillation of our works of love but our history itself that passes into its definitive consummation in God.[50] History is embraced by God in the Christ-event as having eternal meaning. Human freedom and the moral character of our actions have final and definitive significance because they are taken up into God and transformed in Christ.[51]

This line of thought is related to the idea articulated more recently by John Polkinghorne,[52] and built upon by Robert John Russell,[53] that new creation will come from the old (*ex vetere*), in both *continuity* and *discontinuity* with it. Rahner embraces these positions in his theology of the self-transcendence of the history of the universe in new creation. His thought moves in the same direction when he asks, in another article, whether final consummation will come from within creation or from beyond: Will our final consummation be immanent or transcendent?[54] Again, Rahner insists, this consummation *is* the self-bestowal of God. And this self-bestowal is not only our fulfilment, but also *the principle of the movement* towards this fulfilment. The present is sustained by the future. It is the immanent God who constitutes this future and enables the self-transcendence of the crea-

---

50. Rahner, 'The Theological Problems Entailed', 270.
51. Rahner, 'The Theological Problems Entailed', 271.
52. Polkinghorne, 'Eschatology: Some Questions', in *The Ends of the World and the Ends of God: Science and Theology on Eschatology*, edited by John Polkinghorne and Michael Welker (Harrisberg, Pennsylvania, 2000), 29–41, 38–41; 'Eschatological Credibility', in *Resurrection: Theological and Scientific Assessments*, edited by Ted Peters, Robert John Russell and Michael Welker (Grand Rapids: Eerdmans, 2002), 44–55; *The Faith of a Physicist: Reflections of a Bottom-up Thinker* (Minneapolis: Fortress, 1994), 162–70.
53. Russell, 'Eschatology and Physical Cosmology', in *The Far Future Universe: Eschatology from a Cosmic Perspective*, edited by George FR Ellis (Philadelphia: Templeton, 2002), 266–315, 283; 'Bodily Resurrection', in *Resurrection: Theological and Scientific Assessments*, Peters, Russell and Welker, 3–30, 14–28.
54. Rahner, 'Immanent and Transcendent Consummation', 273–89.

ture into this future. This means that our final consummation is *both* immanent and transcendent.

What of the consummation of the universe as a whole? As always, Rahner insists that matter and spirit constitute a unity. If one were to consider matter as such, in the abstract, it would never reach its consummation. But the material world has always been sustained by the creative impulse of self-transcendence by which it tends towards the spirit. This impetus is nothing other than the impetus of the divine self-bestowal. The incarnation of the Word is present in this creative impulse from the beginning. The material world is not something to be cast aside as a transitory stage in the journey of the spirit. The material world itself is to be transformed in Christ. From the beginning, this movement of the universe towards consummation has been one of self-bestowing love Because this self-bestowal in love is the most immanent element in every creature, Rahner concludes: 'It is not mere pious lyricism when Dante regards even the sun and the other planets as being moved by that love which is God himself as he who bestows himself'.[55]

Conclusion: Suffering Built-In to the Universe in the Light of Christ

I have been proposing that one partial response to the suffering that is built into our life-bearing universe can be found in a theology of divine action based upon the Christ event. At the centre of this theology is the Christian claim that the resurrection of Jesus Christ is the promise and the beginning of the final healing and divinisation of the whole of creation. How is this theology of divine action related to the loss, suffering and grief caused by the South Asian tsunami? What does it have to say in the light of the natural evil that is built into the universe from its origin? What it offers is an account of a God whose nature is to love and respect the natural world in its emergence and in its integrity, who does not over-rule the natural world, but works in and through its processes bringing all things finally to healing and fulfilment in God's self.

Some key characteristics of this theology of divine action can be summed up in the following points:

---

55. Rahner, 'Immanent and Transcendent Consummation', 289.

1. *It is an act of self-bestowing love, that reaches its culmination only when all things are taken up, healed and divinised in the Trinitarian life of God.*
2. *It takes effect in creation's God-given capacity for self-transcendence.*
3. *It is immanent rather than interventionist. It is better understood as one, differentiated, act rather than many discrete acts.*
4. *This one act (primary causality) embraces both creation and salvation, and finds expression in a variety of created persons, word and events, that can be seen as objective and special divine acts.*
5. *It is compatible with creaturely autonomy and enables it to flourish.*
6. *It is a power-in-love, a love that waits with infinite patience on human freedom and on creaturely integrity in achieving the divine saving purposes.*
7. *This view of divine action offers a partial response to the issue of natural evil. It is understood in the context of a God who acts in fidelity to the divine nature, as self-bestowing love; who is present to each creature, embracing each in love, delighting in each and suffering with each; who is radically respectful of both human freedom and the integrity of natural processes; who waits on the self-transcendence of creaturely processes; who will bring each creature, in a way that is appropriate to each, to redemption and fulfilment in the divine Communion.*

This approach raises at least three fundamental questions that cannot be addressed here. First, how precisely can resurrection be thought of in non-interventionist terms? This question clearly sets an important agenda for further theological work. Second, how can Christian eschatological hope be reconciled with cosmology's bleak predictions about the future of the universe? This is an issue facing all Christian eschatologies, one that has been taken up directly by Bob Russell in recent work.[56] Third, how do we go beyond Rahner's thought about the material universe being transformed in Christ to think about the eschatological fulfilment of non-human biological creatures? Does God really care about every sparrow that falls to the ground? Else-

---

56. Russell, 'Bodily Resurrection', 3–30; 'Eschatology and Physical Cosmology', 66–315.

where, I have attempted some response to this question,[57] arguing that we can think of the Spirit of God not only accompanying every sparrow with love in its life and its death, delighting in it and suffering with it, but also as bringing it to a redemptive fulfilment in the Trinitarian life of God.

In my view, this concept of divine action is one partial but important response, on the basis of the Christian sources, to the suffering built-in to the universe. It has something to say at both the level of the science-theology dialogue of this volume and at a pastoral level. At the level of the science-theology dialogue, the theology of divine action developed here is in creative dialogue with the science-religion discussion of divine action in the nineties, where divine action is understood as both general and special, as non-interventionist, and as not only subjective but also objective. It adds to the discussion a dynamic notion of God's creative act as eschatological self-bestowal and as working in and through creaturely self-transcendence.

This approach offers a further contribution to the general discussion with the argument that God's omnipotence is redefined by the cross and resurrection: divine omnipotence is understood not as the capacity to do absolutely anything, but as the divine capacity to act in fidelity to the divine nature. This nature is one that lovingly respects and waits on the integrity of human freedom and the autonomy of nature and will bring all to fulfilment in and through the process. This view of divine action offers a thoroughly eschatological theology in the notion of divine bestowal that works in and through every aspect of creation, grace, incarnation and final fulfilment. It involves a promise not just to human beings but to the whole of creation as one creation. All will be taken up into God and transformed in Christ. All will be divinised.

At a pastoral level, this theology of divine action provides a viable alternative to an interventionist God who arbitrarily brings suffering to some and healing to others. It sees God as working in and through natural processes in a way that waits upon and fully respects the integrity of the processes and the freedom of human beings. It sees God as lovingly accompanying each creature in its life and its death; it sees the cross as revealing a God who enters into the pain of the world

---

57. 'Every Sparrow that Falls to the Ground: The Cost of Evolution and the Christ-Event', in this volume

and suffers with suffering creation; it sees the resurrection as a promise that creaturely suffering and death will be redeemed and healed as each creature finds its meaning and fulfilment in God's self-bestowing love. In this kind of theology, standing as it does in the Christian tradition, what is argued for is the plausibility of holding that while we do not fully understand why suffering is built into the universe, we can still entrust ourselves, our universe and all its creatures in faith, hope and in love, to the absolute mystery of self-bestowing love.

Miracles and the Laws of Nature

Evolutionary biology points to the way competition, predation, death and extinction are built into the 3.8 billion year history of life. This intensifies the old problem of how we think about God and God's action in the context of suffering and loss. One aspect of this discussion is that of miracles. Does God sometimes overturn or bypass the laws of nature? If so, then why not more often? The Christian tradition of miracles can seem to suggest that God occasionally and arbitrarily intervenes to save people while allowing others to perish.

In this article, I will ask how the Christian tradition of miracles is to be understood: Does it mean that God is to be thought of as miraculously intervening in the natural world to preserve some from tsunamis while allowing others to suffer them? Or are we to think of God, even the God who works miracles, as respecting and working consistently in and through the processes of the natural world? Much of the pastoral practice of the church reinforces the idea of a God who can and does intervene in an occasional way to overturn nature. I believe that an alternative theology is needed, and will suggest an approach to a theology of miracles that does not involve an interventionist view of God.

With Johann Baptist Metz I believe that the miracles that are crucial to the Christian tradition are those connected with the coming of revelation in Jesus Christ.[1] I will begin with a brief exploration of miracles in the life of Jesus, using the historical work of John Meier. Then I will turn to the classical treatment of miracles in the work of

---

1. Johann Baptist Metz, 'Miracle', in *Encyclopedia of Theology: A Concise Sacramentum Mundi*, edited by Karl Rahner (London: Burns & Oates, 1975), 962.

Aquinas. This will lead into a discussion of the meaning of the laws of nature, taking up ideas developed by William Stoeger. Finally, in dialogue with the thought of Karl Rahner, I will suggest a view of divine action that makes room for the miraculous but without the idea of occasional intervention.

The Miracles of Jesus

It is obvious from any kind of reading of the Gospels that the evangelists see Jesus as a wonder worker. Alan Richardson has pointed out that in Mark's Gospel, for example, 209 verses out of a total of 666 deal directly or indirectly with miracles.[2] This fact has not deterred some of those involved in the various quests for the historical Jesus from avoiding or minimizing the miracles. A counter to this is offered in the work of John P Meier. He devotes 529 closely argued pages of his second volume of *A Marginal View* to Jesus' miracles.[3] I find Meier a helpful guide to the historicity of the miracles, and will focus on a key insights that are helpful for my purposes on the general question of Jesus as a miracle worker, followed by brief comments on the healing of Bartimaeus, the raising of Lazarus and the walking on the water.

Before considering particular miracle stories, Meier addresses the global question: Did Jesus perform extraordinary deeds that were considered by himself and others as miracles? His response is governed by the criteria he uses throughout his work on the historical Jesus. First, he finds that the criteria of multiple attestation of sources comes into play, because every Gospel source (Mark, Q, M, L and John), every evangelist in redactional summaries, and Josephus, all attest to Jesus as a miracle work. In considering multiple attestation of literary forms, he finds that miracles are attested to in exorcism stories, healing stories, nature miracles, summary statements, parables, dispute stories and in Jesus' mandate to the disciples. The criterion of coherence also plays an important role. Meier finds coherence between Jesus' exorcisms and his sayings, between his healings and

---

2. Alan Richardson, *The Miracle-Stories of the Gospels* (London: SCM Press, 1941), 36.
3. John P Meier, *A Marginal Jew: Rethinking the Historical Jesus. Volume Two: Mentor, Message, and Miracles* (New York: Doubleday, 1994).

sayings, and between the signs and discourses in the Gospel of John. In general, Jesus' miracles are coherent with the picture of one who gained a large number of disciples and aroused much interest.

The criterion of discontinuity (between Jesus and both Judaism and early Christianity) is of limited value, since there are accounts of both Jewish and early Christian miracle workers. What is distinctive of Jesus, however, is the combination of preacher, parabler, proclaimer of the kingdom, plus miracle worker actualizing his own proclamation. Meier finds the criterion of embarrassment (where the Christian community preserves material it finds awkward) has a limited but significant use in the Beelzebul incident, where Jesus' exorcisms lead to the charge of him being in league with the devil (Mk 3:20–30; Matt 12:22–32). Finally, Meier turns to the criterion of consistency with Jesus' rejection and death: he finds that the miracles fit well with his execution, in that they would have stirred up excitement and thus been an aggravating circumstance contributing to his death.

The application of these criteria to the general question of Jesus as a miracle worker leads Meier to an unambiguous conclusion:

> Viewed globally, the tradition of Jesus' miracles is more firmly supported by the criteria of historicity than are a number of other well well-known and readily accepted traditions about his life and ministry . . . If the miracle tradition from Jesus' public ministry were to be rejected *in toto* as unhistorical, so should every other Gospel tradition about him.[4]

According to Meier, then, Jesus did see himself and was seen by others as a wonder worker in the cause of the Reign of God.

In his detailed discussion of the healing of Bartimaeus, Meier finds that the application of criteria suggest that the Bartimaeus story is one of the 'strongest candidates for the report of a specific miracle going back to the historical Jesus'.[5] In his analysis of the Lazarus story, he finds it impossible to say exactly what happened, but he does think it reflects early material, and that it is likely that this story 'goes back ultimately to some event involving Lazarus, a disciple of Jesus, and that this event was believed by Jesus' disciples even during his lifetime

---

4. Meier, *A Marginal Jew*, 630.
5. Meier, *A Marginal Jew*, 690.

to be a miracle of raising the dead'.[6] Meier's treatment of the walking on the water leads him to the conclusion that 'the walking on the water is most likely from start to finish a creation of the early church, a christological confession in narrative form'.[7] He sees it as a narrative comment on the feeding of the five thousand, which would have symbolised the eucharistic experience of the early Christians: 'What I am suggesting is that, to a small church struggling in the night of a hostile world and feeling bereft of Christ's presence, the walking on the water likewise symbolized the experience of Christ in the eucharist.'[8]

This sample of some of Meier's insights and results leads me to conclude that we do need to think of Jesus as a miracle worker, whose healing ministry proclaims and anticipates the coming Reign of God. We do need to think of him as bringing healing to individuals like Bartimaeus. It seems he was thought of as restoring Lazarus to life, although we cannot know whether Lazarus was clinically dead in today's terms. We need not think of him as walking on the water during his lifetime, but can see this as expressing the action of the risen Christ, perhaps in and through the eucharistic experience of the early church. I will take this as a reasonable assessment of the data that a theology of miracles needs to address and begin this work with insights from Thomas Aquinas.

Aquinas on the Dignity of Secondary Causes

For Aquinas, God's nature is to exist, and God's proper effect is to cause existence (*esse*) in all other things. God causes this effect in creatures not just when they begin to exist, but at every moment in which they are maintained in existence. Because nothing is more deeply interior to an entity than its existence, God must exist in all things and be present to them at their most interior level.[9] All things exist only as created by God *ex nihilo*. All things depend on God entirely for their existence at every point. They find in God not only the cause of their being (efficient cause), but their end (final cause).

---

6. Meier, *A Marginal Jew*, 831.
7. Meier, *A Marginal Jew*, 921.
8. Meier, *A Marginal Jew*, 923.
9. Thomas Aquinas, *Summa theologiae* 1a.8.1. Quotations are from the Blackfriars edition (London: Blackfriars in conjunction with Eyre & Spottiswoode, 1964–80).

God's providence governs all creatures towards their end which is participation in the goodness of God.

According to Aquinas, God commonly works through creatures that are themselves truly causal. He calls these secondary causes. God is the primary cause who is always providentially at work in all created causes. It is by God's power that every other power acts.[10] While God enables creaturely causes to exist and to have effect, Aquinas sees secondary causes as genuinely causal in their own right. It is through these secondary causes that God cares for creation: 'Divine Providence works through intermediaries. For God governs the lower though the higher, not from any impotence on his part, but from the abundance of his goodness imparting to creatures the dignity of causing'.[11] God respects the dignity of secondary causes, and bestows on them their own integrity.

Aquinas thus opposes the view, sometimes called Occasionalism, which sees God as the only real cause at work in the universe. He is also opposes what will come to be called Deism, the idea that God is involved in creating things at the beginning, but takes no further part in the functioning of the universe. For him God's providence and God's government are always and everywhere at work, taking effect through the range of secondary causes. He challenges those who would say that God acts alone without intermediaries:

> But this is impossible, and first because it would deprive creation of its pattern of cause and effect, which in turn would imply lack of power in the creator, since an agent's power is the source of its giving an effect a causative capability. It is impossible, secondly, because if the active powers that are observed in creatures accomplished nothing, there would be no point to their have received such powers. Indeed if all creatures are utterly devoid of any activity of their own, then they themselves would seem to have a pointless existence, since everything exists for the sake of its operation.[12]

To the argument that God works through secondary causes because God wants creatures to have the dignity of genuine causes, Aquinas

---

10. Aquinas, *De potentia* 3.7
11. Aquinas, *Summa theologiae* 1a.22.3.
12. Aquinas, *Summa theologiae* 1a.105.6.

adds two further arguments. First, God's creative power would be diminished if God did not enable creatures to participate in causing. Second, if created causative powers do not genuinely accomplish their operations they would seem to have a pointless existence. They would lack meaning and integrity.

These arguments can be brought to bear on contemporary controversies. The proponents of 'intelligent design', for example, seek to show that there are instances of 'irreducible complexity' in the natural world that cannot be accounted for by Darwinian evolution, and that require the intervention of a designer.[13] It seems to me that one who thinks like Aquinas would not be inclined to support this line of thought. Aquinas would find no need to search for a place where God intervenes as designer because God is found in every dimension of creation: God 'acts interiorly in all things', because 'God is the cause of *esse*, which is innermost in all things'.[14] In today's context, it would be consistent with Aquinas to see God's creativity finding its most profound expression in evolutionary history, by enabling creaturely processes to have their own dignity and integrity as genuine causes of novelty in the world. It is worth noting that this is not necessarily the position of all contemporary followers of Aquinas. W Norris Clarke, a well-regarded Thomist philosopher, is remarkably sympathetic to 'irreducible complexity'.[15] My reading of Aquinas suggests, by contrast, that it reflects all the more glory to God if God enables life to evolve through natural processes, which have their own integrity, and which are to be accounted for empirically by the natural sciences, including Darwinian evolutionary theory.

How does Aquinas think about miracles? He tells us that miracles have as their purpose the manifestation of God's grace.[16] They are signs of grace and manifestations of the Spirit (1 Cor 12:7). Like most people of faith of the thirteenth century, Aquinas takes it for granted that miracles occur. He notes that the word miracle comes from the word *admiratio*, suggesting the wonder that accompanies the experience of something whose cause is hidden from us.[17]

---

13. Michael Behe, *Darwin's Black Box: The Biochemical Challenge to Evolution.* (New York: Free Press, 1996).
14. Aquinas, *Summa theologiae* 1a.105.6
15. W Norris Clarke, *The One and the Many: A Contemporary Thomistic Metaphysics* (Notre Dame, Indiana: University of Notre Dame Press, 2001), 255.
16. Aquinas, *Summa theologiae* 1a.104.3.
17. Aquinas, *Summa theologiae* 1a.105.7.

A real miracle, he tells us, has its cause absolutely hidden, because its cause is God. He sees miracles as involving the action of God replacing secondary causes. They are 'exceptions to the pattern in nature'.[18] They occur in a manner that 'surpasses the capabilities of nature'.[19] A miracle can exceed the capability of nature in three ways: in the kind of thing done; in the person who does it; and in the manner and order in which it is done.[20] In every case, a miracle is an event that occurs *only* through God's action, and without a secondary cause:

> Thus if we look to the world's order as it depends on the first cause, God cannot act against it, because then he would be doing something contrary to his foreknowledge, his will or his goodness. But if we take the order in things as it depends upon any of the secondary causes, then God can act apart from it; he is not subject to that order but rather it is subject to him, as issuing from him not out of necessity of nature, but by the decision of his will. He could in fact have established another sort of pattern in the world; hence when he so wills, he can act apart from the given order, producing, for example, the effects of secondary causes without them or some effects that surpass the powers of these causes.[21]

As Brian Davies puts it, for Aquinas, a miracle occurs because of what is *not* present, a secondary cause.[22] He sees two theses flowing from Aquinas's view of miracles. First, no one but God can work a miracle. In so far as holy people are involved, it is not that they work miracles, but that God brings about miracles at their request.[23] Second, in working miracles God does not do violence to the natural order. All the events that occur in the universe are the effect of God's will. If God brings about something miraculous in the natural order this is no more a violation of the natural order than the fact that the order exists in the first place.[24]

---

18. Aquinas, *Summa theologiae* 1a.105.7 ad1.
19. Aquinas, *Summa theologiae* 1a.105.7 ad 2.
20. Aquinas, *Summa theologiae* 1a.105.8.
21. Aquinas, *Summa theologiae* 1a.105.6.
22. Brian Davies, *The Thought of Thomas Aquinas* (Oxford: Clarendon Press, 1992), 174.
23. Aquinas, *Summa theologiae* 1a.110.4 ad 10.
24. Davies, *The Thought of Thomas Aquinas*, 173.

I think Davies is right to insist that for Aquinas, God's miracles surpass the natural order but do not do violence to it. What is not explored by Aquinas, however, is the possibility that God may so respect the unfolding of the processes of the natural order that even in miracles God works in and through the laws of nature. What if God, out of loving fidelity to creatures, always waits patiently on the unfolding of creaturely processes as God waits upon human freedom? What if God works *consistently* through secondary causes? I find Aquinas's concept of primary and secondary causality indispensable and foundational in the current dialogue between science and theology, and the same is true of his view of God's respect for the integrity of secondary causes. I also embrace his view of miracles as wonderful manifestations of the Spirit. But I will depart from his view that in miracles God replaces secondary causes, to explore the idea that miracles might be seen as wonderful manifestations of the Spirit that occur through secondary causes. God's respect for the integrity of secondary causes, so clearly defended by Aquinas, may mean that even in miracles God acts in and through the law of nature. Taking this proposal further will mean attempting to clarify what is meant by these laws of nature.

The Laws of Nature

In a series of articles, cosmologist and philosopher William Stoeger has explored the meaning and ontological status of the laws of nature.[25]

---

25. William R Stoeger, 'Contemporary Physics and the Ontological Status of the Laws of Nature', in *Quantum Cosmology and the Laws of Nature: Scientific Perspectives on Divine Action,* edited by Robert John Russell, Nancey Murphy and CJ Isham (Vatican Observatory/ Center for Theology and the Natural Sciences, Vatican City State/Berkeley California, 1993), 209–34, William R Stoeger, 'The Mind-Brain Problem, the Laws of Nature and Constitutive Relationships', in *Neuroscience and the Person: Scientific Perspectives on Divine Action,* edited by Robert John Russell, Nancey Murphy, Theo C Meyering, and Michael A Arbib (Vatican Observatory/ Center for Theology and the Natural Sciences, Vatican City State/Berkeley California, 1999), 129–46; Willliam R Stoeger, 'Epistemological and Ontological Issues Arising from Quantum Theory', in *Quantum Mechanics: Scientific Perspectives on Divine Action,* edited by Robert John Russell, Philip Clayton, Kirk Wegter-McNelly and John Polkinghorne (Vatican Observatory/ Center for Theology and the Natural Sciences, Vatican City State/Berkeley California, 2001), 81–98.

I will focus on three questions addressed in his work. The first asks: To what extent do well-confirmed scientific theories, and the laws of nature they embody, describe what occurs in reality? Stoeger accepts that some theories, which because of their success have the status of laws, offer a detailed model of fundamental patterns of order and causal influence observed in the physical and chemical world. These theories have been molded, modified and refined through continual observation and experiment. Such theories and their laws have a 'very strong basis' in observed reality.[26]

But Stoeger insists that our observations do not reveal the whole of the reality under scrutiny. Some aspects, even some of the most fundamental, remain hidden. Science focuses on stable and characteristic features that are accessible to it. It seeks what is universalisable and what is relevant to the questions of the scientist. It isolates and simplifies aspects of reality and models them with concepts such as mass and velocity. The design of a research program and the interpretation of its results are limited by the heuristic anticipation of the researcher. Much of the reality of the matter under observation is missed.

Even with physical levels that seem well modeled in laws and theories, there is much that escapes comprehension, including aspects of the quantum level of realty. In the physics of complex systems, 'order and chaos nourish one another with a strange reciprocity'.[27] The turbulence of flowing fluids is difficult to model in detail or to compress algorithmically. These problems only increase in biology, neurophysiology, psychology, economics, politics and sociology, where reality escapes all attempts to describe it in the law-like and rigidly predictable ways of physics and mathematics. Stoeger concludes that there is an enormous difference between using the language of laws of nature to speak of *scientific theories*, which are always partial and limited, and using this same language to point to the relationships, processes and causal interconnections of the *natural world itself*.

A second, related question concerns the function of the laws of nature: Do they *prescribe* the way reality behaves or merely describe it? They certainly describe the behaviour of the natural world in cer-

---

26. Stoeger, 'Contemporary Physics and the Ontological Status of the Laws of Nature', 223.
27. Stoeger, 'Contemporary Physics and the Ontological Status of the Laws of Nature', 224.

tain circumstances and attribute this behaviour to particular causes and influences. But do the laws force or constrain the behaviour? While it is common to assume that they do, Stoeger argues that the laws cannot be said to be the source of the behaviour. They simply model or describe it. Of course, one reason why the laws of nature have been assumed to be prescriptive is that they were originally thought of as God's laws, governing the physical world as God's commandments govern human conduct.

Stoeger sees the laws of nature as human descriptions of observed regularities:

> In a way, saying that something is a 'law of nature' is simply a way of indicating that it is so fundamental to the description of the detailed workings of physical, chemical or biological systems that it never is observed not to hold when those systems are properly isolated and simplified and certain conditions are fulfilled.[28]

There is no reason to assume that the law is the *cause* of the regularity that is observed. It is a description of the regularity and of its fundamental character.

There are times when a source of behaviour is found to be grounded in the next level of physical process and structure, as when the laws of chemical reactions are explained at the level of atomic structure. These deeper explanatory connections can provide intermediate, detailed descriptions that causally link phenomena that had seemed unconnected, but they never explain completely why reality is the way it is: 'Rather, they explain that, since it is this way, it has to have these relationships with what appear to be more fundamental realities'.[29] The models give the appearance of imparting necessity, but this apparent necessity does not come from the models, but is hidden in the observed entities and their regularities. The ultimate source of the regularity we observe is not the model we articulate. The model itself does not tell us why this model holds and not some other. While the theories and laws of nature can describe reality well

---

28. Stoeger, 'Contemporary Physics and the Ontological Status of the Laws of Nature', 225.
29. Stoeger, 'Contemporary Physics and the Ontological Status of the Laws of Nature', 225.

and point to intermediate causal connections between different levels of reality, they do not prescribe reality. They do not cause it to be the way it is.

The third question concerns the independent existence of our models and laws: Do they have an existence outside our minds? Are they more than our approximations of what is manifest in the physical phenomena being observed? Stoeger is opposed to the Platonic view that would give these laws an independent and pre-existing reality. He finds no scientific or philosophical reason to see the laws of nature as constituting an underlying plan or pattern of physical reality: 'The most we can say is that there are regularities and inter-relationships in reality as it is in itself—a fundamental order—which are imperfectly reflected in our models and laws.'[30] These models are in some cases highly successful, but they are remain imperfect and limited. The models represent in an idealized way the structures and relationships between the phenomena under study, but they always leave a great deal out:

> It is an illusion to believe that these incredibly rich representations of the phenomena are unconstructed isomorphisms we merely *discover* in the real world. Instead they are *constructed*—painstakingly so—and there is no evidence that they are isomorphic with structures in the real world as it is in itself.[31]

Our scientific models are the result of imaginative and conceptual abstraction guided by continued observation and experiment. There is no justification for the idea that they correspond in a direct way to the entities, structures and relationships of physical reality as it is in itself.

This whole line of argument means that there is a need to distinguish between two possible meanings of the laws of nature: 'We may mean the regularities, relationships, processes and structures in nature: (1) *as we know, understand and model them*; or (2) *as they actually function in reality*, which is much more than we know, under-

---

30. Stoeger, 'Contemporary Physics and the Ontological Status of the Laws of Nature', 221.
31. Stoeger, 'Contemporary Physics and the Ontological Status of the Laws of Nature', 216.

stand or have adequately modeled.'[32] The laws of nature as we know them are provisional, imperfect and limited, and not well equipped to deal with important areas of life, including not only the metaphysical, but also the mental, the interpersonal, the aesthetic and the religious. The existence of parts of reality that defy scientific analysis, such as personal relationships or deeply held values, is an indication, not that these phenomena are illusory, but that the laws of nature, meaning the natural sciences as we know them, do not model or describe central aspects of reality.[33]

This clarification has important consequences for a theology of miracles. It means that a marvelous manifestation of the Spirit, such as an act of healing, may take us beyond the laws of nature understood in the first sense—as our limited models of reality. But it may not be beyond the laws of nature understood in the second sense, as the relationships and processes that function in reality, which are more than we have fully understood or adequately modeled. And, of course, all of these patterns of relationship and causality that escape our present models are, theologically, secondary causes. This opens us the possibility that miracles may occur through a whole range of secondary causes that our current science cannot model or cannot model well.

A Theological Approach

Johann Baptist Metz offers a further insight into miracles by insisting that they function symbolically. They are not only signs but also mediations of the coming Reign of God. They display the Reign of God as 'actually and effectively present'.[34] Metz approaches miracles from the perspective of human intersubjectivity. The miracles of the Gospels are not the reports of detached observers, but the testimony of believers. They are of their very nature signs, that bear on salvation. It is of the essence of miracles that they are attested to by those who are subjectively affected by them. Within the dynamics of faith, they contain a promise and a call. A miracle does not compel assent.

---

32. Stoeger, 'The Mind-Brain Problem, the Laws of Nature and Constitutive Relationships', 130.
33. Stoeger, 'The Mind-Brain Problem, the Laws of Nature and Constitutive Relationships', 134–5.
34. Metz, 'Miracle', 963.

It is not experienced in the way of the methodical observation of the natural sciences. It is a sign that summons a person to commitment to the way of the Reign of God.

Rahner's approach is similar. He sees a miracle as a sign and manifestation of God's salvific activity in revelation and grace. It is a manifestation in historical tangibility of grace that is addressed to specific persons. Miracles are specific, directed towards particular addressees: 'They are not *facta bruta* but an address to a knowing subject in a quite definitive historical situation'.[35] A miracle occurs in a theological sense when someone experiences God's self-communication in a particular configuration of events, in such a way that God's self-communication participates immediately in the event. In such a miraculous event, God's self-communication comes to appearance and witnesses to itself.[36] It is a wonderful call of God in and through specific events.

What is needed to experience the miraculous, Rahner says, is 'a person who is willing to allow himself to be called in the depths of his existence, who is free and open to the singularly wonder-ful in his life'.[37] The recipient needs a willingness to believe, to have eyes to see and ears to hear. Such a person keeps alive a humble and receptive wonder in the concrete events of her existence. She can find in historical events a call from God and be empowered and obligated by them to a historical dialogue with God. This is, after all, the Gospel presupposition for a miracle: 'Your faith has made you whole.'

Rahner suggests the idea proposed here, that we can do without the notion of miracles violating the laws of nature. He points to the multi-layered nature of our experience of the world. The more fundamental levels of reality are subsumed into the higher without violating what is proper to the lower but becoming something new. So the physical is subsumed into the chemical and the biological, and in us the material, chemical and biological is subsumed into human freedom, without losing the integrity of the lower levels. Rahner sees something analogous happening with regard to God's action in the world. The natural world, with its processes and laws, is created by God as part of the process of God's self-bestowal to the world. It is

---

35. Karl Rahner, *Foundations of Christian Faith: An Introduction to the Idea of Christianity* (New York: Seabury, 1978), 258.
36. Rahner, *Foundations of Christian Faith,* 261.
37. Rahner, *Foundations of Christian Faith,* 263.

not that God creates a world that is other from God so that, in order to communicate, God needs to intervene in the world from time to time. Rather the natural world, with its processes and laws, exists within God's one act of self-bestowal. The laws of nature are part of God's own self-giving. They are an element within grace.[38] God does not need to break these laws or overturn them in order to communicate to human persons in specific circumstances. The natural world with its laws is the means of God's self-revelation. God can give marvelous signs of grace to God's people without violating natural laws.

Rahner's thought here can be further developed by the distinction Stoeger makes between the two meanings of the laws of nature. It is not simply the natural world as our theories model it that is the vehicle for God's self-communication. It is the far more mysterious world of nature itself, much of which is beyond our understanding and modeling, which is the vehicle of God's self-manifestations. And, in terms of Aquinas's theology, this is all the world of secondary causes. If a miracle is a wonderful manifestation and sign of God's grace, there is every reason to think it can take effect in the natural world, some of which is beyond our modeling, but which has its own God-given integrity as a world of interacting secondary causes. God's grace takes effect in a way that fully respects the integrity of nature at the physical and biological level as well as at the level of human freedom.

This line of thought suggests that miracles are marvels of God's gracious self-communication that occur in different ways. Some may occur at levels beyond the laws we know at present governing physics, chemistry and biology. A person suffering from cancer might pray with her community for healing from a cancer and find herself miraculously restored to health. This need not be taken as God acting in an interventionist way without secondary causes. It may well be God acting in and through secondary causes that we do not fully understand. It may be that science will one day understand more clearly how common prayer, or human solidarity and love, can sometimes contribute to biological healing. Other miracles may occur in ways that are consistent with contemporary science. A person cured from illness, in a way that science can explain, who finds God providentially at work in this cure, so that it becomes for her a call and address by God, might well see this as a miracle, a wonderful manifestation

---

38. Rahner, *Foundations of Christian Faith*, 261.

and sign of the Spirit of God. A person might receive, as a gift, the capacity to make peace in a damaged relationship and experience this as a miracle of grace. Such events do not impact on any known law of nature, but they are marvelous manifestation of the Spirit.

The proposal I have made is to extend Aquinas's view of God's respect for secondary causes to suggest that we might be able to think of God working consistently through secondary causes, even when God works miracles in our lives. This puts me in the company of Pope John XXII. When Aquinas's canonization was being discussed, the paucity of miracles was raised as an objection, and the pope is said to have replied that every question Thomas Aquinas answered was a miracle.[39] Certainly, Aquinas's body of work, the Spirit-led expression of his faith, hope and love and the integrity of his commitment to truth, constitutes a miracle in the sense proposed here, as a marvelous manifestation of the Spirit.

---

39. Simon Tugwell, editor and translator, *Albert and Thomas: Selected Writings* (New York: Paulist Press, New York, 1988), 259.

Towards a Theology of Divine Action: William R Stoeger, SJ, on the Laws of Nature

William Stoeger, a Jesuit of the California province, was a staff scientist of the Vatican Observatory Research Group in Tucson until his death on 24 March 2014. He specialised in theoretical cosmology, high energy astrophysics, and in the interrelationship between science, philosophy and theology. He earned his PhD in astrophysics from the University of Cambridge, where he was a classmate of Stephen Hawking and studied under Astronomer Royal Sir Martin Rees. Guy Consolmagno, another US Jesuit on the Vatican Observatory staff, points out that Stoeger's scientific output was prolific and highly regarded—including the publication of two major papers on cosmology or general relativity each year, most recently on the interconnection between theoretical cosmology and the observed structure of the universe, as seen in distant galaxies.[1]

There is another side to Stoeger's academic work—his contributions to the dialogue between theology and science. One aspect of this was his long-standing and faithful commitment to the 'Theology and Science' topic sessions of the conventions of the Catholic Theological Society of America. Another aspect, the focus of this article, was his role in a series of research conferences on divine action that gathered scientists, philosophers and theologians from around the world. These conferences began when Pope John Paul II asked the Vatican Observatory to further the science-theology dialogue by organising a conference to celebrate the 300th anniversary of Isaac

---

1. Guy Consolmagno, 'Across the Universe: Big Bang Bill', in *Tablet*, 268 (April 26, 2014): 36.

Newton's *Principia*,² at which key participants began to consider the possibility of a series of such conferences. To test the feasibility of this idea, Stoeger, of the Vatican Observatory, and Robert John Russell, of the Centre for Theology and the Natural Sciences at Berkeley (CTNS), organised an initial conference at Castel Gandolfo outside Rome in September 1987. The publication that resulted from this conference, with an opening message from John Paul II, is a wonderfully rich resource in the dialogue between science and theology from the late 20th century.³

The success of this conference led George Coyne, SJ, director of the Vatican Observatory, to propose that a series of five such conferences be held over a decade. A long-term steering committee was set up made up of Stoeger, Russell and Nancey Murphy from Fuller Theological Seminary. Coyne invited CTNS to co-sponsor the series of research conferences with the Vatican Observatory.⁴ It was agreed that the organising theological theme would be the nature of divine action, and that this theme would be taken up in the light of advances in five particular scientific areas: quantum cosmology, chaos and complexity, evolutionary and molecular biology, neuroscience and quantum mechanics. The focus would be not simply on God's continuous creative act, but on the Christian conviction of God's particular acts in the history of salvation and in human lives ('special divine action').

Stoeger's contribution involved not only planning, organisation and co-editing of volumes that emerged from the colloquia, but also his own substantial essays in each volume. In one of these, he develops his own approach to a noninterventionist theology of divine action in relation to Aquinas's theology of primary and secondary

---

2. See *Newton and the New Direction in Science: Proceedings of the Cracow Conference*, edited by George V Coyne, Mochał Heller, and J Życiński (Vatican City: Vatican Observatory, 1988).
3. *Physics, Philosophy and Theology: A Common Quest for Understanding*, edited by Robert John Russell, William R Stoeger, and George Coyne (Vatican City: Vatican Observatory, 1988).
4. For an account of these developments see Robert John Russell, "Introduction," in *Quantum Cosmology and the Laws of Nature: Scientific Perspectives on Divine Action*, ed. Robert John Russell, Nancey Murphy, and CJ Isham (Vatican City: Vatican Observatory; Berkeley CA: Center for Theology and the Natural Sciences (CTNS), 1993) 1–32.

causality.⁵ Apart from Stephen Happel, Stoeger was something of a lone voice in embracing a Thomist account.⁶ A substantial group of scholars (including Russell, Murphy, George Ellis and Thomas Tracy) explored the idea that God acts in the indeterminacy of quantum events to bring about particular outcomes in the macro world. Others, such as Ian Barbour, contributed insights from Whiteheadian process theology. John Polkinghorne saw God as acting through the openness of nature, by the top-down imparting of information. Arthur Peacocke saw God as acting in and through every aspect of nature, acting on the system as a whole, by analogy with a whole-part or top-down cause.

Stoeger's contributions to the various conferences and volumes, I propose, do far more than articulate a standard Thomist account of divine action. They provide a highly fruitful development of the Thomist position and offer a basis for further theological developments. My intention in engaging with his works here is to show, first, that three of his five contributions can be read as organically developing a fundamental argument: that the laws of nature as we know them through the sciences are constructed models of what occurs in nature; that they are not isomorphic with the natural world; and that the complex and rich reality of the world around us far exceeds our capacity to model it in our scientific theories and laws. This line of thought, then, suggests the possibility that God may be acting not only through the laws we know but also in the natural world that is far beyond our current laws.

Stoeger's three contributions represent a detailed engagement with the various sciences and complex philosophical explorations. Each of the articles works in a particular scientific context, shaped by the theme of the conference in which it was offered. Each sheds light on the other two and enables a better interpretation of them. I hope to show that a reading of these three essays as an interconnected argument offers creative possibilities for a renewed theology of divine

---

5. William R Stoeger, 'Describing God's Action in the World in Light of Scientific Knowledge of Reality', in *Chaos and Complexity: Scientific Perspectives on Divine Action*, edited by Robert John Russell, Nancey Murphy and Arthur R Peacocke (Vatican City: Vatican Observatory; Berkeley, CA: CTNS, 1995), 239–61.
6. Stephen Happel, 'Divine Providence and Instrumentality: Metaphors for Time in Self-Organizing Systems and Divine Action', in *Chaos and Complexity*, 177–203.

action that builds on the Thomist tradition.⁷ My reading of Stoeger's work does not attempt to represent the detail and complexity of the original articles; nor is it simply a summary; rather, it is an attempt to demonstrate the power and scope of the sustained argument at work in the series.

My second intention here is to propose that Stoeger's argument constitutes an important breakthrough in the theology of divine action, one that, though largely unrecognized in the literature, is highly significant not only for the science-theology field but also for broader Catholic theology. If Stoeger is judged to be right in his claim, then many aspects of theology would be impacted. If his insights, so deeply based in the sciences, were to find acceptance in the Catholic theology of creation, incarnation, providence and miracles, for example, then new possibilities might well open up for dialogue with contemporary culture and for evangelisation in today's world. The claim I am making, then, is that Stoeger's argument constitutes an important legacy to twenty-first century theology, one that calls for wide discussion and debate in Catholic theology.

In my last section, I attempt to show the consequences of this legacy by taking up just one example, the theology of miracles. In what follows, then, I offer a reading of Stoeger's three papers in turn, focusing on the first where he lays out his general position, and then more briefly on his essays on neuroscience and quantum mechanics. In the final section, I will point to the importance of these insights for a contemporary theology of divine action, focusing on miracles as one important aspect of God's action in the world.

The Ontological Status of the Laws of Nature

In the first of his three essays,⁸ Stoeger explores what he sees as the fundamental question underlying all discussion between science and theology: How should we think about the laws of nature? His answer

---

7. Stoeger's fifth paper, not directly related to the three on the laws of nature, is 'The Immanent Directionality of the Evolutionary Process, and Its Relationship to Teleology', in *Evolutionary and Molecular Biology: Scientific Perspectives on Divine Action*, edited by Robert John Russell, William R Stoeger and Francisco J Ayala (Vatican City: Vatican Observatory; Berkeley CA: CTNS, 1998), 239–61.
8. William R Stoeger, 'Contemporary Physics and the Ontological Status of the Laws of Nature', in *Quantum Cosmology and the Laws of Nature*, 209–34.

involves an extended argument for three interrelated positions. First, the laws of nature are to be seen as approximate models and idealised constructions of nature, which are never complete and never isomorphic descriptions of the far more complex world to which they refer. Second, the laws are descriptive rather than prescriptive; although they describe fundamental regularities in nature, they are not the source of the regularities they describe, nor the source of their physical necessity. Third, the laws do not exist independently of the reality they describe, thus ruling out a pre-existing or 'Platonic' interpretation of the laws of nature.

Stoeger argues for these positions in two steps, beginning with the experience of the natural sciences and then moving to a more philosophical articulation of his position. He begins his argument by reflecting on highly successful scientific theories in physics. Even with such theories, he points out, we have the almost continual experience of 'replacing or subsuming laws and well-confirmed theories by more comprehensive ones, which more adequately describe the relevant aspects of phenomena under a wide range of conditions'.[9] A prime example is Newton's theory of gravitation, which has now been subsumed as a limited case of Einstein's general relativity. Newton's theory is still regarded as valid, and as giving correct predictions for relatively weak gravitational fields such as obtain on Earth, and for velocities that are much below the speed of light. But the new theory, general relativity, gives a completely revised description of the underlying reality. The movement between the two theories represents a radical paradigm shift, which is adopted only on the basis of controlled experiments and careful observations. The new theory and laws describe a larger range of conditions than the older one, and predict further phenomena that can be tested. Still, the new theory may itself be replaced by another. In the case of gravity, it is possible that general relativity will be replaced by a quantum theory of gravity—the topic of the conference and the volume in which Stoeger's essay appears.

The recognition of such paradigm shifts should lead us to question the common practice of speaking of 'laws of nature' as if they were complete and immutable explanations of the regularities and the interrelationships that are found in physical reality. By contrast,

---

9. Stoeger, 'Contemporary Physics', 212.

Stoeger insists that the experience of major paradigm shifts in science, as in the instance of gravity, leads to the conclusion that the laws and theories involved are actually models, or 'approximate descriptions', even if they are detailed and accurate descriptions.[10]

With the case of gravity, we have at least two theories and two sets of laws that work equally well in certain circumstances. Which one better represents physical reality as it is in itself? The answer to this question, Stoeger argues, depends on our criteria for what is judged as better, for what constitutes a good representation, and for what we think reality is in itself. Since Stoeger insists that we do not have access to physical reality independently from the phenomena we can observe, our observations of them are necessarily 'theory laden' in the way we design experiments, make observations and interpret results. Such reflections, he suggests, warn against the illusions to which we are subject when we talk about our scientific theories and laws of nature: we can easily talk as if they were complete descriptions of nature itself.

Stoeger points out that there are often free parameters or constants in our theories or laws that are not determined by laws themselves. These and other factors he discusses lead him to conclude that our best theories and laws have an incomplete, approximate and descriptive character. They represent reality but do so only partially: 'They reveal but they also hide aspects of physical reality'.[11] He points to theoretical entities and concepts like temperature, entropy, electrons, photons and attributes of particles such as mass, spin and charge. What is the relationship between these abstract theoretical entities and the phenomena they describe and to some extent explain? Stoeger responds:

> It is really that of a model to the very rich and full patterns of kinematic, dynamic and structural behavior we observe. The model represents in an idealized and imperfect way the structures we find manifested in the phenomena and the detailed qualitative and quantitative relationships which appear to exist among them. However, it leaves a great deal out too—and sometimes it leaves out sophistications

---

10. Stoeger, 'Contemporary Physics', 212.
11. Stoeger, 'Contemporary Physics', 215.

and precisions we desperately wish to include, but do not know how. It is an illusion to believe that these incredibly rich representations of the phenomena are unconstructed isomorphisms we merely *discover* in the world. Instead they are *constructed*—painstakingly so—and there is no evidence that they are isomorphic with structures in the real world as it is in itself.[12]

The reason we are successful with such theories and their mathematical models is that there are levels of reality in which the dominant behaviour is relatively simple and uncomplicated, as, for example, in the movement of planets around the sun. But there are other situations, such as the dynamic behaviour of biological systems, that are too complicated for such straightforward modelling, where it is impossible or extremely difficult to isolate the laws from the highly complex states of the systems and the boundary conditions. Stoeger points out that in biology, whether in the functional or evolutionary disciplines, laws are rarely spoken of as they are in physics, and then only in analogous ways because the complexity of biological systems, universality, explanatory power, simplicity and predictability are all far more problematic in biology than they are in physics.[13]

Stoeger moves from a phenomenological reflection on the experience of the sciences to a more philosophical analysis and formulation. I will first summarise his comments on the three questions identified at the beginning of this section.

Question 1: To what extent do successful and well-confirmed physical theories and the laws they embody describe reality in itself? Stoeger makes it clear that such theories do have a very strong basis in observed reality, but that they do not describe physical reality as it is in itself. They do not reveal all the features of the reality under observation, not even its most fundamental features. Many of these remain hidden from us because: (1) our science tends to focus on stable and characteristic features; (2) that are observed at energies we are able to detect; (3) that we can isolate, simplify, and model in concepts such as mass, velocity and energy; (4) that are relevant to our interests in

---

12. Stoeger, 'Contemporary Physics', 216.
13. Stoeger refers here to Ernst Mayr, 'Is Biology an Autonomous Science?', in *Toward a New Philosophy of Biology*, edited by Ernst Mayr (Cambridge, MA: Harvard University, 1988), 8–23.

performing experiments and constructing theories; and (5) that are framed by our heuristic anticipations in designing and interpreting experiments.

While some parts of reality can be successfully modelled—they are 'algorithmically compressible'[14]—other important areas are not. This is true, for example, even of complex physical systems found throughout the natural world in such everyday realities as fluids exhibiting strong turbulence. In these systems, 'order and chaos nourish one another with a strange reciprocity'.[15] It becomes extremely difficult to model or algorithmically compress the observed reality. Stoeger writes: 'As we move into the science of complex chemical molecules, into biology, neurophysiology, psychology, economics, politics, and sociology, these problems increase and prevent us from describing phenomena in anything like the lawlike and rigidly predictable way to which we are accustomed in physics and mathematics.'[16] For Stoeger, then, our laws of nature and the theories that enshrine them are carefully constructed models, incomplete and imperfect descriptions of what we observe in the far more complex world around us.

Question 2: Given that many of our physical theories and their laws are successful and well-confirmed by the evidence, do such laws of nature *prescribe* the behaviour we observe in nature? They can certainly give the impression of doing so, because they are painstakingly accurate descriptions of a hierarchy of interrelated phenomena isolatable and characterised by highly regular behaviour that can be generalised in law-like terms. But, Stoeger argues, this impression is an illusion. There is no justification for claiming that the laws are the source of behavior we see in nature, or that they exercise constraints on the behaviour. He points out that one of the reasons why laws of nature came to be seen as prescriptive is that they were originally thought of as God's laws. While this metaphor may have some application to the regularities of the natural world seen as God's creation, Stoeger insists it should not be applied literally to constructed laws of nature. Such laws are descriptive rather than prescriptive:

---

14. A physical system is said to be algorithmically compressible when it can be modelled mathematically.
15. Stoeger, 'Contemporary Physics', 224.
16. Stoeger, 'Contemporary Physics', 224.

> In a way, saying that something is a 'law of nature' is simply a way of indicating that it is so fundamental to the description of the detailed workings of physical, chemical or biological systems that it never is observed not to hold when those systems are properly isolated and simplified and certain conditions are fulfilled. But there seems to be little support for the position that the law is the cause of the regularity observed or that it forces physical, chemical or biological entities to behave in the way they do.[17]

A law is simply a description of the regularity and its fundamental character. What enforces this regularity is not the description. Sometimes an intermediate cause of law-like behaviour is revealed in another level of physical process that is a consequence of relationships at a more fundamental level. An example is the way laws of chemical reactions are now seen as grounded in the deeper level of atomic structure. But, Stoeger insists, these deeper connections do not explain in any complete way why reality is the way it is. The models we make can give the impression of imparting necessity, 'but the apparent necessity does not come from the models; it is hidden in the observed realities and in the entities which adhere to them. Its ultimate source is not accessible to our probing.'[18]

Question 3: To what extent can the laws of nature be endowed in a justified way with an existence independent of the objects they govern?[19] Based on his answers to the previous two questions, Stoeger sees it as difficult to justify the claim that the laws have an independent existence. In fact, he thinks the claim does not make sense, since the laws belong to the models and to the entities that constitute them. The question rests on the confusion between our laws and the regularities and relationship of nature itself. It also rests on the unwarranted philosophical assumption that the regularities of nature are based on something pre-existent, like a blueprint for a building. Hence Stoeger

---

17. Stoeger, 'Contemporary Physics', 225.
18. Stoeger, 'Contemporary Physics', 225.
19. Stoeger discusses two further questions: on the possibility of postulating other sets of laws in an alternative set of entities or ensembles of other universes, and on finding a single overarching fundamental law of the universe. I leave them aside here in order to follow his key ideas through the three essays and to situate them in relation to the theology of divine action.

rejects a Platonic view of the laws of nature on the basis that is has no scientific or philosophical justification.

Stoeger then argues for a general epistemological position that can be called an 'empirical realism', because he sees the theories, laws and models of science as having a firm basis in reality. Such scientific knowledge is knowledge that is widely shared, tested in experiment and against the predictions it makes, and continually reassessed. But he also claims that his own epistemological position is 'weakly objective', because it is a brand of realism that does not claim to know physical reality as it is itself.[20] With this assessment, Stoeger endorses Bernard D'Espagnat's view of the limits of our knowledge in the light of quantum mechanics,[21] and he builds on the insights of Bas van Fraassen, particularly in the rejection of the idea that the laws of nature enforce a physical necessity.[22]

At the end of this first of his three essays, Stoeger points out that the conception of the laws of nature he has outlined offers a context for discussing God's action in the universe, a context quite different from that of a strongly realist view. Stoeger nevertheless insists that not only is it still appropriate to think of God working through the laws of nature, but that it is now also possible to think of God acting principally not through 'our laws' but rather through 'the underlying relationship and regularities in nature itself, of which 'our laws' are but imperfect and idealized models'.[23] Through revelation, we Christians see God as acting in the particular and the personal. And, in the light of the argument advanced here, the Creator can be thought of as acting continuously in and through the complex and rich interrelationships of the physical world that our laws only partially model and describe.

The Laws of Nature and the Mind/Brain Problem

Stoeger's second essay applies his thinking about the laws of nature to the problem of how we understand the relationship between the

---

20. Stoeger, 'Contemporary Physics', 230.
21. Bernard D'Espagnat, *Reality and the Physicist* (Cambridge, UK: Cambridge University, 1989).
22. Bas C Van Fraassen, *Laws and Symmetry* (Oxford: Clarendon, 1989).
23. Stoeger, 'Contemporary Physics', 234.

brain and mental states.[24] He does not seek to resolve this extremely complex problem, but to clear the ground by clarifying certain key concepts. I highlight two aspects of his work here: his clarification of the concepts of the physical and the mental or spiritual and his understanding of constitutive relationships.[25]

Stoeger begins with a reformulation of the crucial distinction he has established between two possible meanings of the laws of nature: 'We may mean the regularities, relationships, processes, and structure in nature: (1) as we know, understand, and model them; or (2) as they actually function in reality, which is much more than we know, understand, or have adequately modelled'.[26] He goes on to speak of 'our laws of nature' to describe the first, and 'the laws of nature' to describe the second. He proposes that this distinction is particularly helpful in dealing with the mind-brain problem.

Stoeger begins by considering the relationship between the physical and the nonphysical aspects of reality, between matter and spirit, and particularly between the brain and the mind. He points out that 'matter' is not a well-defined scientific concept, but the concepts of 'mass' and 'energy' are. He asks about the characteristics of matter or, more specifically, of mass energy. He proposes that we need to include not only life but also mental capacity as potential properties of matter, even though we do not yet understand the laws of nature that enable matter to give rise to these characteristics. Of course, matter possesses these characteristics only when it is organised in specific ways. Mind, or spirit, exists only in relation to matter that is organised in a 'highly neurological way'.[27] Mind is not immaterial, in the sense of being separate from matter or independent of matter. It might possibly be called immaterial in common speech, but this is because it involves qualities of matter that go beyond what we can model or understand in our current science.

---

24. William R Stoeger, 'The Mind-Brain Problem, the Laws of Nature, and Constitutive Relationships', in *Neuroscience and the Person: Scientific Perspectives on Divine Action*, edited by Robert John Russell *et al* (Vatican City: Vatican Observatory; Berkeley CA: CTNS, 1999), 129–46.
25. This means I will deal only in passing with other important concepts that Stoeger develops, particularly his work on reducibility, emergence and supervenience.
26. Stoeger, 'Mind-Brain Problem', 130.
27. Stoeger, 'Mind-Brain Problem', 134.

Central to the brain-mind question, Stoeger insists, is the fact that our scientific understanding of the issues is so limited. We certainly know that the mind is related to the brain and to physical processes and events, but we do not know how: 'What we must admit is that we really do not understand the capacities of the physical and the mental when it is neurologically organized.'[28] We know that matter in the form of the brain is necessary for our experiences of mind or spirit. But we have no adequate scientific account of the interrelationship between the brain and the mind. Our laws of nature as they currently exist do not adequately account for the relationship between the brain and the mind, or for the experience of oneself as self-conscious and free, or for interpersonal relationships, let alone for religious experiences.

Having insisted that our current science faces severe limits in talking about the brain-mind relationship, Stoeger then offers a fresh way of looking at the issue through 'constitutive relationships'.[29] This expression refers to the way realities from an atom to a cell, to a molecule, to an organ like the brain, and far beyond to the universe can be described in terms of nested hierarchical structures. The relationships between entities at one level constitute new entities at another level. Constitutive relationships involve all the relationships and interactions, both internal and environmental, that incorporate components at one level into a more complex whole at another level. These constitutive relationships are the foundation for the unity of an entity or organism and for its properties and behaviour. These relationships can enable something new to emerge, something more than a simple aggregation (such as a pile of logs). When the characteristics of an entity are essentially different from those of its components, when it cannot be reduced to its parts. Stoeger speaks of the new entity as mereologically irreducible.[30] It functions as a new, distinct whole, with properties not found in its components. When this occurs, Stoeger proposes that it be considered an emergent property.[31]

---

28. Stoeger, 'Mind-Brain Problem', 134.
29. Stoeger, 'Mind-Brain Problem', 136–7.
30. Based on the Greek word for part, *meros*.
31. Mereological irreducibility is thus distinct from causal irreducibility. Causal irreducibility occurs when higher level causes are not determined solely by causes operating at a more fundamental level, but by external causes or top-down causes. Something that is mereologically irreducible and therefore emergent may or may not be causally irreducible.

Another concept Stoeger uses at this point is supervenience, which, for him, refers to the dependence of higher level states or properties on lower level states or properties. The higher level properties, however, are not generally reducible to the lower level properties. In this way, 'chemical properties are "supervenient"—or "supervene"—on physical properties, and mental states are "supervenient" on brain states'.[32] Higher level entities that supervene or more fundamental entities are formed by their constitutive relationships, which organise the fundamental entities into more complex entities, whose characteristics and behaviours cannot be predicted by knowledge of the fundamental entities.

For Stoeger, then, mental states supervene on brain states, but mental states are not simply determined by brain states. While they depend on brain states, they are determined by all the constitutive relationships at the level of the mental states—their relationships with one another and with their environment. Stoeger points out that many researchers in philosophy of mind and neurophysiology have been preoccupied with a bottom-up approach, but, he insists, this cannot show us the full picture: 'The full picture—concerning these crucial constitutive relationships to which we have been appealing—must also essentially involve the "top down" orientation. This means that the character of the brain states themselves is strongly influenced by the mind and consciousness, as well as by the body and its components'.[33] He goes on to show how the human mind depends not only on the body but also on all the relationships of a human life, very much including the interpersonal relationships:

> For instance, if we take the example of the human brain, it is certainly obvious that some of its constitutive relationships specify how it is constructed from individual neurons into certain types of neuron bundles, which in turn are part of larger, highly differentiated neuron groups or brain areas such as the cerebral cortex, the amygdala, the hippocampus, etc. However, what also essentially specifies that it is a human brain is its relationship with the rest of the human body, not only at the present moment but also at previous moments in

---

32. Stoeger, 'Mind-Brain Problem', 142.
33. Stoeger, 'Mind-Brain Problem', 144.

the body's history, including its conception from a particular egg and a particular sperm cell, its fetal development, and its infancy. This automatically involves the fact that this body is or was a living human person interacting with his or her environment, with other persons, and with society as a whole. Thus, the brain is the brain of a particular person, its capabilities—in terms of its brain states and the bodily, personal, and mental behavior they support—depend on an enormous variety of relationships.[34]

The mind involves not only dependency on a complex pattern of evolving brain states, but also all the relationships with the outside world that make up a person's life, including the social world. Leading neuroscientist Michael Gazzaniga says something similar:

> In the end, my argument is that all of life's experiences, personal and social, impact our emergent mental system. These experiences are powerful experiences modulating the mind. They not only constrain our brains but also reveal that it is the interaction of the two layers of brain and mind that provide our conscious reality, or moment in real time.[35]

To know and describe these relationships and their impact on brain states in detail does not seem possible at this stage, and may never be possible. Some of the constitutive relationships involved in the brain-mind problem are not accessible to science because of science's analytic and reductionist methods. Stoeger suggests that some constitutive relationships, including those involving states of consciousness, may not be accessible to science on principle.[36]

At the end of this essay, Stoeger returns to his fundamental question: 'What are the laws of nature—what are the constitutive relationships—effecting such a unified, sophisticated, and dynamic kind of organisation?'[37] In his view, our current laws of nature have revealed a very great deal about the brain, and make it clear that the mind is

---

34. Stoeger, 'Mind-Brain Problem', 145.
35. Michael S Gazzaniga, *Who's in Charge: Free Will and the Science of the Brain* (New York: HarperCollins, 2011, 2012), 218.
36. Stoeger, 'Mind-Brain Problem', 146.
37. Stoeger, 'Mind-Brain Problem', 146.

dependent on brain states, but do not take us far in dealing either with mind or with the personal. When we consider the mind, or consciousness, or the nature of a person, or interpersonal life, to say nothing of the relationship with God, our laws of nature are severely limited in what they can tell us about the far greater and more mysterious reality in which we participate.

The Laws of Nature in the Light of Quantum Theory

In his third essay, Stoeger turns to the counterintuitive world of quantum mechanics.[38] He asks: To what extent does quantum theory give us access to the underlying reality? He proposes, first, that at the quantum level, we are dealing with aspects of reality that are independent of our measurements. The fact that, in our interactions with the quantum level, we find that this level of reality is resistant to our common assumptions is one indicator of this independence. Another indicator is the further fact that quantum theory successfully predicts and explains a whole range of other phenomena. The second part of Stoeger's proposal is that our knowledge of the underlying states is indirect—it is mediated through our measurements and through the theory. This means that a great deal of reality at the quantum level may completely escape our detection.

Stoeger discusses key features of quantum theory, including the following four: (1) *Uncertainty* points to the fact that we cannot simultaneously measure both the position and the momentum of a particle. (2) *Complementarity* means that, in different types of measurement, a given quantum system may sometime manifest itself as a wave and at other times as a particle. (3) *The Problem of Measurement* springs from the fact that when a measurement is performed, only one of the possible outcomes at the quantum level is realised at the macro level—the wavefunction collapses to yield just one outcome. (4) *Decoherence* concerns the interaction between the shadowy, uncertain, but rich in potentialities, quantum level and the macro level, where only some of the potentialities at the quantum level are

---

38. William R Stoeger, 'Epistemological and Ontological Issues Arising from Quantum Theory', in *Quantum Mechanics: Scientific Perspectives on Divine Action*, edited by Robert John Russell *et al* (Vatican City: Vatican Observatory; Berkeley CA: CTNS, 2001), 81–98.

realised. In this interaction, Stoeger writes, we find 'objective chance, objective probability, and objective indefiniteness'.[39]

Stoeger argues for the Copenhagen interpretation of quantum theory, which points to the objective character of chance, indefiniteness and probability. In this interpretation it is only measurement, or interaction with the macroscopic world, that endows quantum systems with definite meaning and properties. He points out, however, that there is an increasing awareness that we must consider macroscopic objects themselves as quantum systems, so that all physical reality is understood as possessing a quantum character.

What does this say about our capacity to know reality as it is in itself? Stoeger believes: (1) there is a reality that exists independently of our knowing it, and that this reality is at least partially responsible for what we observe at both the quantum and classical levels. (2) We can say that we can have some limited knowledge of reality at the quantum level through this reality's manifestation of itself in our instruments of observation. We are therefore able to provisionally model what is knowable through the theoretical apparatus of quantum physics. And (3) we cannot know the objects or entities of the quantum world as they exist in themselves; they are 'veiled' and partially hidden from view:

> We cannot say that the basic properties that characterize quantum reality as we observe it are actually possessed by the underlying quantum entities themselves. We can only say that there are properties of the underlying quantum entities we represent by wave functions—that yield the properties we observe in our measurements when we interact with them using a macroscopic apparatus. Those observed properties are, in a sense, projections of the underlying quantum properties into the world of macroscopic experience through the interaction of quantum entities with macroscopic entities.[40]

At the quantum level, then, there must be properties that underlie and generate what we observe in quantum physics, such as uncer-

---

39. Stoeger, 'Epistemological and Ontological Issues Arising from Quantum Theory', 91.
40. Stoeger, 'Epistemological and Ontological Issues Arising from Quantum Theory', 93.

tainty and complementarity. We can tentatively model this underlying reality, but this modelling means that something in the theory stands for, without necessarily describing, the underlying reality: 'We are blocked ... from asserting that such underlying properties actually describe the properties of the underlying quantum realities as they are'.[41] Our knowledge of the underlying reality remains indirect and incomplete. We have good reason to believe, however, that what we observe in quantum physics is consistent with the underlying properties of the quantum world.

Stoeger does not believe that the wavefunction of quantum physics is an objective reality, but he holds that from a philosophical point of view it represents or stands for the hidden underlying objective reality. He believes that our knowledge of reality through quantum physics can be characterised as 'weakly objective', in the sense that we know that this reality exists and manifests itself through our interactions with it, but we do not grasp reality as it is in itself.[42] The completeness attributed to the wavefunction applies only to our knowledge of it, to the properties we can observe; it does not represent everything about the underlying reality. What do we find is that quantum physics, along with aspects of reality studied in the other sciences, reveals a world that is 'profoundly relational and interactive', where the systems and entities that make them up exist in interrelationship with one another, and where potentialities are realised only through these relationships.[43]

Stoeger sees these reflections on quantum physics as strongly reinforcing his earlier conclusions that, first, the laws of nature we formulate are imperfect and incomplete descriptions of the regularities, structures, relationships, and process of nature in itself, and second, that our laws of nature are descriptive rather than prescriptive. The quantum laws of nature do not directly describe what goes on 'behind the veil' at the level of the underlying reality.[44] Stoeger brings his work

---

41. Stoeger, 'Epistemological and Ontological Issues Arising from Quantum Theory', 94.
42. Stoeger, 'Epistemological and Ontological Issues Arising from Quantum Theory', 94.
43. Stoeger, 'Epistemological and Ontological Issues Arising from Quantum Theory', 95.
44. Stoeger, 'Epistemological and Ontological Issues Arising from Quantum Theory', 95.

to a conclusion with three comments on divine action in the light of this view of the laws of nature:

1. God's universal creative action must take place, in part, 'behind the veil', at the quantum level, in laws of nature, in regularities, processes and relationships, to which we have little access.
2. There are similar, 'veiled' realities at other levels of the natural world where we do not know the laws of nature as they actually function—even approximately. These include consciousness and the interpersonal, which are discussed in the second of the three essays. Even more to the point, Stoeger notes, are the relationships between the transcendent Creator and human persons and communities, through experiences and manifestation of transcendence. It is here, he says, that God's special action seems to be focussed. God's action appears in our world as partially 'veiled'. Because it is partially veiled, the appearance of God's action can certainly reflect something of the divine reality, but God's action appears to us only on this side of the veil.
3. Because it seems that God's special divine action is almost always effected in terms of God's personal relationship with human persons, it will involve top-down influences on the physical causal structure. It thus transcends the causes that we can perceive and model adequately in our physical sciences. This happens, of course, even in our inter-human relationships, but is far more pronounced if we think of the utterly transcendent and spiritual God in interrelationship with human persons.

What is the connection, the 'causal joint' between God and creatures in special divine action as well as divine creative action? By way of answer, Stoeger returns to his earlier article on divine action: The causal nexus is the 'active, richly differentiated, profoundly immanent (because it is transcendent) presence of God in created beings and their relationships'.[45] God's action through secondary causes springs from the inclusion of creatures in God's own existence and relationships as Trinity: 'The presence of God in each entity constitutes the

---

45. Stoeger, 'Epistemological and Ontological Issues Arising from Quantum Theory', 97. See also Stoeger, 'Describing God's Action in the World in Light of Scientific Knowledge of Reality', in *Chaos and Complexity*, 253-4.

direct, the immediate, relationship of that entity with God, and therefore is the channel of divine influence in secondary causes'.[46] God acts, Stoeger proposes, not simply through the laws of nature as we know them, but through the laws of nature as they function in reality, including all the regularities, processes and relationships of the natural world, many of which are hidden from our eyes or glimpsed only fleetingly.

Consequences for Theology: The Expansion of Our View of Secondary Causes

Stoeger was convinced that philosophy plays an indispensable mediating role in the relationship between science and theology. His three essays on the laws of nature explored here form a helpful philosophical mediation between science and the Christian theology of divine action and, more specifically, a fresh mediation between contemporary science and Aquinas's theology of a God who acts consistently through created causes.

A great deal of Christian theology involves divine action, including God's continuing creative act, God's providential care, divine revelation, the experience of God's grace, the incarnation, the resurrection, the promise of the transformation of human beings and, with them, the whole of creation, and miracles. The question, central for the discussion between science and theology, is how God's actions are to be understood. Are they to be understood in an interventionist sense as God overturning laws of nature, or as putting them aside, in order to accomplish God's purposes? Or may we think of God acting in a way that fully respects the laws of nature, acting lovingly and effectively but in a noninterventionist way? Here I focus on one important example of divine action, that of miracles, proposing that Stoeger's account of the laws of nature helps us understand miracles in a noninterventionist but genuinely theological way that builds on Aquinas.[47]

---

46. Stoeger, 'Epistemological and Ontological Issues', 97–8.
47. I have developed a broader theology of divine action in *How God Acts: Creation, Redemption and Special Divine Action* (Minneapolis: Fortress, 2010).

Aquinas holds that God is present to all things at their most interior level, enabling them to exist and act at every moment.[48] God's very nature is to exist, and God causes existence (*esse*) in all other beings. Nothing is more deeply interior to an entity than its existence. God is found in every dimension of creation: God 'acts interiorly in all things', because 'God is the cause of *esse*, which is innermost in all things'.[49] All things exist only as created by God *ex nihilo* at every moment. They depend on God entirely for their existence and action at every moment. Following the language of Aristotle, but with his own profound theological convictions, Aquinas calls all the interacting causes found in the empirical world *secondary* causes. God, then, is the *primary* cause, the Creator always acting providentially in and through created causes. It is by God's power that every other power acts.[50]

God is not a cause like creaturely causes, but the uncreated ground of all creaturely causality. When God is described as a primary cause, the word 'cause' is used only analogously to refer to the absolutely unique relationship between Creator and creatures, by which God confers existence on all things and enables them to be, to act, and to become. There is an infinite difference, then, between God's action and the actions of secondary causes in the world. Secondary causes include all the interacting causes found in empirical reality, absolutely all the patterns of relationship found in the natural world, everything studied by the sciences, everything that could ever be studied by the sciences in the future.

According to Aquinas, God delights in creatures being truly causal in their own right: 'Divine Providence works through intermediaries. For God governs the lower through the higher, not from any impotence on his part, but from the abundance of his goodness imparting to creatures the dignity of causing'.[51] God so loves and respects the dignity of creatures that God wants them to be fully causal, respecting their integrity, their dignity and their proper autonomy. Aquinas opposes those who would say that God acts alone and without intermediaries:

---

48. Thomas Aquinas, *Summa theologiae* (hereafter *ST*) 1, q 8, a 1. I am using the Blackfriars translation: Thomas Aquinas, *Summa theologiae* (London: Blackfriars in conjunction with Eyre & Spottiswoode, 1964–1980).
49. *ST* 1, q 105, a 6.
50. Thomas Aquinas, *Quaestiones disputatae de potentia dei* q 3, a 7.
51. *ST* 1, q 22, a 3.

> But this is impossible, and first because it would deprive creation of its pattern of cause and effect, which in turn would imply lack of power in the creator, since an agent's power is the source of its giving an effect a causative capability. It is impossible, secondly, because if the active powers that are observed in creatures accomplished nothing, there would be no point to their having received such powers. Indeed if all creatures are utterly devoid of any activity of their own, then they themselves would seem to have a pointless existence, since everything exists for the sake of its operation.[52]

God's love and respect for creation, therefore, is such that God wants creation to have its own pattern of cause and effect. God wants creaturely causes to have their own integrity and their own proper autonomy.

In the context of this deep respect for creaturely causes, how does Aquinas think about miracles? In a miracle, he says, the action of God replaces secondary causes. This means that miracles are 'exceptions to the pattern in nature',[53] which occur in a manner that 'surpasses the capabilities of nature'.[54] Aquinas sees a miracle as an event that occurs without a secondary cause:

> But if we take the order in things as it depends upon any of the secondary causes, then God can act apart from it; he is not subject to that order but rather it is subject to him, as issuing from him not out of necessity of nature, but the decision of his will. He could in fact have established another sort of pattern in the world; hence when he so wills, he can act apart from the given order, producing, for example, the effects of secondary causes without them or some effects that surpass the powers of these causes.[55]

In Aquinas's theology, as Brian Davies rightly points out, miracles surpass the natural order but do not do violence to it.[56] If God brings

---

52. *ST* 1, q 105, a 6.
53. *ST* 1, q 105, a 7 ad 1.
54. *ST* 1, q 105, a 7 ad 2.
55. *ST* 1, q 105, a 6.
56. Brian Davies, *The Thought of Thomas Aquinas* (Oxford: Clarendon, 1992), 173.

about something miraculous in the natural order this is no more a violation of the natural order than the fact that the order exists in the first place.[57]

While this is true, it is precisely at this point that Stoeger's insights into the laws of nature enable us to go further than Aquinas. In my view, Aquinas's thought is indispensable in the dialogue between science and theology, with his concept of primary and secondary causality and his view of God's profound respect for secondary causes. But what if God works through secondary causes even in the case of many of the events in the Gospels and in our lives that we rightly see as miracles, as marvellous gifts of God?

Stoeger's distinction between the laws of nature as we know them and model them and the laws of nature understood as the regularities, potentialities and processes of the natural world itself greatly expands our understanding of the ways God works through the natural world. Stoeger's distinction enables us to see more clearly that, in thinking about God's action, we are not limited to the two alternatives: divine action that is either in conformity with our laws of nature or not. It is not simply a choice between God's working through our laws of nature or God's overturning or bypassing them. God might be working through all the unknown or partly known possibilities of the natural world that far surpass what we already know and model.

Stoeger's enormous expansion of the laws of nature applies with equal force to what Aquinas calls secondary causes, which are simply all the interactions we perceive in the empirical world. When we extend our understanding of these interactions to include those that contemporary science glimpses, such as those operating in the brain-mind relationship, and those at work at the quantum level, those that we simply do not know at all, then the range of secondary causes is mightily extended. Here, too, in and through the natural world, including the many aspects of the natural world not yet mapped by our scientific laws, God may work marvels for God's people.

What I am proposing here, then, does not mean any kind of rejection of the theology of miracles. As John Meier has shown at length, miracles cannot be dismissed from the gospel narratives without completely distorting their accounts of Jesus. Miracles are intrinsic

---

57. Davies, *The Thought of Thomas Aquinas*, 173.

to his life and work.[58] And the experience of miracles has been part of Christian life through all the ages since. The position taken here is that miracles do occur as marvellous acts of God in our history. The question is whether miracles are necessarily acts of God that occur without secondary causes. Stoeger's account of the laws of nature creates room for God to be seen as, at least possibly, acting in miracles through secondary causes, through aspects of nature that we have not mapped with our scientific theories.

Such an interpretation, then, would support Karl Rahner's contention that there is no reason why the laws of nature would need to be abolished or suspended if God's self-communication were to take place through laws that are, because of God's creative act, the very precondition for this divine self-giving.[59] This interpretation of Stoeger would also support the position of Gerhard Lohfink, who writes of the existence of Jesus as altogether in harmony with the will of God, so that in his miracles he 'called upon the powers of this world, extending into a profound depth that is impenetrable for us today'.[60] He goes on to say that 'no one can define where the limits of "nature" in this sphere lie, unless one would lay claim to having an absolutely complete and comprehensive knowledge of all the powers at work in nature. Who would dare to make such an assertion?'[61]

Building on Stoeger's insights, I have sought to show that the vehicle for God's action in creation, grace, incarnation and miracles is not simply the world our sciences model with our discovered laws of nature. Rather, the vehicle of God's self-manifestations and actions, even in the case of miracles, is the wonderful, far more mysterious world of nature itself including those aspects of the natural world that still escape our scientific modelling.

---

58. John P Meier, *A Marginal Jew: Rethinking the Historical Jesus*, volume 2, *Mentor, Message, and Miracles* (New York: Doubleday, 1994), 509–1038.
59. Karl Rahner, *Foundations of Christian Faith* (New York Seabury, 1978), 261.
60. Gerhard Lohfink, *Jesus of Nazareth: What He Wanted, Who He Was* (Collegeville, MN: Liturgical, 2012), 142.
61. Lohfink, *Jesus of Nazareth*. 142-3.

D.   In Dialogue with Karl Rahner

Resurrection and the Costs of Evolution: A Dialogue with Rahner on Non-Interventionist Theology

Suffering that springs from natural causes, such as the South Asian tsunami of 26 December 2004, has always raised hard questions for Christian theology. In the current dialogue between science and theology, the issue of the suffering of human and non-human creatures takes on a new intensity, with science making it clear how predation, competition for survival, death and extinction are built into the 3.8 billion year history of life on Earth. Without creatures drawing energy from their environment there could be no emergence of life. Without death and the succession of generations there could be no evolution: there would be no eyes, wings, or human brains. The evolution of life in its abundance and beauty is accompanied by terrible costs to human beings and to other species.

The costs are built into the process. They are built into the biology, geology and the underlying physics of a dynamic life-bearing planet. The costs of evolution are built into an emergent universe. This pushes theology to a deeper reflection on the nature of God's action. Theology needs to respond, however inadequately, to the idea that so much that is beautiful and good arises by way of increasing complexity through emergent processes that involve tragic loss. We know, as no generation has known before us, that these costs are intrinsic to the processes that give rise to life on Earth in its beauty, fecundity and diversity.

In response to this, a theology of creation has to be able to offer a view of God working creatively in and through the natural world to bring it to healing and wholeness. I think that there are at least three requirements for such a response. First, with Robert John Russell and others in the science-theology dialogue, I am convinced that a theological response to the costs of evolution must involve eschatology, even though the claims of Christian eschatology exist in some tension with the predictions of scientific cosmology.[1] What is needed is an objective and powerful theology of both resurrection and the final fulfillment of creation. God's action in creating an emergent universe needs to be understood in the light of the resurrection and its promise that all things will be transformed and redeemed in Christ (Rom 8:19–23; Col 1:20; Eph 1:10; Rev 21:5). A merely psychological or subjective theology of the resurrection cannot offer hope to creation. Only a theology of resurrection that is eschatologically transformative can begin to respond to the suffering that is built into an evolutionary universe.

A second requirement, I will propose, is that this divine action be understood in a non-interventionist way. Of course, it has long been recognised that science becomes impossible if God is thought of as intervening in such a way as to compete with or to overturn the regularities of nature. In addition to this, the theological problem of suffering is made far worse if God is thought of as arbitrarily intervening to send suffering to some creatures and not to others. Christian theology today has the task of facing up to the way in which a particular theology of divine action, one that runs deep in the Christian tradition, can contribute to the pain of those who suffer because of its implicit theological model of an interventionist God, a God who chooses freely to send sufferings to some and lovingly to protect others. Such a theology can contribute to a sense of alienation from God. The culture of an interventionist God is reinforced, sometimes explicitly and sometimes implicitly, by many aspects of church life. The scientific insight the costs of evolution are built into an emergent universe presents theology with the challenge of finding an alternative to a God who can be thought of as freely modifying the dynamics of tectonic plates to save some from a tsunami, while causing others to suffer it.

The third requirement for a theology of divine action that might offer some response to the costs of evolution, in my view, is that it would involve an understanding of God's power as constrained by

---

1. See for example Robert John Russell 'Bodily Resurrection, Eschatology and Scientific Cosmology: The Mutual Interaction of Christian Theology and Science', in *Resurrection: Theological and Scientific Perspectives*, edited by Ted Peters, Robert John Russell and Michael Welker (Grand Rapids: Eerdmans, 2002), 3–30.

God's love and respect for creatures. Such a view of divine power can be based on the way the power of God is revealed and defined in Jesus of Nazareth, above all in his death and resurrection. In the cross, divine omnipotence is revealed as the transcendent divine capacity to give oneself in love. The cross does not reveal the absence of divine power but its true nature. Only an omnipotent love can give itself away in radical vulnerability.[2] Theology had always taught that God can act only in accordance with the divine nature, and this nature is revealed in the Christ-event as radical love. It can be argued that the God revealed in the cross and resurrection is a God whose nature it is to respect the proper autonomy of creatures, to work through them and to bring them to fulfilment. In such a view of divine power, the love that defines the divine nature is understood as a love that *waits upon* creation, living with its processes, accompanying each creature in love, rejoicing in every emergence, suffering with every suffering creature, and promising to bring all to healing and fullness of life.

In what follows, I will assume the position on divine power outlined here, which I have discussed in more detail in other places.[3] My focus will be the other two requirements, eschatological power and non-intervention, as they apply to the resurrection. Many would think of the resurrection as the hardest case for a non-interventionist theology of divine action. I will ask: Can the resurrection be understood as an act of God that is objective and powerfully transformative but is also non-interventionist? Before addressing this question directly, I will situate my own approach to divine action, which is grounded in the tradition of Karl Rahner, in the context of the wider discussion of divine action and non-interventionist theology that took place in the nineties of the last century.

Non-Interventionist Theologies of Divine Action

In September 1987 the Vatican Observatory, at the initiative of Pope John Paul, held an important international conference on science and religion that resulted in the publication *Physics, Philosophy and*

---

2. On this see Walter Kasper, *The God of Jesus Christ* (London: SCM, 1983), 195.
3. See for example Denis Edwards, 'Every Sparrow that Falls to the Ground: The Costs of Evolution and the Christ-Event', in *Ecotheology: The Journal of Religion, Nature and the Environment* 11 (March 2006): 103–23 in this volume; *Ecology at the Heart of Faith* (Maryknoll, NY: Orbis, 2006), 39–45.

Theology.[4] Building on this work, George Coyne SJ, the director of the Observatory, invited Robert John Russell and the Centre for Theology and the Natural Sciences at Berkeley to co-sponsor with the Observatory a series of research conferences and publications. These conferences took up the theme of divine action, exploring it first in relation to quantum cosmology, followed by chaos and complexity, evolutionary and molecular biology, neuroscience and the person, and quantum mechanics.[5]

In these discussions, a number of participants agreed that a theology of divine action needed to include not only God's continuous creative act (*creatio continua*), but also special and objective divine acts, which would include personal providence and the Christ-event. At the same time, they sought to articulate a theology of divine action in which God acted without violating or overturning the laws of nature. Over a number of conferences, a consensus emerged around a form of divine action that was special and objective, but non-interventionist – in the sense of not violating or suspending the laws of nature.[6] Within this consensus there are at least five positions taken.

First, Ian Barbour, Charles Birch and John Haught represent the perspective of process theology, and they understand divine action as

---

4. Robert J Russell, William R Stoeger SJ and George V Coyne SJ, editors, *Physics, Philosophy and Theology: A Common Quest for Understanding* (Vatican City State: Vatican Observatory Publications, 1988).
5. Robert J Russell, Nancey C Murphy and Chris J Isham, editors, *Quantum Cosmology and the Laws of Nature: Scientific Perspectives on Divine Action*, second edition (Vatican City State; Berkeley, Calif: Vatican Observatory; Center for Theology and the Natural Sciences, 1996); Robert J Russell, Nancey C Murphy and Arthur Peacocke, editors, *Chaos and Complexity: Scientific Perspectives on Divine Action* (Vatican City State; Berkeley, Calif: Vatican Observatory; Center for Theology and the Natural Sciences, 1995); Robert J Russell, William R Stoeger SJ and Francisco J Ayala, editors, *Evolutionary and Molecular Biology: Scientific Perspectives on Divine Action* (Vatican City State; Berkeley, Calif: Vatican Observatory; Center for Theology and the Natural Sciences, 1998); Robert J Russell, Nancey C Murphy, Theo C Meyering and Michael A Arbib, editors, *Neuroscience and the Person: Scientific Perspectives on Divine Action* (Vatican City State; Berkeley, Calif: Vatican Observatory; Center for Theology and the Natural Sciences, 1999); Robert John Russell, Philip Clayton, Kirk Wegter-McNelly and John Polkinghorne, editors, *Quantum Mechanics: Scientific Perspectives on Divine Action* (Vatican City State; Berkeley, Calif: Vatican Observatory; Center for Theology and the Natural Sciences, 2001).
6. See Robert J Russell, 'Introduction', in *Chaos and Complexity*, 9–13.

the inviting lure of God, which is operative in every actual occasion, but which does not determine the outcome in an exclusive way. Second, a number of authors, including Robert Russell, Nancey Murphy, George Ellis and Thomas Tracy explore the idea that God acts in the indeterminacy of quantum events to bring about one of a number of possible outcomes.[7] A third position is taken by John Polkinghorne: God can be thought of as acting in the openness of chaotic and complex systems to bring about outcomes through the top-down imparting of information. Fourth, Arthur Peacocke sees God as acting in and through and under every aspect of nature, acting on the system as a whole, by way of analogy with a 'top-down' or 'whole-part' cause in nature. Finally, William Stoeger SJ and Stephen Happel understand God as acting in and through secondary causes: Stoeger sees the triune God acting in every aspect of creation, through God's immanent and differentiated presence to all things, including those laws of nature of which we have a partial understanding and those processes and regularities of nature that are still unknown to us.

My proposal begins from this last position (Stoeger), which I see as compatible in many respects with the fourth position (Peacocke).[8] I am drawn to Stoeger's position because it clearly respects the abso-

---

7. Murphy sees God as acting in all quantum events, not as the sole determiner of events, but in a mediated action, in the sense that God always acts together with nature at the quantum level. Tracy suggests seeing God as acting in some rather than all quantum events, in order to bring about the effects of God's providence. Russell proposes that God acts in all quantum events until the appearance of life and consciousness, and then God increasingly refrains from determining outcomes, leaving room for top-down causality in conscious creatures, particularly in humans. For a summary of these views see Russell, 'Divine Action and Quantum Mechanics: A Fresh Assessment', in *Quantum Mechanics*, 293–328.

8. Those who see God as determining one of several possible outcomes, either at the quantum level (Russell and Murphy) or at the macro level (Polkinghorne), increase the intensity of the theodicy problem. Murphy and Ellis respond to this with a kenotic theology in *On the Moral Nature of the Universe: Theology, Cosmology and Ethics* (Minneapolis, Minn: Fortress Press, 1996). Polkinghorne explores the issue in a number of places including 'Kenotic Creation and Divine Action', in *The Work of Love: Creation as Kenosis*, edited by John Polkinghorne (Grand Rapids: Eerdmans, 2001), 90–106. Russell acknowledges that 'theology becomes a particularly intense issue in light of the present thesis regarding a noninterventionist approach to objective, special divine action' and argues that the response is to be found in a Trinitarian theology of resurrection and final transformation ('Divine Action and Quantum Mechanics', 319, 322–3).

lute transcendence and radical mystery of God's action and because I continue to be attracted by Aquinas's idea that God acts through intermediate secondary causes 'not from any impotence on his part, but from the abundance of his goodness imparting to creatures also the *dignity of causing*.'[9] Aquinas, of course, allows for the exception of miracles, where he sees God acting without a secondary cause.[10] I will not take up a theology of miracles in general here, but simply focus on the resurrection and ask: Can God be thought of as working consistently through secondary causes even in the resurrection? Can the resurrection be seen as a non-interventionist divine action in the sense that here too God acts through secondary causes? Can God be understood as working in the resurrection through the laws and constants of nature rather than as violating, suspending, or bypassing them?

In Rahner's work, there are suggestions for a theology of divine action that can extend this discussion of non-interventionist divine action. Such a theology would stand within the perspective of the Thomist tradition, seeing God as acting through secondary causes because God gives to creatures the dignity of causing, but as opposed to Thomas's view of miracles, would argue that it is possible to think of God as consistently working through secondary causes. Rahner discusses the issue of divine action briefly in his *Foundations of Christian Faith*. He points out that if we are to experience God, it cannot be as one element in the world, but as the very ground of the world. We find God in the openness to mystery that occurs in our experience of created realities, but, if this is so, then God must be 'embedded' in this world to begin with.[11] What is seen as an 'intervention' of God is really to be understood as the historical expression of God's self-communicating presence that it always intrinsic to the world. Rahner says that every 'intervention', although it is a free and unpredictable act of God, actually makes concrete and historical the one intervention by

---

9. *Summa theologiae* 1a.22.3. Translation by Thomas Gilby OP in *Saint Thomas Aquinas Summa Theologiae* V (London: Blackfriars, 1967), 99. Central to this tradition is the idea that God does not act as one cause among creaturely causes, but as the ground of all created causes. It is worth noting that Polkinghorne takes an opposing view, stating that 'I have come to believe that *the Creator's kenotic love includes allowing divine special providence to act as a cause among causes*' (Polkinghorne, 'Kenotic Creation and Divine Action', 104).
10. *Summa theologiae* 1a.105 6, 8.
11. Rahner, *Foundations of Christian Faith*, 87.

which God has embedded God's self in the world from the beginning as its 'self-communicating ground'.[12]

In Rahner's view there certainly are *special* acts of God, but these are 'objectifications' of God's one self-bestowing action. In these special acts of God, a created reality mediates and expresses the immanent presence and love of God. Because creatures really do express the divine action, Rahner speaks of *objective,* special divine acts. However, he sees these events as capable of being recognised as special only within the context of subjective experience of grace.[13] In such divine acts, the one self-bestowing act of God finds objective expression in and through a range of created secondary causes. These include words, persons, and events. To those with eyes to see, these become symbolic mediations of the divine.

Rahner offers a 'modest' example of a special divine action. When a person has a 'good idea' that proves effective and is experienced as a gift from God, there may well be a natural explanation for the good idea. But it can still be seen as an act of God, in the sense that in it a person encounters the God who is present and really mediated in this event of a good idea. When a good idea is experienced as the place of encounter with the ground of all reality, it can be understood as willed by God, as God-given, and hence inspired. It becomes, in Rahner's view, a genuine experience of God's special providence.

In a later (1980) book, co-authored with Karl-Heinz Weger, Rahner comments explicitly on interventionist and non-interventionist approaches to divine action and speaks of a 'fundamental change' away from an interventionist view of God.[14] He acknowledges that while in traditional theology, God was understood as the ever-present, immanent, all-embracing and ultimate ground of being, traditional theology also assumed that there were interventions of God that could be located at certain points of space and time. In fact, the traditional idea of the history of salvation was 'based mainly on the model of interventions by God'. This interventionist model coexisted with a more universal view of God as the 'deepest energy of the world', and the two models were never completely reconciled.[15]

---

12. Rahner, *Foundations of Christian Faith*.
13. Rahner, *Foundations of Christian Faith*, 88.
14. Rahner, Karl and Karl-Heinz Weger, *Our Christian Faith* (London: Burns and Oates, 1980), 57.
15. Rahner and Weger, *Our Christian Faith*, 77.

While Rahner has no wish to condemn the older approach, and while he too holds for a history of salvation and of particular and special revelation, above all in Jesus Christ, he argues for the emergence of a 'universalist basic model' of divine action. In this universalist model, God in God's free grace has always and everywhere 'communicated himself to his creation as its innermost energy and works in the world from the inside out'.[16] Rahner wants to show that, without interpreting Christianity in a naturalist way, it is possible 'with all due caution and modesty, to do without a particularist model of external intervention by God into his world at particular points of space and time'.[17]

In this kind of theology, Jesus can be seen as the one who makes God's deepest promise historically accessible and irreversible. Because this promise of God is already the fundamental energy at work in all things in the universe, Rahner believes it is possible to understand the event of Christ without the image of intervention.[18] The resurrection of Jesus gives expression to this promise that is always at work in creation. It is certainly an event of revelation, but not one coming from 'outside'.[19]

Rahner simply states this claim. I will attempt to explore it further, asking: Can the resurrection itself be understood in non-interventionist terms without diminishing its eschatological promise? I will propose that four lines of thought in Rahner's theology suggest an affirmative answer: his theology of resurrection as part of the one divine act of self-bestowal, his evolutionary Christology, his sacramental or symbolic theology of salvation, and his understanding of resurrection as ontological transformation.

---

16. Rahner and Weger, *Our Christian Faith*, 78–9.
17. Rahner and Weger, *Our Christian Faith*, 84.
18. 'The event of God's promise of himself in Jesus makes that deepest promise by God of himself to the world historically accessible and irreversible. It is always and everywhere the fundamental energy and force of the world and its history. It is therefore perfectly possible to understand the event of Jesus without the aid of images of an intervention in the world from outside. In doing without such an image, however, we must let history really be history and clearly realise that this deepest energy and power of the world and its history is God in his sovereign freedom, who, by his free promise of himself, has made himself this deepest energy and force of the world.' Rahner and Weger, *Our Christian Faith*, 103–4.
19. Rahner and Weger, *Our Christian Faith*, 111.

Resurrection within the *One* Divine Act

Rahner sees divine action in terms of God's self-bestowal to creation. He looks to the heart of Christian revelation and finds that God gives God's self to us in the Word made flesh and in the Spirit poured out in grace. He sees this Trinitarian self-giving as involving not just incarnation and grace, but creation and final fulfilment. The self-giving of God defines every aspect of God's action. This means that the scientific story of the emergence of the universe and the evolution of life is to be seen as part of a larger story of divine self-bestowal.[20] God creates in order to give God's self to creation as its final fulfilment. This fulfilment will be the salvation not only of human beings but also of the whole creation. God wills to bestow God's very self in love, and creation comes to be as the addressee of this self-bestowal.[21]

In the theological tradition, there have been two schools of thought regarding the relationship between creation and the Christ-event. One school tends to see the Christ-event as a second act after creation, brought about because of sin and the need for redemption. The other school, associated with the Franciscan theology exemplified in Duns Scotus (126–1308), holds that God freely chooses, from the beginning, to create a world in which the Word would be made flesh. Rahner adopts this Franciscan theology and sees creation, incarnation and final fulfilment as united in one great act of divine self-bestowal. The incarnation is not thought of as an add-on to creation. It is not simply a remedy for sin, although it is this. The Christ-event is the irreversible beginning of God's self-giving to creation that will find its fulfilment only when the whole of creation is transformed in Christ. Divine action is *one* act, one act of self-bestowing love in which there are distinct elements that include creation, incarnation and final fulfilment.[22]

---

20. Rahner, 'Christology in the Setting of Modern Man's Understanding of Himself and of His World', in *Theological Investigations* 11 (New York: Seabury, 1974) 215–29, at 219. I am building here on an earlier article 'Resurrection of the Body and Transformation of the Universe in the Theology of Karl Rahner', forthcoming in *Philosophy and Theology*.
21. Rahner, 'Resurrection', in *Encyclopedia of Theology: A Concise Sacramentum Mundi*, edited by Karl Rahner (London: Burns and Oates, 1975), 1430–42, at 1442.
22. This means that creation and incarnation are 'two moments and two phases of the *one* process of God's self-giving and self-expression, although it is an intrinsically differentiated process'. (Rahner, *Foundations*, 197).

Rahner insists that what is most specific to the Christian view of God is the idea of a God who bestows God's very self to creation.[23] This is a God who creates creatures that are *capax infiniti*, who without being consumed in the fire of divinity, are able to receive God's life as their own fulfilment. Christianity insists against pantheism on the distinction between creation and God, but this does not mean that there is a distance between God and creatures. God's being is the distinction.[24] But this same transcendent creator is radically interior to each creature in self-bestowing love. God is the very core of the world's reality and the world is truly the fate of God. Creation is intrinsically directed towards self-bestowal. It is not simply that God creates something other, but that God freely communicates God's own reality to the other. The universe emerges in the process of God's self-bestowal. Rahner sees this self-bestowal of the transcendent God as 'the most immanent factor in the creature'.[25]

In this concept, creation is intrinsically oriented to the resurrection of Christ and intrinsically oriented to final fulfilment. It is eschatological from the ground up. This view of God acting in one act of self-bestowal constitutes a first line of thought that can build towards an inside-out rather than an interventionist theology of resurrection. If God acts in one differentiated act, this suggests that the resurrection is not an intervention of God from without, but the central dimension of this one act by which God creates, saves and brings all to fulfilment. This leads to a second line of thought that can contribute to a non-interventionist theology of resurrection, that of evolutionary Christology.

Resurrection within evolutionary Christology

While divine action can be considered from God's side as divine self-bestowal, it can also be considered from the perspective of its effect

---

23. Rahner, 'The Specific Character of the Christian Concept of God', in *Theological Investigations* 21 (New York: Crossroad, 1988), 185–95.
24. 'God is not merely the one who as creator establishes a world distant from himself as something different, but rather he is the one who gives himself away to this world and who has his own fate in and with this world. God is not only himself the giver, but he is also the gift' (Rahner, 'The Specific Character' 191). See also his 'Christology in the Setting', 224.
25. Rahner, 'Immanent and Transcendent Consummation of the World', in *Theological Investigations* 10 (London: Darton, Longman & Todd, 1973), 273–89, at 281.

in the creature, as enabling creaturely self-transcendence. According to Rahner, the effect of God's immanent presence is that creation has the capacity to transcend itself. This concept is worked out in Rahner's anthropology and is central to his evolutionary Christology, but it functions in much of his work.[26] With the concept of divine self-bestowal, it provides a way of grasping the radical unity of God's one act. It is God present in self-bestowal who enables creaturely self-transcendence. Divine self-bestowal and creaturely self-transcendence characterise not only creation, grace and incarnation, but also final consummation.[27]

The ancient theological tradition has always had a theology of continuous creation. It saw God as sustaining all creatures in being (*conservatio*) and enabling them to act (*concursus*). Rahner transforms this into a theology of becoming. God not only enables creatures to exist, but enables them to transcend themselves, to become something new. In his evolutionary Christology, he begins from the fundamental *unity* he finds in creation. All of creation is united in its one origin in God, in its self-realisation as one united world, and in its one future in God. Within this unity, there are transitions to the *new* in the history of the universe, particularly when matter becomes life, and when life becomes self-conscious spirit. Rahner argues for a theology of God's creative act as enabling the active self-transcendence of creation. This capacity is truly intrinsic to creation, but it occurs through the creative power of the immanent God. The presence and constant 'pressure' of the divine being enables the creature to become more than it is in itself.[28] This 'pressure' is not something that can be discerned by the natural sciences, but is the interior, dynamic relationship of all things in the evolving universe to their Creator.

The material universe transcends itself in the emergence of life, and life transcends itself in the human. In human beings, the universe becomes open to self-consciousness, freedom and a personal relationship with God in grace. Rahner sees the Christ-event in this con-

---

26. See Rahner, *Hominisation: The Evolutionary Origin of Man as a Theological Problem* (London: Burns and Oates, 1965), 98–101; 'Christology within an Evolutionary View of the World', in *Theological Investigations* 5 (London: Darton, Longman & Todd), 157–92; *Foundations of Christian Faith* 178–203.
27. Rahner, 'Christology in the Setting', 223–6.
28. Rahner, 'Natural Science and Christian Faith', in *Theological Investigations* 21 (New York: Crossroad, 1988), 16–55, at 37.

text, as the definitive self-transcendence of the created universe into God.[29] Jesus in his created humanity is a part of evolutionary history, a part that is completely and uniquely open to the divine bestowal. If the Christ-event is considered from below, it can be seen as the self-transcendence of the evolving universe into God. If it is considered from above, it can be seen as God's irreversible self-bestowal to creation. In this one person, there is found the irreversible self-communication of God to creatures and the definitive human acceptance of this communication. Because of this, Jesus Christ is understood as absolute saviour.[30]

Jesus' creaturely life of self-giving love culminates in his death as a radical act of love for God and for others. In the resurrection, God radically and irreversibly takes creation to God's self. The life, death and resurrection of Christ are always to be seen together. In this paschal event, part of evolutionary history gives itself completely into God and is taken up and transformed in God, as the beginning of the transformation of all things.

Together, the death and resurrection are to be seen as the culminating moment of the self-transcendence of creation to God, and as the irreversible self-bestowal of God to creation. Within the context of an evolutionary Christology, the resurrection can be seen not as an intervention from without, but as the free and unpredictable breaking forth of that divine self-bestowal to the world that has been immanent in creation from the very beginning in the presence to creation of the Creator Spirit.

Resurrection as Real Symbol of Salvation

A third dimension of Rahner's theology that supports a view of resurrection that is both objective and non-interventionist is found in his concept of salvation. The Christian tradition has always claimed that Jesus died and was raised up 'for us'. Rahner asks how this is to be understood. In what sense is the paschal event the cause of our salvation?

---

29. In Jesus, we find the 'initial beginning and definitive triumph of the movement of the world's self-transcendence into absolute closeness to the mystery of God' (Rahner, *Foundations*, 181).
30. Rahner, *Foundations*, 193.

Rahner finds that the biblical concept of redemption through the sacrificial blood of Christ fails to communicate in the cultural contexts of today. It 'smacks of mythology' when an angry God seems to insist on reparation for the offence done and then becomes a forgiving God as a result of a bloody sacrifice.[31] Rahner also rejects Anselm's theory of satisfaction as meaningful for today: it assumes that the sins of the world are an infinite offence against God, because of the dignity of the one offended; it assumes that the satisfaction is of infinite value because it is measured by the dignity of the person making satisfaction. These assumptions are difficult to justify in today's world.[32] Rahner acknowledges that these theologies can be meaningful when they are properly understood in their historical context, but he sees them as secondary and derivative in relation to the primary experience of salvation in Christ.

Rahner thinks that a more contemporary theology of salvation is needed. A fundamental requirement for such a theology would be that it shows clearly that God is the cause of salvation. What needs to be avoided is any suggestion that the cross changes God from being a God of wrath to a God of grace. Christ's death and resurrection do not cause God to begin to love us sinners. They are the expression and consequence of God's divine love. They give expression to God's eternal will to save. Rahner suggests a theology of salvation in which the Christ-event has a causality of a quasi-sacramental and real symbolic nature.[33] The life, death and resurrection taken together can be seen as the real symbol in which God's saving will reaches its full and irrevocable realisation and manifestation in the world. Rahner's concept of the real symbol is a strong one. It involves not only the revelation of salvation but its accomplishment.

Jesus' life finds its climax in the surrender to God in his death and in God's acceptance of this in the resurrection. The event of Christ's life, death and resurrection is both the symbol and the radical accomplishment of God's saving love. Jesus, who is one of us, who has given himself in death to God, is raised up by God. This is the irreversible

---

31. Rahner and Weger, *Our Christian Faith*, 114.
32. Rahner and Weger, *Our Christian Faith*, 114–15.
33. Rahner, *Foundations,* 282–5; 'The Theology of the Symbol', in *Theological Investigations* 4 (London: Darton, Longman & Todd), 221–52; 'Salvation', in *Encyclopedia of Theology*, 1499–530, at 1527.

manifestation of God's saving love for our world. In the Christ-event, God's salvific will is made present in the world 'historically, really and irrevocably'.[34] The universal experience of the Spirit in grace is always ordered to the Word made flesh, to Jesus' life, death and resurrection. The grace of the Spirit is always the grace of Christ. In this sense, Christ is the final cause of the Spirit, and the Spirit is always the Spirit of Jesus Christ.[35]

In this framework, the resurrection is not an event that comes from outside, but the expression in history of God's will to save, which has been operative in creation from the beginning and will find its fulfilment in the transformation of the whole creation. The resurrection is the radical expression of the promise of God, and the beginning of the fulfilment of the promise. It is the real symbol, the expression and the reality, of God's saving, self-bestowing love at work in the world. It is the bringing to visibility and to an initial accomplishment of the self-bestowing love that has always been present to every aspect of the universe and its creatures.

It is of the essence of the church to be the visible sign and agent of the resurrection at work in the world.[36] The risen Christ is encountered today in the experience of grace that occurs in the mediation of the church, above all in the Word of God, in the Eucharist and in the other sacraments. But these sacraments are linked to the mysticism of everyday life. They 'awaken, deepen, strengthen, and bring to full expression' the sacramental experiences of everyday life.[37] Christians go out from the Eucharist and encounter the resurrected Christ in words, persons and events in this world. In the light of the Word, they meet the risen one in the transcendental experience of grace that occurs in daily life. The experience of the risen one is not the experience of an intervention from without but a meeting with the mystery of God incarnate in Christ that occurs in and through our encounters with fellow creatures in the world. It has a sacramental structure.

---

34. Karl Rahner, *Foundations*, 284.
35. Rahner, *Foundations*, 317.
36. See Karl Rahner, *Meditations on the Sacraments* (New York: Seabury, 1977), xv.
37. Harvey D Egan, *Karl Rahner: Mystic of Everyday Life* (New York: Crossroad, 1998), 163.

Resurrection as Ontological Transformation

A fourth line of thought concerns the objectivity of the resurrection and its impact on creation. It is all too easy to maintain a non-interventionist theology of resurrection in a reductivist model, where the resurrection is understood simply in terms of the subjective experience of the disciples. Such a reductivist theology, in my view, not only fails to represent the Christian tradition adequately, but also fails to provide a basis for the eschatological transformation of creation. It has little to offer suffering creation.

Rahner's robust and objective claims about the resurrection and its eschatological impact are developed by working with a theology of salvation in Christ that is strong in the East, divinisation. Rahner asks why the theology of the resurrection, when compared to its New Testament origins, has suffered such an 'astonishing process of shrinkage' in the theology of the West.[38] He thinks that a central reason for this shrinkage was the adoption by the West of a purely juridical notion of redemption: Jesus, because of his full divinity and full humanity, is able to make proper satisfaction for human sin. In this kind of theology, the focus is on the cross, rather than the resurrection.

In the East, by contrast, the resurrection plays a central role in the theology of salvation. Salvation occurs because God takes humanity and the whole creation to God's self in the incarnation. The incarnation culminates in the death and resurrection of Christ and these events promise final fulfilment. The resurrection transforms humanity and creation from within. This theology of resurrection is more concerned with ontological change than with legal relation. Because God embraces creaturely life in the incarnation, and above all in its culmination in resurrection, creaturely life is changed forever. Human beings and in some way the whole of creation are taken up into God. Rahner takes three inter-related themes from the Eastern model: salvation as ontological rather than juridical, salvation as involving the divinisation of humans and the whole creation, and the resurrection of Christ as the beginning of this divinising transfiguration.

In this ontological model of the redemption, God adopts creaturely reality as God's own in the incarnation and this culminates in the res-

---

38. Rahner, 'Dogmatic Questions on Easter', in *Theological Investigations* 4 (London: Darton, Longman and Todd, 1974), 121–33, at 122.

urrection of the crucified.³⁹ In the life and death of Jesus, a piece of this world, part of creaturely reality, is handed over fully in freedom into God in complete obedience and love and in the resurrection this creaturely reality is fully taken up into God. In the resurrection, God irrevocably adopts creaturely reality as God's own reality, divinising and transfiguring the creature. Because of the unity of the one world that springs from the Creator, this is an event for the whole creation. What occurs in Jesus, as part of the physical, biological and human world, is *ontologically* and not simply juridically the 'beginning of the glorification and divinization of the whole of reality'.⁴⁰ It is 'the beginning of the transformation of the world as an ontologically interconnected occurrence'.⁴¹

The resurrection of Christ is understood not only as a unique and radical transformation of the crucified, but also as the beginning of the transformation of all things in God. It is not the revival of a corpse to live again in the old way but the 'eschatological victory of God's grace in the world'.⁴² Rahner insists that our future participation in resurrection life will be a completely unforeseeable and unimaginable transfiguration of our spiritual, bodily, social selves. He sees continuing identity in resurrection life as provided not by the molecules that make up our bodies before death, which in this life are always subject to metabolic processes, but by the free, spiritual subject, that can be called the soul. This means that finding a corpse in a grave could not be taken as evidence that there is no resurrection.⁴³

Christ in his risen, bodily reality is the hidden presence that gives meaning and direction to the universe. The transfiguration of the world has begun in the risen Christ and is 'ripening and developing' to that point where it will become manifest in the final fulfilment of

---

39. 'The redemption was felt to be a real ontological process which began in the incarnation and ends not so much in the forgiveness of sins as in the divinization of the world and first demonstrates its victorious might, not so much in the expiation of sin on the cross as in the resurrection of Christ' (Rahner, 'Dogmatic Questions on Easter', 126).
40. Rahner, 'Dogmatic Questions on Easter', 129.
41. Rahner, 'Resurrection', 1442.
42. Rahner, 'Jesus' Resurrection', in *Theological Investigations* 17 (New York: Crossroad, 1981), 16–23, at 22.
43. Rahner, 'The Intermediate State', in *Theological Investigations* 17 (New York: Crossroad, 1981), 114–34, at 120.

all things.[44] Clearly this is not a theology with a purely psychological or interior understanding of the resurrection and its effects. It has no interest in a reductivist view of the resurrection. It makes the very large claim that the resurrection is the central event in the history of the universe, that it is the irreversible expression of God's saving love in our world, and that it has already begun transforming the whole of creation from within. But, as I have been attempting to show, this large claim is made about a divine action that springs from the God who is always at work from within creation, rather than being seen as some kind of intervention from without. It is seen as the radical transformation, unpredictable fulfilment and the real meaning and goal of God's work of creation, rather than as a miracle that overturns the natural world and its laws.

Resurrection: Transformation but Non-Interventionist

The proposal being made here is that, in order to respond to the issue of suffering built into creation, a theology of divine action is needed that is both eschatological and non-interventionist. This raises the test case of the resurrection. Many have understood this as the greatest of divine interventions. Is the resurrection to be seen as an intervention from without? Rahner thinks not, but does not argue the case. I have been attempting to show that there are four lines of thought from within Rahner's theology that support a non-interventionist, but still objective and powerful theology of resurrection. These involve seeing the resurrection as a dimension of God's *one* divine act of self-bestowal, as within the framework of an evolutionary Christology, as real symbol of God's universal saving love and as an ontological event, the beginning of the divinising transformation of all things. Taken together, these give general plausibility to the claim that the resurrection can be seen as an objective but non-interventionist act of God.

In order to take this argument a little further, however, it will be necessary to consider some of the particular ways in which the resurrection impinges on human beings and on other creatures. Can these impacts of the resurrection be considered as objective and non-inter-

---

44. Rahner, 'The Festival of the Future of the World', in *Theological Investigations 7* (London: Darton, Longman & Todd), 181–5, at 184.

ventionist? I will take up briefly two important ways in which the resurrection impacts on creation; first, the experience of the risen Christ by the first disciples and, second, the ontological transformation of creation that the resurrection involves.

Clearly the encounter between the first disciples and the risen one had a distinctive character. Many of the disciples who encountered Jesus beyond death had walked with him in Galilee and accompanied him to Jerusalem. Their experience was distinct because they had known him in life and death and now knew him as the risen one. It was distinct from later Christian experience in a second way, in that it had a church-founding character. For both these reasons, their witness is irreplaceable and unique. All later Christian life depends upon their experience and their testimony. But were their experiences of the risen one miraculous interventions in the sense that they broke the laws of nature? Or did they take place in and through the laws of nature, and thus in and through secondary causes?

Historically, there is no evidence that can tell us exactly what kind of experience was involved in the appearances of the risen Christ to the first disciples. Theologically, however, there is good reason to think that these encounters were not the same as the everyday experience of other persons in our lives, or of Jesus during his lifetime. As Rahner insists, the experience of the risen Christ cannot be thought of as one among other ordinary experiences, but must be seen as an experience that is *sui generis*:

> Such a resurrection, into a human existence finalized and bringing history to fulfillment, is essentially an object of knowledge of an absolutely unique kind. It is essentially other than the return of a dead man to his previous biological life, to space and time which form the dimensions of history unfulfilled. Hence it is not in any way an ordinary object of experience, which could be subsumed under the common condition and possibilities of experience.[45]

Granted this, I believe that it is possible and appropriate to understand the appearances of the risen Christ in a non-interventionist way. They might be seen as unique revelatory encounters with the

---

45. Rahner, 'Resurrection', 1431.

risen Christ that occur in a way that is related to our own experience of God in grace. Rahner makes this suggestion. He says that the best analogy for understanding the appearances may be the experience of Christ in the Spirit that Christians have today, rather than imaginative visions or everyday sense experience.[46] Rahner gave much of his theological life to articulating the nature of the experience of God, as transcendental experiences that occur in and through the experience of creaturely realities in the world. I have discussed this in detail elsewhere and here simply note that this experience is an experience of grace in which God really does act, but which is experienced by us in a truly human and creaturely way.[47]

The appearances of the risen Christ may have the structure of a transcendental experience that occurs in and through the experience of created realities, where the one encountered is recognised as Jesus who had walked with the disciples in Galilee but who is now radically transformed as the power of new creation. The encounters with the risen Christ may have been mediated by the communion of the church, the Word of God, the breaking of the bread, the natural world, the love of another human being or the experience of prayer. What matters is that they were experienced as unique revelations of the crucified, risen from the dead as the power of new life from God. Such experiences can be understood in a non-interventionist way, and yet at the same time be thought of as church-founding encounters with Jesus, in which the risen one reveals himself as alive beyond death with the fullness of bodily life, transformed in God and embodying resurrection life.

The second question that needs to be addressed at this stage concerns the ontological change that the resurrection promises and initiates. If the resurrection is the beginning of the transformation of the whole creation in Christ, how does this impact on the laws of nature? Does it involve an overturning of laws of nature or the appearance of new laws of nature? On the basis of the theology developed above, there is no need to see God as overturning natural laws or as intro-

---

46. Rahner says: 'So far as the nature of this experience is accessible to us, it is to be explained after the manner of our experience of the powerful Spirit of the living Lord rather than in a way which either likens this experience too closely to mystical visions of an imaginative kind in later times, or understands it as an almost physical sense experience' (*Foundations*, 276).
47. Denis Edwards, *Human Experience of God* (New York: Paulist Press, 1983).

ducing new ones, since God has been creatively involved with every aspect of the universe from the beginning precisely as the one who would raise Jesus from the dead and bring all creation to its consummation. This had always been the very meaning of creation, that for which the processes and regularities of the natural world exist. The God of resurrection, the God who will transform all things in Christ, is the God of creation. God is present in the Spirit to every creature in the long history of the universe as the God of self-bestowing resurrection love. God creates a universe that is capable of being transformed from within. As Robert John Russell says, God creates a universe that is transformable by resurrection:

> Our starting point is that the new creation is not a replacement of the old creation, or a second and separate creation *ex nihilo*. Instead, God will transform God's creation, the universe, into the new creation *ex vetere*, to use Polkinghorne's phrase. It follows that God must have created the universe *such that it is transformable*, that is, that it can be transformed by God's action. Specifically, God must have created it precisely with those conditions and characteristics that it needs as preconditions in order to be transformable by God's new act.[48]

Because God creates a universe capable of being transformed in new creation, there is no need to understand what Rahner calls the ontological change of resurrection as an intervention. Rather it can be seen as the instantiation of potentialities that God had placed in the natural world from the beginning, potentialities that have always been directed towards resurrection and new creation. In a series of articles, William Stoeger has distinguished between two meanings of 'the laws of nature': on the one hand, the phrase refers to the laws contained in our scientific theories, which are only a partial description of reality; on the other, it can refer to something far wider, the relationships, processes and causal connections of the natural world

---

48. Russell, 'Bodily Resurrection, Eschatology, and Scientific Cosmology', 21. At a conference on the resurrection held at St Mark's in Canberra in March 2006, Russell explored the possibility that the resurrection might involve new laws of nature.

itself, much of which escapes our theories.[49] The laws of nature as we know them are provisional and imperfect and not well suited at this stage to deal with important areas of life, including the mental, the interpersonal, the aesthetic and the religious, all of which are part of the natural world. This makes it quite possible to think that the eschatological transformation of creation begun in the resurrection may occur through secondary causes that exist in the natural world but which are not mapped, or not mapped well, by our scientific theories.

The impact of the resurrection on the universe might be seen as a new and, to us, unforeseeable instantiation of potentialities of nature that are already built into God's creation from the beginning. This view fits well with Rahner's idea that the eschatological consummation of the universe will take place as the act of God, but that this is an act which works in and through the self-transcendence of creation. God is at work as the power of the future in every aspect of creation. In God's final act, God will embrace the whole of creation in self-bestowing love, but this love is already 'the most immanent element in every creature'.[50]

At the beginning of this article I proposed that a theology of divine action that can make some kind of response to the suffering of creation might have at least three characteristics: 1. It would offer eschatological hope for the redemption of creation; 2. It would be a non-interventionist theology, so that God is not thought of as freely choosing to send suffering to some and saving others from suffering; 3. It would understand divine power to be defined by the cross and resurrection as a power that by nature finds expression in love and respect for creatures, a power that waits upon creation, lives with its processes and accompanies each creature in love.

My focus has been on the first two of these characteristics as they apply to the all-important case of the resurrection. I have argued for a theology of resurrection that makes strong objective claims about Christ's resurrection and its liberating eschatological consequences. At the same time, I have proposed that the resurrection can be under-

---

49. William R Stoeger SJ, 'Contemporary Physics and the Ontological Status of the Laws of Nature', in *Quantum Cosmology and the Laws of Nature*, 209–34; 'The Mind-Brain Problem, the Laws of Nature and Constitutive Relationships', in *Neuroscience and the Person*, 129–46; 'Epistemological and Ontological Issues Arising from Quantum Theory', in *Quantum Mechanics* 81–98.
50. Karl Rahner, 'Immanent and Transcendent Consummation', 289.

stood in non-interventionist terms as the central expression in our history of God's one act that embraces creation and redemption, an act which consistently finds expression through secondary causes. I see this combination of objectivity with non-intervention in a theology of resurrection as a partial theological response to the suffering of creation.

The physicist Paul Davies is a learned and helpful contributor to the discussions between science and theology. Many years ago, after expressing openness to the idea of a Creator, he was asked: What do you think about Christianity? His response was to say that Christianity is based on the miracle of the resurrection, and as a scientist he did not hold for exceptions to the laws of nature. My own theological response, framed inwardly at the time and made more explicit here, is that the resurrection is not best thought of as a miracle that overturns the laws of nature. It is far more than this. It is the event that gives meaning and direction to the whole universe and to all of its laws. It does not come from without but from within, from the presence of the creative, saving God who enables creation not only to emerge and unfold, but to come to its final fulfilment.

Resurrection of the Body and Transformation of the Universe in the Theology of Karl Rahner

It is remarkable how much attention Rahner gives to the dialogue between science and theology in his late essays. Many of the articles in volume 21 of his *Theological Investigations* either explore or touch upon this interaction.[1] In one of these articles, Rahner outlines an agenda for Christology. Among other things, he identifies a need to develop the thought of Teilhard de Chardin with more precision and clarity, showing the intelligible and orthodox connection between Jesus of Nazareth and Christ as the Omega point of world evolution.[2] In another article on the redemption, he points to the need for a soteriology that is worked out in relation to contemporary cosmology.[3] What Rahner seems to be calling for at the end of his life is a truly *systematic* theology of the risen Christ in relation to the evolving universe.

My proposal is that Rahner had already long been involved in the work of constructing such a theology. His contributions on this theme are widely spread throughout his work, appearing in short articles on a variety of topics. My focus will not be on the range of Rahner's eschatology—an excellent synthesis of this can be found in Peter Phan's critical study[4]—but on his view of the relationship between the resurrection of Christ and the transformation of the universe.

---

1. Karl Rahner, *Theological Investigations*. 23 volumes. (London, Baltimore and New York: Darton, Longman & Todd and The Seabury Press, 1961–1992). Abbreviated hereafter as *TI*.
2. Rahner, 'Christology Today', in *TI* 21: 220–7, at 227.
3. Rahner, 'The Christian Understanding of the Redemption', *TI* 21, 239–54, at 252.
4. Peter Phan, *Eternity in Time: A Study of Karl Rahner's Eschatology* (London and Toronto: Associated University Presses, 1988).

I will attempt to gather his thought into a short synthesis, built up around six interrelated systematic elements. By considering his work in this way, I hope to show how Rahner's various and scattered contributions form a coherent theology. I will argue that the first two elements, divine self-bestowal and creation's self-transcendence, form the twin systematic foundations for the rest. I will conclude with brief reflections on the significance of Rahner's contribution and with a discussion of three critical issues.

Self-Bestowal as the Meaning and Purpose of Creation

Rahner sees God as creating in order to give God's self to creation as its fulfilment. God wills to bestow God's very self in love, and creation comes to be as the addressee of this self-bestowal. This means that grace and incarnation are not thought of as additions to creation. They are not simply a remedy for human sin, although they are this. With the Franciscan school exemplified in Scotus, Rahner holds that incarnation is built into God's decision to create. Creation exists because God wants to give God's self in love to a world of creatures. Creation and incarnation are united in one great act of divine self-communication. They are to be seen as 'two moments and two phases of the *one* process of God's self-giving and self-expression, although it is an intrinsically differentiated process'.[5]

The means that Rahner will always see the story of the universe, and everything that science can tell us about its long history, as part of a larger story, the story of salvation. The creation of the universe was 'from the outset an element in that wider and more radical decision of God's will to impart himself to that which is other than himself and not divine'.[6] The history of salvation 'is ultimately the ground of the history of nature and does not simply unfold against the static background of a nature unaffected by it'.[7] The story of the universe exists *within* a larger vision of the divine purpose.

---

5. Rahner, *Foundations of Christian Faith*, translated by William V Dych (New York: Seabury Press, 1978), 197.
6. Rahner, 'Christology in the Setting of Modern Man's Understanding of Himself and of his World', *TI*: 215–29, at 219.
7. Rahner, 'Resurrection: D. Theology', in *Encyclopedia of Theology: A Concise Sacramentum Mundi*, edited by Karl Rahner (London: Burns and Oates, insert year here), 1440–2, at 1442. Abbreviated hereafter as *ET*.

The theme of divine self-communication is at the centre of Rahner's early work on grace[8] and, later, is the fundamental principle that provides the structure for his *Foundations of Christian Faith*. Towards the end of his life, he returns to the theme of God's self-giving in creation, arguing that this is what is most specific to the Christian view of God.[9] This God creates creatures who are *capax infiniti*, who without being consumed in the fire of divinity, are able to receive God's life as their own fulfilment:

> God is not merely the one who as creator establishes a world distant from himself as something different, but rather he is the one who gives himself away to this world and who has his own fate in and with this world. God is not only himself the giver, but he is also the gift. For a pantheistic understanding of existence this statement may be completely obvious. For a Christian understanding of God, in which God and the world are not fused but remain separate for all eternity, this is the most tremendous statement that can be made about God at all. Only when this statement is made, when, within a concept of God that makes a radical distinction between God and the world, God himself is still the very core of the world's reality and world is truly the fate of God himself only then is a concept of God attained that is truly Christian.[10]

The immense, breathtaking history of the universe derives its ultimate meaning from the fact that in this history God gives God's self in grace to free human creatures, this history is directed to the transformation and fulfilment not just of human beings but the whole universe in God, and this future is not only promised but already begun in the life, death and resurrection of Jesus Christ.[11] God creates in order to give God's self to creatures in what we call grace, incarnation and final consummation.

---

8. Rahner, 'Concerning the Relationship between Nature and Grace', *TI* 1: 297–317; 'Some Implications of the Scholastic Concept of Uncreated Grace', *TI* 1: 319–45. 297–317.
9. Rahner, 'Natural Science and Christian Faith', *TI* 21: 55; 'Book of God – Book of Human Beings', *TI* 22: 214–24; 'The Specific Character of the Christian Concept of God', *TI* 21: 185–95.
10. Rahner, 'The Specific Character of the Christian Concept of God', 191.
11. Rahner, 'The Book of God—Book of Human Beings', 223.

How is God's creative presence to creatures to be understood? Rahner rejects the notion that it can be understood simply on the model of efficient causality. This model is based on the relationship between finite beings that are distinct from one another prior to the causal relationship. Rahner finds in the theology of grace a better model for understanding the nature of God's immanence to creation. In grace, God freely gives God's self to us as our fulfilment. This cannot be understood simply as efficient causality whereby one finite entity achieves an effect in another. It is better understood as quasi-formal causality, by which the indwelling God, while remaining radically transcendent, really determines our being. Rahner points out that Christianity's insistence, against pantheism, on the difference between God and the world does not mean that there is a distance between God and the creature. Rather, God in God's being *is* this difference.[12] Because God is God and not a created cause, neither divine transcendence nor creaturely freedom is compromised. Creaturely freedom flourishes and grows in direct relationship to intimacy with God.

On the basis that creation is one and that the one history of creation is directed to divine self-bestowal, Rahner proposes that the divine indwelling characteristic of grace is an appropriate analogy for characterising the fundamental relationship that God has with the world in general: What is true of grace is always valid 'in an analogous way for the relationship between God's absolute being and being which originates from him'.[13] This means that Rahner can say that the creative immanence of God to the world is of such a kind that 'the reality of God himself is imparted to the world as its supreme specification'.[14]

In Rahner's vision, creation is intrinsically directed towards self-bestowal. It is not simply that God creates something different over against God's self, but that God freely communicates God's own reality to the other. The universe emerges in the process of God's self-bestowal. God is immanent to the world in self-giving love. The

---

12. Rahner, 'Christology in the Setting', 224.
13. Rahner, 'Natural Science and Christian Faith', 21, 36.
14. Rahner, 'Christology in the Setting', 225.

self-bestowal of God, as the absolutely transcendent, 'is the most immanent factor in the creature'.[15]

Self-Transcendence as the Way God Acts

A second fundamental concept, alongside the idea of creation as divine self-bestowal, is that of creation's self-transcendence. This concept is worked out in Rahner's anthropology[16] and particularly in his evolutionary Christology,[17] but it functions in many aspects of his theology. Like the concept of divine self-bestowal, it provides a way of grasping the radical unity of God's one and undivided act that involves both creation and redemption.

Traditional theology understood creation as God sustaining creatures in being (*conservatio*) and enabling them to act (*concursus*). Rahner transforms this theology of creation from a more or less static theology into a theology of becoming, a theology of self-transcendence. In his evolutionary Christology, Rahner begins from the fundamental *unity* he finds in creation. All of creation is united in its one origin in God, in its self-realisation as one united world, and in its one future in God. In this context, he reflects on the transitions to the *new* in the history of the universe, particularly when matter becomes life, and when life becomes self-conscious spirit.

This emergence of the new is in need of explanation, not only at the level of science, which has its own integrity, but also at the level of theology. God's creative act needs to be understood not only as enabling the universe to exist, but also as enabling it to *become*. Rahner argues for a theology of the active self-transcendence of creation, a dynamism that is truly intrinsic to creation, but which occurs through the creative power of the immanent God. In a late article, he writes of the 'constant pressure' of the divine being that enables creation to become more than it is in itself.[18] This 'pressure' does not belong to the essence of the finite being and it cannot be discerned by

---

15. Rahner, 'Immanent and Transcendent Consummation of the World', *TI* 10: 273–89, at 281.
16. Rahner, *Hominisation: The Evolutionary Origin of Man as a Theological Problem* (London: Burns and Oates, 1965).
17. Rahner, 'Christology within an Evolutionary View of the World', *TI* 5: 157–92; *Foundations*, 178–203.
18. Rahner, 'Natural Science and Christian Faith', 37.

the natural sciences. It is understood in terms of the interior, dynamic relationship of all things in the evolving universe to their Creator.

The material universe transcends itself in the emergence of life, and life transcends itself in the human. In human beings, the universe becomes open to self-consciousness, freedom and a truly personal response to God. Rahner writes: 'The one material cosmos is the *single* body as it were of a *multiple* self-presence of this very cosmos and its orientation towards its absolute and infinite ground'.[19] The experience of God's self-communication in grace is the foretaste and promise of union with God in glory and the transformation of the whole of reality in God.

Within this context, Rahner sees the Christ-event as the definitive self-transcendence of the created universe into God. Jesus is a part of evolutionary history that is radically open to the divine bestowal. He is part of the process of the world's becoming that gives itself radically into divine love. In Jesus, we find the 'initial beginning and definitive triumph of the movement of the world's self-transcendence into absolute closeness to the mystery of God'.[20] If the Christ-event is considered from below, it can be seen as the self-transcendence of the evolving universe into God. If it is considered from above, it can be seen as God's irreversible self-bestowal to creation. In this one person, we find the irreversible self-communication of God to creatures and the definitive human acceptance of this communication. This is Rahner's concept of Jesus as absolute saviour.[21]

In one of his articles, Rahner speaks of the *two* ways in which the theology of God's creative immanence needs to be developed. The first is the idea outlined in this section, that the immanent God gives to creatures themselves the capacity to transcend themselves.[22] The second is the concept discussed in the previous section, that the immanent God's 'basic act (an act which also includes God's creativity) is the self-bestowal of God upon that which is not divine'.[23] I think it can be concluded that, for Rahner, these are *two consistent and fundamental characteristics of divine action*. On the one hand, divine action is an act of divine self-bestowal. On the other hand, this divine

---

19. Rahner, *Foundations*, 189.
20. Rahner, *Foundations*, 181.
21. Rahner, *Foundations*, 193.
22. Rahner, 'Christology in the Setting', 223.
23. Rahner, 'Christology in the Setting', 226.

action works dynamically through the *self*-transcendence of creatures. These two aspects of divine action are mutually inter-related. It is God present in self-bestowal who enables creaturely *self*-transcendence. As always for Rahner, divine action and creaturely action are not in competition. God's action enables creaturely cause and effect to flourish. As will become clear in what follows, God's action, understood as divine self-bestowal and creaturely self-transcendence, characterises not only creation, grace and incarnation, but also the final consummation of all things in Christ.

The Resurrection of Christ as the Beginning of the Transformation of the Universe

In his theology of the resurrection, Rahner moves beyond a Christian apologetics that would seek to prove the reality of resurrection on the basis of the appearances and particularly the empty tomb. He replaces the old apologetics with a theology of transcendental hope. He argues that, in the light of the resurrection of Jesus, a universal human hope for resurrection can be discerned. In every authentic act of human freedom and commitment he finds an implicit hope for definitive and eternal meaning and validity. This hope includes a longing for the eternal life of the whole embodied person. Eternity is understood, not as time spinning on endlessly, but as the final and definitive fulfilment of human freedom. Eternity 'comes to be in time as its own mature fruit'.[24] The transcendental hope of resurrection is the gift of God's grace. This grace-filled experience of hope provides the context in which Jesus' resurrection becomes credible. In this way, the resurrection is both the ground of faith and the object of faith.[25]

Although the empty tomb belongs to the oldest tradition of the New Testament, it does not provide real knowledge of Jesus' resurrection. It expresses a conviction that exists for other reasons – that Jesus is alive. This conviction is more basic and primary than the stories of the appearances, which communicate the experience of salvation in the risen one by means of concepts drawn from time and space.[26]

---

24. Rahner, *Foundations of Christian Faith*, 271; 'Christology in the Setting', 288–308; 'Eternity from Time', *TI* 19: 169–77.
25. Rahner, *Foundations of Christian Faith*, 268–74; 'Jesus' Resurrection', *TI* 17: 16–23.
26. Rahner, 'Jesus' Resurrection', 17, 19–20.

Rahner insists that the resurrection of Christ is a unique and radical transformation of the crucified. It is not the revival of a corpse to live again in the old way, but the 'eschatological victory of God's grace in the world'.[27] He sees our participation in resurrection life as a transfiguration of our spiritual and bodily selves. Continuing identity in resurrection life is provided not by the molecules that make up our bodies before death, which in this life are always subject to metabolic processes, but by the free, spiritual subject, that can be called the soul. This means, Rahner says, that finding a corpse in a grave could not be taken as evidence that there is no resurrection.[28]

In an article written in the 1950s, Rahner explores doctrinal questions concerning the resurrection.[29] He notes the central place given to Christ's death in Western theology and the marginal place allotted to the resurrection. He points out that, when compared with its New Testament origins, the theology of resurrection has suffered an 'astonishing process of shrinkage'.[30] A central reason for this shrinkage is the Western adoption of a purely juridical *interpretation of the redemption*. Jesus Christ, because of his full divinity and full humanity, is seen as able to make proper satisfaction for the insult offered to God by human sin. In this kind of theology, there is little place for the resurrection. It points to the personal bliss of Jesus in his glorified humanity but offers little else.

Rahner contrasts this with the theology of the East, where the resurrection plays a fundamental role in the theology of salvation: 'The redemption was felt to be a real ontological process which began in the incarnation and ends not so much in the forgiveness of sins as in the divinisation of the world and first demonstrates its victorious might, not so much in the expiation of sin on the cross as in the resurrection of Christ'.[31] Rahner finds three related themes in this theology of the East, each of which will play an important role in his thought: salvation as ontological rather than juridical, the idea of the divinisation of the world, and the resurrection of Christ as the beginning of this divinising transfiguration.

---

27. Rahner, 'Jesus' Resurrection', 22.
28. Rahner, 'The Intermediate State', *TI* 12: 114–24, at 120.
29. Rahner, 'Dogmatic Questions on Easter', *TI* 4: 121–33.
30. Rahner, 'Dogmatic Questions on Easter', 122.
31. Rahner, 'Dogmatic Questions on Easter', 126.

He sets out on this line of thought from what has been central to the theology of the West, Good Friday. He focuses, however, on the death of Jesus itself, rather than on the sufferings that precede it. When theology's focus is on the moral character of Christ's dying, Rahner notes, 'then one has missed the death by a hairs-breadth'.[32] He sees death as the final act of a human being by which the whole of a person's life is gathered up in a free decision that can ripen into eternal life. If this is so, then the death of Christ is not simply one moral act among others performed before death. It is, rather, 'the totality of Christ in act, the definitive act of his freedom, the complete integration of his time on earth with his human eternity'.[33] In this context, the resurrection can be seen not simply as an event that occurs after Jesus' death, but rather as a manifestation of what happens in the death, as Jesus freely hands his whole bodily existence into the mystery of a loving God.

In the death of Jesus, a piece of this world is handed over freely into God, in complete obedience and love, and is fully taken up into God. This event is salvific for the whole of reality: 'This is Easter, and the redemption of the world'.[34] The resurrection is not simply a juridical event in which God accepts Jesus' self-giving, but *essentially* the event in which God irrevocably adopts creaturely reality as God's own reality. This adoption occurs by God's primordial act, which has 'already' found expression in the incarnation of the Word. It is this that culminates in the resurrection, when God divinises and transfigures the creature.

Because of the unity of the world that springs from the Creator, this is an event for the whole world. What occurs in Jesus, as part of the physical, biological and human world, is *ontologically* and not simply juridically, 'the embryonically final beginning of the glorification and divinization of the whole of reality'.[35] In a world which is a single inter-related dynamic of divine self-bestowal, the resurrection of Jesus is not simply an exemplary cause of final resurrection. It is, as Rahner states in his *Encyclopedia of Theology*, 'the beginning of the transformation of the world as an ontologically interconnected

---

32. Rahner, 'Dogmatic Questions on Easter', 127.
33. Rahner, 'Dogmatic Questions on Easter', 128.
34. Rahner, 'Dogmatic Questions on Easter', 128.
35. Rahner, 'Dogmatic Questions on Easter', 129.

occurrence'.³⁶ In the resurrection of Jesus, the final destiny of the world is decided and already begun. Jesus risen is the 'pledge and beginning of the perfect fulfilment of the world'. He is the 'representative of the new cosmos'. As the risen one, he is freed from 'the limiting individuality of the unglorified body', and in his new state is present to all of creation. His final glorious return, then, will be 'the disclosure of this relation to world attained by Jesus in his resurrection'.³⁷

The history of Jesus that reaches its completion in death, the matured and final reality of his temporal life, abides in the resurrection life. It abides as possessing a real salvific function. The saving significance of his life is fully accepted by God and set free to work in the transformation of the world. The transfigured reality of Christ remains the mediator to the immediacy of God.³⁸ Here and elsewhere, Rahner holds to the theological principle that the humanity of Jesus has enduring significance for the salvation of the world.³⁹ Jesus is 'the gate and the door, the Alpha and the Omega'.⁴⁰ He is forever the openness of created reality to God.

In an article that appears in the second volume of the *Investigations*, Rahner explores the meaning of the doctrine of bodily resurrection for the future of the universe.⁴¹ He asks: What is meant by the resurrection of the body? What is the minimum that is meant? His response is that the body here means the whole embodied person taken up into eternal life by God. Those who die in God are not to be thought of as taken away from the body or from creation. No matter how hard it is to imagine, they remain united with the reality and fate and events of the world. It is worth noting that in his theology of death, Rahner suggests that one who dies does not so much become *acosmic* as *pancosmic*.⁴² Later in his career, he will replace this with Gisbert Greshake's idea of resurrection of the whole person in death.⁴³

---

36. Rahner, 'Resurrection: D. Theology', 1142.
37. Rahner, 'Resurrection: D. Theology', 1142.
38. Rahner, 'Dogmatic Questions on Easter', 131–3.
39. Rahner, 'The Eternal Significance of the Humanity of Jesus for our Salvation', *TI* 3: 35–46.
40. Rahner, 'The Eternal Significance of the Humanity of Jesus', 43.
41. Rahner, 'Resurrection of the Body', *TI* 2: 203–16.
42. Rahner, *On the Theology of Death* (London: Burns and Oates, 1961), 20
43. Rahner, 'The Intermediate State', 114–24; Silvano Zucal, *La Teologia della Morte in Karl Rahner* (Bologna: Instituto di Scienze Religiose, 1982), 6.

Rahner suggests that contemporary cosmology may help us to think theologically about the final state of the universe. In the past, the universe was thought of as a series of heavenly spheres and as more or less unchanging. Eternal life could be thought of as movement from one place to another, from the everyday sphere to the heavenly sphere. With the scientific picture of an evolving universe, Rahner thinks we are in better place to conceive of a God-given final state of the universe as a whole. He recognises the complexity of the relationship between the predictions of science and Christian eschatology.[44] But he insists that the Second Coming of Christ will not be enacted for human beings on the stage of an unchanged world. It will take place at the moment of the perfecting of the world into the reality that Christ already possesses. Then, it will be seen that 'the world as a whole flows into his Resurrection and into the transfiguration of his body'. Christ then, 'will be revealed to all reality and, within it, to every one of its parts in its own way, as the innermost secret of all the world and of all history'.[45]

For Rahner, resurrection of the body and the transformation of the world are to be understood together. Both are beyond imagination. We look to the risen Christ and find that resurrection is not simply the revival of a corpse but radical transformation (1 Cor 15:44). Even so, Rahner argues, because Christ is risen, we can think of heaven as a *place*, even though it is not part of our present space.[46] He thinks of the risen Christ as creating the new place that we call heaven.[47] Even though we cannot imagine such a place, we can conceive of it. He notes that physics can teach us about things that can be conceived of even though they cannot be imagined pictorially. He insists that in the consummation of all things in Christ, everything will be transformed, and 'it will then be equally correct to call the new reality a new heaven or a new earth'.[48]

In a meditation on Holy Saturday, Rahner ponders the risen Christ as the hidden presence that gives meaning and direction to all things in the universe: 'Christ is already at the heart and centre of all

---

44. Rahner, 'Resurrection of the Body', 212.
45. Rahner, 'Resurrection of the Body', 213.
46. Rahner, 'Resurrection of the Body', 215.
47. Karl Rahner, 'The Interpretation of the Dogma of the Assumption', *TI* 1:215–27, at 222.
48. Rahner, 'Resurrection of the Body', 215.

the poor things of this earth, which we cannot do without because the earth is our mother. He is present in the blind hope of all creatures who, without knowing it, are striving to participate in the glorification of his body'.[49] In a reflection on the Ascension, he claims that Christians are really 'the most sublime of materialists' and 'more crassly materialist' than those who call themselves so. Christians hold that matter will last forever, and be glorified for ever in Christ. But it will undergo a radical transformation, 'the depths of which we can only sense with fear and trembling in that process which we experience as our death'.[50] The transfiguration of the world has begun in the risen Christ and is 'ripening and developing to that point where it will become manifest'.[51]

God as Absolute Future: The *Docta Ignorantia Futuri*

This strong position on the promise of final transformation is accompanied by an equally strong insistence that we know very little about its content. At one point, Rahner says that to think we could picture our final and definitive state 'would be still more absurd than to suppose that the caterpillar could imagine what it would be like to be a butterfly'.[52] He takes up this theme in a systematic way in his influential essay on the hermeneutics of eschatological statements,[53] material that he incorporates into his *Foundations of Christian Faith*.[54] At the centre of his approach to the interpretation of the biblical and traditional depictions of the future, is the thesis that *the future of the world in God remains radically hidden to us.*

The future is announced and promised in Christ, but it is announced and promised precisely as hidden mystery. This future is nothing else than the coming of the incomprehensible God. Rahner insists that it is the essence of the eschatological for it to be hidden in its revelation. It is revealed only as 'the dawn and the approach of mystery as such'.[55] This conviction provides Rahner with a basis for

---

49. Rahner, 'Hidden Victory', *TI* 151–8, at 157.
50. Rahner, 'The Festival of the Future of the World', *TI* 7, 181–5, at 183.
51. Rahner, 'The Festival of the Future of the World', 184.
52. Rahner, 'Hidden Victory', 156.
53. Rahner, 'The Hermeneutics of Eschatological Assertions', 323–46.
54. Rahner, *Foundations of Christian Faith*, 431–7.
55. Rahner, 'The Hermeneutics of Eschatological Assertions', 330.

distinguishing between genuine eschatological utterances and what he calls, rather loosely and inaccurately, apocalyptic ones. While genuine eschatology preserves the mystery, a false apocalyptic presents the future as if it were the literal report of a spectator.

This idea is interlinked with a central theme in Rahner's eschatology: the future is to be understood as an inner moment of the present. All genuine knowledge of God's future is knowledge of the eschatological present. The future is the fulfilment of salvation already given in God's self-communication in Christ and in the grace of the Spirit. As William Thompson says, for Rahner the future remains 'uncontrollable and hidden yet also present, something we really look forward to, something in the presence of which we hope, dare, trust, and surrender ourselves'.[56] According to Rahner, what we encounter in the experience of grace is the God who is absolute future.

In articles that explore the Christian concept of the future in relation to the Marxist utopian vision and the predictions of futurologists, Rahner distinguishes this *absolute* future from all *this-worldly* futures.[57] He sees the absolute future as God's self-bestowal. It is the consummation of creation and redemption that is promised and initiated in the life, death and resurrection of Jesus. By contrast, all 'this-worldly' futures occur in the ordinary dimensions of time and space as particular events or states of this world. Each of them, by definition, remains open to a further future.

Christianity proclaims that the becoming of the universe will end, not in emptiness, but in the divine self-bestowal. This absolute future is already a constitutive element of the unfolding of the universe. It has found irrevocable expression and been made visible in Jesus Christ. His resurrection is the promise and the beginning of the absolute future, the transformation of all things in Christ. Rahner sees the real nature of the human as defined by the possibility of attaining this absolute future. We are not defined by this or that goal that then opens out towards something else, but by God coming towards us as our absolute future. Absolute future is another name for God. It

---

56. William M Thompson, 'The Hope for Humanity: Rahner's Eschatology', in *A World of Grace: An Introduction to the Themes and Foundations of Karl Rahner's Theology*, edited by Leo O'Donovan (New York: Seabury Press, 1980), 158.
57. Rahner, 'Marxist Utopia and the Christian Future of Man', *TI* 6: 59–68; 'A Fragmentary Aspect of a Theological Evaluation of the Concept of the Future', *TI* 10: 235–41; 'The Question of the Future', *TI* 12: 181–201.

points to the fullness of reality, which not only comes towards us but is also 'the sustaining ground of the dynamism towards the future'.[58]

God, then, is known not as one object among others that we might plan for the future, but as the ground of this whole projection towards the future. This means there is only one real question we humans must face: Is the future to which we project ourselves simply more of the same, made up of specific and limited realities, no matter how well planned or manipulated? Or does the infinite, unsurpassable future as such come toward us? Rahner argues that Christianity opts for the second possibility. The absolute future of God comes to each person. It is offered to each and its acceptance is the ultimate task for each.

According to Rahner, Christianity is 'the attitude of abiding openness to the question of the absolute future which seeks to bestow itself, which has definitively promised itself as coming in Jesus Christ, and which is called God'.[59] The content of Christian preaching consists of the question of the absolute future and, properly speaking, *of nothing else*.[60] This is not to ignore what is revealed in Jesus, but to recognise that in him, as the crucified and risen one, God has entered into our world as absolute future. Even in final blessedness, God will remain the eternal mystery to which human beings commit themselves in the ecstasy of love. Christianity in its essence is openness to the question of the absolute future.

Because of this, it is essential to the church and a fundamental task of theology to act as the guardian of the '*docta ignorantia futuri*'.[61] Rahner uses the language of learned ignorance, associated with Nicholas of Cusa, to point to theology's critical role of resisting closure with regard to the future. Keeping open the question of the future is theology's most basic task. It is the theme that is always and everywhere proper to the theologian. The Christian is called to *both* stand before God as absolute future and to love thy neighbour by working toward 'this-worldly' future goals. Rahner calls this interaction between the absolute future and planning of a 'this-worldly' future the 'utopian' factor. The Christian form of the utopian involves both a genuine commitment to this world and openness to the absolute future, in such a way that each conditions the other.

---

58. Rahner, 'Marxist Utopia and the Christian Future of Man', *TI* 6, 59–88, at 62.
59. Rahner, 'The Question of the Future', *TI* 12, 181-201, at 190.
60. Rahner, 'The Question of the Future', 188–9.
61. Rahner, 'The Question of the Future', 181, 198.

The *docta ignorantia futuri* provides the basis for a critical stance before what exists in the present. It questions the assumption that what already exists is the only right state of affairs. While Christians may not agree on specific plans for the future, they have in common a commitment to the unknown in the future they plan for.[62] We are always called beyond the present into God's future. Hope in the absolute future not only liberates us from reifying the present, but also from the mindless quest for novelty. God as absolute future is, consciously or unconsciously, both motive and critique of our strivings toward a 'this-worldly' future

Human Action as Finally Significant

Rahner sees Christians as called to participate in action aimed at a just and peaceful future and, in the light of this, he takes up the two important issues of ideology and the final significance of human actions. He understands ideology in the negative sense as 'a fundamental closure in face of the "wholeness" of reality, one which turns a partial aspect into an absolute'.[63] He sees it as the task of Christianity, as the religion of the absolute future, to unmask and reject all forms of ideology. Rahner describes three forms of ideology. First, an ideology of *immanence* converts finite areas of experience into absolutes. This includes what are commonly referred to as ideologies, such as nationalism, 'blood and soil', racism and materialism. Second, an ideology of *transmanence* totalises the ultimate and the infinite so that the relative and the finite are cheated out of their rights. An example is quietism, where concern for the divine removes motivation for engagement with ordinary life. Third, an ideology of *transcendence* sees ideology everywhere and is thus unable to commit to anything. The result is relativism and the unrestrained 'openness' that avoids all serious engagement.

While Rahner acknowledges that Christianity can function as an ideology, he argues that in itself it is not an ideology because essentially it is nothing but the absolute and forgiving nearness of God in grace. This God unmasks as worthless idols all ideologies of immanence, whether they concern nation, race, pleasure or anything else.

---

62. Rahner, 'The Question of the Future', 201.
63. Rahner, 'Ideology and Christianity, *TI* 6: 43–58, at 44.

Furthermore, Christianity is called to resist all ideologies that seek to rise above history, either as transmanence or transcendence, because the centre of Christianity is Jesus of Nazareth in his concrete history and the experience of the Holy Spirit that is always mediated by history.

Rahner holds that Christianity has no utopian vision of its own.[64] It contains some general norms, but nothing that amounts to a specific programme for the future. Because of this, Christians are called to tolerance with regard to differing views of the future within the church and to co-operate with others in planning and pursuing political agendas. What Christianity must reject is any political programme in which nation, race, class, money, pleasure or any vision or plan is absolutised. It is always called to oppose sacrificing and butchering human beings here and now for the sake of a dream of the future. It also has the responsibility to defend the dignity and value of those who can make no tangible contributions to such causes.

In an article exploring the notion of the 'new earth',[65] Rahner faces the question put by Marxism: How seriously do Christians take the world of justice, peace and integrity that they are trying to achieve? What is the relationship between the coming of God as our absolute future and the world that we attempt to construct? Rahner responds by means of his fundamental principles of divine self-bestowal and creaturely self-transcendence. The coming Reign of God will not simply be the outcome of the history planned and accomplished by humans. Nor will it simply come upon us from outside. It will be the deed of God, but this deed of God is to be understood as the *self-transcendence* of history.

In response to Marxism, then, Rahner argues that there is a dialectical tension between the two statements that human history will endure and that human history will be radically transformed. It is this tension that 'maintains in us an openness to the future while still according a radical importance to the present'. With this qualification in mind, Rahner makes the strong claim that 'history itself constructs its own final and definitive state'. What endures, he states, is 'the *work* of love as expressed in the concrete in human history'. It is

---

64. Rahner, 'Marxist Utopia and the Christian Future of Man', 65.
65. Rahner, 'The Theological Problems entailed in the Idea of the "New Earth"', *TI* 10; 260–72.

not merely some distillation of our works of love but our history itself that 'passes into definitive consummation in God'.[66] What confirms this, for Rahner, is that history is embraced by God in the Christ-event as having eternal meaning. From the perspective of the human, Rahner argues that if human freedom and the moral character of our actions are to have final and definitive existence, history itself must have enduring significance. On the basis of these arguments, he insists that human acts have final significance as taken up into God and transformed in Christ.[67]

In a related article, Rahner asks whether our final consummation will come from within or from outside ourselves.[68] Will our final consummation be immanent or transcendent? Rahner again points out that this consummation is the self-bestowal of God, who is not only *causa efficiens*, but *causa quasi-formalis* of this consummation. This divine self-bestowal is not only our fulfilment, but also the principle of the movement towards this fulfilment. The present is sustained by the future. It is the immanent God who constitutes this future and enables the self-transcendence of the creature into this future. This means that the final consummation for individuals and for the human community is both immanent and transcendent.

What of the consummation of the universe as a whole? As always, Rahner insists that matter and spirit constitute a unity. He says that if one were to consider matter as such, in the abstract, it would never reach its consummation. But the material world has always been sustained by the creative impulse of self-transcendence by which it tends towards the spirit. This impetus is nothing other than the impetus of the divine self-bestowal. The incarnation of the Word in the world of matter is present in this creative impulse from the beginning. Rahner insists that the material world is not something to be cast aside as a transitory stage in the journey of the spirit. The material world itself is to be transformed in Christ.

Again, Rahner points out that we cannot form an imaginary picture of what this will be like. What can be said it that from the beginning this movement towards consummation has been 'sustained by divine power, which consists in the love that bestows itself absolutely

---

66. Rahner, 'Immanent and Transcendent Consummation of the World', 270.
67. Rahner, 'Immanent and Transcendent Consummation of the World', 271.
68. Rahner, 'Immanent and Transcendent Consummation of the World', 273–89.

in freedom'.[69] Rahner says that this self-bestowal in love is 'the most immanent element in every creature'. Therefore, he can conclude: 'It is not mere pious lyricism when Dante regards even the sun and the other planets as being moved by that love which is God himself as he who bestows himself'.[70]

Hope as Trust in God in the Midst of Perplexity

If God's self-bestowal is our absolute future, then hope is the grace-filled human response. Rahner sees hope as a theological virtue which, like faith and love, is directed to God in God's self. Hope bears on God who has promised God's self to us in Christ. It is the acceptance of our orientation toward the incalculable and uncontrollable God. It is the act by which, in what occurs to us in life, we base ourselves on that which is beyond our powers to control. It is the act 'in which the uncontrollable is made present as that which sanctifies, blesses and constitutes salvation without losing its character as radically beyond our powers to control, precisely because this salvific future is hoped for but not manipulated or controlled'.[71]

In the death of Christ, understood as the most radical act of hope, the grace of God is definitively established in our world. This grace 'finds its unique historical manifestation in Christ precisely as crucified, and thereby as surrendering himself in the most radical sense to the disposing hand of God'.[72] All our acts of hope spring from the grace of God made manifest in Christ and find their fulfilment in the God revealed in Christ as our absolute future. Those who commit themselves, even implicitly, to the uncontrollable, are committing themselves to the blessed one and to salvation.

Hope finds its deepest expression in death, which Rahner understands as the culmination of a life lived in faith, love and hope. But Christian hope involves the whole of life, lived with what Rahner calls a 'continually revolutionary attitude'. He points out that the position of Christianity on this issue is the exact opposite of what is often thought both outside and inside the church:

---

69. Rahner, 'Immanent and Transcendent Consummation of the World', 289.
70. Rahner, 'Immanent and Transcendent Consummation of the World', 289.
71. Rahner, 'On the Theology of Hope', 245.
72. Rahner, 'On the Theology of Hope', 255.

> The hope that is directed towards the absolute future of God, towards that eschatological salvation which is God himself as absolute, is not entertained in order to justify an attitude of conservatism, which from motives of anxiety, prefers a certain present to an unknown future and so petrifies everything. It is not the 'opium of the people' which soothes them in their present circumstances even though these are painful. Rather it is that which commands them, and at the same time empowers them, to have trust enough constantly to undertake anew an exodus out of the present into the future.[73]

Those who hope are called to set out ever anew from social structures that have become 'petrified, old and empty'.[74] Christianity offers an imperative to Christians to venture into the future with other people of good will, using every bit of intelligence and common sense. It lives in hope before a God, who as the absolute future, relativises and reveals the finite limits of all human plans and programmes.

In two late articles, Rahner offers some reflections on the gap between the utopia we long for and the reality we experience.[75] We dream of a world of justice and love, yet find ourselves in a world where selfishness and violence seem pervasive. We strive for structural change designed to overcome inequality and corruption, but find inequality and corruption reappearing in our new constructions. Rahner identifies two false responses to this kind of situation. One is that of the *idealist*, who finds reality hopelessly wanting and seeks to escape it. This is the response of the snob, the aesthete, the 'ideas person', the romantic and the religious escapist. The second false response is that of the *realist*. This includes those who take their stance in the shabbiness of life, in the survival of the fittest, and make the most out of it for themselves. Rahner observes: 'We might add, of course, that there are such closet realists in the Church'.[76]

Both the 'pseudo-idealist' and the 'pseudo-realist' seek to escape the tension and the perplexity of existence. Rahner argues that genuine hope will not collapse the tension between what we hope for and

---

73. Rahner, 'On the Theology of Hope', 257.
74. Rahner, 'On the Theology of Hope', 259.
75. Rahner, 'Utopia and Reality: The Shape of Christian Existence Caught between the Ideal and the Real', in *TI* 22: 26–42; 'Christian Pessimism', *TI* 22: 155–62.
76. Rahner, 'Utopia and Reality', 29.

what we experience. Hope lives in the tension. It lives with the perplexity. The Christian stands before that utopia which is the absolute, eternal and incomprehensible God. And this absolute future reveals all other realities as inescapably relative and finite. It is precisely this incomprehensible God who challenges us to love the Earth and its creatures. Christian hope exists in the tension between this utopia and our everyday commitments and loving actions.

Rahner sees perplexity as built into the human condition. It is part of a world of finitude and sin. But, writing in the early eighties, Rahner argues that the experience of perplexity is growing in intensity. Our technology makes us more and more powerful, but the results are ever more ambiguous. We are flooded with information from the sciences and from other sources, but decisions seem more difficult than ever. We are confronted with so many points of view that we can find ourselves lost. Rahner comments: 'Today only the simpleminded and the foolish know what should be done by individuals and groups'.[77] At the same time, 'dissonant voices urge us to do a thousand things at once'.[78]

In this context, Rahner advocates a 'Christian pessimism' that accepts perplexity and refuses to allow it to be repressed.[79] He points to Paul's saying that we are 'perplexed but not driven to despair' (2 Cor 4:8). We can hope in the midst of perplexity because God comes toward us as the all-embracing mystery of love. And we know that perplexity is built into existence because we arrive at God's definitive realm only by passing through death, the 'ultimate and all-embracing enigma of human existence'.[80]

This kind of Christian pessimism can liberate us from the feeling that it all depends on ourselves, that with a bit more effort everything would be alright. It is not the pretext for cheap resignation, but liberates us to act wisely and lovingly: 'Its function is to explain situations in which we can act realistically, fight and win partial victories, and soberly and courageously accept partial defeats'.[81] We are perplexed but do not despair because we already experience the Spirit of God, the anticipation of the fullness of the divine self-bestowal.

---

77. Rahner, 'Utopia and Reality', 34.
78. Rahner, 'Utopia and Reality', 35.
79. Rahner, 'Christian Pessimism', 155.
80. Rahner, 'Christian Pessimism', 158.
81. Rahner, 'Christian Pessimism', 158.

Because of this gift of the Spirit, Christianity is a message of 'joy, courage and unshakeable confidence'. We Christians have the responsibility to 'bring about a foretaste of God's eternal reign through our solidarity, unselfishness, willingness to share and love of peace'.[82] The grace of God does not completely remove the complexity, but enables it to become the occasion and the mediation of the mystery of God. In this grace, we can know that all our complexities are but 'forerunners and first instalments of the perplexity that consists of losing ourselves entirely through love in the mystery that is God'.[83]

Reflections

In this article, I have discussed Rahner's many, widely-spread, contributions to a theology of resurrection and the transformation of the universe in terms of six inter-related systematic themes: self-bestowal as the meaning and purpose of creation; self-transcendence as the way of divine action; resurrection as the beginning of the transformation of the universe; God as Absolute Future; human action as finally significant; hope as trust in God in the midst of perplexity. I will conclude with some comments on Rahner's achievement and with three critical reflections.

1. Rahner's contributions form a thoroughly coherent and systematic theology. As Peter Phan has said, the coherence and unity of Rahner's theology is 'utterly astonishing'.[84] I agree with Phan's description of a gradual evolution in Rahner's eschatology from existentialist and interpersonal concerns to a sharper focus on socio-political issues and on God as absolute future.[85] In my view, this evolution confirms the dynamic creativity of a theology that is able to respond to new contexts and issues in a way that is integrated, consistent and plausible.
2. More than any other major Catholic theologian, Rahner engages in a fruitful, sustained and systematic dialogue with the worldviews of contemporary cosmology and evolutionary biology.

---

82. Rahner, 'Christian Pessimism', 160.
83. Rahner, 'Christian Pessimism', 161.
84. Phan, *Eternity in Time*, 210.
85. Phan, *Eternity in Time*, 26–39, 201, 209.

3. At the beginning of this article, I referred to Rahner's call for a theology that is able to establish an 'intelligible and orthodox' connection between Jesus of Nazareth and the cosmic Christ, between soteriology and cosmology. In my judgment his theology establishes this connection, and provides a basis for further development.
4. I have proposed that the interlinked ideas of God's self-bestowal and creation's self-transcendence are the foundations on which the structure of Rahner's theology is built. They form the basis for a Rahnerian concept of divine action. They govern his view of creation, grace, incarnation and final consummation. The complex issue of divine action has been widely discussed in the science-theology dialogue of the last twenty years, and I believe that Rahner's theology has something valuable to contribute to the discussion.
5. Rahner's insistence on the transformation of the material universe in Christ offers a foundation for the development of an ecological theology. It is also at this point, as I will indicate below, that I think his theology needs critical assessment and development.
6. I believe that Rahner's theology of the future can speak plausibly of the resurrection promise in today's world. Particularly valuable is his insistence of *both* the promise of radical transformation and the *docta ignorantia futuri*. In a context where many Christians seem to have abandoned the Christian promise as mythological and implausible, Rahner offers a way forward in his view of God as absolute future and in his insistence on what we do not know about this future. And, in a context where other large and influential groups of Christians make alarmingly confident and specific predictions about the future, Rahner's insistence on the *docta ignorantia futuri* is urgently needed.
7. Rahner's theology of God as absolute future offers a truly Christian basis for a political theology that unmasks all ideologies as worthless idols, yet sees our limited historical actions as having final meaning.
8. His theology of hope in the midst of perplexity offers an important resource for a Christian praxis, whether it be in the struggle for social justice, in ecological commitment or in the life of the church. As Rahner says, its function is 'to explain situations in

which we can act realistically, fight and win partial victories, and soberly and courageously accept partial defeats'.[86]

Three critical issues come to mind in this re-reading of Rahner: the difference between the scientific predictions of the future of the universe and the Christian promise; the theological status of non-human living creatures; and the role of the Holy Spirit in the divine work of creation and salvation.

Science and Theology

Rahner's theology of the transformation of the universe in Christ comes up sharply against the scientific predictions of the future of the universe. His claim for theology is a strong one. He does not envisage theology as taking the scientific history of nature as a given, and then showing how the events of salvation unfold against this background. His claim is, rather, that 'it is the history of salvation that is the ground of the history of nature'.[87] The universe comes to be as part of the process of God's self-bestowal. Rahner has a robust stance that stands by the theology of divine self-bestowal as the meaning of creation, salvation and final consummation.

When science puts before us the vision of a universe that has been expanding for many billions of years, a story of life evolving by way of natural selection, and a view of the human mind as profoundly dependent on the emergence of the physical brain, Rahner finds these insights to be congruent with the Christian tradition. He responds by constructing a theology of God-given self-transcendence at work from within creatures, in the emergence of the universe, of life and of the human.

But Rahner's theology is not infinitely flexible. He declares that were the natural scientist to declare that the material world will disappear at the end through a gravitational collapse then the theologian would have to protest.[88] He would find equal difficulty with any absolute claim, based on the current cosmological view, that the universe will expand forever in endless, bleak dissipation. Rahner's protest, of

---

86. Rahner, 'Christian Pessimism', 158.
87. Rahner, 'Resurrection: D. Theology', *ET*: 1442.
88. Rahner, 'Natural Science and Christian Faith', 55.

course, would be based on the purely theological conviction that the world of matter is to find its fulfilment in God. His further conviction that God's future for the universe will come *from within*, by way of self-transcendence, sharpens the point.

The clash between scientific predictions of the future of the universe and Christian eschatology is recognised as a pressing issue in the field of science and religion by specialists such as Robert John Russell.[89] It is clear that Rahner's theology leads to this critical point. There may be important resources in his theology to move forward on this issue, in his theology of resurrection as radical transformation, his theology of self-transcendence and of God as absolute future.

Ecology and Theology

A second key issue concerns the relationship of non-human living creatures to God. This is a burning question for ecological theology, made more urgent by the knowledge we now have of the 3.5 billion year history of life, and of the competition, predation, death and extinction that are intrinsic to it. Michael Petty has presented a strong argument that while Rahner is not explicitly responding to the ecological crisis, 'his theology is profoundly ecological in that he brings to each theological problem and issue a fundamental vision which sees all reality, God the world, and human being, as interrelated.'[90] I agree with Petty's argument and, in a less fully developed way, have suggested something similar.[91] But while Rahner provides a foundation for ecological theology, I do not see his theology as truly ecological because he does not deal fully and directly with the issues raised by non-human life. Rahner deals explicitly with biological life in a few places, such as in his theology of evolution[92] and in a short article

---

89. Robert John Russell, 'Bodily Resurrection, Eschatology, and Scientific Cosmology: The Mutual Interaction of Christian Theology and Science', in *Resurrection: Theological and Scientific Assessments*, edited by Ted Peters, Robert John Russell and Michael Welker (Grand Rapids: Eerdmans, 2002), 3–30.; 'Eschatology and Physical Cosmology: A Preliminary Reflection', in *The Far Future Universe: Eschatology from a Cosmic Perspective*, edited by George FR Ellis (Philadelphia: Templeton Foundation, 2002), 266–315.
90. Michael W Petty, *A Faith that Loves the Earth: The Ecological Theology of Karl Rahner* (Lanham: University Press of America, 1996), 39, 170.
91. Denis Edwards, *Jesus and the Cosmos* (New York: Paulist Press, 1991).
92. Rahner, 'Evolution: II Theological', *Encyclopedia of Theology*, 478–88.

'The Secret of Life',[93] but by and large his evolutionary vision, magnificent as it is, seems to by-pass non-human living creatures.

Part of the issue, I suspect, is that Rahner thinks continuously and strongly in the metaphysical categories of matter and spirit, and he sees the whole of creation finding its fulfilment in the human. He powerfully defends the unity of the human person, the importance of the body and, as this article has shown, the world of matter. However, as a scientist friend observes, matter is not finally a scientific concept. Science is interested in atoms, molecules and organisms. And ecological theology is interested in organisms, species, eco-systems and the interconnections of the living systems of our planet.

In my view, Rahner's theology needs expansion to account for God's relationship with non-human living creatures. It must be admitted that his theology, while it is undoubtedly a theology of final consummation of the *whole* creation, is centred on human beings as the self-transcendence of creation. I think it is possible to agree with Rahner about the unique dignity of the human—as the locus of the incarnation and grace—and still argue for a divine valuing of and joy in all the manifestations of life. Rahner thinks in relational terms, seeing the whole of creation as geared to God's self-bestowal in love. He sees the recipients of this bestowal as human beings, who are the universe come to consciousness and freedom, and the whole material universe that will in some way be taken up into God. But what of God's relationship to ants, eagles and whales?

Rahner insists that the God of the universe is present in God's entirety and omnipotence everywhere in the universe, 'even in the fir needle that the tiny ant is dragging along'.[94] This presence of God, according to Rahner, is always the presence of the God who bestows God's self in love. But what does it mean for the ant? In particular, what does it mean in face of what we know of the pain of non-human creation? In my view, nothing ought to be taken from Rahner's truly wonderful view of God's self-bestowal to human beings. But what needs articulating is an understanding of the way God relates, in creating and redeeming love, to other creatures in ways that respect their specific nature and identity.

---

93. Rahner, 'The Secret of Life', *TI* 6: 141–52.
94. Rahner, 'Book of God—Book of Human Beings', 215.

The Creator Spirit

Rahner's theology of divine self-bestowal is radically Trinitarian: God bestows God's self in the Spirit poured out in grace and in the Word made flesh in Christ Jesus. But, as David Coffey has pointed out, this Trinitarian structure could be made more explicit.[95] In re-reading Rahner's contributions to a theology of resurrection and the transformation of creation, I am struck by the paucity of references to the Holy Spirit. My own theological conviction is that the Spirit of God is to be seen as the immanent presence of God to creatures, as the Creator Spirit at work in creation, grace, the incarnation, the church and in the final transformation of all things.[96] In particular, I think it can be argued that Rahner's theology of God's immanence at work in all things, as self-bestowing love and as empowering creaturely self-transcendence, can be understood in fully Trinitarian terms as the presence and action of the Creator Spirit.

Rahner might well be happy with this suggestion. In one of his 'short formulas' of faith, he describes the absolute future bestowing itself over history as in a special sense the Spirit of God. He tells us that this Spirit at work in our history can be characterised as 'love, freedom, and a newness that constantly takes us by surprise'. In his meditation on the Ascension, Rahner reflects on the dynamism at the heart of creation in richly Trinitarian terms:

> And already for this world as a whole the process of fermentation has already commenced which will bring it to this momentous conclusion. It is already filled with the forces of this indescribable transformation. And this inner dynamism in it is called, as Paul boldly confirms for us in speaking of the resurrection of the flesh, the holy *Pneuma* of God. It is a free grace. It is not the sort of entity which the world could lay claim to as something proper to itself, something belonging to it autonomously and as of right. But it is the true, the ultimate perfection of the world in all its power, which brooded and hovered over the primordial chaos, and which

---

95. David Coffey, 'The Spirit of Christ as Entelechy', in *Philosophy and Theology* 13 (2001): 363–98
96. Denis Edwards, *Breath of Life: A Theology of the Creator Spirit* (Maryknoll, New York: Orbis Books, 2004).

will preserve all things and perfect all things which were and are. And this power of all powers, this meaning which is the ultimate meaning of all meanings, is now present at the very heart and centre of all reality including material reality, and has already, in the glorified Son, brought the beginning for the world triumphantly to its final goal of perfection.[97]

In my view, this view of the role of the holy Pneuma at work in creation can be read back into Rahner's whole theology of divine self-bestowal and creaturely self-transcendence. It is the life-giving Breath of God who is the immanent source of the new, the empowering love of God transforming all things in Christ from within.

---

97. Rahner, 'The Festival of the Future of the World', 184.

Teilhard's Vision as Agenda for Rahner's Christology

Pierre Teilhard de Chardin (1881–1955) was not only a geologist and paleontologist but also a Jesuit priest who developed an integrated vision of the inner relationship between the Omega of evolution and the Christ of Christian faith. In this article, I will ask the question: To what extent did his younger Jesuit confrere, Karl Rahner (1904– 1984), who was not a scientist but a theologian, take up and develop the agenda set by Teilhard?[1] I will begin to explore this question by examining Teilhard's view of the relationship between the Omega of evolution and Jesus Christ, focusing particularly on Teilhard's two late essays, 'The Heart of Matter' and 'The Christic'. Then I will trace Rahner's explicit comments on Teilhard's work, and propose that Rahner set himself a theological agenda with regard to Teilhard's vision. After noting the different methodological approaches of Teilhard and Rahner, I will explore how fundamental aspects of Rahner's Christology develop Teilhard's vision.

Teilhard on Evolution and Christ

At the end of his life, Teilhard looked back and traced the development of his thought in *The Heart of Matter*. In a first line of thought, he describes how, beginning from his early love of matter, his personal discovery of evolution enabled him to begin to see how 'Mat-

---

1. This article had its origin in a paper delivered at the 'International Symposium in Commemoration of the 400th Anniversary of Matteo Ricci 1552–1610: The Genesis and Development of East-West Dialogue', held at Fu Jen Catholic University, Taipei, Taiwan, April 2010.

ter is the matrix of Spirit', and 'Spirit is the higher state of matter'.[2] What became central for him was the conviction that the evolutionary law of complexity-consciousness does not stop with the biosphere but continues into the noosphere, the sphere of the human mind and of interpersonal consciousness and love. He became convinced that evolution now takes the form of a movement toward a global convergence and union of the human, to a point of irreversibility that he called Omega. He saw the universe, the whole world of matter, as in the process of becoming fully personalised in this Omega Point.

In a second line of thought, Teilhard reflects on the emergence of the 'Christic' in his life. Beginning from his early initiation into the symbol of the heart of Christ, he began to discover how the fire of love symbolised in this heart permeated everything in the universe. This discovery coincided with a view of God not simply as the God above, but as the God ahead, the God who draws all things to their completion in Christ. The incarnation of God in Jesus Christ reveals a God who is radically involved with matter. The risen Christ, sharing in the divine immensity, is at work in the whole of creation.

Teilhard tells us that his vision of reality was formed when he was able to understand together his insight into evolution of the cosmos to the point of Omega and his conviction of the presence of Christ in all things. Then he was able to see the cosmic and the Christic not only as converging, but as one:

> The cosmic sense and the christic sense: these two axes were born in me quite independently of one another, it would seem, and it was only after a long time and a great deal of hard work that I finally came to understand how, through and beyond the Human, the two were linked together, converged upon one another, and were in fact one and the same.[3]

On the one side, based on his scientific training, Teilhard saw a vision of a universe that was becoming personalised through convergence. On the other side, based on his theological commitment, he saw a vision of a person, Christ, who was becoming universalised. The result in him was his conviction of Christ as the very heart of the evolving matter of the universe: 'To Christify matter:

---

2. Pierre Teilhard de Chardin, *The Heart of Matter* (San Diego: Harcourt, 1978), 35.
3. Teilhard, *The Heart of Matter*, 40.

that sums up the whole venture of my innermost being'.[4] This process of Christification happens through the energy of incarnation, flowing into, illuminating and giving warmth to the universe of matter. He insists that this action of the risen Christ occurs not in a metaphysical sense, but in a physical sense.[5] For Teilhard, there is a wonderful confluence between Christ, who can be seen as 'evolver', and the cosmic centre that emerges from evolution. In this way, he says, the 'heart of a universalised Christ' coincides with the heart of 'amorised matter'.[6]

Just two months before his death, Teilhard began to write 'The Christic', which he saw as bringing together the quintessence of *Le Milieu Divin*, 'The Mass on the World', and 'The Heart of Matter'. In this essay, he argues that there is more in the total Christ than humanity and divinity. There is also the whole creation. He speaks of creation as a third 'aspect' or 'function' of Christ, and as 'in a true sense of the words', a third 'nature' of Christ.[7] Teilhard asks himself how such an 'immensified' view of the Christ avoids depersonalising him. He finds the answer to this precisely in the union between the Omega of evolution and the Christ, since this constitutes a Divine Milieu in which all opposition between the universal and the personal is wiped out. What is most cosmic is now most personal and what is most personal is most cosmic. For Teilhard, then, cosmogenesis reveals itself first in biogenesis and then in noogenesis, and culminates only in a true christogenesis.

Teilhard's work was resisted by some other biologists, and not simply because of his bold linking of evolution with Christ. The philosopher of science, Ernan McMullin, has pointed to a neo-Lamarckian tendency in Teilhard that may help to explain the violence of the opposition to him on the part of some leading neo-Darwinian biologists.[8] Teilhard divides the energies that propel the universe forward

---

4. Teilhard, *The Heart of Matter*, 47.
5. Teilhard, *The Heart of Matter*, 48.
6. Teilhard, *The Heart of Matter*, 49.
7. Pierre Teilhard de Chardin, 'The Christic', in *The Heart of Matter*, 93.
8. Ernan McMullin, 'Natural Science and Belief in a Creator: Historical Notes', in *Physics, Philosophy and Theology: A Common Quest for Understanding*, edited by Robert John Russell, William R Stoeger and George V Coyne (Vatican City State: Vatican Observatory, 1988), 49–79, at 68–70.

into two types, tangential and radial.⁹ Tangential energies are those that are normally associated with the natural sciences. But Teilhard introduces another form of energy, the radial, as necessary to account for the evolutionary process. This radial energy is fundamentally psychic in nature. It can be discerned by seeing the larger patterns of evolutionary process, rather than through the normal modes of inference at work in biology. Teilhard himself writes of this as a neo-Lamarckian addition to Darwinism.¹⁰ Rahner, by contrast, will see God as acting at a metaphysical level through secondary causes, in a way that is not accessible to science, which does not fill gaps in the scientific account, and which leaves science with its own integrity.

Towards the end of *The Christic*, Teilhard asks himself why is it that he seems to be the only one who has seen this vision: 'How is it, then, that as I look around, still dazzled by what I have seen, I find that I am almost the only person of my kind to have *seen*? And so I cannot, when asked, quote a single writer, a single work, that gives a clearly expressed description of the wonderful "Diaphany" that has transfigured everything for me?'¹¹ This is a poignant question, made all the more so by the difficulties Teilhard experienced with restrictions on his theological work by church authorities during his lifetime. Since Teilhard wrote 'The Christic', of course, other theologians, including Henri de Lubac, have taken up and defended his vision and, in our own time, scholars working in the area of science and theology, such as John Haught, continue build creatively on his thought.¹² I will focus on some key aspects of Rahner's response to Teilhard's vision.¹³

---

9. Pierre Teilhard de Chardin, *The Human Phenomenon*, translated by Sarah Appleton-Weber (Brighton: Sussex Academic Press, 1999, 2003), xxii, 30–2, 37, 227–32.
10. See his footnote in *The Human Phenomenon*, 97–8.
11. Teilhard, 'The Christic', 100.
12. See two recent books by John F Haught *Christianity and Science: Towards a Theology of Nature* (Maryknoll, NY: Orbis Books, 2007), particularly 65–81, and *Making Sense of Evolution: Darwin, God, and the Drama of Life* (Louisville: Westminster John Knox Press, 2010), particularly 137–48.
13. Some of these themes have been taken up in a thesis by HK Kodikuthiyil, 'Faith Engaged in Dialogue with Science. A Comparative Study of Pierre Teilhard de Chardin's and Karl Rahner's Reception of the Theory of Evolution' (PhD dissertation, Catholic University of Leuven, 1998). See also Leo O'Donovan, 'Der Dialog mit dem Darwinismus. Zur theologishen Verwendung des evolutiven Weltbilds bei Karl Rahner', in *Wagnis Theologie*, edited by Herbert Vorgrimler (Freiberg: Herder, 1979), 15–29.

Rahner's Explicit Comments on Teilhard

Cardinal Karl Lehmann was Rahner's assistant from 1964 to 1967. In an interview, he notes that Rahner did not see himself as a disciple of Martin Heidegger, Joseph Maréchal, or any other thinker, and then he goes on to speak of Rahner's relationship to the thought of Teilhard:

> It is also difficult to document where Rahner is dependent on someone else's thought. There are only faint clues, not that he wanted to cover that up, but his primary concern was his own independent thinking. Many maintain, for example, that he borrowed much from Pierre Teilhard de Chardin. That's not true. He did not read much Teilhard de Chardin, but he did have a seminar in Innsbruck on him. When others made their presentations during the seminar it stimulated new ideas for Rahner to think about.[14]

Rahner himself seems to have agreed that while he had not read Teilhard closely, he had been influenced by his ideas in a more general way. In response to an interviewer, Rahner recalled how a Dutch theologian had complained that while Rahner's thought had been largely inspired by Teilhard, Rahner had failed to acknowledge Teilhard. Rahner comments:

> I could only answer that at least up to that time I had read practically nothing of Teilhard de Chardin. But if you concluded from this that Rahner's theology is independent of Teilhard, I would answer that I don't make any such claim. I would conjecture that in the investigation of someone's thought, that there is obviously an 'atmospheric communication' of a non-literary kind.[15]

---

14. Karl Lehmann 'He Simply was Unique: In Conversation with Karl Cardinal Lehmann, Mainz', in *Encounters with Karl Rahner: Remembrances of Rahner by Those Who Know Him*, edited and translated by Andreas R Batlogg and Melvin E Michalski (Milwaukee: Marquette University Press, 2009), 111–34, at 118.
15. Karl Rahner, 'The Importance of Thomas Aquinas: Interview with Jan van den Eijnden, Insbruck (May 1982)', in *Faith in a Wintry Season: Conversations and Interviews with Karl Rahner in the Last Years of his Life*, edited by Paul Imhof and Hubert Biallowons, translated by Harvey Egan (New York: Crossroads, 1990), 41–58, at 53.

It is this atmospheric communication and its effects in Rahner's Christology that I will explore in the rest of this article. Rahner is sparing in his direct references to other thinkers, but in fact he does mention Teilhard de Chardin many times. Sometimes Rahner refers to Teilhard simply as an example, as when he lists Teilhard with Augustine, Aquinas and Pascal, as orthodox Christian thinkers who have different understandings of the human.[16] In another instance, reflecting on the future of the Jesuits on the two hundredth anniversary of their suppression in 1773, Rahner invokes the name of Teilhard to bring to mind the way Jesuits have been seen in 'leftist' or 'progressive' terms.[17] In an article where he is discussing the difficulty of theologians and natural scientists finding common ground, Rahner writes: 'So it happens, for example, that a Teilhard de Chardin is recognized by theologians as a natural scientist but not as a philosopher and theologian, whereas the natural scientist will think of him as a theologian who has not quite managed to keep up to date with the most recent findings of the natural sciences'.[18]

In a late article on natural science and faith, Rahner speaks of the church's resistance to the heliocentric system of Copernicus and then says of Teilhard: 'In reprimanding Teilhard de Chardin and repressing his endeavors it manifested too little understanding for an ontology in which created being is conceived in principle and in the very beginning as being which is in the process of becoming within an entire evolution of the cosmos, which is still in the process of becoming'.[19] In one of his important articles on Christology and evolution, Rahner describes his understanding of the self-transcendence of matter to spirit and, in a footnote, points out that 'a similar line of thought, though developed from a different starting-point, is to be found

---

16. Karl Rahner, 'Christian Humanism', in *Theological Investigations* 9 (London: Darton, Longman & Todd, 1972).
17. Karl Rahner, 'The Jesuits and their Future', in *Karl Rahner: Spiritual Writings* edited by Philip Endean (Maryknoll, NY: Orbis, 2004), 169–75, at 170.
18. Karl Rahner, 'A Small Question Regarding the Contemporary Pluralism in the Intellectual Situation of Catholics and the Church', in *Theological Investigations*, 6 (London: Darton, Longman & Todd, 1969), 21–30, at 25.
19. Karl Rahner, 'Natural Science and Reasonable Faith: Theological Perspectives for Dialogue with the Natural Sciences', in *Theological Investigations* 21 (New York: Crossroad, 1988), 16-55, at 25.

in Teilhard de Chardin's *Man's Place in Nature*.[20] Rahner also consciously uses Teilhard's language of Christ as 'Omega Point'.[21] In his article on evolution in *Sacramentum Mundi*, Rahner uses Teilhard's concepts of the 'noosphere' and speaks of the relationship between growth in 'complexity' and in 'interiority', in a way that seems to echo Teilhard's law of complexity-consciousness.[22] Naturally, Rahner refers to Teilhard's work in the introduction he agreed to write to Robert North's book, *Teilhard and the Creation of the Soul*.[23]

Rahner's most fundamental contribution to an evolutionary Christology is undoubtedly his 'Christology within an Evolutionary View of the World', first published in English in 1966. It contains three references to Teilhard. In the first, Rahner makes an important methodological distinction between his own work and that of Teilhard:

> To put it another way: we will try to avoid those theorems with which you are familiar from your study of Teilhard de Chardin. If we arrive at some of the same conclusions as he does, then all to the good. Yet we do not feel ourselves either dependent on him or obliged to him. We want to confine ourselves to those things which any theologian could say if he brings his theological reflection to bear on the questions posed by the modern evolutionary view of the world.[24]

I read this as Rahner saying that he may well arrive at some of the same conclusions as Teilhard, but he will attempt to get there on the basis of a theological methodology, rather than through the unitary approach of Teilhard and his attempt at a full integration of science

---

20. Karl Rahner, 'Christology in the Setting of Modern Man's Understanding of Himself and of his World', *Theological Investigations* 11(London: Darton, Longman & Todd, 1974), 215–29, at 218.
21. On Christ as omega-point, see Rahner's 'Thoughts on the Possibility of Belief Today', in *Theological Investigations* 5 (London: Darton, Longman & Todd, 1966), 3–22, at 13; 'Evolution: II Theological', in *Encyclopedia of Theology: A Concise Sacramentum Mundi* (London: Burns and Oates, 1975), 478–84, at 481.
22. Rahner, 'Evolution: II Theological', 481.
23. Robert North, *Teilhard and the Creation of the Soul* (Milwaukee: Bruce Publishing Company, 1967), ix.
24. Karl Rahner, 'Christology within an Evolutionary View of the World', in *Theological Investigations* 5 (London: Darton, Longman & Todd, 1966), 157–92, at 159–60.

and theology. In a second reference to Teilhard in this same article, Rahner says that he can go no further in applying his concept of self-transcendence without 'the more a-posteriori method proper to the natural sciences and with the aid of concepts such as are developed by Teilhard, for instance'.[25] In the final reference, Rahner defends Teilhard against the accusation that he does not have a proper concept of sin: 'It is also well-known that Teilhard has been reproached with rendering sin harmless in this way—a reproach which H de Lubac has surely invalidated most lucidly in his most recent book about Teilhard'.[26]

In a late discussion on the love of Jesus, Rahner points to the difficulty of connecting the Teilhardian Christ-Omega with Jesus of Nazareth, and with the Jesus whom Christians seek to love here and now.[27] Finally, about the same time, in 1982, Rahner published a short article on 'Christology Today' where he said, among other things: 'It would do no harm for a present-day Christology to take up the ideas of a Teilhard de Chardin and to elaborate them with more precision and clarity, even though in his work it is not very easy to find an intelligible and orthodox connection between Jesus of Nazareth and the cosmic Christ, the Omega Point of world evolution'.[28] I see this comment as more than a suggestion for other theologians. I propose that it might be seen as a description of what Rahner had tried to do in his own theology. He had taken up aspects of Teilhard's agenda, and tried to develop these in ways that showed their intelligibility and their orthodoxy in the light of the Christian tradition. Before exploring three of the ways in which Rahner took up this project in his Christology, I will make a brief comment on their very different methodologies.

Two Methodologies

Teilhard's methodology can be characterised as a unitary one. He brings together science, the inter-personal and the religious into

---

25. Rahner, 'Christology within an Evolutionary View', 167.
26. Rahner, 'Christology within an Evolutionary View', 185.
27. Karl Rahner, *The Love of Jesus and the Love of Neighbour* (New York; Crossroad, 1983), 20.
28. Karl Rahner 'Christology Today', in *Theological Investigations* XXI (New York: Crossroad, 1988), 220–7, at 227.

a unity of knowledge. Thomas King, a helpful guide to Teilhard's thought, points out that, for Teilhard, the unifying theme of all knowledge is evolution. Evolution does not remain simply a biological concept but becomes a universal one. Evolution is understood as far broader than biology, but biology still remains dominant in Teilhard's thought. As King says, 'By his broad understanding of evolution Teilhard is introducing a biological model by which to understand the universe'.[29] Teilhard sees the universe in bodily terms, as an organism, and then unites all fields of knowledge within his biological and evolutionary model. He sees everything as inter-related and understands these inter-relations as increasing and progressively converging in evolutionary process. As opposed to reductionists of both materialist and idealist kinds, Teilhard seeks to manifest a unity of the without and the within, of the bodily and the spiritual. He sees the material and biological universe coming to consciousness in the human. In the human, the universe can itself turn to God in love.

Rahner's methodology is radically different. It is true that he shares with Teilhard a great unifying vision of God's action in creation, redemption and in final fulfilment, which I will discuss in the next section. But Rahner's methodology can be distinguished from Teilhard's in four important ways. First, unlike Teilhard, Rahner sees God's action with regard to creation as occurring not at the physical or psychic level, but at the metaphysical level of a God who acts dynamically in and through created entities. In principle, this divine action is not open to scientific investigation. Second, Rahner writes only as a systematic theologian thinking within the Christian tradition, who seeks always to show the way that new theological approaches and insights remain faithful to what is central to the tradition. Third, while Rahner has a strong sense of the reciprocity of matter and spirit, and hence of science and theology, and while he engages with science creatively and often, he does this in a dialogical stance, conscious of the difference between science and religion, rather than through any attempt at the kind of full integration that Teilhard undertakes.[30] Finally, as opposed to Teilhard's unitary

---

29. Thomas M King, 'Teilhard's Unity of Knowledge', in *Teilhard in the 21st Century: The Emerging Spirit of Earth*, edited by Arthur Fabel and Donald St John (Maryknoll, NY: Orbis, 2003), 34.
30. See Karl Rahner, 'Natural Science and Reasonable Faith', in *Theological Investigations* 21 (New York: Crossroad, 1988), 16–55.

approach to knowledge, Rahner insists over and over again on the irreducible pluralism of knowledge today in all disciplines, including theology. He is deeply convinced that any one thinker can have only a partial approach to truth.[31] With their different methodologies in mind, I turn now to consider three ways in which Rahner builds on Teilhard in his Christology.

Divine Self-Bestowal: The Unity of Creation and Redemption

In Christian theology, there have been two traditional views about the relationship between Christ and the whole creation. In one view, the incarnation is thought to have caused as a remedy for human sin. In the other, associated with Franciscan theology, particularly Duns Scotus (c 1266–1308), God's plan of creation always had the incarnation of Christ as its centre. Long ago, NM Wildiers drew attention to the importance of this Scotist position for Teilhard de Chardin.[32] Rahner, too, follows this Scotist line of thought and develops it. He holds that God freely chooses, from the beginning, to create a world in which the Word would be made flesh and the Spirit poured out.[33] It would be hard to overestimate the importance of this insight for Rahner's theology. Harvey Egan has said that the briefest possible summary of Rahner's theological enterprise can be found in 'his creative appropriation of Scotus's view that God creates in order to communicate *self* and that creation exists in order to be the recipient of God's free gift of self'.[34]

One of Rahner's most characteristic theological concepts is his idea of divine self-bestowal. What is revealed in the Christ-event, in the life, death and resurrection of Jesus and in Pentecost, is a God who gives God's self to us in the Word made flesh and in the Spirit poured out in grace. God is revealed as a God who bestows God's

---

31. See, for example, Karl Rahner, 'Pluralism in Theology and the Unity of the Creed in the Church', in *Theological Investigations*, 11, 3–23.
32. NM Wildiers, *An Introduction to Teilhard de Chardin* (London: Collins, 1968), 130–41.
33. Karl Rahner, 'Christology within an Evolutionary View of the World', in *Theological Investigations* 5 (Baltimore: Helicon Press, 1966), 184–7.
34. Harvey D Egan, 'Theology and Spirituality', in Declan Marmion and Mary E Hines, *The Cambridge Companion to Karl Rahner* (Cambridge: Cambridge University Press, 2005), 16.

very self to creatures. Based on what is revealed in Christ, Rahner sees this divine self-bestowal as defining every aspect of God's action in creation and redemption. The story of the universe and of life on Earth, and everything that science can tell us about its evolution history, is part of a larger story, the story of divine self-bestowal.[35] When God wills to bestow God's self in love, creation comes to be as the addressee of this self-bestowal. This means that the story of salvation is the real ground of the history of nature, and not simply something that unfolds against the background of nature.[36] The evolution of the universe, and of life on Earth, exists *within* this larger vision of the divine purpose to give God's self to us.

Once sin exists, of course, the incarnation is the radical event of divine forgiveness and reconciliation. But at a more original level, the incarnation expresses the meaning and purpose of creation, the self-bestowal of God to a world of creatures. Creation and incarnation are not separate and independent acts of God, but are, in all their distinctiveness, united in the one act of God: they are 'two moments and two phases of the *one* process of God's self-giving and self-expression, although it is an intrinsically differentiated process'.[37] For Karl Rahner, self-bestowal in love characterises God's action in creation, grace, incarnation and the final fulfilment of all things in Christ. In this radically Trinitarian theology of self-bestowal, I believe that Rahner achieves what Teilhard sought, a way of showing the inner connection between creation and Christology, that is thoroughly theological and deeply grounded in God's self-revelation.

Evolutionary Christology—Creation's Self-Transcendence

Working simply as a theologian, Rahner asks how Christology might be understood in terms of the evolutionary worldview proposed by contemporary science. At the heart of his contribution on this issue is his concept of self-transcendence. Rahner comes to this concept in a transformation of scholastic theology's understanding of the God-

---

35. Karl Rahner, 'Christology in the Setting of Modern Man's Understanding of himself and of his World,' *Theological Investigations* 11 (New York: Seabury Press, 1974), 219.
36. Karl Rahner, 'Resurrection: D. Theology', in *Encyclopedia of Theology: A Concise Sacramentum Mundi* (London: Burns and Oates, 1975), 1442.
37. *Foundations of Christian Faith*, 197.

world relationship that builds on Aquinas. In this view, God's action with regard to creatures had been understood as the dynamic creative presence by which God sustains creatures in being (*conservatio*) and enables them to act (*concursus*). Rahner takes up and develops this fundamental metaphysical position into something new with his concept that God gives to creation itself the capacity for self-transcendence. In this new vision, divine self-bestowal and creaturely self-transcendence are mutually inter-related. It is precisely the creative presence of God in self-bestowing love that enables created entities to go beyond what they are to become something new.

Rahner's idea of the God-given self-transcendence of creatures is explored particularly in his evolutionary Christology, but it functions in his anthropology, his eschatology and many aspects of his work.[38] In all the transitions to the *new* in the history of the universe, particularly when matter becomes life, and when life becomes self-conscious spirit, Rahner proposes an evolutionary dynamism that is truly intrinsic to creation, but which occurs through the creative, saving power of the immanent God. The idea of *self*-transcendence indicates that at the empirical level, the emergence of the new is completely open to explanation in scientific terms. But at a deeper, theological and metaphysical level, it is the immanent presence of the divine being that enables creation to become more than it is in itself.

Rahner proposes the following pattern of evolutionary self-transcendence that brings out the inner connection between evolution and Christology. The material universe transcends itself in the emergence of life, and life transcends itself in the human. In human beings, the universe further transcends itself, becoming self-conscious and free and capable of personal response to God's self-bestowal in grace. The Christ-event is the radical self-transcendence of the created universe into God. In his humanity, Jesus, like us, is part of the evolutionary history of life on Earth, and a product of a long history of the universe. As a creature, and unlike us, Jesus in his life and death is wholly open to God, and lives a radical free response of love to God's self-bestowal.

---

38. Karl Rahner, *Hominisation: The Evolutionary Origin of Man as a Theological Problem* (London: Burns and Oates, 1965), 98–101; 'Christology within an Evolutionary View of the World', in *Theological Investigations* 5 (Baltimore: Helicon Press, 1969), 157–92; *Foundations*, 178–203.

Considered from below, Jesus Christ can be seen as the self-transcendence of the evolving universe into God, the culmination of the process of evolutionary emergence, although one that has not yet reached its final fulfilment. Considered from above, Jesus Christ can be seen as God's irreversible bestowal of God's very self to creation. In this one person, we find the event of salvation: God's irreversible self-giving to creatures and full creaturely acceptance of this self-bestowal, united in the one person.[39]

In this theology, Rahner builds an evolutionary theology in a critical engagement with two fundamental parts of the Christian tradition. First, he engages with Aquinas's metaphysical view of the God-world relationship, transforming it with his concept of self-transcendence. In doing so, he preserves Aquinas's view of a God who works consistently through secondary causes. God is not seen as an interventionist, but as one who works in and through the regularities and the laws studied by the sciences.[40] This means that God is not an alternative to what science can discover. Gaps in science are to be filled by science, not by invoking God. God is not an alternative to natural selection, but works through natural selection, through randomness and lawfulness, through all the processes of nature, which it is the role of science, not theology, to discover.

The second aspect of the tradition that Rahner takes up, and transforms, in this theology is the Christological teaching of the Council of Chalcedon. Rahner's view of Jesus as both the evolutionary self-transcendence of creation to God and God's self-bestowal to creation, united in the one person, as the event of our salvation, respects and dynamically develops the doctrine of the two natures united in the one person of Chalcedon.

Resurrection as Deifying Transformation of Creation

A third fundamental dimension of Rahner's evolutionary thought is his eschatological theology of the resurrection of Christ. He contrasts the traditional, Western, juridical focus on the death of Jesus with the theology of the East, where the resurrection plays a fundamental

---

39. Rahner, *Foundations of Christian Faith*, 193.
40. Karl Rahner and Karl-Heinz Weger, *Our Christian Faith* (London: Burns and Oats, 1980), 78–9.

role in the theology of salvation: 'The redemption was felt to be a real ontological process which began in the incarnation and ends not so much in the forgiveness of sins as in the divinization of the world and first demonstrates its victorious might, not so much in the expiation of sin on the cross as in the resurrection of Christ'.[41] Along with this Eastern theology, Rahner sees salvation as ontological rather than juridical, understands salvation as a deification that involves human beings and with them the whole creation, and sees the resurrection of Christ as the beginning of this divinising transfiguration. He thus locates a basis for something like the Teilhardian vision in the theology of great Eastern thinkers like Irenaeus and Athanasius.

According to Rahner, what happens in the death of Jesus is that a piece of this evolutionary, fleshly world is handed over freely into God, in complete obedience and love. In the resurrection, God irrevocably adopts creaturely evolutionary reality as God's own reality. Because of the unity of the world that springs from the Creator, this is an event for the whole world. What occurs in the resurrection of Jesus, as part of the physical, biological and human world, is *ontologically* and not simply juridically, 'the embryonically final beginning of the glorification and divinisation of the whole of reality'.[42] As Rahner puts it in another place, the resurrection is 'the beginning of the transformation of the world as an ontologically interconnected occurrence'.[43] The final destiny of the world is not only promised, but already begun. The risen Christ is the 'pledge and beginning of the perfect fulfillment of the world'. He is the 'representative of the new cosmos'.[44]

On this basis, Rahner holds that we Christians are really 'the most sublime of materialists'. Matter will last forever, and be glorified forever in Christ. But, Rahner believes, it will also undergo a transformation, 'the depths of which we can only sense with fear and trembling in that process which we experience as our death'.[45] In this way, Rahner holds with Teilhard, that the transfiguration of the world

---

41. Karl Rahner, 'Dogmatic Questions on Easter', in *Theological Investigations* 4 (London: Darton, Longman and Todd, 197), 126.
42. Rahner, 'Dogmatic Questions on Easter', 129.
43. Rahner, 'Resurrection: D Theology', 1142.
44. Rahner, 'Resurrection: D Theology', 1142.
45. Karl Rahner, 'The Festival of the Future of the World', in *Theological Investigations*, 7 (London: Darton, Longman and Todd, 1971), 183.

has already begun in the risen Christ and is 'ripening and developing to that point where it will become manifest'.[46] In dialogue with Eastern patristic theology, Rahner argues that the resurrection of the Crucified is the beginning of the transfiguration in Christ, not only of humanity, but with them, in ways that are appropriate to different creatures, of the whole universe.

Conclusion

Earlier, I referred to Teilhard's lament that he could not quote a single writer that gave expression to the insight into the relationship between Christ and evolution that had transfigured everything for him. I have proposed that Rahner can be counted as one who does this. I also referred to Rahner's suggestion at the end of his life that present-day Christology should take up the ideas of a Teilhard de Chardin, elaborate them with precision and clarity, and show an intelligible and orthodox connection between Jesus of Nazareth and the cosmic. It has been proposed that this formed something of an agenda for Rahner throughout his life. Rahner stays with a more traditional metaphysical notion of divine action than Teilhard, and I think this enables his theology better to respect the integrity of science, including neo-Darwinism. And he places evolutionary theology with a profoundly Trinitarian and incarnational theology of a God who bestows God's self to us in the Word and the Spirit.

At the same time, he transforms the metaphysical tradition of divine action by showing how God's self-bestowal enables creation to transcend itself in evolutionary emergence. In a way that is faithful to Chalcedon, he shows how Jesus Christ can be understood as both the evolutionary self-transcendence of the universe to God, and God's radical self-bestowal to the universe, united in one person. Finally, he builds on the Eastern patristic tradition to show the resurrection of Jesus can be seen as the beginning of the deifying transformation of human beings and with them of the whole universe in Christ. Rahner takes up some of Teilhard's agenda in a theology of divine self-bestowal, a self-bestowal in love that enables not only creaturely self-transcendence but also the transfiguring deification of human beings and of the whole universe in Christ.

---

46. Rahner, 'The Festival of the Future of the World', 184.

Climate Change and the Theology of Karl Rahner: A Hermeneutical Dialogue

In many different parts of the world, theologians have been engaged in responding to ecological issues, some specifically focusing on climate change. My intention here is the modest one of attempting to clarify the kind of dialogue involved in this emergent ecological theology. In particular, I will ask about the hermeneutical principles involved in bringing a scientifically informed ecological consciousness into creative dialogue with the Christian tradition. In order to pursue this aim, I think it is helpful to be specific and concrete, and so I will take up one example of a major ecological issue that confronts us, climate change, and engage with one specific interpretation of the Christian tradition, the theology of Karl Rahner.

One of the positions I will advocate is that just as there are two sides to a real conversation, so there ought to be two sides in a theology that engages with ecology. There are examples of ecological hermeneutics that are one-sided where, for example, ecological insights are seen as challenging aspects of the Christian tradition, but this tradition appears to have nothing to add to the conversation. On the other hand, there are Christian theologies that ignore or marginalise ecological concerns. Both perspectives will need to be engaged critically in an authentic ecological theology. An ecological consciousness has the possibility of not only raising crucial questions for Christian theology, but also of opening up fruitful new perspectives. An ecological theology will not only raise critical questions about assumptions within the ecological movement, but may also give insight into the meaning and the value of God's creation. A creative dialogue between these perspectives may lead to a critically aware ecological theology that has something to say in the context of global climate change.

Global climate change involves many disciplines besides science and theology, including those of economics and politics. For the sake of clarity, my focus will be restricted to the interaction between a scientifically informed ecological consciousness and theology. Obviously, this can only offer a partial view of the whole. But I hope it can clarify some aspects of the dialogue that goes on in the work of ecological theology. As a small step in this direction, I will attempt to articulate hermeneutical principles that emerge from a scientifically informed consciousness of global climate change, on the one hand, and from the theology of Karl Rahner, on the other.

A Scientifically Informed Consciousness of Climate Change

What does a scientifically informed consciousness bring to the task of constructing a Christian ecological theology that can offer a response to the issue of global climate change? My proposal is that a scientific consciousness can be thought of as bringing to the table one general challenge to theology and five more specific hermeneutical principles.

A General Challenge

An ecological consciousness confronts theology with a stark challenge: *Global climate change, understood in relation to all its associated ecological and human issues, is the most urgent issue facing the community of life on our planet in the twenty-first century and therefore it is also an issue that Christian theology must address.* In our time, we see the loss of Arctic sea-ice, the northern permafrost thaw, the retreat of glaciers that are the sources of great rivers and the thermal expansion of the ocean. It seems clear that large areas of our planet will become far hotter while others will be subject to more violent storms and floods. While some species will be able to migrate to new habitats, many others will become extinct as their habitats are lost. Human beings will be displaced and many will be forced to become refugees. Great food growing areas will become subject to extreme drought, flooding or inundation by the seas. Water will become very scarce in many parts of the planet. There is a real danger of wars over sources of water and over land for food, as well as over the sources of energy. The continuing loss of biodiversity challenges us at every level. All the other major issues facing the human community, from the inequality between rich and poor in our world to the threat of nuclear war, are inextricably interconnected with the issue of global climate change.

There can be little doubt that global climate change, in the context of the other issues with which it interconnects, is a great challenge we face in this century. Responding to it will require all the creative energy, good will and co-operation that the human community can muster. When the human community faces this kind of challenge, it involves the deepest dimensions of the human. Religious faith, including Christian faith, is challenged to ask itself two critical questions: 1. Do its formulations and practices contribute to the problems facing the community? 2. In what ways might its traditions and liturgies become a source of energy, life and motivation for a genuine ecological commitment in this new time? A scientific and ecological consciousness puts to theology a challenge to rethink its doctrines and practices in the light of the global crisis facing our planet.

Five Interpretative Principles

An ecological consciousness can also be seen as offering specific contributions to the discussion. I will propose that it can offer at least five further guiding ideas or interpretative principles for the building of a genuine ecological theology in the context of global climate change.

1. *Global climate change needs to be addressed from within a scientific worldview, which includes an understanding of the observable universe as expanding and evolving, and of life on Earth as evolving by means of natural selection.*

An ecological consciousness is necessarily informed by the biological sciences, all of which are shaped by the theory of evolution. Biologists have a common vision of life as beginning about 3.8 billion years ago with simple bacterial cells, and emerging through the evolution of complex cells into multicellular creatures, and then into all forms of life, including dinosaurs, flying reptiles, mammals, birds and flowering plants. About four million years ago, chimpanzee-like apes gave rise to various hominid species (the *Australopithecines*), and then, with a large increase in brain size, to various species of *Homo*, including *Homo erectus*, and about 200,000 years ago, to modern humans. Everything is interconnected in the history of life and everything depends upon evolution, which is driven at least in large part by natural selection.

Life on Earth is unthinkable without the stars, something now recognised in the establishment of departments of Astrobiology at NASA and various universities. It was only through the work of Einstein and Hubble in the early first decades of the twentieth century that we came to know that our universe is not static but expanding. We can now trace it back to a time when it was extremely small, hot and dense 13.7 billion years ago. Biological life is deeply connected to the story of the universe. We are a carbon-based life-form and all the carbon atoms that make us up, along with the nitrogen and oxygen, are produced by the process of nucleosynthesis in stars. An ecological consciousness is informed by the story of the universe offered by scientific cosmology and of life offered by evolutionary biology.

What questions or challenges does this principle bring to the dialogue with theology? Obviously, it challenges a theology that is content to simply repeat what has been said in the past. The cosmological worldview taken for granted by the Bible, Augustine or Aquinas cannot be taken for granted today. The theological insights contained in the ancient classical texts may be as relevant as ever, but they need to be rethought from within a new worldview. We know wonderful things about the dynamic nature of God's creation and its evolutionary emergence that were not available to Paul, Augustine or Aquinas. An ecological theology will need to be a theology articulated within a consciousness of the 13.8 billion-year history of the observable universe and the 3.7 billion-year history of life on Earth. This is not only a challenge, but an opportunity for theology to speak about God's action in creation and salvation in ways that take seriously the new, dynamic understanding of the world available to us. An ecological theology will be one that takes seriously the story of the universe and of life given to us by the sciences.

2. *The regular shifts in the global climate, the current scientific consensus on human-induced climate change, and the provisional and revisable nature of this science need to be taken into account.*

In a scientific approach to climate change, our present experience of climate change is situated in a larger context of regular shifts in the global climate, caused by variations in green house gasses, plate tectonics, volcanism, solar radiation and the Earth's orbit. Since the 1970s, scientists have linked long-term climate change to three variations in the orbit of the Earth around the Sun (the Milankovitch theory). These variations occur in predictable cycles. One cycle, caused by a wobble in the axis of the Earth's rotation, called precession, occurs every 22,000 years. The others, caused by the tilt in the Earth's rotational axis and by the shape of its orbit, occur every 41,000 and 100,000 years. These three cycles alter the distribution of solar energy reaching the Earth. Over the last three million years, these variations have produced a series of ice ages followed by warmer interglacial periods. The last ice age was about 20,000 years ago and the present interglacial period (the Holocene) is well advanced.

The Intergovernmental Panel on Climate Change, in its Fourth Assessment Report (2007) concludes that global warming has accelerated over recent decades and there is new and stronger evidence that it is to be attributed to an increase in greenhouse gasses caused by human activities. By the end of the twenty-first century, average world temperatures are likely to be between 1.4 and 5.8 degrees higher than in 1990. The IPCC predictions are tentative and revisable. Its conclusions are based on a current consensus in peer-reviewed science. Many of the challenges and attacks directed against the IPCC that appear in the media are not based on peer-reviewed climate science. When theology engages with climate science, I think it needs to engage with what appears to be the best information available from peer-reviewed science. It must also recognise that science is revisable in the light of further evidence. In discussions on climate, theology engages not with what is certain or absolute, but what is provisional.

3. *The costs of evolution are intrinsic to the process of the emergence of life on Earth. Suffering is built into the natural world.*

The earthquakes and tsunamis that have killed hundreds of thousands of people in recent years are caused by the meeting of tectonic plates. It is this dynamic system of tectonic plates that allows for the emergence of mountain ranges, rivers, rainforests and fertile plains, providing habitats that allow life to evolve in new ways. The evolution of life, with its abundance and beauty, is accompanied by terrible costs to human beings and to other species. The costs are built into the universe and its laws. Evolutionary emergence involves not only co-operation but also competition for resources. The pattern of evolution depends on death, and the continuing cycle of generation. The diversity of life, with all its beauty and goodness, arises by way of increasing complexity through emergent processes that involve tragic loss. The costs are evident in the history of life with its predation, death and extinctions. We know, as no generation has known before us, that these costs are intrinsic to the processes that give rise to life on Earth in all its wonderful diversity.

This principle challenges a tendency to see the ecological as always harmonious, peaceful and in balance. What is natural can also be ugly and it can be painful. This principle challenges all romantic notions of the natural world. It challenges Christian theology, not to abandon its conviction of the goodness and beauty of creation, but to see it for what it really is in all its complexity. It also puts suffering at the centre of a Christian theology of creation. Suffering, death, and the extinction of species that have occurred throughout evolutionary history cannot be seen, in the way that an earlier theology might have seen them, as the outcome of human sin, but are part of the way God has created the diversity of life. This new insight into the suffering built into creation sets an important agenda for twenty-first century theology. It needs to return to the age-old issue of suffering. It needs to respond to the costs built into evolutionary emergence by God and to do this in the light of its deepest insights into the meaning of Christ and his promise.

4. *Other living creatures are to be valued not only because of their usefulness to human beings but because they possess intrinsic value.*

One of the fundamental claims of ecological ethics is that the value of life-forms is not determined simply by their value for humans. Holmes Rolston III, a founding contributor to the new field of environmental ethics, has argued for the objective intrinsic value of the natural world by means of an analysis that is based closely on the biological sciences. At the level of each organism, he finds a life being defended and valued. Because the genetic set for an organism is conserved primarily at the species level, Rolston sees the species as well as the organism as being the object of moral consideration. At the level of the ecosystem, and the biosphere of the planet, Rolston finds not only intrinsic value but 'systemic' value, above all in the natural world's capacity to evolve diverse and complex life-forms. He finds value in living things from the tiniest organism to the biotic community of Earth, and insists that this value is objectively there in the natural world and that it makes moral claims on human beings.[1]

What this principle challenges is uncritical anthropocentrism, whether it appears in the biblical texts, in the Christian theological tradition or in the life of the churches. Uncritical anthropocentrism is the view that other creatures exist only to serve human beings. The principle of intrinsic value does not, in my view, rule out a strong view of the unique dignity of the human person. It supports the idea that other creatures also have their own unique dignity and value. This principle is a fruitful one for Christian theology. It is congruent with, and can be brought into creative dialogue with, fundamental biblical positions: that the Creator holds all things in existence, finds all of creation good and enables it to flourish in all its fertility and abundance (Gen 1:20-31); that God loves and cares for each creature (Wis 11:24; Lk 12:6); that the diversity of creatures is the self-expression of God (Ps 104:24); that, in God's eschatological future, each creature, in the heavens, on earth, under the earth and in the sea will sing praise to the one seated on the throne and to the Lamb (Rev 5:13).

5. *All the forms of life on Earth are interconnected in one web of life, and are interrelated with the land, the seas, the rivers and the atmosphere.*

This is perhaps the most pervasive principle at work in an ecological consciousness. The Earth is a place of abundant and exuberant life. The five to ten million species that inhabit our planet have emerged over the last 600,000 years. They have a common heritage that goes back to the origins of bacterial life more than 3.8 billion years ago. They have evolved in relationship to each other, interconnected in delicate ecological systems. They are interdependent not only with each other, but also with the Earth's atmosphere, its seas, rivers and lakes and the land itself. Human actions, such as ruthless fishing practices, the dumping of industrial and urban waste, the destruction of river systems and uncontrolled land-clearing destroy both known

---

1. Holmes Rolston III, *Genesis, Genes and God; Values and their Origins in Natural and Human History* (Cambridge: Cambridge University Press, 1999), 38-53.

and unknown species and make Earth a more sterile and dangerous place.

This principle is a critical principle that can guide human action into an ecological future. At a deeper level, it points to the idea that our very identity is that we exist only in relation to others, to other human beings, to other species, and to all that supports life on our planet. When we act as if we can disconnect ourselves from the rest of biological life, we ignore our true nature as interdependent in the community of life on our planet. While this challenges the individualism found in some interpretations of the Christian tradition, it can be a stimulus for conversation with the deepest traditions of Christian faith, which finds an inter-relational view of reality grounded in an inter-relational view of God as a God of mutual relations. In a fully ecological theology, the ecological relationships that characterise life on Earth can be understood as springing from the relational life of the Trinity.

From the Perspective of Rahner's Interpretation of the Christian Tradition

So far, I have proposed that from the perspective of an ecological consciousness, a general challenge is offered to Christian theology along with five interpretative principles that can contribute to the building of an ecological theology. Turning now to Rahner's thought, I will suggest one fundamental theological stance and five further interpretative principles that can contribute to this same project.

A Fundamental Theological Stance

It was proposed above that the issue of global climate change is a fundamental issue facing the human community in the twenty-first century and, as such, is an urgent issue for Christian theology. *The fundamental response offered in the theology of Karl Rahner is that it is precisely in the engagement with what confronts us in our daily and communal lives, such as global climate change, that we encounter the mystery of God.* Rahner holds that when we go out of ourselves to our world, in knowledge, love and commitment, we find ourselves also open to the infinite mystery that transcends all objects of immediate experience. This experience of radical openness to mystery is always mediated by our knowledge and love of other persons and entities in our world. It is in our engagement with our world, with persons, with issues, with great challenges like climate change, that we are brought to a sense of the incomprehensible mystery in which all of this dwells. Rahner insists that because of revelation, we can this as truly the place of grace, the place of the Holy Spirit. [2]

When we engage with the world, when we are drawn to an awareness of our planetary community of life, there is an openness to holy mystery in our knowledge of our fragile planet. We know our limited and finite planet only against a horizon that is boundless. When we are drawn to loving commitment to the Earth and its creatures, our love opens out beyond itself to a love that is without limits. Rahner insists that the boundlessness of the human heart and mind that occurs in our engagement with our world is the place of God's grace. God has freely chosen to give God's self to us and we encounter this God in our knowledge of, love for and commitment to the Earth and its creatures. To adapt Rahner's words from his famous article on the unity of love of God and love of neighbour: We can only love the God that we do not see by loving the planetary community that we do see. And to truly be committed in love for the community of life on our planet is already to love, at least implicitly, the living God.[3]

We encounter the living God in negative as well as positive experiences of our engagement with our world. Involvement with the issue of global climate change will lead, at least at times, to the experience of failure and frustration, and living with ambiguity, unable to control the outcome of political decisions. Rahner would say that when we resist cynicism and despair, and continue our commitment, continuing to hope and to act, then this is the place of God and God's liberating grace.[4] And also when we are taken out of ourselves by the exuberant life of a rain forest, or by the song of a single bird, or by the experience of human solidarity, this too can be a place for encountering God's Spirit. To see this as the silent

---

2. See Karl Rahner, *Foundations of Christian Faith: An Introduction to the Idea of Christianity* (New York: Seabury, 1978), 51–71.
3. Karl Rahner, 'Reflections on the Unity of Love of Neighbour and the Love of God', in *Theological Investigations* 6 (New York: Seabury, 1969), 231–49.
4. See Karl Rahner, 'Experience of the Holy Spirit', in *Theological Investigations* 18 (New York: Crossroad, 1983), 189–210.

presence of God, to give ourselves to this holy one is to be involved with what Rahner calls the mysticism of everyday life.[5] In terms of this discussion, it might be said what Rahner's theology offers to the discussion of climate change at the most fundamental level, is the idea that there is a genuine mysticism of commitment to the Earth and all its creatures.

Five Further Interpretative Ideas from Rahner's Theology

What I have been describing above is sometimes called Rahner's transcendental method. It refers to the way he consistently seeks to see our experiences in this world as the place where we encounter a gracious and mysterious God. But, as scholars like Francis Schüssler Fiorenza point out, Rahner's work is not limited to any one methodology.[6] He uses a variety of approaches. In particular, he consistently sees the Word made flesh in Jesus of Nazareth as the norm for his theology. Everything, including the experience of grace in everyday life, is understood from the perspective of the Christ-event. There is a Christological centre to Rahner's theology. Based on his view of God's self-communication in Christ, five further interpretative principles can be found in Rahner's theology.

1. *The creation of the universe and the Incarnation can be seen as distinct dimensions of the one act of divine self-bestowal in love.*

According to Rahner, the central insight of Christianity is that God gives God's self to us in the Word made flesh and in the Spirit poured out in grace. God is revealed to us as a God who bestows God's self. God gives God's self to creatures. Based on what is revealed in Christ, Rahner sees this self-bestowal as defining every aspect of God's action in creation, redemption and final fulfilment. The story of the universe, and everything that science can tell us about its evolution, is part of a larger story, the story of divine self-bestowal. He sees the creation of the universe as an element in the radical decision of God

---

5. Rahner, 'Experience of the Holy Spirit', 203.
6. Francis Schüssler Fiorenza, 'Method in Theology', in *The Cambridge Companion to Karl Rahner*, edited by Declan Marmion and Mary E Hines (Cambridge: Cambridge University Press, 2005), 65–82.

to give God's self in love to that which is not divine.[7] When God wills to bestow God's self in love, creation comes to be as the addressee of this self-bestowal. Rahner insists that the story of salvation is the real ground of the history of nature, and not simply something that unfolds against the background of nature.[8] The history of the evolution of the universe, and of life on our planet, exists *within* this larger vision of the divine purpose.

In this theology, the incarnation is not something that comes about simply as a remedy for sin. It is not simply a corrective for a creation that has gone wrong. It is not thought of as an add-on, or as an afterthought, to creation. With the Franciscan school of theology, exemplified in Duns Scotus (1266–1308), Rahner holds that God freely chooses, from the beginning, to create a world in which the Word would be made flesh and the Spirit poured out.[9] Harvey Egan finds that the briefest possible summary of Rahner's theological enterprise is found in 'his creative appropriation of Scotus's view that God creates in order to communicate *self* and that creation exists in order to be the recipient of Gods free gift of self'.[10] Once sin exists, the incarnation is the great expression of divine forgiveness. But even more radically, the incarnation expresses the meaning and purpose of creation, divine self-bestowal. Creation and incarnation are united in the one act of God: they are 'two moments and two phases of the *one* process of God's self-giving and self-expression, although it is an intrinsically differentiated process'.[11]

This principle challenges two opposed theological positions. On the one hand, it challenges a theological tradition that centres the whole redemptive act of God in Christ on human sin, and atonement for human sin. On the other hand, it also challenges some of the proponents of creation spirituality, who tend to reject or aban-

---

7. Karl Rahner, 'Christology in the Setting of Modern Man's Understanding of himself and of his World', in *Theological Investigations* 11 (New York: Seabury Press, 1974), 219.
8. Karl Rahner, 'Resurrection: D Theology', in *Encyclopedia of Theology: A Concise Sacramentum Mundi* (London: Burns and Oates, 1975), 1442.
9. Karl Rahner, 'Christology within an Evolutionary View of the World', in *Theological Investigations* 5 (Baltimore: Helicon Press, 1966), 184–7.
10. Harvey D Egan, 'Theology and Spirituality', in *The Cambridge Companion to Karl Rahner,* edited by Declan Marmion and Mary E Hines (Cambridge: Cambridge University Press, 2005), 16.
11. *Foundations of Christian Faith*, 197.

don the theology of redemption as dangerously anthropocentric. This principle proposes a theology in which creation and redemption are held together as inseparable dimensions of God's one act of self-giving love. This, in turn, can provide the foundation for a theology of redemption that involves the whole creation.

2. *God's act of redemption involves the deification of human beings and with them the whole creation.*

Rahner sees the incarnation and creation itself from the perspective of the resurrection. He contrasts the Western juridical notion of redemption focused on the death of Jesus with the theology of the East, where the resurrection plays a fundamental role in the theology of salvation: 'The redemption was felt to be a real ontological process which began in the incarnation and ends not so much in the forgiveness of sins as in the divinization of the world and first demonstrates its victorious might, not so much in the expiation of sin on the cross as in the resurrection of Christ'.[12] There are three themes in this Eastern theology that are fundamental for Rahner's thought: salvation as ontological rather than juridical, the idea of the divinisation of the world, and the resurrection of Christ as the beginning of this divinising transfiguration.

In the death of Jesus, a piece of this world is handed over freely into God, in complete obedience and love, and is fully taken up into God. In the resurrection, God irrevocably adopts creaturely reality as God's own reality. Because of the unity of the world that springs from the Creator, this is an event for the whole world. What occurs in Jesus, as part of the physical, biological and human world, is *ontologically* and not simply juridically, 'the embryonically final beginning of the glorification and divinization of the whole of reality'.[13] The resurrection is 'the beginning of the transformation of the world as an ontologically interconnected occurrence'.[14] The final destiny of the world is decided and already begun. The risen Christ is the 'pledge

---

12. Karl Rahner, 'Dogmatic Questions on Easter', in *Theological Investigations* 4 (London: Darton, Longman and Todd, 197), 126.
13. Rahner, 'Dogmatic Questions on Easter', 129.
14. Rahner, 'Resurrection: D. Theology', 1142.

and beginning of the perfect fulfilment of the world'. He is the 'representative of the new cosmos'.[15]

This means that we Christians are really 'the most sublime of materialists'. Christians hold that matter will last forever, and be glorified forever in Christ. It will, however, undergo a radical transformation, 'the depths of which we can only sense with fear and trembling in that process which we experience as our death'.[16] The transfiguration of the world has begun in the risen Christ and is 'ripening and developing to that point where it will become manifest'.[17] This position challenges any theology of the redemption that limits the meaning of Christ to human beings, because it sees the whole creation as involved in God's work of redemption and deification. At the same time, however, because it gives a radically central place to the incarnation and the resurrection, it sees God as forever united to humanity in Christ, and challenges claims, sometimes put forward from an ecological perspective, that undermine the dignity of the human being.

What it offers is a theology of redemptive deification that involves the whole creation, clearly fundamental for a Christian ecological theology. It opens up the possibility of pursuing questions not considered by Rahner: To what extent might we think of the incarnation as a deep incarnation in the sense that God embraces and transforms not only human flesh, but all flesh, the whole of our evolutionary history, and the interconnected web of life? How do we think of the final salvation not only of matter, but also of nonhuman biological creatures, both species and individuals?

3. *The transcendent God's relationship with creation is characterised by radical immanence.*

Rahner is a theologian convinced that we stand before a God who is an abiding, absolute and incomprehensible mystery to us, a mystery that theology can approach only by means of analogy. In his final theological reflection, Rahner writes: 'theologians are worthy of the title only when they do not seek to reassure themselves that they are providing clear and lucid discourse, but rather when they

---

15. Rahner, 'Resurrection: D. Theology', 1142.
16. Karl Rahner, 'The Festival of the Future of the World', in *Theological Investigations* 7 (London: Darton, Longman and Todd, 1971), 183.
17. Rahner, 'The Festival of the Future of the World', 184.

are experiencing and witnessing, with both terror and bliss to the analogical back and forth between affirmation and negation before the abyss of God's incomprehensibility'.[18] In stressing the divine transcendence, Rahner is not unique, but stands in the great theological tradition of the Gregory of Nyssa, Augustine and Aquinas. It is precisely and only because God is radically transcendent that God can be, as Augustine says, more interior to me than I am to myself. God's radical immanence to creatures is the fruit of divine transcendence.

Rahner goes further when, in a late article he asks himself: what is most specific to the Christian view of God? His answer is the idea that God bestows God's very self to creation.[19] God creates creatures that are able to receive God's life as their own fulfilment: 'Only when this statement is made, when, within a concept of God that makes a radical distinction between God and the world, God himself is still the very core of the world's reality and world is truly the fate of God himself, only then is the concept of God attained that is truly Christian'.[20] Rahner makes the staggering claim that *God's self-giving is the very core of the world's reality and the world is truly the fate of God*. This claim is based on the conviction that in creation, incarnation and in its culmination in resurrection, God commits God's self to this world, to this universe and its creatures, and does this eternally.

Rahner sees God's action on creation not according to the model of efficient causality, but that of formal causality: God creates through self-bestowal. God gives God's self to us and we are made a new creation. God, then, does not create simply by producing something different from God's self, as a carpenter makes a table. Rather, God creates by communicating God's own divine reality and making it a constitutive element in the fulfilment of the creature. God remains God but radically determines our being, and we are transformed from within. We become a 'new creation' (2 Cor 5:17) and are made

---

18. Karl Rahner, 'Experiences of a Catholic Theologian', in *The Cambridge Companion to Karl Rahner*, edited by Declan Marmion and Mary E Hines (Cambridge: Cambridge University Press, 2005), 301.
19. Karl Rahner, 'The Specific Character of the Christian Concept of God', in *Theological Investigations* 21 (New York: Crossroad, 1988), 185–95.
20. Rahner, 'The Specific Character of the Christian Concept of God', 191.

'participants of the divine nature' (2 Pet 1:4).[21] This relationship that Rahner sees as characteristic of grace, he sees as an appropriate analogy for the relationship that God has with *the whole universe and all its creatures.*[22] God is creatively present to every entity and process of the universe, in such a way that 'the reality of God himself is imparted to the world as its supreme specification'.[23] Self-bestowal is not only the goal of creation, but that which moves creation from within to the goal. This self-bestowal of the transcendent God is 'the most immanent factor in the creature'.[24]

Because of its stress on the absolute transcendence of God, Rahner's theology questions tendencies in ecological and scientific thought, which seem to make the universe into the Creator, or which would make evolution itself into something divine, or which suggest that the creativity of nature is 'God enough'. It insists on the transcendent God who creates through secondary causes, which include the universe itself, evolution and the creativity of nature. With the idea that this God gives God's self to the universe of creatures in such a way that this self-giving is the very core of the world's reality and the world is the fate of God, this theological vision questions the widespread idea that transcendence is opposed to immanence, and that there is some kind of need to move from a theology of transcendence to one of immanence. What Rahner's theology offers is a vision of God who is present in self-giving love to every aspect of creation, to every galaxy and to each insect in a rainforest, as the source of its existence, its creativity and its final fulfilment.

---

21. See Rahner, *Foundations of Christian Faith,* 120–3. In some works, Rahner calls this *quasi*-formal causality, with the *quasi* indicating the uniqueness of this kind of formal causality, in which both divine transcendence and creaturely integrity are fully maintained. See Rahner, 'Natural Science and Christian Faith', in *Theological Investigations* 21 (New York: Crossroad, 1988), 35–6.
22. What is true of grace is always valid 'in an analogous way for the relationship between God's absolute being and being which originates from him'. Karl Rahner, 'Natural Science and Christian Faith', 36.
23. Rahner, 'Christology in the Setting', 225.
24. Karl Rahner, 'Immanent and Transcendent Consummation of the World', in *Theological Investigations* 10 (London: Darton, Longmann & Todd), 281.

4. *God acts through in a noninterventionist way through creaturely causes.*

Thomas Aquinas saw God as working through creatures that are themselves truly causal, which he calls secondary causes. God is the primary cause who is always creatively and providentially at work in all created causes. It is by God's power that every other power acts. While God enables creaturely causes to exist and to have effect, Aquinas insists that secondary causes are genuinely causal in their own right. It is through these secondary causes which have their own proper independence that God cares for creation: 'Divine Providence works through intermediaries. For God governs the lower though the higher, not from any impotence on his part, but from the abundance of his goodness imparting to creatures *the dignity of causing*'.²⁵ God respects the dignity of secondary causes, and bestows on them their own integrity. According to Aquinas, God works consistently through secondary causes, except for the case of miracle, where God acts without secondary causes.

Rahner develops the tradition of Aquinas. He proposes that the great events of the history of salvation as well as special divine acts in our lives might be understood in noninterventionist terms. They are instances where God freely brings to particular, concrete and historical expression that one act by which God is immanent to creation from the beginning: 'God in his free grace, from the very beginning and always and everywhere, has communicated himself to his creation as its innermost energy and works in the world from the inside out'.²⁶ God is never simply one object amongst others in our world, but is 'embedded' in this world from its origin.²⁷ A special act of God is an 'objectification' of God's one self-bestowing action. In such a divine act, a created reality expresses and mediates the immanent action of God. Because a created entity reality really does give expression to divine action, it is appropriate to speak of *objective,* special divine action.²⁸ God's actions in creation, in the history of salvation and in our own lives can be understood as God acting through sec-

---

25. Aquinas, *Summa theologiae* 1a.22.3.
26. Karl Rahner and Karl-Heinz Weger, *Our Christian Faith* (London: Burns and Oats, 1980), 78–9.
27. Rahner, *Foundations of Christian Faith*, 87.
28. Rahner, *Foundations of Christian Faith*, 88.

ondary causes. And these secondary causes have their own integrity and proper autonomy.

A fundamental principle of the God-world relationship, grounded in the tradition of Aquinas, and one that Rahner often repeats, is expressed in the axiom: *Radical dependence on God and the genuine autonomy of the creature are directly and not inversely related.*[29] The closer creatures are to God, the more they can be truly themselves. Creaturely integrity and autonomy are not diminished by this relationship of ongoing creation, but are enabled to flourish.

This view of divine action challenges not only creationism, but also recent attempts at the more sophisticated theory of 'intelligent design'. If one holds, with Aquinas and Rahner, that in creating God acts consistently through secondary causes, then God is not an alternative to what science can discover. Gaps in science are to be filled by science, not by invoking God. God is not an alternative to natural selection, but works through natural selection, through randomness and lawfulness, through all the processes of nature, which is the role of science, not theology, to discover. This view of divine action can also respond to the scientific critics of religion who suppose that, if science can explain, for example, the origin of life on Earth, then this will do away with the idea of a Creator. What this theology supports is a healthy and creative relationship between science and theology. A theology that sees God as acting in and through secondary causes does not compete with science, but delights in the discoveries of science, seeing them as pointing to the way God creates. It sees God acting in and through the whole of creation, enabling the universe and all the entities that make it up to exist, to interact creatively, and to evolve.

5. *God creates by giving to creation itself the capacity for self-transcendence.*

The concept of divine self-bestowal describes the divine act from the side of God. Rahner proposes a second principle that describes this same act from the perspective of its impact on creatures: *creation has the capacity for self-transcendence.* Self-transcendence means that an entity is enabled to go beyond what it is to become something new. This idea is explored in Rahner's anthropology and evolution-

---

29. See, for example, Rahner, *Foundations of Christian Faith*, 78–9.

ary Christology, but it functions in many aspects of his work.[30] He considers the transitions to the *new* in the history of the universe, particularly when matter becomes life, and when life becomes self-conscious spirit. He argues that the traditional view, that God confers existence and the capacity to act on all things, needs to be developed to take account of an evolutionary universe. Rahner proposes an evolutionary dynamism that is truly intrinsic to creation, but which occurs through the creative power of the immanent God. The idea of *self*-transcendence indicates that at the empirical level of science, the emergence of the new is completely open to explanation at the scientific level.

In this view, the Creator not only enables things to exist and act, but also enables them to become something radically new, as when life first appears in a lifeless universe. The immanent presence and 'pressure' of the divine being enables creation to become more than it is in itself. Rahner proposes a large pattern of evolutionary self-transcendence, one that brings out the inner connection between evolution and Christology. The material universe transcends itself in the emergence of life, and life transcends itself in the human. In human beings, the universe becomes open to self-consciousness and freedom, and to a fully personal response to God's self-bestowal in grace. The Christ-event is the radical self-transcendence of the created universe into God. As a creature, Jesus in his life and death lives the radical response of love to God's self-bestowal. In his humanity he is, like us, part of the evolutionary history of life on Earth, and a product of a long history of the universe. Unlike us, he is wholly open to God. If the Christ-event is considered from below, it can be seen as the self-transcendence of the evolving universe into God. Jesus, in his life, death and resurrection, is the culmination of the process of evolutionary emergence, one that has not yet reached its final fulfilment. If considered from above, Jesus Christ can be seen as God's irreversible self-bestowal to creation. In this one person, we find the event of salvation: God's irreversible self-communication to creatures and full creaturely acceptance of this self-bestowal.[31]

---

30. Karl Rahner, *Hominisation: The Evolutionary Origin of Man as a Theological Problem* (London: Burns and Oates, 1965), 98–101; 'Christology within an Evolutionary View of the World', in *Theological Investigations* 5 (Baltimore: Helicon Press, 1969), 157–92; *Foundations of Christian Faith*, 178–203.
31. Rahner, *Foundations of Christian Faith*, 193.

This view of divine action seeks to situate Christology within an evolutionary view of the world. It puts a question to Christian theologies that ignore the scientific revolutions associated with the discovery of the expansion of the universe and the evolutionary history of life on Earth. It is a response, at least in part, to evolutionary thinkers who attack Christianity for what they see as opposition to evolution. What it offers is the beginning of an engagement between the evolutionary scientific worldview and the heart of Christian faith. Such an engagement will not only be essential for all those who inhabit this worldview and want to be committed to faith in Jesus Christ, but it will also be the necessary foundation for an ecological theology.

Conclusion

A scientifically informed ecological consciousness brings to the dialogue, first of all, a sense of global climate change as an urgent issue that theology needs to address. It brings five further hermeneutical principles: the worldview of big bang cosmology and evolutionary biology; the science of climate change and its provisional nature; the costs of evolution; the intrinsic value of nonhuman creation; and the interconnectedness of all things.

Karl Rahner's theology brings a theology of grace which enables us to see engagement with the issue of global climate change as the place of God. It, too, can be seen as offering five further hermeneutical principles that can contribute to an ecological theology: creation and redemption as distinct dimensions of God's one act of self-bestowal; redemption as the deification of human beings and the whole creation; God's relationship to creation characterised by radical transcendence and radical immanence; God's action as non-interventionist action through secondary causes; God's creation as enabling creaturely emergence through self-transcendence.

This theology not only offers profound theological meaning to ecological commitment, but also raises questions that can challenge common assumptions in the ecological movement. It questions, for example, the tendency to make Earth, or the universe, into God. And it resists the tendency to undermine the unique value of human beings before God—even as it proposes that other creatures have intrinsic value. It seeks to replace anthropocentrism not with geocentrism or biocentrism, but with theocentrism. As Michael Petty has said, Rahner's theology is 'profoundly ecological in that he brings to each theological problem and issue a fundamental vision which sees all reality, God the world, and human being, as interrelated'.[32]

At the same time, the ecological consciousness I have described challenges Rahner's theology at several points and invites further developments. In particular, it raises questions about biology. While Rahner certainly takes matter seriously, he seldom discusses animals or the biological world in general. And he does not take up the issue of nonhuman suffering. The costs of evolution, put before us by contemporary science, call for a renewed ecologically aware theology of divine action. In these and other ways, ecological consciousness helps set the agenda for theology.

In this paper, I have attempted not to do an ecological theology that responds to climate change, but simply to tease out some of the hermeneutic issues involved. It has been proposed that such a theology needs to be based, at least in part, on a creative dialogue between a scientifically informed ecological consciousness and a consciousness informed and shaped by the Christian tradition. Such a dialogue will need to be two-sided, so that interpretative ideas that spring from both sides can shape the theological outcome. Hearing from both sides of the dialogue allows critical questions from one side to raise challenges for the other, and creates the possibility that insights from both sides might contribute to a new and in part unforeseeable outcome, a truly ecological theology that responds to the great issues of our time.

---

32. Michael W Petty, *A Faith that Loves the Earth: The Ecological Theology of Karl Rahner* (Lanham: University Press of America, 1996), 39.

E. In Dialogue with Athanasius

Athanasius: The Word of God in Creation and Salvation

Athanasius (c 296–373) was born in the great city of Alexandria, where he served as a deacon, priest and bishop. As a deacon, he accompanied his bishop, Alexander, to the Council of Nicaea in 325, where the views of Arius, priest of Alexandria, were rejected and condemned. Athanasius became bishop of Alexandria at about the age of thirty, in 328. As a bishop, he was in continual conflict with a schismatic group called the Melitians, who took a rigorous approach to apostasy and represented a challenge to his authority. He became the leading defender of pro-Nicaean theology and a vigorous opponent of those who held anti-Nicaean views, whom he called collectively 'Arians'. Athanasius was bishop of Alexandria for forty-six years, but because of the changing politics of the empire, he spent seventeen of these years in five different periods of exile. He was a powerful advocate of Nicaea's teaching that the Word who becomes flesh in Jesus of Nazareth is fully and eternally divine.

The inter-relationship between creation and salvation is central to everything for Athanasius. The Word of creation is the Word of our redemption. He has an unambiguous and radical theology of creation out of nothing. The world of creatures exists from nothing at every moment. As Alvyn Pettersen says, for Athanasius, 'creation is both very fragile, but most wonderful'. Of itself it is completely unstable, but because it participates in the creative Word, it something sublime—'Creation is from the world's side a continuous receiving of God who gives all that it is and has'.[1] Athanasius is clear that the Word is not something intermediate between the whole world of creatures and the uncreated God. He insists that the Word of God, through

---

1. Alvyn Pettersen, *Athanasius* (London: Geoffrey Chapman, 1995), 25.

whom all creation exists, belongs fully to God. This fully divine Word takes our bodily reality as his own and, through his death and resurrection, transforms and deifies our creaturely, bodily reality.

Khaled Anatolios describes the relationship between creation and salvation as the 'architectonic center' of Athanasius's Christological vision: 'His conception of the relation between God and creation may thus be considered as the architectonic center of Athanasius's theological vision; his account of this relation provides the overarching framework in which his various doctrines acquire their distinctive resonance.'[2] The central focus of this relation between creation and God is Christological. In Athanasius's view, it is Christology that radically unites God and the world of creatures. As Anatolios puts it, 'His account of the relationship between God and creation is thus ultimately a Christology conceived in the most universal terms.'[3]

In Athanasius's thought there is a profound, inner connection between the doctrine of creation (understood as God's creative act) and the doctrine of salvation, because the Word of creation is the Word of our redemption and deification. There is also a radical link between salvation and all creation (understood as the universe of created entities) because the Word embraces bodily existence in a world of creatures and transforms this world from within. I will explore some of these connections as they are found in three of Athanasius's works. First, I will outline the structure of his thought, which he lays out in his early double work *Against the Greeks—On the Incarnation*. Then, I will briefly take up some insights on deification through the Word from his *Orations against the Arians*. Finally, I will focus on his view of the Holy Spirit in creation and deification as found in his *Letters to Serapion*.

Against the Greeks—On the Incarnation: The Structure of Athanasius's Thought

Athanasius's early double work provides a view of his system of thought. In *Against the Greeks*, he discusses how human beings fell from their ability to know God and turned from the worship of the true God into idolatry. Then, in *On the Incarnation*, he focuses on

---

2. Kahled Anatolios, *Athanasius* (London: Routledge, 2004), 39.
3. Anatolios, *Athanasius*, 40.

redemption in Christ, the conquering of death and our restoration to communion with God. For Athanasius, incarnational theology is not, as it is for some contemporary theologians, an alternative to a theology of Christ's death and resurrection. Athanasius makes it fully explicit that his incarnational theology is precisely a theology of the cross. Both books begin with an explanation of their purpose, where the reader is told that they are written as a defence of the cross of Christ. In the introduction to *Against the Greeks*, Athanasius says of those pagans who scorn the cross, that 'in slandering the cross they do not see that its power has filled the whole world, and that through it the effects of the knowledge of God have been revealed to all'.

Recent commentators have described Athanasius's double work as first and foremost 'an apology for the Cross'.[4] He says of those who reject the cross of Christ that 'if they really applied their minds to his divinity they would not have mocked at so great a thing, but would have recognised that he was the Saviour of the universe and the cross was not the ruin but the salvation of creation'.[5] I find it significant that here, at the beginning of his major work, Athanasius speaks of the one on the cross as 'the Saviour of the universe' and of the cross as 'the salvation of creation'. The emphasis created by combining 'Saviour of the universe' with 'the salvation of creation' suggests that Athanasius has more than humanity in view. There is no doubt that, throughout his work, Athanasius's primary focus is on humanity. But I am proposing that here, and in texts to be considered later, he sees humanity as part of a world of creatures, and sees salvation in Christ as embracing humanity with the rest of creation.

In *Against the Greeks*, Athanasius looks back from the cross to the origin of evil. It is in this way, Behr notes, that he expounds the 'Word of the Cross'.[6] What Athanasius finds is that human beings were created for communion with God, through contemplation of God's Word and Image. He finds that evil is not God's will. It did not exist from the beginning but comes about through human sin. Human beings were created to contemplate God in the Word revealed in creation. They turned instead to idolatry, making creatures into gods.

---

4. John Behr, *The Nicene Faith: Part 1 True God of True God* (Crestwood, NY: St Vladimir's Seminary Press, 2004), 171; Anatolios, *Athanasius*, 28.
5. Athanasius, *Greeks* 1, translated in Robert Thomson, *Athanasius:* Contra Gentes *and* De Incarnatione (Oxford: Clarendon Press, 1971), 3–5.
6. Behr, *The Nicene Faith: Part 1 True God of True God*, 173.

Athanasius goes to great lengths to describe the perversity of the history of idolatry. Opposed to this disastrous, idolatrous attitude to the natural world, Athanasius puts the Christian view of the one God who creates all things through the Word: 'Who then is he, if not the all-holy Father of Christ, beyond all created being, who as supreme steersman, through his own Wisdom and his own Word, our Lord and Saviour Christ, guides and orders the universe for our salvation, and acts as seems best to him.'[7] This Wisdom/Word is not a creature, but the 'living and acting God, the very Word of the good God of the universe, who is other than created things and all creation; he is rather the sole and individual Word of the good Father, who has ordered all this universe and illuminates it with his providence.'[8]

Athanasius thinks that what the unbeliever can see of creation should be proof that everything has come into existence through the Word and Wisdom of God. Every aspect of creation bears the imprint of the uncreated Word. Nothing would exist if it were not created by this divine Wisdom:

> He, the power of God and wisdom of God, turns the heaven, has suspended the earth, and by his own will has set it resting on nothing. Illuminated by him, the sun gives light to the world, and the moon receives its measure of light. Through him water is suspended in the clouds, rains water the earth, the sea is confined, and the earth is covered with verdure in all kinds of plants.[9]

More than anyone before him, Athanasius develops the doctrine of creation *ex nihilo*. The universe of creatures is not only originally created out of nothing, but also rests on nothing. It is held in being over an abyss of nothing by God's creative will in the Word:

> For the nature of created things, having come into being from nothing, is unstable, and is weak and mortal when considered by itself; but the God of all is good and excellent by nature. Therefore he is also kind. For a good being would be envious of no one, so he envies nobody existence

---

7. Athanasius, *Greeks* 40, in Thomson, *Athanasius*, 111.
8. Athanasius, *Greeks* 40, in Thomson, *Athanasius*, 111.
9. Athanasius, *Greeks* 40, in Thomson, *Athanasius*, 113.

> but rather wishes everyone to exist, in order to exercise his kindness. So seeing that all created nature according to its own definition is in a state of flux and dissolution, therefore to prevent this happening and the universe dissolving back into nothing, after making everything by his own eternal Word and bringing creation into existence, he did not abandon it to be carried away and suffer through its own nature, lest it run the risk of returning to nothing. But being good, he governs and establishes the whole world through his Word who is himself God, in order that creation, illuminated by the leadership, providence and ordering of the Word, may be able to remain firm, since it shares in the Word who is truly from the Father and is aided by him to exist, and lest it suffer what would happen, I mean a relapse into nonexistence, if it were not protected by the Word.[10]

The Word of the Cross is the very same Wisdom of God who not only enables the whole universe of creatures to exist but also brings them into a beautiful harmony. As a musician tunes a lyre and skillfully produces a single melody from many diverse notes, so 'the Wisdom of God, holding the universe like a lyre', draws together the wonderful variety of created things 'thus producing in beauty and harmony a single world and a single order within it'. Athanasius insists that the Wisdom of God acts in the whole creation, in a fully divine way, 'unmoved with the Father' but, by Wisdom's intrinsic being, moving everything as seems good to the Father.[11]

In *On the Incarnation*, Athanasius tells his readers that he needs to begin his discussion of the redemption by first speaking of the creation of the universe. In this way, he says, it will become apparent that it is fitting that the renewal of creation 'is effected by the Word who created it from the beginning'.[12] Again he insists on creation *ex nihilo*. Against various competing philosophies of creation, he argues that God does not depend on pre-existing matter, but rather creates the matter from which all created things come into being. Here and elsewhere, Athanasius defends his view that the Creator, who is 'the Father of Christ', creates all things through the eternal Word, by

---

10. Athanasius, *Greeks* 41, in Thomson, *Athanasius*, 113–115
11. Athanasius, *Greeks* 42, in Thomson, *Athanasius*, 117.
12. Athanasius, *Incarnation* 1, in Thomson, *Athanasius*, 137.

pointing to the 'all-inclusive' text: 'All things came into being through him, and without him not one thing came into being' (Jn 1:3).[13]

Athanasius then undertakes a full discussion of the reason for the incarnation. He offers two analyses. First, in sections 3–10, he discusses the incarnation as overcoming death and bringing resurrection life. Then, in sections 11–19, he describes it as renewing the image of God in us and so enabling us to know God. The first analysis takes the reader again to God's act of creation. Building on Genesis and the *Shepherd of Hermas*, Athanasius says that because God is good, and 'envies nothing its existence', God 'made everything out of nothing through his own Word, our Lord Jesus Christ'. He then narrows his focus to the creation of human beings:

> And among these creatures, of all those on earth he had special pity for the human race, and seeing that by the definition of its own existence it would be unable to exist for ever, he gave it an added grace, not simply creating humans like all irrational animals on the earth, but making them in his own image and giving them also a share in the power of his own Word, so that having as it were shadows of the Word and being rational, they might be able to remain in felicity and live the true life in paradise, which is really that of the saints.[14]

Like all other creatures, human beings would exist from nothing, held in existence only through the creative Word. And, like all other creatures, they would be destined for death. But God, in creating them, gave them a special grace, making them in the divine image, empowering them by the Word, and freeing them from death. Human beings were also given free will, and the capacity to reject grace, so God gave them a law that was meant to preserve them in grace. Keeping this law would mean their joy and immortality, but 'if they transgressed and turned away (from the law) and became wicked, they would know that they would suffer the natural corruption consequent on death, and would no longer live in paradise, but in future dying outside it would remain in death and corruption'.[15]

---

13. Athanasius, *Incarnation* 2, in Thompson, *Athanasius*, 139.
14. Athanasius, *Incarnation* 3, in Thompson, *Athanasius*, 141, slightly modified.
15. Athanasius, *Incarnation* 3, in Thompson, *Athanasius*, 141–3.

Humans were granted 'the grace of the Word' to live a divine life,[16] but turned away from God, rejected the law of God, and were reduced to their natural, mortal state, facing death and corruption. Sin everywhere increased—'they became insatiable in sinning'; 'the whole earth was filled with murders and violence'; 'cities warred with cities, and peoples rose up against peoples'.[17] In this context, Athanasius reflects upon the divine response to sin. On the one hand, God would not be truthful if, having said that sin results in death, this did not happen. On the other hand, it would not be worthy of the goodness of God if the human being, who had been created by God and partaken in the Word, were to be abandoned to corruption and come to nothing. Athanasius asks: 'what should God, who is good, have done?'

How was God to respond to a humanity become prisoner to natural corruption, and deprived of the grace of being in the divine image? The Word of God who had created the universe from nothing would be the one to bring about new creation: 'For since he is the Word of the Father and above everyone, consequently he alone was able both to recreate the universe and be worthy to suffer for all and to be an advocate on our behalf before the Father.'[18] Athanasius tells us that it is for this reason that the Word of God, who fills the universe, comes to our realm. The Creator of the universe took a body like ours from the Virgin, as an instrument for our salvation:

> And thus taking a body like ours, since all were liable to the corruption of death, and surrendering it to death on behalf of all, he offered it to the Father. And this he did in his loving kindness in order that as all die in him, the law concerning the corruption in humanity might be abolished—since its power was concluded in the Lord's body and it will never again have influence over humans who are like him—and in order that, as humans had turned to corruption, he might turn them back into incorruption and might give them life for death, in that he had made the body his own, and by the grace of resurrection had rid them of death as straw is destroyed by fire.[19]

---

16. Athanasius, *Incarnation* 5, in Thompson, *Athanasius,* 145.
17. Athanasius, *Incarnation* 5, in Thomson, *Athanasius,* 147.
18. Athanasius, *Incarnation* 7, in Thomson, *Athanasius,* 151.
19. Athanasius, *Incarnation* 8, in Thomson, *Athanasius,* 153.

Athanasius compares the coming of the Word into a bodily world to a great king who enters a city and dwells in one of its houses. Such a city is honoured and respected and remains safe from enemies and bandits. The Word come to us, takes a human body and gives his life as a sacrifice on behalf of bodies like his own. We human beings are no longer condemned to death but are destined for life, when we share in the resurrection of the Word made flesh. This, Athanasius tells us, 'is the primary cause of the incarnation of the Saviour'.[20]

He then offers his second explanation for the incarnation, based upon the knowledge of God. Originally, human beings, creatures made from nothing, would have had no real knowledge or understanding of the God who created them, or of the Word by whom they had been made. God, therefore, 'since he is good, bestowed on them his own image, our Lord Jesus Christ, and he made them according to his own image and likeness, in order that, understanding through such grace the image, I mean the Word of the Father, they might be able through him to gain some notion about the Father, and recognizing the Maker, might live a happy and truly blessed life'.[21] But, of course, human beings turned away from God, lost the concept of God, and made idols for themselves.

Athanasius points out that God had not hidden God's self, but had provided manifold ways of self-revelation: through the grace of being in the image, they were enabled to know the Word, and through the Word the Father; through creation: 'They could lift their eyes to the immensity of heaven, and discerning the harmony of creation know its ruler, the Word of the Father'; and through God's gift of the law and the prophets of Israel, they could learn of 'God the Creator of the universe, the Father of Christ'.[22] But, in spite all of this, human beings rejected the knowledge of God and chose the path of irrationality. Again, Athanasius asks the question: what was God to do? In the divine mercy, God would renew humanity made in the divine image in order that human beings might once again be able to know God. This would occur through the coming in the body of the very image of God, our Saviour Jesus Christ. The Word of God, the Image of the Father, takes a mortal body in order that death might be destroyed

---

20. Athanasius, *Incarnation* 10, in Thomson, *Athanasius*, 159.
21. Athanasius, *Incarnation* 11, in Thomson, *Athanasius*, 161.
22. Athanasius, *Incarnation* 12, in Thomson, *Athanasius*, 163.

and that human beings might be renewed in the image. The Word comes to our realms to restore, renew and find those who were lost, through the forgiveness of sins.

God is revealed in creation, yet human beings were blind and confused, so the Word is revealed in the body so that 'those who were unwilling to know him by his providence and government of the universe, yet by the works done through the body might know the Word of God who was in the body, and through him the Father'.[23] Human beings had been led astray by their senses to worship what they could see and touch. The Word comes in the senses, teaching the truth of God through the actions of the body, through his words and deeds and ultimately his cross and resurrection. In the body, and through the senses, in his life and in the signs he does in his ministry, we meet the one who is not merely a human being but the Word and Wisdom of the true God.

Athanasius points out that the eternal Word is not enclosed in the body, but continues to act creatively and providentially in the whole universe. And while the Word is in the whole universe, the Word is not contained by creation, but contains everything else: 'For he was not bound to the body, but rather he controlled it, so he was in it and in everything, and outside creation, and was only at rest in the Father. And the most amazing thing is this, that he both lived as a man, and as the Word gave life to everything, and as the Son was with the Father.'[24] Throughout his double work, Athanasius continually links the Word of creation with the Word of the incarnation. He concludes his second discussion of the reason for the incarnation by returning to his 'apology for the cross', pointing out that creation itself witnesses to the death of Jesus:

> Nor did he cause creation itself to be silent, but, what is most amazing, even at his death—or rather at the victory over death, I mean the cross—the whole of creation was confessing that he who was known and suffered in the body was not simply a man, but the Son of God and Saviour of all. For the sun turned back, and the earth shook, and the mountains were rent, and all were terrified; and these things showed that Christ who

---

23. Athanasius, *Incarnation* 14, in Thomson, *Athanasius*, 169.
24. Athanasius, *Incarnation* 17, in Thomson, *Athanasius*, 175.

was on the cross was God, and that the whole of creation was his handmaid and was witnessing in fear to the coming of his master. So in this way God the Word revealed himself to men through his works.[25]

As Behr notes: 'Creation not only witnesses to the divinity of Jesus Christ, as the one who governs and orders the creation, but, Athanasius points out, it witnesses to the divinity of the one who died on the cross.'[26] The whole creation witnesses to The Word comes to us. Athanasius goes on to say of Christ's death that 'this is the chief point of our faith' and 'absolutely everyone talks about it'.[27] Of course, the cross includes resurrection. It is the transformation of death that is its point. When Athanasius deals with the resurrection in *On the Incarnation*, his focus is not on the appearances of the risen Christ, but on the way the Body of Christ, the Church, witnesses to the resurrection:

> That death has been dissolved and that the cross was a victory over it that it is no longer powerful but truly dead, is demonstrated in no uncertain manner and is clearly credible by the fact that it is despised by all Christ's disciples and everyone treads it underfoot and no longer fears it, but with the sign of the cross and with Christian faith they trample on it as a dead thing . . . Likewise, if anyone is disbelieving and still – after such great things, after so many have become martyrs in Christ, after the scorn shown everyday to death by heroes in Christ . . . if anyone were to watch men and women and young children eagerly rushing to death for their devotion to Christ . . . Let no one doubt that death has been destroyed by Christ and its corruption broken and brought to an end . . . So what has been said above is no small proof that death has been destroyed and that the cross of Christ is the victory over it.[28]

The witness of those who belong to the body of Christ is the prime visible 'proof' of the transformation of death by the cross of Christ. The works of the risen Christ are revealed in his body, in the lives of

---

25. Athanasius, *Incarnation* 19, in Thomson, *Athanasius*, 181.
26. Behr, *The Nicene Faith: Part 1 True God of True God*, 200.
27. Athanasius, *Incarnation* 19, in Thomson, *Athanasius*, 181.
28. Athanasius, *Incarnation* 27–30, in Thomson, *Athanasius*, 199–207.

Christians. Those who live in Christ demonstrate Christ's victory over death. Behr notes that here and elsewhere, there is 'an identity of the body assumed by the Word with all human beings, an identity now manifest in those who put on Christ, so giving a far broader scope, than is often done, to what is meant by incarnation'.[29] The Word of creation, the one who called it into being in the first place, is the one who renews it by coming into creation in the body, and this bodily presence of the Word is continued today in his body the church.

Against the Arians: Salvation as Deification

Athanasius began his *Orations Against the Arians* in Rome during his second exile, in about 339. Lewis Ayres has described how he constructs 'Arianism', drawing his anti-Nicene enemies into an increasingly sophisticated account that presents them as perpetuating a theology that stems from Arius. Athanasius claims that Eusebius of Nicomedia is the partial author of 'Arianism' and he spends much of his time refuting Asterius, whom he treats as the 'standard-bearer' of this heresy.[30] Unlike his earlier double work, which never mentions Arius, the *Orations* are directly opposed to the non-Nicenes whom Athanasius portrays as 'Arians'. He is concerned to counter the biblical arguments of his opponents, particularly the claim that Proverbs 8:22 proves that the Wisdom/Word of God is a creature, by demonstrating that a proper, ecclesial, reading of the Scriptures shows that Christ is the eternal Wisdom/Word of God who is divine by nature. The focus becomes more Trinitarian, although Athanasius's view of the incarnation always provides the structure of his thought.

A further difference from his earlier works, one on which I will focus, is that in these writings Athanasius freely uses the language of deification to defend the divinity of the Word. The first time this word appears to describe the transformation of creatures in Christ is in the well-known exchange formula of *On the Incarnation* 54: 'For he became human that we might become divine.'[31] In his anti-Arian writings he uses deification far more widely. In the thirty instances

---

29. Behr, *The Nicene Faith: Part 1 True God of True God*, 206.
30. Lewis Ayres, *Nicaea and its Legacy: An Approach to Fourth-Century Trinitarian Theology* (Oxford: Oxford University Press, 2004), 107.
31. Athanasius, *Incarnation* 19, in Thomson, *Athanasius*, 269 (modified).

where Athanasius speaks of deification in Christ, he uses the verb *theopoieō*, and the noun he coins, *theopoiēsis*.[32] In the *Orations*, he offers a view of salvation as the divine condescension of the Word that effects the deification of humanity: 'So he was not a human being and later became God. But, being God, he later became a human being in order that we may be divinized'.[33]

Athanasius sees deification as a radical ontological change that occurs in creaturely reality when the Word is made flesh. Because of the incarnation there is a divine transformation already at work in humanity and in the world. Through the flesh assumed by the Logos, God communicates divine life to all flesh in principle. It is then transmitted in practice to human individuals in the life of the Spirit. In the once-for-all ontological transformation that occurs in the incarnation, the body of Jesus is the instrument (*organon*) for the salvation of all.

Athanasius strongly opposes the Arian view that the Word of God is deified, and insists that the Word is the source of deification and is not subject to deification. He points out that even in the past, long before the birth of the Saviour, the Word of God was the source of deification: it is only through the eternal Word that Moses and others were long ago adopted and deified as children of God.[34] Athanasius does, however, see a very important deification at work in the incarnation; a deification, not of the eternal Word, but of the bodily humanity of Jesus. This deification of the created humanity of Christ is fundamental to our salvation: 'For the Word was not lessened by his taking a body, so that he would seek to receive grace, but rather he divinized what he put on, and, what's more, he gave this to the human race'.[35]

Athanasius has a range of words to describe the one who takes a body on our behalf, speaking not only of the eternal *Word*, but also often of the *Wisdom* of God, the *Image* of God, and the *Radiance* of

---

32. Norman Russell, *The Doctrine of Deification in the Greek Patristic Tradition* (Oxford: Oxford University Press, 2004), 168. In his early work, Athanasius also uses the word deification about twenty times in a negative sense to describe the pagan deification of creatures.
33. Athanasius, *Orations* 1:39. I am using the translation in Anatolios, *Athanasius*, 96.
34. Athanasius, *Orations* 1.39, in Anatolios, *Athanasius*, 96.
35. Athanasius, *Orations* 1:42, in Anatolios, *Athanasius*, 99.

the Divine Light: He is the one, true 'Word, Radiance and Wisdom of the Father, of which all things that come to be participate and are sanctified, in the Spirit'.[36] Several times he picks up Irenaeus's metaphor for the Word as the *Hand* of God: 'Just as the light enlightens all things by its radiance, and apart from the radiance nothing would be enlightened, so also the Father worked all things in the Word, as by a hand, and does nothing without him'.[37]

The Word of God takes on fallen flesh and as a result we share in his deified flesh. For Athanasius, there is a solidarity in the flesh: both the body of Christ and our fleshly humanity are deified:

> He took to himself the body that was human and had a beginning so that he who is its creator may renew it and thus divinize it in himself and lead all of us into the kingdom of heaven, in accordance with his own likeness ... But humanity would not have been deified if joined to a creature, or unless the Son was true God. And humanity would not come into the presence of the Father unless the one who put on the body was his true Word by nature. Just as we would not have been freed from sin and the curse unless the flesh which the Word put was human by nature–for there would be no communion for us with what is other than human–so also humanity would not have been deified unless the Word who became flesh was by nature from the Father and true and proper (*idios*) to him. Therefore the conjoining that came about was such as to join what is human by nature to what is of the nature of divinity, so that humanity's salvation and deification might be secured.[38]

It is central to Athanasius's thought that the Word is proper (*idios*) to the being of the Father, and that this eternal divine word 'appropriated' created human nature, so that henceforth humanity was not external to the Word's being, but has become the Word's own.[39] For

---

36. Athanasius, *Orations* 1:46, in Anatolios, *Athanasius,* 103.
37. Athanasius, *Orations* 2:31, in Anatolios, *Athanasius,* 125–6. See also *Orations* 2:71, in Anatolios, *Athanasius,* 164–5, where Athanasius points to biblical texts on the hand of God, and *On the Council of Nicaea* (*De Decretis*) 7, in Anatolios, *Athanasius,* 184.
38. Athanasius, *Orations* 2:70, in Anatolios, 163.
39. On this see Anatolios, *Athanasius,* 67.

Athanasius, there is a wonderful divine condescension, a gratuitous descending love of God, at work in both creation and redemption. In the divine act of creation, the Word condescended (*sunkatabas*) that creatures, who otherwise would not have been able to withstand the Word's nature as unmitigated splendour of the Father, might be 'supported, strengthened and carried into being'.[40] Then, by the Word's further condescension (*sunkatabantos*) in the incarnation, creation is adopted and redeemed, so that Athanasius sees the Scripture speaking of the Word as the firstborn of creation in both senses.

The deification of our humanity is about us becoming fully human in a way that is faithful to God's intention. As Thomas Weinandy puts it, 'deification is not then the changing of our human nature into something other than it is, that is, into another kind of being'. Rather, for Athanasius, it is 'the making of humankind into what it was meant to be from the very beginning'.[41] We are made into the image of the Word, taken into the divine life of the Trinity, and enabled to be the human beings that God wants us to be. This whole process occurs only through the action of the Holy Spirit in us, and in Christian life it is lived out in word and sacrament.

In the *Orations against the Arians*, Athanasius constantly connects the Word of creation with the Word of redemption and deification, insisting that the Word is not a creature, but the Word through whom all things are created. Very many times he points to the texts that tells us that it is through the Word that all things come to be (Jn 1:30) and that this Word is before all things and is the one in whom all things hold together (Col 1:17). In his second *Oration*, he unambiguously includes the whole creation in the liberation that comes through Christ's death and resurrection:

> Then again, if he is a creature and all creation 'came to be through him' (Jn 1:3) and 'had its consistence in him' (Col 1:17), how can he both create the creation and be one of the things which have their consistence in him? Such a conception of theirs is manifestly absurd. The truth that refutes them is that he is called 'firstborn among many brothers' (Rom 8:29) because of the kinship of the flesh, and 'firstborn

---

40. Athanasius, *Orations* 2:64, in Anatolios, *Athanasius*, 158.
41. Thomas Weinandy, *Athanasius: A Theological Introduction* (Aldershot, Hampshire: Ashgate, 2007), 99.

> from the dead' (Col 1:18) because the resurrection of the dead comes from him and after him, and 'firstborn of all creation' (Col 1:15) because of the Father's love for humanity, on account of which he not only gave consistence to all things in his Word but brought it about that the creation itself, of which the apostle says that it 'awaits the revelation of the children of God', will at a certain point be delivered 'from the bondage of corruption into the glorious freedom of the children of God' (Rom 8, 19, 21). The Lord will be the firstborn of this creation which is delivered and of all those who are made children, so that by his being called 'first', that which is after him may abide, united to the Word as to a foundational origin and beginning.[42]

Here, Athanasius makes explicit his conviction not only that all things are created in the Word, and not only that the Word enables all things to exist at every point, but also, with Paul in Romans 8, that the whole of creation is to be liberated with human beings in Christ. The creation itself is destined to be transformed in Christ. The risen Christ is firstborn, the foundational origin and beginning of the deliverance of *both* the broader creation discussed by Paul and human beings who are made children of God.[43]

In Athanasius's view, when 'the God of the universe' created us through the Word and gave us freedom, the Creator foresaw our disobedience, and 'being the lover of humanity', prepared beforehand the economy of our salvation in the Word in whom we were created.[44] The relationship between the Wisdom/Word revealed in creation and the Wisdom/Word of the incarnation and redemption is brought out beautifully in the last few pages of the second *Oration*. First, Athanasius points to the Wisdom revealed in all the creatures around us:

> Therefore, the only-begotten and true Wisdom of God is the creator and maker of all things. For it says: 'In wisdom

---

42. Athanasius, *Orations* 2:63, in Anatolios, *Athanasius,* 157.
43. Athanasius returns to a discussion of the groaning of creation in *Orations* 2:72, this time arguing that the Son is other than the whole world of creatures that await their freedom, since he is the one who is to bring freedom and salvation to all creatures.
44. Athanasius, *Orations* 2:75, in Anatolios, *Athanasius,* 168.

you have made all things' and 'the earth is filled with your creation' (Ps 104:24). But in order that creatures may not only be but also thrive in well-being, it pleased God to have his own Wisdom condescend to creatures. Therefore he placed in each and every creature and in the totality of creation a certain imprint (*typon*) and reflection of the Image of Wisdom, so that the things that come into being may prove to be works that are wise and worthy of God.[45]

Then Athanasius turns to the presence of the Wisdom of God in the human heart. He sees holy Wisdom as coming to human beings in a special interior way. The wisdom that comes into being in us is the gift of divine Wisdom by which we come to knowledge of God: 'Thus we become recipients of the Creator-Wisdom, and through her we are able to know her Father'.[46] But the Wisdom revealed in creation and in our own hearts is not enough. God wanted to do even more for us:

> For God willed to make himself known no longer as in previous times through the image and shadow of wisdom, which is in creatures, but has made the true Wisdom herself take flesh and become a mortal human being and endure the death of the cross, so that henceforth all those who put their faith in him may be saved. But it is the same Wisdom of God, who previously manifested herself, and her Father through herself, by means of her image in creatures—and thus is said to be 'created'—but which later on, being Word, became flesh (Jn 1:14) as John said.[47]

For Athanasius, then, there is a four-fold presence of divine Wisdom in our world:[48] Wisdom is revealed in the created world since

---

45. Athanasius, *Orations* 2:78, in Anatolios, *Athanasius*, 171.
46. Athanasius, *Orations* 2:78, in Anatolios, *Athanasius*, 171.
47. Athanasius, *Orations* 2:81, in Anatolios, *Athanasius*, 174. As Anatolios notes: 'In Athanasius's Greek, the personal pronoun switches from feminine when the subject is Wisdom (*Sophia*) to masculine when the subject is the Word (*Logos*) or the human being (*anthropos*) which the Word became.' Anatolios, *Athanasius*, 267, n 173.
48. On Athanasius's theology of divine self-revelation see Pettersen, *Athanasius*, 37–61.

all creatures in some way bear the imprint of the Creator; Wisdom is revealed explicitly in the Scriptures; Wisdom is found in the depths of the human soul, in the human being made in the divine image; and finally, because divine generosity knows no boundaries, Wisdom herself takes flesh in our midst to secure the salvation and deification of human beings and with them the rest of creation.

The fruitfulness of creation and redemption is grounded in the fruitfulness of the divine life. Athanasius argues, against the Arians, that the dynamic fruitfulness of God's creation can only have sprung by God's free choice from a God who was already, eternally, generative: 'But if, according to them, the divine essence itself is not fruitful but barren, like a light that does not shine and a fountain that is dry, how are they not ashamed to say that God has creative energy'.[49] For Athanasius, the foundation of his theology of both creation and redemption is found in the fruitfulness of the divine life where the Father eternally generates the Son.[50] And, as Athanasius makes more explicit in the text to be considered next, the Holy Spirit shares fully in this dynamic divine life. It is a truly Trinitarian fruitfulness of the one God that gives rise to creation and salvation through the Word and in the Spirit.

Letters to Serapion on the Holy Spirit: Creation and Salvation in the Spirit

About 357, during his third exile, living with a monastic community in the Egyptian desert, Athanasius wrote the *Letters to Serapion on the Holy Spirit*. He wrote in response to a request from a friend and supporter, Bishop Serapion of Thmuis. Serapion was concerned about a group of Christians who accepted the divinity of the Son, but rejected the divinity of the Holy Spirit, holding that the Spirit was unlike the Father and the Son in being. Athanasius begins by responding to the particular biblical texts used by this group to support their position. He argues that they use an inappropriate figurative form of interpretation, or 'trope', and he calls these opponents 'Tropici'.

These Tropici had argued that, if the Spirit were not a creature, this would lead to the absurdity of the Spirit being considered a brother

---

49. Athanasius, *Against the Gentiles*, 10, Thomson, 159.
50. See Weinandy, *Athanasius: A Theological Introduction*, 79–80.

or a son of the Son, and so compromise the notion of the Son as only-begotten. Athanasius responds by pointing to the apophatic mystery of God and to the radical difference between the life of the triune God and human family relationships. He goes on to provide a biblical reading that demonstrates how the Spirit's work in creation and salvation is identified with the divine agency of the Father and the Son. As the Scriptures witness to the full divinity of the Word, so they witness to the full divinity of the Holy Spirit. This work constitutes the first extended treatment of the divinity of the Holy Spirit, one which would be an important influence on Basil of Caesarea's *On the Holy Spirit* and bear fruit in the First Council of Constantinople in 381.

The Holy Spirit, Athanasius claims, is the one in whom the whole creation is sanctified and renewed, pointing to Psalm 104:30: 'When you send forth your spirit, they are created; and you renew the face of the ground'. He mines the Scriptures to show that the Holy Spirit is the life-giver (Rom 8:11; Jn 4:14; 7:39), the anointing (1 Jn 2:27) and the seal (Eph 1:13). When we become sealed by the Holy Spirit, Athanasius tells us, 'we properly become sharers in the divine nature, as Peter says (2 Pet 1:4), and so the whole creation participates of the Word, in the Spirit'.[51] If we become participants in the divine nature through the Word and in the Spirit, how can the Spirit be anything but divine? If the Spirit divinises, the Spirit must possess the divine nature:

> And for a still clearer negation of this heresy, the psalmist sings in the one-hundred-and-third psalm, as we have previously quoted: 'You will take away their spirit and they will perish and return to their dust. You will send forth your spirit and they will be created, and you will renew the face of the earth' (Ps 104:29–30). And Paul writes to Titus: 'Through the bath of regeneration and the renewal of the Holy Spirit, which he poured out richly upon us through Jesus Christ' (Titus 3:5–6). But if the Father creates and renews all things through the Son and in the Holy Spirit, what likeness of kinship can there be between creatures and the Creator? Or how can it at all be the case that the one in whom everything is created is a creature?[52]

---

51. Athanasius, *Serapion* 1:23, in Anatolios, *Athanasius,* 223.
52. Athanasius, *Serapion* 1:24, in Anatolios, *Athanasius,* 223–4.

When Athanasius says that 'The Father creates and renews all things through the Son and in the Holy Spirit', he encapsulates a great deal of his theology: the full divinity of both the Son and the Spirit; the unity of Father, Son and Spirit in the divine actions of creation and redemption; and the distinction of Father, Son and Spirit in these divine actions. He also reveals the way he thinks about the inter-relationship between creation and new creation. As all things are created through the Word and in the Spirit, so all are redeemed and transformed through the Word and in the Spirit. The Spirit does not belong to creation but to God: 'If the Son belongs (*idios*) to the being of the Father because he is from the Father, then necessarily the Spirit also, who is said to be from God, belongs (*idion*) to the being of the Son'.[53] Athanasius presents his argument for the divinity of the Spirit again in the following text:

> Therefore it is in the Spirit that the Word glorifies creation and presents it to the Father by divinising it and granting it adoption. But the one who binds creation to the Word could not be among the creatures and the one who bestows sonship upon creation could not be foreign to the Son. Otherwise it would be necessary to look for another spirit to unite this one to the Word. But that is senseless. Therefore the Spirit it not among the things that have come into being but belongs (*idion*) to the divinity of the Father, and is the one in whom the Word divinizes the things that have come into being. But the one in whom creation is divinized cannot be extrinsic to the divinity of the Father.[54]

Because the Holy Spirit is the one who 'binds creation to the Word', the one who unites us as adopted daughters and sons with the divine Son, and the one in whom the Word deifies and glorifies creation and presents it to the Father, the Spirit can only be divine. Clearly, again, creation and new creation are held together in one vision of God's Trinitarian action through the Word and in the Spirit. In this text, Athanasius speaks freely of the deification of creation. It seems that here, too, Athanasius is thinking not just of the deification of human

---

53. Athanasius, *Serapion* 1:25, in Anatolios, *Athanasius,* 224.
54. Athanasius, *Serapion* 1:25, in Anatolios, *Athanasius,* 225.

beings, but of the deification with them, in some way, of the whole creaturely world.[55]

Athanasius points to the texts from *The Wisdom of Solomon* that speak of the universal role of the Spirit in the whole of the universe: 'the Spirit of the Lord fills the whole world' (Wis 1:7); and 'Your incorruptible Spirit is in all things' (Wis 12:1). God's work of ongoing creation is the work of the Word and the Spirit. He applies the Nicaean *homoousios* to the Spirit: the Holy Spirit, he says, 'belongs (*idion*) to the one Word, and accordingly belongs (*idion*) to the one God and is of the same being (*homoousion*)'.[56] The Trinity is indivisible in its nature and its activity (*energeia*) is one: 'For the Father does all things though the Word and in the Holy Spirit'.[57] As for our participation in the life of new creation, our communion in the gifts given through the Word occurs only in the Spirit—'it is by our participation in the Spirit that we have the love of the Father and the grace of the Son and communion of the Spirit itself'.[58] For Athanasius, Word and Spirit are inseparable.[59]

Rowan Williams sums up Athanasius's view: 'Only God can deify, only the unequivocally divine savior can decisively transform our lives, only the creator can re-create.'[60] He says that, for Athanasius, what is truly distinctive of Christian identity is the idea of new creation as an event that makes a radical, decisive and unforeseen difference to our world, as something brought out of nothing, life from death. And if God not only creates, but also deifies and transfigures

---

55. I think this reading is supported by my earlier reference (in note 39) to the *Orations* where Athanasius points to the deliverance of the whole creation in Romans 8:21.
56. Athanasius, *Serapion* 1:27, in Anatolios, *Athanasius*, 227. While RPC Hanson, *The Search for the Christian Doctrine of God: The Arian Controversy 318-381* (Edinburgh: T&T Clark, 1988), 752, n 70, points to another reference in *Letters* 2:6, and CRB Shapland, C.R.B. (1951), *The Letters of Saint Athanasius Concerning the Holy Spirit* (London: Epworth Press, 1951), 133, n 7, finds a reference in Letters 3:1, Anatolios sees this as the only instance of Athanasius's direct application of the *homoousios* to the Holy Spirit. In both the other cases, it is applied to the Son's relation to the Father. Anatolios, *Athanasius*, 277, n 39.
57. Athanasius, *Serapion* 1:28, in Anatolios, *Athanasius*, 227.
58. Athanasius, *Serapion* 1:30, in Anatolios, *Athanasius*, 230.
59. Athanasius, *Serapion* 1:31, in Anatolios, *Athanasius*, 230, and 1:33, in Anatolios, *Athanasius*, 233.
60. Rowan Williams, *Arius: Heresy and Tradition* (London: Darton, Longman and Todd, 1987), 240.

the human condition and in some way the whole world of creatures, in and through the Word and the Spirit of God, then Word and Spirit belong to the very being of God.

Conclusion

The relationship between the created world and salvation structures Athanasius's Christological vision. He sees the universe of creatures as created out of nothing, and as resting on nothing in itself. But because of God's generosity, creatures are continually held in being and ordered by the uncreated Word, through which they were made. Every creature bears the imprint of this divine Word. Human beings were given the unique grace of being made in the divine image and therefore possessing eternal life. But they turned away from God to idolatry and lost eternal life. God's generosity was such that God's Word became flesh, taking up a body destined for death, and through the death and resurrection of this Word made flesh, human beings and with them the whole creation were transformed. Salvation takes the form of forgiveness, resurrection life, adoption and deification in the Word. The Word of creation is the Word of salvation. It is the Spirit of God who binds creatures to the Word in both creation and salvation. So for Athanasius, God creates and deifies all things through the Word and in the Holy Spirit. This deification involves the divine adoption of human creatures, and also the transformation and glorification, with them, of the rest of God's creatures.

Incarnation and the Natural World: Explorations in the Tradition of Athanasius

For some Christian communities, the celebration of Easter begins on Holy Saturday night with the lighting of the paschal candle from the Easter fire. Then, in the light cast by the candle enthroned high on its stand, they listen to the reading of the Scriptures, beginning with the story of the creation of the world from the opening chapter of Genesis. They look back on the creation of the universe of creatures and on the history of salvation and see it all illuminated by the light of the crucified and risen Christ. This seems a particularly good image for the particular way in which Christian theology sees the natural world from the perspective of the Word made flesh.

With many, but not all, other theologians today, I follow the theological tradition, associated with Maximus the Confessor (580–662) in the East, and with Duns Scotus (1266–1308) in the West, which understands the incarnation as eternally God's intention in the creation of a world of creatures. The incarnation is not, then, only a remedy for sin, a corrective for a world gone wrong. Of course, in our sinful world, the life, death and resurrection of Jesus is an unthinkable act of divine mercy and forgiveness. But even if there were no sin, creation and incarnation are linked in God's eternal purpose. God creates a world of creatures in order to bestow God's self upon them in the Word made flesh and the Spirit poured out.[1] Creation and incarnation are radically interconnected as distinct dimensions of God's one act of divine self-bestowal.

---

1. Karl Rahner, 'Christology in the Setting of Modern Man's Understanding of Himself and of the World', in *Theological Investigations* 1 (London: Darton, Longman & Todd, 1974), 219–20.

In the contemporary discussion between science and theology and in the attempt to develop a theology that can engage with ecological issues, however, there is a tendency to appeal simply to the theology of creation. Christology, and the theology of salvation, play a minor role, or they are bracketed out of the discussion altogether. But a theology that is truly Christian cannot bracket out the incarnation. A Christian theology of creation cannot exist for long alone, disconnected to Christology. Creation and incarnation are intimately interconnected and mutually interdependent in the Christian tradition. This raises a fundamental question: What is the meaning of the Word made flesh for the rest of the natural world?

I will begin to explore this question, which I see as at the heart of a Christian ecological theology, with insights from Athanasius, focusing first on his theology of creation, particularly his view that the whole natural world exists only because it participates of the Word, in the Spirit. In the second section, I turn to his theology of salvation, and the way he sees the natural world participating in deification through the incarnation of this same Word. Then I will explore two implications of Athanasius's thought for today: the first, on God's eternal commitment to the natural world, in dialogue with Karl Rahner and Thomas Torrance; the second, on God's engagement with the particular, in dialogue with Sandra Schneiders and Niels Gregersen.

Athanasius: The Natural World Exists through Partaking of the Word in the Spirit

Athanasius begins his theology of incarnation not from the pre-existing Word of God, but from the cross of Jesus Christ. Recent commentators have pointed out how both volumes of his foundational work, *Against the Gentiles* and *on the Incarnation*, begin as an 'apology for the cross' against its mockers.[2] In 'slandering the cross', Athanasius writes, the mockers do not see that 'its power has filled the whole world'. They fail to understand that the one on the cross is 'the Saviour of the universe and that the cross was not the ruin but the salvation of

---

2. Khaled Anatolios, *Athanasius: The Coherence of his Thought* (London: Routledge, 1998), 28; John Behr, 'The Nicene Faith: Part One: True God of True God', in *The Formation of Christian Theology*, volume 2 (Crestwood NY: St Vladimir's Seminary Press, 2004), 171.

creation'.³ For Athanasius, it is the Jesus of flesh and blood, the one on the cross, who is the Word of God and the Saviour of the creation. It is from the perspective of Jesus who lived among us, who was crucified and rose from the dead, that Athanasius looks back to God's creation of the universe of creatures. As John Behr says, 'It is the Word of the Cross, or the Word on the Cross, that Athanasius expounds by describing how all things have come into being by and for him; it is Christ himself that Athanasius is reflecting on, not the creation accounts in and of themselves'.⁴

Athanasius describes the divine act of creation twice, focusing on the creation of the whole world in *Against the Gentiles* and on that of humanity in *On the Incarnation* and, in the process, makes a major contribution to the development of the theology of *creatio ex nihilo*. He sees the whole universe of creatures as coming into being from absolutely nothing simply by the will of God. Creation has no reason in itself for its existence. It rests on nothing but the Wisdom of God: 'He, the power of God and wisdom of God, turns the heaven, has suspended the earth, and by his own will has set it resting on nothing'.⁵ Athanasius uses 'Word' and 'Wisdom' interchangeably, along with 'Son', and sometimes 'Radiance' and 'Hand', to speak of the one in whom all things are created.

It is not only that the universe of creatures was originally created out of nothing, but also that in itself creation remains inherently unstable. It is continually held in being over an abyss of nothing by God's creative Wisdom. For Athanasius, creatures exist only because they *partake of* the creative Wisdom/Word of God:

> After making everything by his own eternal Word and bringing creation into existence, he did not abandon it to be carried away and suffer through its own nature, lest it run the risk of returning to nothing. But being good, he governs and establishes the whole world through his Word who is himself God, in order that creation, illuminated by the leadership, providence and ordering of the Word, may be able to remain

---

3. Athanasius of Alexandria. *Against the Gentiles* 1, with translation in Robert Thomson, *Athanasius:* Contra Gentes *and* De Incarnatione (Oxford: Clarendon Press, 1971), 1-3.
4. Behr, *The Nicene Faith*, 181-2.
5. Athanasius, *Against the Gentiles,* Thompson, 113.

firm, since it *partakes of* (*metalambanousa*) the Word who is truly from the Father and is aided by him to exist, and lest it suffer what would happen, I mean a relapse into nonexistence, if it were not protected by the Word.[6]

Creation exists and remains firm because it partakes of the Word of the Father. It is the Word who enables the whole universe of creatures to exist, who leads the creation, provides for it and governs it. The Word of the Father is 'present in all things and extends his power everywhere' and 'gives life and protection to everything, everywhere, to each individually and to all together'.[7]

The creative Wisdom of God keeps all the diverse element of creation in balance. There is nothing created that does not come into being and subsist in and through Wisdom. According to Athanasius, it is through this divine Wisdom that the oceans are kept safely in their place and the land is covered with all the different kinds of green vegetation. The Wisdom of God brings the diversity of creatures into balance and beautiful harmony. As a musician tunes a lyre and skillfully produces a single melody from many diverse notes, so 'the Wisdom of God, holding the universe like a lyre', draws together the wonderful variety of created things 'thus producing in beauty and harmony a single world and a single order within it'.[8] Creatures who participate in divine Wisdom participate in the Father and thus have their existence in a community of creation.

When Athanasius describes the creation of human beings in *On the Incarnation*, he sees them as given a unique divine grace, of being made in the divine image and participating in the Word in such a way as to be made sharers in eternal life. But by sinfully rejecting God's law, and the special grace that they were given, they have lost the gift of eternal life. God's extraordinarily generous response to this predicament is to send the Word in the flesh, in a body subject to corruption and death, to bring about forgiveness and to overcome death in the power of the resurrection. The overcoming of death, Athanasius tells us, 'is the primary cause of the incarnation of the Saviour'.[9] The

---

6. Athanasius, *Against the Gentiles*, 41, Thompson, 113–15.
7. Athanasius, *Against the Gentiles*, 41, Thompson, 114–15.
8. Athanasius, *Against the Gentiles*, 42, Thompson, 117.
9. Athanasius, *On the Incarnation*, with translation in Robert Thomson, *Athanasius: Contra Gentes and* De Incarnatione (Oxford: Clarendon Press, 1971), 159.

second major reason for the incarnation is that human beings who had failed to recognise the Word of God spoken in the whole creation might now come to know 'the Word of God who was in the body, and through him the Father'.[10]

Participation in the Word of God is central to all of this: first, all the creatures of the universe are held firm and enabled to exist only by partaking of the Word; second, human beings were given a special grace at their creation of participating in the Word in a unique way, and so sharing eternal life; third, faced with human sin and the rejection of this special grace, God does even more—sending the Word in the flesh that sin might be forgiven and human beings, and with them all creation, might be renewed and transformed by participating in the very Word made flesh.

Athanasius's early two-volume work is very much focused on the Word/Wisdom of God. When, much later, around 357, he shifts his attention to a defense of the divinity of the Holy Spirit, in his *Letters to Serapion*, we find him articulating his full Trinitarian theology of participation. He writes that it is the Holy Spirit who activates (*energoun*) everything that is worked by the Father through the Son: 'For there is nothing that is not brought into being and actuated through the Word, in the Spirit'.[11] The Holy Spirit is the one who binds creation to the Word.[12] (*Serap.* 1:25, Anatolios, 225). All the various creatures exist only because they partake of the Word in the Holy Spirit. At the heart of all this is Athanasius's conviction that the Holy Spirit, far from being a creature as his opponents suppose, is the one in whom all creatures are created and transformed: 'The Father creates and renews all things through the Son and in the Holy Spirit'.[13]

Athanasius: The Natural World Participates in Deification

Partaking of the Word, in the Spirit, so central to Athanasius's theology of creation, is also central to his theology of deification (or 'divin-

---

10. Athanasius, *On the Incarnation*, 16, Thompson, 169.
11. Athanasius of Alexandria, *Letters to Serapion on the Holy Spirit*, translated in CRB Shapland, *The Letters of Saint Athanasius Concerning the Holy Spirit* (London: Epworth Press, 1951), Letter 1:15–33 translated in Khaled Anatolios, *Athanasius* (London: Routledge, 2004), 212–33, at 230.
12. Athanasius, *Letters to Serapion on the Holy Spirit*, 1:25; Anatolios, *Athanasius*, 225.
13. Athanasius, *Letters to Serapion on the Holy Spirit*, 1:24; Anatolios, *Athanasius*, 224.

isation'). His first usage of the language of deification is in his *On the Incarnation,* in the well-known exchange formula: 'For he became human that we might become divine'.[14] Later, in his anti-Arian writings he uses frequently both the verb *theopoieō*, and the noun he coins, *theopoiēsis*, to defend the eternal divinity, and divine condescension, of the Word, who is made flesh to bring about our deification: 'So he was not a human being and later became God. But, being God, he later became a human being in order that we may be divinised'.[15]

Athanasius not only uses deification language more freely than his predecessors, but also clarifies its meaning. Norman Russell points out that he constantly pairs the word deification with a series of other key words that explain its meaning, including adoption, renewal, salvation, sanctification, grace, transcendence, illumination and vivification.[16] Athanasius also deepens the theological meaning of deification by insisting, against Origen, and later Arian views, that the Word is *not* deified but is always the source of deification. Again, against Origen who speaks of the deification of the *nous*, for Athanasius it is the body, the flesh, or humanity that is deified.

While rejecting the idea that the Word of God is deified, Athanasius insists that the bodily humanity of Jesus *is* deified by its union with the Word. It is precisely this deification of Christ's creaturely humanity by the Word that enables the deification of our humanity: 'For the Word was not lessened by his taking a body, so that he would seek to receive grace, but rather he divinized what he put on, and, what's more, he gave this to the human race'.[17]

For Athanasius, deification is a radical ontological transformation in creaturely reality. He does not ignore what is sometimes called the ethical aspect of deification, growth in holiness, but his emphasis is much more on the ontological change that comes through the incarnation. Because of the incarnation there is a divine transformation already at work in humanity and in the world. Through the flesh assumed by the Logos, God communicates divine life to all flesh in principle. This divine life is then transmitted in practice to individu-

---

14. Athanasius, *On the Incarnation,* 54.
15. Athanasius of Alexandria, *Orations against the Arians,* 1:39, selections translated in Khaled Anatolios, *Athanasius* (London: Routledge, 2004), 87–175, at 96.
16. Norman Russell, *The Doctrine of Deification in the Greek Patristic Tradition* (Oxford: Oxford University Press, 2004), 177–8.
17. Athanasius, *Orations against the Arians,* 1:42; Anatolios, *Athanasius,* 99.

als through baptism and in the life of the Spirit. In this deifying transformation, the bodily humanity of Jesus is seen as the instrument (*organon*) for the salvation of all.

Athanasius constantly connects the creative Word with the deifying Word. He makes no sharp division between God's creative act and God's deifying act. He sees the whole natural world as sharing, in its own way, with human beings in salvation in Christ. In his second *Oration against the Arians* he builds on Romans 8:19–23 to include, completely unambiguously, the whole creation in the liberation that comes about through Christ's resurrection:

> The truth that refutes them is that he is called 'firstborn among many brothers' (Rom 8:29) because of the kinship of the flesh, and 'firstborn from the dead' (Col 1:18) because the resurrection of the dead comes from him and after him, and 'firstborn of all creation' (Col 1:15) because of the Father's love for humanity, on account of which he not only gave consistence to all things in his Word but brought it about that the creation itself, of which the apostle says that it 'awaits the revelation of the children of God', will at a certain point be delivered 'from the bondage of corruption into the glorious freedom of the children of God' (Rom 8, 19, 21).[18]

In characteristic fashion, Athanasius then goes on to link together creation's deliverance and the divine adoption of human beings, stating that the risen Christ will be the first-born of the wider creation delivered from the bondage of corruption and the first-born of human beings made children of God. Christ is called 'first', he says, to indicate that which comes after him (humanity and the rest of creation) 'may abide, united to the Word as to a foundational origin and beginning'.[19]

When discussing the deifying adoption of human beings, Athanasius often speaks of non-human creatures as also participating of the Word in the Spirit. Examples of this are found in his *Letters to Serapion*. Speaking of human beings as being saved and sealed with the Holy Spirit, he writes: 'When we are sealed in this way, we properly become sharers in the divine nature, as Peter says (2 Pet 1:4), and so

---

18. Athanasius, *Orations against the Arians*, 2:63; Anatolios, *Athanasius*, 157.
19. Athanasius, *Orations against the Arians*, 2:63; Anatolios, *Athanasius*, 157.

the whole creation *participates of* (*metechei*) the Word, in the Spirit'.[20] In a context where the whole focus is on human beings participating in deification, Athanasius moves immediately to speak of the whole creation partaking of the Word in the Spirit. RHB Shapland, in the notes to his translation of these letters, makes the comment that this reference to the whole creation sharing in *salvation* by partaking of the Word in the Spirit seems a natural extension of the statement that Athanasius makes in *Against the Nations* (quoted earlier) that creatures owe their very *existence* to their partaking of the Word.[21]

Athanasius moves back and forth between creation and deification. When he speaks of the deification and adoption of human beings he seems naturally to bring in the wider creation, assuming that the whole creation will share with human beings in glorification and deification. The close interconnection between the glorification of creation and human adoption and deification is evident in the following text from his *Letters to Serapion*:

> Therefore, it is in the Spirit that the Word glorifies creation and presents it to the Father by divinizing it and granting it adoption. But the one who binds creation to the Word could not be among the creatures and the one who bestows sonship upon creation could not be foreign to the Son. Otherwise, it would be necessary to look for another spirit to unite this one to the Word. But that is senseless. Therefore, the Spirit is not among the things that have come into being but belongs (*idion*) to the divinity of the Father, and is the one in whom the Word divinizes the things that have come into being. But the one in whom creation is divinized cannot be extrinsic to the divinity of the Father.[22]

Clearly for Athanasius, it is the Holy Spirit who 'binds' creatures to the Word, who bestows adoption on human beings, and who is the one in whom the Word deifies creation.

There are important distinctions to be made between the participation of the Word, in the Spirit, that occurs in different creatures.

---

20. Athanasius, *Letters to Serapion on the Holy Spirit*, 1:23; Anatolios, *Athanasius*, 223.
21. CRB Shapland, *The Letters of Saint Athanasius Concerning the Holy Spirit* (London: Epworth Press, 1951), 124–5, n 15.
22. Athanasius, *Letters to Serapion on the Holy Spirit*, 1:25; Anatolios, *Athanasius*, 225.

As later Greek theologians have pointed out, there are distinctions in creaturely receptivity to participation in divine communion. The receptivity of a human being is different to that of a tree. But both participate of the Word in the Spirit. And, of course, the way a saint participates of the Word in the Spirit is different to that of a sinner. In his reflections on this theme in Gregory Palamas, Doru Costache notes: 'All are in God yet not all are equally receptive to God's presence. The Spirit shines wholly and continually to all creation yet the receptive capabilities vary from one being to another'.[23] God is radically and fully present to each creature, but creatures participate of the Word in the Spirit in distinct ways because of their distinct forms of receptivity to divine life.

In summary, for Athanasius, both the creation of a world of creatures and their deifying fulfilment are seen as partaking of the Word in the Spirit. This is neatly encapsulated in Athanasius' sentence quoted earlier: 'The Father creates and renews all things through the Word and in the Spirit'.[24] From the perspective of the cross and resurrection, Athanasius sees God's act of creating, sustaining, providing for, and governing a world of creatures as occurring through their partaking of the Word in the Spirit. He sees the incarnation as bringing about the deifying transformation of mortal human nature by participation in the Word, through the Spirit. And he believes that in its own way the natural world will be healed and glorified, participating with human beings in their deifying adoption as daughters and sons of God.

For Athanasius, Christ is the one, true 'Word, Radiance and Wisdom of the Father, of which all things that come to be participate and are sanctified, in the Spirit'.[25] The incarnational theology found in Athanasius relates to the natural world in two interrelated ways: on the one hand, starting from the cross of Christ, this theology looks back to see the whole natural world as existing only because it participates in the creative Word through the Spirit; on the other hand, it sees the natural world as, in its own proper ways, now enabled to

---

23. Doru Costache, 'Experiencing the Divine Life: Levels of Participation in St Gregory Palamas' *On the Divine and Deifying Transformation*', in *Phronema* 26/1 (2011): 9–25 at 17.
24. Athanasius, *Letters to Serapion on the Holy Spirit*, 1:24; Anatolios, *Athanasius*, 224.
25. Athanasius, *Orations against the Arians*, 1:46; Anatolios, *Athanasius*, 103.

participate with human beings in the deifying transformation that comes through the incarnation of the Word in the Spirit. In the next sections, I will explore briefly two consequences of this theology of deifying incarnation.

The Eternal Commitment of God to Matter and Flesh

One consequence of this kind of thoroughly incarnational theology is that God is understood as becoming *forever* a God of matter and flesh. The Word is made flesh and matter and flesh are irrevocably taken to God and embedded in the divine Trinity. The incarnation and its culmination in the resurrection and ascension of the crucified Jesus mean that the Word of God is forever matter, forever flesh, forever a creature, forever part of a universe of creatures, but part of all of this that is now radically transfigured. The risen Christ is the first-born of the new creation. He is the beginning of the deifying transformation of the whole universe of creatures in God.

This is a theme that runs through many of Rahner's writings. In 1950, for example, he published a short article entitled 'A Faith that Loves the Earth', in which he ponders the meaning of Christ's resurrection. He sees Jesus as descending in his death to the 'heart of the earth' (Matt 12:40), entering fully into the place of creaturely impermanence and death. By his own death, Christ has become the heart of this earthly reality. He is 'God's heart at the center of the world'. In the resurrection, Christ does not abandon this embrace of earthly reality. Because he is raised precisely in the body, he is the beginning of the liberating and life-giving transformation of all creaturely reality, of all matter and all flesh:

> No, he is risen in his body. That means: He has begun to transfigure this world into himself; he has accepted this world forever; he has been born anew as a child of this earth, but of an earth that is transfigured, freed, unlimited, an earth that in him will last forever and is delivered from death and impermanence for good. He is risen not to show that he is leaving the tomb of the earth forever, but that this very tomb of the dead—which is the body and the earth—has been completely transformed into the glorious, incomprehensible home of the living God and the divine soul of the son. By

rising, he has not left the dwelling of the earth, since he still has his body, though in a final and transfigured way, and is a part of the earth, a part that still belongs to the earth and is connected to earth's nature and destiny.[26]

The new forces of a transfigured world are already at work in the resurrection of Jesus, and they are conquering impermanence, death and sin at their very core. While we continue to experience suffering and sin in the world, Christian faith holds that they have actually been defeated deep down at their very source. At this level, there is no longer any distance between God and the world. Christ is already at the heart of the nameless yearning of all creatures that are waiting to participate in the transfiguration of Christ's body. Christ is at the heart of Earth's history, at the heart not only of love and generosity, but also of tears, death, defeats and even sin, as radical mercy, unbounded love and the promise of life.

As Christians we do not, or at least should not, think that we need to escape from matter and flesh in order to love God. We are called to love the things of Earth and God *together*, because in the resurrection of Jesus 'God has shown that he has adopted the earth forever'.[27] Tertullian said long ago that the flesh is the connecting point, the hinge, of salvation: *Caro cardo salutis*. The Christian claim is not that we find God by going to God in the transcendent spiritual world beyond, but that God has come to us in the flesh. And it is as creatures of flesh that we are transformed in Christ. Since the incarnation, we know that 'Mother Earth has brought forth only creatures that will be transfigured, for his resurrection is the beginning of the resurrection of all flesh'.[28]

In another essay, this time a late one, Rahner asks himself the question: what is specific to the Christian view of God? The answer he finds is precisely the idea that God gives God's very self to creation in the Word made flesh and in the Spirit poured out. What is truly characteristic of Christianity, Rahner claims, is that while maintaining the radical distinction between God and the world, it understands God's

---

26. Karl Rahner, 'A Faith that Loves the Earth', in *The Mystical Way in Everyday Life: Sermons, Essays and Prayers: Karl Rahner, SJ*, edited and translated by Annemarie S Kidder (Maryknoll, NY: Orbis Books, 2010), 52–8, at 55.
27. Rahner, 'A Faith that Loves the Earth', 58.
28. Rahner, 'A Faith that Loves the Earth', 58.

self-giving as the very core of the world's reality and the world as truly the fate of God. He writes:

> God is not merely the one who as creator establishes a world distant from himself as something different, but rather he is the one who gives himself away to this world and who has his own fate in and with this world. God is not only himself the giver, but he is also the gift. For a pantheistic understanding of existence this statement may be completely obvious. For a Christian understanding of God, in which God and the world are not fused but remain separate for all eternity, this is the most tremendous statement that can be made about God at all. Only when this statement is made, when, within a concept of God that makes a radical distinction between God and the world, God himself is still the very core of the world's reality and world is truly the fate of God himself, only then is the concept of God attained that is truly Christian.[29]

The idea that God is the 'core' of the world's reality and that the world is the 'fate' of God challenges many everyday assumptions about how God relates to creation. In this view of the incarnation, the Word is made flesh and flesh is taken to God irrevocably. The resurrection and ascension of the crucified Jesus means that the Word of God is forever flesh, forever a creature, forever part of evolutionary history on this planet, and forever part of a universe of creatures. In creation, incarnation and its culmination in resurrection, God commits God's self to this world, to this universe and its creatures, and does this eternally. In the risen Jesus, part of the biological community of Earth is already forever with God, as the sign and promise of the future of all things in God.

Rahner, a Jesuit theologian in the Roman Catholic tradition, deeply involved in rethinking the heritage of Aquinas, found the largely juridical interpretation of the incarnation in Western theology inadequate, and turned to the Eastern tradition of deification for a richer theology of the meaning of Christ. Thomas Torrance, a minister of the Church of Scotland, strongly influenced by Calvin and by his teacher Karl Barth, represents a different church tradition to

---

29. Karl Rahner, 'The Specific Character of the Christian Concept of God', in *Theological Investigations,* 21 (New York: Crossroad, 1988), 189–95 at 191.

Rahner. But Torrance, too, draws on Eastern patristic theology and his Trinitarian theology builds explicitly on Athanasius.

Torrance writes of the meaning of incarnation: 'Through his cross and resurrection the incarnate Saviour penetrated into the ontological depths of creation where in death created being borders upon non-being, and set it upon a new basis, that of Grace in the triumph of God's holy Love in what the Bible speaks of as a new heaven and a new earth'.[30] In the Christ-event, the new creation is inaugurated in the midst of the old. This is an event that embraces all times: 'The incarnation was not just a transient episode in the interaction of God with the world, but has taken place once-for-all in a way that reaches backward through time and forward through time, from the end to the beginning and from the beginning to the end'.[31]

The Creator of the universe of creatures has once for all become incarnate in it. The incarnation means that the whole universe is brought to share in the freedom of the Creator in the differentiated way appropriate to each creature. God irreversibly binds the created universe to God's own being. The Creator Spirit holds and sustains the creature in an open-ended relation towards the living God as the true fulfilment of the creature. Torrance sees the incarnation of the Wisdom/Word of God as meaning that 'God has decisively bound himself to the created universe and the created universe to himself, with such an unbreakable bond that the Christian hope of redemption and recreation extends not just to human beings but to the universe as a whole'.[32]

The claim made by Torrance and by Rahner is a large one, but it is one that I see as building authentically on the Christian conviction, articulated so powerfully in the work of Athanasius, that Jesus Christ is the eternal Wisdom/Word of God, who is made flesh that we and with us other creatures might be saved and deified in him. His incarnation constitutes an unbreakable bond with the whole creation, to all creatures of all times and all places.

In creation, incarnation, and in its culmination in resurrection, God commits God's very self to this world, to this universe and its creatures, and does this eternally. In the risen Jesus, part of this bio-

---

30. Thomas Torrance, *The Christian Doctrine of God: One Being Three Persons* (Edinburgh: T&T Clark, 1996), 214.
31. Torrance, *The Christian Doctrine of God*, 216.
32. Torrance, *The Christian Doctrine of God*, 244.

logical community of Earth, of this evolutionary history, and this material universe, is already forever with God, as the sign and promise of the deifying fulfilment and transformation of all things in God. In the Creator Spirit, this same divine Wisdom is already at work in the whole universe of creatures bringing them to their liberation and completion in God.

The Scandal of God's Engagement with the Particular

The very particularity of the incarnation of God in one human being can seem far too specific and too limited to offer meaning for the whole of reality. This is sometimes called the 'scandal of particularity'. This scandal is greatly exacerbated by exposure to contemporary science. When cosmologists tell us that our observable universe has been expanding and evolving over the last 13.7 billion years, that our Milky Way Galaxy is made up of something like 200 billion stars more or less like our Sun, and that there are more than 100 billion galaxies in the observable universe, then Christian claims about the incarnation can appear too confined, too specific and too concrete. When we think, in addition, not only of the pluralism of religions on our planet, but also of the possibility of intelligent and religious life on other planets, then it is understandable that some have backed away from universal claims for Jesus Christ and, like Wesley Wildman, opted for what he calls more 'modest' Christologies.[33]

But as biblical scholar Sandra Schneiders has said, everything depends on the kind of interpretation that we make of Jesus. One way of interpreting him is 'to *reduce* Jesus to his particularity as a first century Jewish male who lived a short life in one small country, was executed, and is now a figure of history whom we admire and even imitate but with whom we cannot relate personally and whom we must not universalise'.[34] Once Jesus is understood simply as a great human being and moral example, then this leads inevitably to the conclusion that he cannot have meaning for the whole of human history, let alone for the universe that science puts before us. Then, he

---

33. Wesley Wildman, *Fidelity with Plausibility: Modest Christologies in the Twentieth Century* (Albany, NY: State University of New York Press, 1998).
34. Sandra Schneiders, 'The Word in the World', in *Pacifica* 23 (2010): 247–66 at 263.

becomes 'substantively irrelevant for the scientifically and interreligiously enlightened contemporary person'.[35]

A second way of interpreting Jesus is 'to take utterly seriously the faith of the Church that Jesus *is the Wisdom of God incarnate*'.[36] In the biblical and patristic tradition, Wisdom is the immanence of the transcendent God who is present and active in all creation. Wisdom creates, sustains and brings the universe of creatures to completion and wholeness. It is this wisdom that the biblical and patristic tradition sees as made flesh in Jesus of Nazareth. Schneiders comments that this interpretation of the does not imprison or restrict the infinity of God, but 'focuses' infinity so that in our finitude we can encounter and relate to the absolute mystery of God. Obviously, if, in the particular created humanity of Jesus, the eternal, transcendent, creative, Wisdom of God really does becomes flesh, then something is being said in him that can have the deepest meaning for human beings and their history, for Earth and all its creatures and for the whole universe.

One of the legacies of modernity, I believe, is the tendency to assume the first of these interpretations—to reduce Jesus to prophetic figure. This can happen when theologians and catechists are engaged in a genuine attempt at communicating the gospel in a secular and post-modern world. I am convinced that theologians and catechists need to hold their nerve and claim the great tradition of the transcendent Wisdom of God present to us in the particularity of the human face of Jesus. One of the implications of this, as Schneiders observes, is that *particularity* is revealed as infinitely precious.[37] The God of the whole universe is then seen as the God of this particular laughing kookaburra, this beautiful flowering eucalyptus tree, this vulnerable human person before me.

Divine engagement with the particular extends, I believe, to every aspect of God's creative act in the emergence of the universe and the evolution of life on Earth. In his theological engagement with the sciences of complexity, Niels Gregersen has proposed that the self-organisation that science discovers at work in complex processes be interpreted theologically as the gift of the Creator. The benevolence and generosity of God is such that God bestows on creatures the

---

35. Schneiders, 'The Word in the World', 263.
36. Schneiders, 'The Word in the World', 263.
37. Schneiders, 'The Word in the World', 262.

capacity to make themselves. God designs creation for self-organisation: 'God's design of the *world as whole* favors the emergence of autonomous processes in the *particular course* of evolution, a course at once constrained and propagated by a built-in propensity towards complexification'.[38] From a theological perspective, Gregersen sees the effectiveness of self-organisation as exemplifying a principle of grace written into the structure of the natural world.

In later work, Gregersen reflects on how we might think of the Creator as acting in these emergent processes. He points out that in a self-organising system like a cell there is a constant 'rewiring' that occurs in interaction with the environment, involving an enormous number of steps. These steps are not covered by any one scientific law, but require a variety of interacting scientific explanations.[39] The kind of complexity discovered in self-organising systems at the heart of the natural world suggests a theological conclusion to Gregersen. If God is engaged with every aspect of ongoing creation, then God's engagement is not simply of a general kind. It is better thought of as special divine action that engages with the particulars: 'For if God is not in the particulars, God is not in the whole of reality either'.[40] Gregersen suggests that we can see God as involved in a kenotic way in all the particular details of self-organising creation, 'giving room—from moment to moment, from event to event—to the explorative capacities of God's creatures'.[41]

In the evolution of the universe and in the emergence of life on Earth, divine action involves the historical, the unpredictable and the specific. It involves the specific details of the lives of all living creatures, and in a unique interpersonal way, of human beings. This means we should take seriously the claim of Jesus when he says of sparrows that 'not one of them is forgotten in God's sight' and when

---

38. Neils Henrick Gregersen, 'From Anthropic Design to Self-Organized Complexity', in *From Complexity to Life: On the Emergence of Life and Meaning*, edited by Niels Henrik Gregersen (Oxford: Oxford University Press. 2003), 206–34, at 207–8.
39. Neils Henrick Gregersen, 'Laws of Physics, Principles of Self-Organization, and Natural Capacities: On Explaining a Self-Organizing World', in *Creation: Law and Probability*, edited Fraser Watts (Aldershot, Hampshire, 2008), 81–100, at 97–8.
40. Gregersen, 'Laws of Physics, Principles of Self-Organization, and Natural Capacities: On Explaining a Self-Organizing World', 98.
41. Gregersen, 'Laws of Physics, Principles of Self-Organization, and Natural Capacities: On Explaining a Self-Organizing World', 98.

he makes a promise to of God's providential care for us: 'But even the hairs on your head are all counted' (Lk 12:6–7).

In giving God's self to us in the Word made flesh and in the gift of the Holy Spirit, God is revealed as a God who is infinitely relational, as a Communion of love that embraces difference. This God is creatively present through the Word and in the Spirit with each creature in all its specificity and accompanies each in love. The incarnation of the Word in the Spirit and its fulfilment in resurrection constitutes an unbreakable commitment by God to bring the whole natural world to its proper, transfigured, deifying fulfilment in the divine life.

Athanasius's *Letters to Serapion*: Resource for a Twenty-First Century Theology of God the Trinity

The aim of this essay is theological rather than strictly historical. What I intend is a dialogue with the insights of Athanasius from the perspective of issues and questions that confront the theology of the Trinity today. I will propose that Athanasius's *Letters to Serapion on the Holy Spirit* can serve as an important resource and something of a model for a contemporary theology of the Trinity. Some of the key questions that arise in Trinitarian theology today have been asked by Karl Rahner in the last century: Can we articulate a theology of the Trinity that is grounded not so much in abstract consideration of God in God's self, but in the Bible and the economy of salvation, in the action of the Trinity in creation and salvation? Is the theology of the Trinity one aspect of theology or the articulation of the whole of Christian existence in the world? How does the theology of the Trinity relate to everyday life, to spirituality and worship?[1]

Another issue concerns the relevance of the Trinity for human personal and political life, arising, for example, out of the social model embraced by, among others, Jürgen Moltmann.[2] In a very different way, the Communion theology of John Zizioulas has led to debate around the question: Does the Trinity offer us a model for human interpersonal life, or is such talk simply a projection of recent personalist concerns back onto the Scriptures and the patristic sources?[3]

---

1. Karl Rahner, *The Trinity* (New York: Herder and Herder, 1970).
2. Jürgen Moltmann, *The Trinity and the Kingdom of God: The Doctrine of God* (London: SCM Press, 1981).
3. John D Zizioulas, *Being as Communion: Studies in Personhood and the Church* (Crestwood: St. Vladimir's Seminary Press); *Communion and Otherness* (London: T&T Clark, 2006).

Feminist theologians, including Elizabeth Johnson, ask: How can we move beyond the exclusive use of male images and language for the divine persons, to a broader range of Trinitarian language that respects the mystery of God and contributes to the full humanity of both women and men made in the divine image?[4] Yet another issue arises from the crisis of life that we face on our planet: How can we articulate a Trinitarian theology of the natural world, which might inspire an authentically Christian stance and praxis with regard to the rest of the created world?[5]

We certainly should not expect to find in Athanasius ready-made answers for such questions, but I believe that he offers, particularly in his *Letters to Serapion*, a biblical theology of the Trinity in action, that can be a productive basis for contemporary theology. While his earlier double work *Against the Greeks—On the Incarnation* is focused on the Word and not the Holy Spirit, his *Orations Against the Arians* contains important elements for a theology of the Spirit and a fully Trinitarian theology. But in the *Letters,* he develops a fully explicit defence of the divinity of the Spirit, explores his understanding of the relationship between the Word and the Spirit, and articulates a theology of God as Trinity in creation and salvation, using the word 'Trinity' (*trias*) more frequently than in his other works.

At the beginning, and near the end, of the first letter, Athanasius refers to living in the desert.[6] The *Letters* come from the period of his third exile (356–62), spent with the monastic communities of the Egyptian wilderness. He writes in response to the request of a friend,

---

4. Elizabeth A Johnson, *She Who Is: The Mystery of God in Feminist Theological Discourse* (New York: Crossroad, 1993).
5. See Denis Edwards, *Partaking of God: Trinity, Evolution and Ecology* (Collegeville: Liturgical Press, 2014).
6. Athanasius of Alexandria, *Letters to Serapion on the Holy Spirit* 1.1.1; 1.33.1. The letters have been translated by CRB Shapland in his *The Letters of Saint Athanasius Concerning the Holy Spirit* (London: Epworth Press, 1951), and in part by Khaled Anatolios, *Athanasius* (London and New York: Routledge, 2004), 214–33. There is a new critical edition in *Athanasius Werke II. Die Dogmatischen Schriften. 4. Lieferung. Epistulae I-IV ad Serapionem*, edited by Dietmar Wyrwa and Savvidis Kyriakos (Berlin: Walter de Gruyter, 2010). I will use the new translation made from this critical edition by Mark DelCogliano, Andrew Radde-Gallwitz and Lewis Ayres, in their *Works on the Spirit: Athanasius and Didymus: Athanasius's Letters to Serapion on the Holy Spirit and Didymus's On the Holy Spirit* (New York: St Vladimir's Seminary Press, 2011). Hereafter abbreviated as 'Ser'.

Serapion, the bishop of Thmuis, who is concerned about a group of Christians who accept the divinity of the Word, but insist that the Spirit is a creature and 'unlike' the Father and the Word.[7] Athanasius calls them 'Tropici', apparently because of their allegorical interpretation of biblical texts. They attempt to show that the Spirit is a creature by appealing to Amos 4:13 and 1 Timothy 5:21, and by the argument that if the Spirit is not a creature, then the Spirit must be considered a brother or a son of the Son of God. In his long first letter, Athanasius begins by rejecting their biblical arguments (1.1–14), and then moves to the theological argument (1.15–33), which, along with his more summary comments on the divinity of the Word and Spirit in the second letter, will be my main focus.[8]

In these *Letters*, which constitute the first major theology of the Holy Spirit we possess, Athanasius sets out to show how in the Scriptures, the Spirit is consistently aligned with the Word and the Father, rather than being presented as a creature. Furthermore, he seeks to demonstrate that the Spirit, rather than receiving from God as creatures do, is actively involved as divine agent in both creation and deification, in a way that is distinct and specific to the Spirit, in the one agency of God the Trinity. In exploring Athanasius's contribution, I will begin from the apophatic dimension of his theology of God and show how this exists within a positive theology that builds upon the biblical symbols for God. Then I will take up in turn: Athanasius's view of the relationship between the Word and the Spirit; his dynamic theology of the Trinity in act, in creation and salvation; his concept of the unity and distinction of the Trinity; and his understanding of the experience of baptism and Christian life in the Trinity.

The Apophatic Dimension of Theological Talk of God

In opposing the central theological argument of the Tropici, Athanasius reveals some of his own convictions about theological method. In particular, he makes clear that in his view theological reasoning needs to include an apophatic dimension. A key argument of the Tropici is

---

7. Thus echoing opponents of Athanasius like Aetius and Eunomius.
8. Of the four traditional letters, the first offers the most complete argument, the second focuses on the divinity of the Word, and the third is largely a summary of the first on the Holy Spirit. Recent commentators see the traditional second and third letters as one document, and thus as the second letter of three.

that those who argue for the divinity of the Spirit will end up in the absurd position of seeing the Holy Spirit as a brother of the Word of God or a son of the Word. Behind this facetious argument, there is the concern that maintaining that the Spirit is divine could compromise the uniqueness of the Word and the biblical teaching that the Word is the 'only-begotten' son (Jn 1:14, 18; 3:16, 18; 1 Jn 4:9).[9]

Athanasius begins his response by showing that it is possible to make such impious rationalising sport of any proper theological position. One might ask, for example: who is the father of God the Father? He insists that all such speculation springs from a false premise – that we can simply base our reasoning about God directly on what we know about human creaturely existence. The Creator is radically other than human creatures. Twice in this context Athanasius quotes from the book of Numbers: 'God is not like a human being' (Num 23:19).[10] He points out that human parenting, with its series of generations, is radically different to what can be said of God. God cannot be divided into parts, but the Son is whole from whole as eternal Image and Radiance of the Father. The Father is not begotten, and the Son does not beget. So it is 'sheer insanity' to think of the Spirit as son or grandson.[11] What we do know from Christian faith, Athanasius says, and it is enough for faithful Christians, is that the Spirit is not a creature, but 'ranked with the Trinity' and 'the whole Trinity is one God'.[12] The Trinity is indivisible and self-consistent in divinity. This is the extent to which our human knowledge reaches—'at this point the cherubim spread the covering of their wings'.[13]

With Paul, Athanasius sees the traditions of faith as to be understood not by human wisdom but by the hearing of faith (Gal 3:2). We have no way of speaking adequately of what is beyond us as created entities. He asks: 'What sort of rational account could worthily interpret what surpasses the nature that has come into existence?'[14] He refers to another Pauline text: 'How unsearchable are his ways! For who has known the mind of the Lord? Or who has been his counsel-

---

9. Anatolios, *Athanasius*, 213.
10. *Ser* 1.15.4; 1.16.5. See also *Ser* 3.6.4; 3.6.5.
11. *Ser* 1.16.5.
12. *Ser* 1.17.1.
13. *Ser* 1.17.2.
14. *Ser* 1.17.2.

lor?' (Rom 11:33–34).[15] We cannot know the divine essence because of the gulf between what is created and limited on the one hand, and the infinite, uncreated Creator of all things on the other. We can, however, know the true God by faith, and thus know that the Trinity is one God, indivisible, homogeneous and holy.

We human beings are not God but God's finite creatures, and as such we cannot possibility comprehend the infinite God. Neither our reason nor our speech is adequate to God: 'For none of the things that have come into existence, least of all us human beings, can speak worthily about what is ineffable'.[16] In Athanasius's view it is highly presumptuous to invent new terms, other than those in the Scriptures, for what is beyond the limits of our speech. After all, he argues, if we cannot explain the created world around us, how can we expect to understand or speak adequately of the uncreated Trinity? He points to the heavens above.[17] How are they constituted? How does the sun exist? What do we know about the stars? Can we explain the nature of trees? What do we know of the rivers, lakes and seas? What do we know of the origins and constitutions of living creatures? Athanasius notes that in spite of our lack of knowledge of how created things exist, we have no trouble acknowledging that they do indeed exist. This distinction should help us, then, understand something about our knowledge of God. As Athanasius sees it, we cannot know how God is, but we can certainly know that God is. In another context, in his *First Letter to Monks*, he says that it is 'impossible to comprehend what God is, yet it is possible to say what he is not'.[18]

Other theologians, such as Gregory of Nazianzus, would adopt this strategy of arguing from the limited knowledge of the natural world to the limits on our knowledge and speech about the Trinity.[19] Even though we now know far more about the observable universe and about the evolutionary emergence of life than theologians of the fourth century, I think this strategy still has its place. The nature and size of the expanding universe, with its hundred billion galaxies, the

---

15. *Ser* 1.17.2.
16. *Ser* 1.17.6.
17. *Ser* 1.18.1.
18. *First Letter to Monks* 2. Robertson, *St Athanasius. Select Works and Letters.* Nicene and Post-Nicene Fathers, second series, volume 4 (Edinburgh: T&T Clark, 1987), 563.
19. Gregory Nazianzus, *Oration* 30.31.

wonder of life on Earth, the mind-boggling world revealed by quantum physics, and many other aspects of the natural world lead us into a deeper sense of mystery and, for people of Christian faith, can point beyond themselves to the incomprehensible mystery of love that is the Holy Trinity.

The Biblical Symbols for the Trinity

If Athanasius is clear that human reason can never comprehend the Holy Trinity, he is equally clear that we do have a source of positive knowledge of the Trinity in the biblical Word of God. His theological method involves, then, a necessary apophatic dimension, but this exists within a positive theology based on the Scriptures. In the biblical texts, we find the foundation for all Christian teaching about the Word and the Spirit and their relation to the Father, in the narrative of God's creative and saving action. One of Athanasius's strategies is to appeal to the Scriptures to support the idea that the Spirit possesses the divine characteristics of unchangeability, incorruptibility and omnipresence. But Athanasius finds further, rich theological insight in exploring the biblical names or symbols (*paradeigmata*) for God, showing how these symbols apply not only to the Father and the Word, but also the Spirit. In his *Orations Against the Arians*, Athanasius says of these symbols:

> Since human nature is not capable of comprehension of God, Scripture has placed before us such symbols (*paradeigmata*) and such images (*eikonas*), so that we may understand from them, however slightly and obscurely, as much as is accessible to us.[20]

In his *First Letter to Serapion* he says that the Scriptures provide us with all we need to know: 'For the examples (*paradeigmata*) on this subject found therein are sufficient and fitting'.[21]

These symbols matter greatly to Athanasius. As a contemporary theologian, I find his capacity to invoke and use the whole Bible for his theological work astonishing. Of course, it is not at all astonishing to specialists in fourth century theology. Athanasius's biblical the-

---

20. Athanasius of Alexandria, *Orations against the Arians* 2.32. I am using the translation in Anatolios, *Athanasius*.
21. *Ser* 1.19.1.

ology is a challenge to the disengaged and abstract nature of much Christian theology of today. One result of his way of doing theology is that his images, taken from the Bible, have a capacity to engage the imagination. They speak of God in beautiful ways. They also constantly bring out the dynamic nature of the eternal life of God the Trinity, and the ordering of Trinitarian being and action. In using these images, Athanasius is seeking to manifest the full divinity of the Word and the Spirit, by showing how what is said of the Father is also said of them. He mines the Scriptures according to his own understanding of good interpretation. For him, this means, in particular, reading the Scriptures inter-textually, and so connecting, for example, what is said of Wisdom in Proverbs 8 with Paul's claim that Christ is our Wisdom (1 Cor 1:24). And it means reading the whole of the Bible in the light of Christ, and in the light of what he sees as the authentic tradition of the church.

Athanasius brings six of these symbols together in the long, complex, paragraph 19 of his *First Letter to Serapion*. In order to enable a better appreciation of their beauty and diversity, I will set them out schematically, followed by Athanasius's biblical quotations.[22] The Trinity, then, can be thought of as:

1. *The Fountain, the River, the Spirit of Whom We Drink.* God is 'the Fountain of living water' (Jer 2:13); 'the River of God is filled with waters' (Ps 65:10); 'we were all made to drink of the one Spirit' (1 Cor12:13); 'they drank of the spiritual Rock that followed them, and the Rock was Christ' (1 Cor 10:4).
2. *The Light, the Radiance, the Illuminating Spirit.* 'Our God is Light' (1 Jn 1:5); Christ is the 'Radiance of his glory, and the Character of his Subsistence' (Heb 1:3); Christ is 'the true Light who enlightens every human being who comes into the world' (Jn 1:9); 'May he give you the Spirit of wisdom and of revelation in the knowledge of him, having the eyes of your hearts enlightened' (Eph 1:17).

---

22. In referring to these biblical texts, I am following the translation of Athanasius's usage in DelCogliano, *Works on the Spirit*, 82–3. On these symbols see Khaled Anatolios, *Retrieving Nicaea: The Development and Meaning of Trinitarian Doctrine* (Grand Rapids: Baker Academic, 2011), 141–3; Peter J Leithart, *Athanasius* (Grand Rapids: Baker Academic, 2011), 41–53.

3. *The Father, the Son, the Spirit who make us Sons and Daughters.* 'You did not receive the spirit of slavery leading you back into fear, but you have received the Spirit of adoptive sonship' (Rom 8:15); 'however many received him, to them he gave the power to become children of God' (Jn 1:12).
4. *Fountain of Wisdom, the Wisdom of God, the Gift of Wisdom.* 'Why is it, O Israel, that you are in the land of enemies? You have forsaken the Fountain of wisdom' (Baruch 3:10,12); God is 'the only wise one' (Rom 16:27); 'Christ is the Power of God and the Wisdom of God' (1 Cor 1:24); The 'Spirit of Wisdom' (Eph 1:7); 'the Lord sets prisoners free; the Lord gives Wisdom to the blind' (Ps 146:7–8).
5. *Source of Life, the Life, Life-Giving Spirit.* 'I am the life' (Jn 14:6); 'It is no longer I who live, but Christ who lives in me' (Gal 2:19–20); 'the one who raised Christ Jesus from the dead will also give life to your mortal bodies through his Spirit who dwells in you' (Rom 8:11).
6. *The Father Works, the Son does the Works of the Father, the Works are accomplished in the Power of the Spirit.* 'The Father who remains in me does his works. Believe me, that I am in the Father and the Father is in me. Otherwise, believe me because of the works themselves' (Jn 14:10–11); 'For I will not dare to speak anything other than what Christ has worked through me to win obedience from the Gentiles, in word and in deed, in the power of signs and wonders, in the power of the Holy Spirit' (Rom 15:18–19).

In his earlier work, focusing on the full divinity of the Word, Athanasius uses the symbols River, Radiance, Son, Wisdom and Life, along with others, including Word, Image, Power and also, following Irenaeus, Hand of God, in order to bring out not only the unity of the divine nature, but also the divine correlationality.[23] He insists that the Father cannot be Father without the Son. There is no Light without its Radiance. There is no Spring without its flowing River. They are absolutely correlational. Athanasius sees these biblical names as pointing to the generativity that is at the heart of Trinitarian life. It is precisely this generativity that gives rise to creation. If the Word were but a creature, then this would undermine the eternal 'generative nature' of

---

23. See, for example, *Orations*, 2:31–32.

God.²⁴ Then the divine essence would be understood as barren rather than fruitful, as a light without its radiance, as a fountain without its flow of living water.

In the *First Letter to Serapion*, Athanasius now takes care to show how the great biblical images for God also include the Spirit. It is the Spirit who enables us to drink living water, to be enlightened by Christ, to become sons and daughters of God, to share in the Wisdom of God, to partake of divine life. It is noticeable that in each case he specifies the work of the Spirit at the point where creation participates in the life of God. The whole argument is that the Spirit can enable our creaturely participation in God only if the Spirit is truly divine, and one with the Father and the Word.

As he does in his earlier defence of the divinity of the Word, so now in defending the divinity of the Spirit, we find in Athanasius 'the direct translation from linguistic correlativity to ontological correlativity'.²⁵ The Three cannot be separated one from the other:

> Seeing that there is such an order (*sustoichia*) and unity in the Holy Trinity, who could separate the Son from the Father, or the Spirit from the Son or from the Father himself? Who could be so audacious as to say that the Trinity is unlike itself (*anomion*) and different in nature (*heterophyē*)? Or that the Son is foreign to the Father in substance (*allotrioousion*)? Or that the Spirit is estranged from the Son?²⁶

Athanasius absolutely rejects all views, such as those of Aetius and Eunomius, which would posit ontological unlikeness in the Trinity. His own argument is from the biblical witness to the common action of the Three. There is no Light without its Radiance, and the Radiance can be experienced only in the Illumination of the Spirit. The Three are inseparable, dynamically correlated in action, as they are also of the one divine nature.

The unity and correlation of the Three cannot be comprehended by the 'demonstration of words' but this does not mean that we need to remain in perplexity or without words for the Trinity, because we can know God the Trinity first of all through faith and then speak

---

24. *Orations*, 2:2.
25. Anatolios, *Retrieving Nicaea*, 142.
26. *Ser* 1.20.1.

faithfully of this God by recourse to the biblical symbols. Peter Leithart points out that the different symbols qualify and correct one another. If unqualified, for example, the Father-Son image might be understood as implying the physicality, and the beginning in time, of human birthing. When it is joined by the symbol of Light, its Radiance, and Illumination, it becomes clear that what Athanasius is describing is an eternal dynamic correlationship—the Father must always have the Son, as Light always has its Radiance. As Leithart says: 'The image of light and radiance thus assists in the apophatic purgation of our thoughts about God as Father and Son. One paradigm cleanses another'.[27] In my view, the variety of these dynamic biblical images can serve a similar function in theology today.

The Spirit Who Shines Forth from the Word

Athanasius points to the words of the risen Christ: 'Receive the Holy Spirit' (Jn 20:22) and says that when the Spirit is given to us by Christ in this way, 'God is in us'.[28] He goes on to refer to two other Johannine texts on divine indwelling in the disciples: 'If we should love one another, God remains in us. In this we know that we remain in him, and he in us, because he has given us of his Spirit' (1 Jn 4:12–13); and 'I and the Father will come and make our home with him' (Jn 14:23). In this line of thought, the indwelling of the Spirit, the Son and the Father in the believer is based upon the mutual indwelling of the divine persons—an anticipation of what will later be called Trinitarian perichoresis. It is in this sense of mutual indwelling that Athanasius writes of the Son as in the Spirit, and the Spirit as the image of the Son—'For as the Son is in the Spirit as in his own Image, so is the Father in the Son'.[29]

The Spirit is described by the same biblical symbols as the Father and the Word, possesses their one divine nature, and participates in the one action of the Father and the Word in creation and salvation.

---

27. Leithart, *Athanasius*, 46.
28. *Ser* 1.19.7.
29. *Ser* 1.20.4. As Anatolios points out (*Athanasius*, 276, note 20), while Irenaeus calls the Spirit image of the Father (*Against the Heresies* 4.7.4), Athanasius speaks of the Spirit as image of the Son not only here but in other places (*Letters to Serapion* 1.24; 4.3), and this identification is also made by Cyril of Alexandria (*Thesaurus* 33) and John Damascene (*On the Orthodox Faith* 1.13).

Athanasius writes for example that 'there is one holiness which comes from the Father through the Son, in the Holy Spirit'.[30] He uses these same three propositions consistently: 'from', 'through', and 'in' indicate Athanasius's understanding of the distinction of roles within the one action of the Trinity towards creation.[31] The divine action of creating and sustaining a world of creatures, and of saving and deifying creaturely beings, springs from the Father, occurs through the Word and takes effect in the Spirit.

Athanasius has more to say about the relationship between the Word of God and the Holy Spirit. He sees the Word as the unique, only-begotten one, who is sent by the Father for our salvation. What, then, of the Spirit?[32] As the Word of God is the only-begotten one, so must the Spirit, the Word's 'living energy and gift which sanctifies and illuminates', also be one, full and perfect and unique.[33] Athanasius tells us that the Spirit 'is given and sent' from the Son. He repeats these verbs, adding another, 'shining forth': The Spirit 'is said to proceed from the Father, because the Spirit shines forth, and is sent, and is given from the Word, who is confessed to be from the Father'.[34] As these quotations show, Athanasius offers a range of words that point to the Spirit's uniqueness and integrity. Each is a relational word, indicating both the Spirit's distinction from, and intimate relationship with, the Word of God: the Spirit is the gift of the Word who sanctifies and illuminates; the Spirit is the one sent by the Word; the Spirit is the living energy of the Word; and the Spirit shines forth from the Word.

He finds a constant relationship and right order between Word and Spirit in a range of biblical texts: on the one hand, the Father sends the Son (Jn 3:16), the Son glorifies the Father (Jn 17:4), hears the Father (Jn 8:26), and comes in the name of the Father (Jn 5:43); on the other hand, the Son sends the Spirit (Jn 16:17), the Spirit glorifies the Son (Jn 16:14), the Spirit receives from the Son (Jn 16:14), the Spirit is sent in the name of the Son (Jn 5:43). Athanasius finds that 'the Spirit's rank and nature vis-à-vis the Son corresponds to the Son's

---

30. Ser 1.20.4.
31. See for example, *Letters to Serapion* 1.9.7; 1.12.3; 1.24.6; 1.25.5; 1.30.4; 1.31.2; 2.14.4. See Shapland, *Letters*, 36–7.
32. Ser 1.20.5.
33. Ser 1.20.5.
34. Ser 1.20.5.

vis-à-vis the Father'.³⁵ The Spirit is no creature but belongs to the one complete divine Trinity:

> [As] the Son, who is in the Father and the Father in him, is not a creature but is proper to (*idios*) the substance (*ousia*) of the Father . . . so too it is incorrect for the Spirit, who is in the Son and the Son in him, to be ranked with creatures or to be separated from the Word, thereby destroying the perfection of the Trinity.³⁶

Anatolios sums up the relations between the Three in Athanasius's view of the biblical pattern: 'in each case the Father is the source, the Son is the outgoing manifestation and imaged content of the source, and the Spirit is the outward actualisation of that content in and towards creation'.³⁷ Each possesses fully the one divine being. As Thomas Weinandy notes, the unity of being and action between the Word and the Spirit, directly founded on the unity of being and action of the Father and the Word, is the hallmark of Athanasius's theology of the Spirit. It gives expression to the biblical theology of mutual indwelling and provides the ontological base for the later development of the concept of perichoresis.³⁸

The Trinity in Act: Creating and Deifying

In reading Athanasius, there is always the sense that the God he describes is the biblical God, who creates the world of creatures and brings salvation to creatures. His theology is always a narrative theology of God who acts. Of course, he is intensely interested in the divine identity of the Word and the Spirit who act in creation and deification. But his focus is not on God in God's self, but always on the true identity of the God acting to create and save. His concern is for the realism of the narrative: it is truly God who acts in the Word and the Spirit.

---

35. *Ser* 1.21.1.
36. *Ser* 1.21.3.
37. Anatolios, *Retrieving Nicaea*, 142–3.
38. Thomas G Weinandy, *Athanasius: A Theological Introduction* (Burlington, VT: Ashgate, 2007), 119.

In his *Letters to Serapion*, however, Athanasius does not proceed by beginning with creation and then turning to salvation. He focuses, rather, on the saving and sanctifying work of God through the Word and in the Spirit, and refers to creation from within this context. But he makes it abundantly clear that he sees the Spirit's work, not as limited to sanctification and deification, but as including creation. He finds the Spirit at work in every aspect of God's action towards creatures. In his *Second Letter* he quotes Psalm 104:30, 'When you send forth your Spirit they are created', and then comments:

> Seeing that this has been written, it is clear that the Spirit is not a creature but is involved in the act of creation. The Father creates all things through the Word in the Spirit. For where the Word is, there also is the Spirit, and the things created through the Word have their strength to exist through the Spirit from the Word. Thus it is written in Psalm 32: 'By the Word of the Lord the heavens were established, and by the Spirit of his mouth all their power' (Ps 32:6).[39]

For Athanasius, the Spirit is always in the Word: 'For the Spirit is not external to the Word, but is in the Word, and through the Word is in God'.[40] The Spirit is not outside the Word in either creation or in salvation, but is in the Word in both. Creation and deification are deeply inter-related in Athanasius's thought, so interconnected that CRB Shapland writes that Athanasius 'thinks of creation and sanctification as one single work'.[41] In his doctrine of creation, outlined in his *Against the Greeks*, creatures exist only because they partake of God, through the Word in the Spirit.[42] His theology of deification, discussed below, is also understood as a partaking of God through the Word and in the Spirit. But deification involves a new, profoundly interior, radically transforming and far more stable, participation in God.

---

39. *Ser* 2.14.1.
40. *Ser* 2.14.4.
41. Shapland, *Letters*, 37.
42. Athanasius of Alexandria, *Against the Greeks* 41 in *Athanasius: Contra Gentes and De Incarnatione*, translated by Robert Thomson (Oxford, UK: Clarendon Press, 1971), 15.

In writing of biblical texts that speak of the Spirit as the 'anointing' and 'seal' (Isa 61:1; 1 Jn 1:27; Eph 1:13), Athanasius argues that if the Holy Spirit is the anointing and the seal of Christ, then the Spirit cannot be a creature, 'but is proper to (*idion*) the Word who anoints and seals'.[43] The seal possesses the form of Christ who seals, while those who are sealed participate in the Spirit who is the seal, and in Christ who seals. So Athanasius says: 'Thus sealed, it is proper that we also become, as Peter says, sharers of the divine nature (2 Peter 1:4). And thus all creation partakes of the Word in the Spirit'.[44] If it is in the Spirit that all things are deified, then one would have to be crazy, Athanasius says, to doubt that the Spirit who deifies creatures possesses the nature of God—'if he divinizes, there can be no doubt that his nature is of God'.[45] It is notable that here, as elsewhere, Athanasius makes no careful distinction between Christians sealed with the Spirit in Baptism, and the creation participating in God. In his notes on this text, Shapland sees this as an extension of what Athanasius says in *Against the Greeks* (quoted above) that creation by its very existence partakes of God.[46] Here and elsewhere, Athanasius sees the deification conferred by the Spirit not as confined to humanity but as extending to the whole creation.[47] In this instance, Athanasius goes on immediately to quote a classic text about the Spirit's work in creating all things (Ps 104:29-30), followed by one that speaks of the Spirit at work in the bath of renewal and regeneration (Titus 3:5-6). This leads him to assert the full divinity of the Spirit by means of one of his classic summary statements—'The Father creates and renews all things through the Word in the Holy Spirit'.[48]

The Tropici had asked: 'If the Spirit is from God, why isn't he also called a son?' Athanasius responds to this 'reckless and audacious' question, by showing that the Spirit is never called son in Scripture, but is called the Spirit, who is in God and from God.[49] Again, he points out that the various dynamic biblical symbols, Son, Wisdom, Truth,

---

43. *Ser* 1.23.6.
44. *Ser* 1.23.7.
45. *Ser* 1.24.4.
46. Shapland, *Letters*, 124–5, n 15.
47. As well as the example considered in the next paragraph, see *Letters to Serapion* 1.31 and 3.4.
48. *Ser* 1.24.6.
49. *Ser* 1.25.1,2.

Power and Glory apply not only to the Word but also to the Spirit: the Spirit is the Spirit of adoption (Rom 8:15; Gal 4:6), the Spirit of Wisdom (Isa 11:2; Eph 1:7), the Spirit of Truth (Jn 14:17; 15:26; 16:13; 1 Jn 4:6), the Spirit of Power and of Glory (1 Pet 4:14). In this way, Athanasius says, 'the Trinity is complete in the Spirit'.[50] He continues:

> So then, in the Spirit the Word glorifies creatures, and after he has divinized them and made them sons of God, he leads them to the Father. But that which joins creatures to the Word cannot be a creature. And that which makes creatures sons cannot be foreign to the Son. Otherwise another spirit would be needed by which this Spirit could be joined to the Word. But this is absurd. And so, the Spirit is not one of the things that have come into existence, but is proper to the divinity of the Father. In him the Word divinizes all that has come into existence. And the one in whom creatures are divinized cannot himself be external to the divinity of the Father.[51]

In this remarkable paragraph, Athanasius describes the work of the Word and the Spirit as the adoption of human beings and the deification of all that has come into existence. He repeatedly says that it is in the Spirit that the Word deifies creatures or 'all that has come into existence'. In the opening sentence, he offers a fully Trinitarian description of the divine eschatological act that involves the transformation of the creation—in the Spirit the Word glorifies creation and presents it to the Father precisely by deifying it. Athanasius specifies his view of the Spirit's role in this deification—the Spirit 'binds creation to the Word'. The Spirit is the bond that unites each creature to the Word and thus enables its proper deification. And, of course, the Spirit is the one who bestows adoptive sonship and daughtership upon human beings, conforming them to Christ.

For Athanasius, all of this shows that the Spirit is not a changeable creature, but truly 'Image of the Word and proper (*idios*) to the Father'.[52] The Spirit, he tells us, 'fills all things and is present in the midst of all things through the Word'.[53] The Spirit is the one in whom

---

50. *Ser* 1.25.3.
51. *Ser* 1.25.5.
52. *Ser* 1.26.6.
53. *Ser* 1.26.7.

creatures participate, not one who participates in God as creatures do. In this context, Athanasius denies that the Spirit could ever be one of the many created entities and directly applies the homoousios to the Spirit: 'the Spirit is neither of the many nor even an angel, but he is the only one. Or rather, he is proper to the one Word and proper to and the same as the one God in substance (*homoousion*)'.[54]

Unity and Distinction in the Trinity Acting

After discussing the biblical evidence at length, Athanasius turns to 'the tradition, teaching, and faith of the Catholic Church from the beginning, which is nothing other than what the Lord gave, the Apostles preached, and the Fathers preserved'.[55] He encapsulates what he sees as this tradition:

> So, the Trinity is holy and perfect, confessed in Father and Son and Holy Spirit. It has nothing foreign or external mixed with it, nor is it composed of Creator and creature, but is entirely given to creating and making. It is self-consistent and indivisible in nature, and it has one activity (*energeia*). The Father does all things through the Word in the Holy Spirit. In this way is the unity of the Holy Trinity preserved, and in this way is the one God preached in the Church, 'who is above all and through all and in all' (Eph 4:6)—'above all', as Father, as beginning (*archē*) and source; 'through all', through the Word; 'in all', in the Holy Spirit. It is not a Trinity in name alone and in linguistic expression, but in truth and actual existence.[56]

Athanasius thus expresses his complete commitment to the unity and indivisibility of the Holy Trinity, and the ontological gap between the divine Three and the world of creatures. This one Trinity is wholly Creator—'entirely given to creating and making'. The Three are involved in the one act of creation, and in all the acts of the Trinity vis-à-vis creation—its activity (*energeia*) is one. Here, as elsewhere, Athanasius refuses to limit the Spirit to sanctification. The radical

---

54. Ser 1.27.3.
55. Ser 1.28.1.
56. Ser 1.28.2–3.

unity of the Trinity is expressed in the unity of action (*energeia*) of God the Trinity.

Yet immediately Athanasius expresses the proper distinctions in this one act: 'For the Father does all things through the Word and in the Holy Spirit', and reinforces this unity in distinction with his quotation from Ephesians. He insists on the reality of the Three in 'truth and actual existence'. He goes on with a strong statement that each of the Three, the Father, Word and Spirit, 'exists and subsists truly', and explicitly distances himself from Sabellian modalism as well as from Greek polytheism.[57] While Athanasius does not use the language of hypostasis of the Three, he clearly affirms the personal distinction and the ontological unity of the Trinity.[58]

Baptism and Christian Life in the Trinity

The Catholic Church, Athanasius says, has always understood that God is Trinity. This is clear from the original commission of the Lord: 'Go and make disciples of all nations, baptising them in the name of the Father and of the Son and of the Holy Spirit' (Matt 28:19). The constant practice of the church has been to baptise in the name of the one God who is 'above all' and 'through all' and 'in all' (Eph 4:6). Those who deny that the Spirit is divine, then, deform the unity of baptism itself along with the unity of the one God. Baptism is an initiation into the Trinity, not a consecration into two who are divine and one who is a creature—'for just as there is one baptism given in Father and Son and Holy Spirit, and just as there is one faith in the Trinity (as the Apostle said), so too the Holy Trinity, which is identical with itself and united in itself, has nothing in it that belongs to things that have come into existence'.[59]

What the Spirit imparts to each in grace is provided from the Father through the Son: 'For all that the Father has is the Son's. Thus what is given by the Son in the Spirit is the gift of the Father'.[60] In the Spirit, we are drawn into the life of the Trinity. As Alvyn Pettersen comments, our deification is fundamentally a relational matter. It is a

---

57. *Ser* 1.28.3–4.
58. See Anatolios, *Retrieving Nicaea*, 145.
59. *Ser* 1.30.2.
60. *Ser* 1.30.5.

participation, in the Spirit, of the Son's relationship with the Father.[61] According to Athanasius, what happens in the life of grace is that when the Spirit is in us, the Word who gives the Spirit is in us, and the Father is in the Word—'I and my Father will come and make our home with him' (Jn 14:23).[62] Athanasius comments on this Johannine text with one of his favourite symbols of the Trinity:

> For wherever there is Light, there is also Radiance; and wherever there is Radiance, there also is its activity (*energeia*) and luminous grace. Once again, this is what Paul taught when he wrote a second letter to the Corinthians, saying: 'The grace of our Lord Jesus Christ, and the love of God, and the fellowship of the Holy Spirit be with you all' (2 Cor 13:13). For this grace and gift given in the Trinity is given by the Father through the Son in the Holy Spirit. Just as the grace given through the Son is from the Father, so too we cannot have fellowship with the gift except in the Holy Spirit. For it is when we participate in the Spirit that we have the love of the Father and the grace of the Son and the fellowship of the Spirit himself.[63]

The grace of the divine indwelling, then, has the same Trinitarian structure as creation—it is grace given 'from the Father, through the Son, in the Holy Spirit'. It is the Spirit who enables our communion in God. According to Athanasius, the Spirit acts in or activates (*energoun*) everything worked by the Father through the Word: 'For there is nothing which is not brought into being and actuated through the Word, in the Spirit'.[64] Both grace and the act of creation are actuated through the Word in the Spirit.

Athanasius uses the same word *energeia* to depict both the action of the Trinity as a whole towards creation, and the specific role of the Spirit.[65] On the one hand, he insists that the Trinity is indivisible and that its activity (*energeia*) is one.[66] On the other hand he writes: 'For

---

61. Alvyn Pettersen, *Athanasius* (London: Geoffrey Chapman, 1995), 193.
62. *Ser* 1.30.5.
63. *Ser* 1.30.5–6.
64. *Ser* 1.31.2.
65. See Anatolios, *Retrieving Nicaea*, 143.
66. *Ser* 1.28.2.

wherever there is Light, there is also Radiance; and wherever there is Radiance, there is also its activity (*energeia*) and luminous grace',[67] and speaks of the Spirit acting in, or activating (*energoun*) everything that is worked by the Father through the Son.[68] He thus identifies the Spirit as the living energy of the Trinity, in the Trinity's engagement with creation.

Anatolios asks how this characterisation of the Spirit holds if the Trinity is considered independently from creation. He points out that this is not the kind of question that Athanasius is motivated to consider. Athanasius thinks in the context of the Trinity's relation with creation and sees the Spirit as the active agent by which the divine life is actualised in creatures. This establishes, in Athanasius's view, first, the divinity of the Spirit and, second, the specific role of the Spirit in Trinitarian action with regard to creation. Anatolios notes that Augustine later takes up the issue of the character of the Spirit independent of the Spirit's work with creatures, and arrives at an understanding of the Spirit in terms of the biblical name of Gift, as eternally 'the Giveable God' (*Deus donabilis*).[69]

For Athanasius, in both creation and grace, 'the Spirit is not divided from the Word'.[70] If both creation and deifying grace are activated from the Father, through the Word and in the Spirit, what of the incarnation itself? Is there a role for the Holy Spirit in the Word becoming flesh? In his *Against the Arians*, Athanasius shows how the Word of God, who is forever God and the supplier of the Spirit, becomes in his humanity the receiver of the Spirit and is deified by the Spirit.[71] Through this openness to the Spirit of the Word made flesh, we too are enabled to become co-receivers of the Spirit, and taken in the position of the Word in relation to the Father.[72] Athanasius can thus be said to have a Spirit Christology,[73] which, of course, is also fully a Word of God Christology. Spirit and Word are inseparable. At

---

67. *Ser* 1.30.5.
68. *Ser* 1.31.6.
69. Anatolios, *Retrieving Nicaea*, 143. See Augustine, *De Trinitiate*, 5.15.16.
70. *Ser* 1.31.3.
71. *Orations*, 1.46-7 (Anatolios, *Athanasius*, 103–5). On this theme of the receptivity of the Word made flesh, see the recent work of Adam Cooper, 'The Gift of Receptivity: St Athanasius on the Security of Salvation', in *Phronema* 28:2 (2013): 1–20.
72. See Anatolios, *Retrieving Nicaea*, 125.
73. See Anatolios, *Retrieving Nicaea*, 134 and following.

the end of the first of his *Letters to Serapion*, after insisting that Word and Spirit both act in the saints and prophets, he briefly summarises his view of the Word and Spirit in the incarnation:

> Thus also when the Word visited the holy Virgin Mary, the Spirit came to her with him, and the Word in the Spirit, formed the body and accommodated it to himself, out of a desire to join and present the created order to the Father through himself and to "reconcile all things in himself, making peace between the things that are in heaven and the things that are on earth (Col 1:20).[74]

Word and Spirit cannot be separated in the incarnation, or in that which the incarnation initiates and brings about, the eschatological reconciliation and transformation of the whole creation.

Conclusion

My proposal has been that Athanasius's *Letters to Serapion* offers a resource and a model for twenty-first century theology of God the Trinity. At the beginning of this essay, I highlighted a series of issues that need to be addressed in a theology of Trinity in the twenty-first century, acknowledging, of course, that we cannot expect to find in Athanasius direct answers to contemporary questions. I believe that what emerges from this discussion of the *Letters* is that Athanasius's Trinitarian theology can offer a foundation for such a contemporary theology. I will conclude by highlighting key aspects of his approach, emerging from this discussion of the *Letters*, which offer suggestions of ways to respond to the issues I raised at the beginning:

1. Athanasius holds the apophatic stance that human reason cannot comprehend the nature of the triune God, within the context of his strong conviction that we have a rich source of positive knowledge of the Trinity in biblical revelation.
2. The Trinity for him is always the Trinity revealed in the economy of creation and salvation.

---

74. *Ser* 1.31.12.

3. Athanasius offers us a variety of biblical symbols and theological language for the Trinity that represent the unspeakable beauty of the God beyond all language, and that can help bring liberation to those oppressed by unrelenting male language, including: Light, Radiance, Enlightening Spirit; Fountain, Stream of Living Water, Spirit of whom we drink; Font of Wisdom herself, Spirit of Wisdom; Father, Son, Adopting Spirit.
4. The Trinity is understood as acting: creating creatures and deifying creatures.
5. Creation and deifying incarnation are understood as intrinsically interconnected.
6. God's action towards creation is understood as radically one, but the Three act in distinct ways within the one act: 'The Father creates and renews all things through the Word in the Holy Spirit.'[75]
7. The actions of the Trinity spring from the eternal dynamic generativity of divine life where the Light always Radiates, the Spring always produces its flowing Stream, the Father eternally generates the Son.
8. Athanasius's theology is a narrative theology of the triune God acting. It is a narrative theology that makes uncompromising ontological claims about the full and eternal divinity of both the Word and the Spirit.
9. For Athanasius, the theology of the Trinity is not understood as an aspect of theology, but as an interpretation of the whole of Christian life, and ultimately as an interpretation of the whole of reality.[76]
10. His view of Trinitarian deification is that by the grace of the indwelling Spirit, human beings are transformed in Christ, and assimilated to him in his relationship to Abba/Father.
11. Athanasius's use of the Johannine texts that speak of mutual indwelling between the Father and the Son in the Spirit, and of divine indwelling in the disciples, shows that Athanasius sees Christian life in terms of relationship and love, and surely offers general theological support for an interpersonal view of human persons within contemporary Trinitarian theology.

---

75. *Ser* 1.24.5.
76. Anatolios, *Retrieving Nicaea*, 8.

12. Athanasius's theology of deification involves not just human beings, but with them, in their own proper ways, all creatures. The natural world is the place of divine indwelling. It exists because it partakes of God, through the Word and in the Spirit. It will be transfigured and fulfilled through Christ in the Spirit.

Where on Earth is God? Exploring an Ecological Theology of the Trinity in the Tradition of Athanasius

The story of the evolution of life involves not only competition for resources but also wonderful co-operation between species and a sustained interaction over billions of years between living creatures and the seas, the atmosphere and the land. We face a global crisis because humans have brought major changes in these systems, which have already led to loss of species and which threaten to bring further large-scale extinctions of other species and great suffering to human communities. Dealing with this crisis of our twenty-first century demands all the resources we have—including those of theology. Christian theology is called to dig deep into its own sources to offer a theological vision that can sustain and nourish an ecological conversion and way of life.

What is needed, I believe, is not simply a theology of God the Creator, but a fully Trinitarian narrative of the Word and Spirit's engagement with a world of creatures, a theology of creation, incarnation and final salvation. Clearly the approach to salvation will need to embrace not only humanity but also the rest of the natural world. It will need to locate humanity within the community of creation.

There are many possible starting points in recent Trinitarian theology, such as in Jurgen Moltmann's explicit engagement with ecology,[1] or Karl Rahner's theology of Trinitarian self-bestowal and creaturely self-transcendence.[2] It would also be possible to build on the openness to science found in the richly Trinitarian theologies

---

1. Jürgen Moltmann, *The Trinity and the Kingdom of God* (London: SCM, 1981); *The Way of Jesus Christ: Christology in Messianic Dimensions* (London: SCM, 1990).
2. Karl Rahner, *Foundations of Christian Faith: An Introduction to the Idea of Christianity* (New York: Seabury Press, 1978).

of Wolfhart Pannenberg[3] or Thomas Torrance.[4] The communion theologies of John Zizioulas,[5] Walter Kasper,[6] Catherine LaCugna[7] or Colin Gunton[8] can open into a theology of the communion of the whole creation in God. John Polkinghorne has taken up this approach, creatively exploring the connection between science and a Trinitarian relational ontology.[9] The Spirit theologies of Elizabeth Johnson[10] or Sigurd Bergmann[11] are already important resources for a renewed theology of creation. Leonardo Boff has shown how his social theology of the Trinity can open out into an eco-justice theology.[12] An alternative, less explicitly Trinitarian, approach is found in Sallie McFague's ecological theology of the Body of God.[13]

My choice is to build on Athanasius, for several reasons. First, his theology of the Trinity is a dynamic one. It is a theology of the Trinity in action, of God creating and saving through the Word and in the Spirit. It is a theology that is biblical, economic and cast in narrative terms of God's action towards creation. Second, for Athanasius, the Trinity is not one aspect of his theology but simply the Christian way

---

3. W Pannenberg, *Systematic Theology,* Volume 2 (Grand Rapids: Eerdmans, 1994).
4. TF Torrance, *The Christian Doctrine of God: One Being Three Persons* (Edinburgh: T&T Clark, 1996).
5. John D. Zizioulas, *Being as Communion: Studies in Personhood and the Church* (Crestwood, NY: St Vladimir's Seminary Press); *Communion and Otherness* (London. T&T Clark, 2006).
6. Walter Kasper, *The God of Jesus Christ* (London: SCM, 1993).
7. Catherine M. LaCugna, *God for Us: The Trinity and Christian Life* (San Francisco: HarperSanFrancisco, 1991).
8. Colin E Gunton, *The Promise of Trinitarian Theology* (Edinburgh: T&T Clark, 1991); *The One, the Three and the Many: God, Creation and the Culture of Modernity* (Cambridge: Cambridge University Press, 1993).
9. John Polkinghorne, *Science and the Trinity: The Christian Encounter with Reality* (London: SPCK, 2004); *The Trinity and an Entangled World: Relationality in Physical Science and Theology* (Grand Rapids: Eerdmans, 2010).
10. Elizabeth A Johnson, *Women, Earth, and Creator Spirit* (Mahwah, NJ: Paulist Press, 1993); *Quest for the Living God: Mapping Frontiers in the Theology of God* (New York: Continuum, 2007).
11. S Bergmann, *Creation Set Free: The Spirit as Liberator of Nature* (Grand Rapids: Eerdmans, 2005).
12. Leonardo Boff, *Trinity and Society* (Maryknoll NY: Orbis Books, 1988); *Cry of the Earth, Cry of the Poor* (Maryknoll NY: Orbis Books, 1997).
13. Sally McFague, S., *Models of God: Theology for an Ecological, Nuclear Age* (Philadephia: Fortress Press, 1987); *The Body of God: An Ecological Theology* (London: SCM, 1993).

of speaking about the whole of reality.[14] Third, his theology holds creation and the saving incarnation together in one theological vision. Fourth, he has a theology of salvation in Christ as deification, which I think is highly relevant for this time, and even though the wider creation is not at the centre of his thought, he includes the rest of the natural world in the deifying transfiguration that occurs in Christ.

Athanasius's concern, of course, is not the twenty-first century ecological crisis, but the defence of the full divinity of the Word, and later of the Spirit, against alternative readings of the biblical story by his opponents, whom Athanasius lumps together as Arians. My proposal is that his theology can be reinterpreted and built upon to offer hope and meaning in a very different context. In the first part of this chapter, I will take up his Trinitarian theology of creation. Then in the second part, I will engage with his understanding of deification and discuss its applications to human beings and to the rest of the natural world. In the third part, I will conclude briefly with what I see as some important ecological consequences of this theology.

Trinity in Act: Creating a Universe of Creatures

Athanasius's Trinitarian theology of creation is grounded in the cross of Christ. Both volumes of his *Against the Greeks-On the Incarnation* begin from the scandal of the cross. Recent commentators describe this foundational double work as an 'apology for the cross' against its mockers.[15] Athanasius's central strategy is to show that the one who dies on the cross is truly the eternal and divine Word of God, who, by entering into death, brings salvation to the whole creation. Those who slander the cross, he says, fail to understand that the crucified Christ is 'the Saviour of the universe and that the cross was not the ruin but the salvation of creation'.[16]

---

14. See K Anatolios, *Retrieving Nicaea: The Development and Meaning of Trinitarian Doctrine* (Grand Rapids: Baker Academic, 2011), 1, 7–8, 11.
15. K Anatolios, *Athanasius: The Coherence of his Thought* (London: Routledge, 1988), 28; J Behr, *The Nicene Faith: Part One: True God of True God, The Formation of Christian Theology*, volume 2 (Crestwood NY: St Vladimir's Seminary Press, 2004), 171.
16. Athanasius of Alexandria, *Against the Greeks*, 1 in *Athanasius*: Contra Gentes *and* De Incarnatione translated by RW Thomson (Oxford: Clarendon Press, 1971), 5. Hereafter abbreviated as '*C gent*'.

It is from the perspective of the cross, then, that Athanasius begins to discuss the role of the Word of God in creating a universe of creatures. John Behr explains: 'It is the Word of the Cross, or the Word on the Cross, that Athanasius expounds by describing how all things have come into being by and for him; it is Christ himself that Athanasius is reflecting on, not the creation accounts in and of themselves.'[17] Athanasius's view of creation is grounded in the incarnation, in the experience of the Word made flesh, above all in the saving death and resurrection of Jesus. For him, creatures exist, only because by God's creative act they continually participate in this very same Word, in the Holy Spirit.

God Creates through the Word in the Spirit

Based on his interpretation of key biblical texts (Jn 1:3; Col 1:16; Heb 1:2-3; 1 Cor 1:24, 8:6; Prov 8:22-31), Athanasius sees God as creating through God's own Word or Wisdom, who has the very being of God, and who is God. Insisting on, and developing, the concept of *creatio ex nihilo*, Athanasius sees creatures as having in themselves absolutely no reason for their own existence. They exist only through the sheer divine benevolence by which God creates a universe of creatures through the Word. All creatures exist out of nothing at every point, which means that they are inherently unstable—apart from their participation in the Word. So creation is not simply something that occurs at the beginning, but is a continuous divine act. It is not only that things are originally brought into existence through the Word, but that each creature continues to exist only by its ongoing participation in the creative Word:

> After making everything by his own eternal Word and bringing creation into existence, he did not abandon it to be carried away and suffer through its own nature, lest it run the risk of returning to nothing. But being good, he governs and establishes the whole world through his Word who is himself God, in order that creation, illuminated by the leadership, providence and ordering of the Word, may be able to remain firm, since *it shares in the Word* who is truly from the Father

---

17. Behr, *The Nicene Faith: Part One*, 181-2.

and is aided by him to exist, and lest it suffer what would happen, I mean a relapse into nonexistence, if it were not protected by the Word. [18]

The words I have highlighted translate the Greek word *metalambánousa*, which can also be translated as 'it participates in the Word'. According to Athanasius, it is participation in the Word that enables each creature to exist and the whole creation to remain firm. The one who is Word and Wisdom of the Father is 'present in all things' and 'gives life and protection to everything, everywhere, to each individually and to all together'.[19] Divine Wisdom brings the diversity of creatures into balance and beautiful harmony, keeps the oceans in place and provides the wonderful variety of green plants of Earth. As a musician tunes a lyre and skilfully produces a single melody from many diverse notes, so 'the Wisdom of God, holding the universe like a lyre', draws together the variety of created things 'thus producing in beauty and harmony a single world and a single order within it'.[20]

What is the role of the Holy Spirit in this ongoing act of creation? After neglecting the Holy Spirit in his early work, Athanasius gives expression to his Spirit theology in his *Orations against the Arians*, and focuses directly on the Spirit in his *Letters to Serapion* – the first substantial theology of the Spirit we possess. In these later works, Athanasius articulates a comprehensive theology of creation as participation in the Trinity. He sees the indwelling Spirit as the divine 'bond' that unites creatures to the Word and, through the Word, to the Father.[21] The Spirit is the divine presence to creatures who activates and energises everything that is worked by the Father through the Son: 'For there is nothing that is not brought into being and actuated through the Word, in the Spirit'.[22]

In the divine act of continuous creation, the Spirit enables each creature to be open to, and to receive, the creative Word. Creation is a

---

18. *C gent*, 41, Thomson, *Athanasius*, 114–15.
19. *C gent*, 41, Thomson, *Athanasius*, 115.
20. *C gent*, 42, Thomson, *Athanasius*, 117.
21. Athanasius of Alexandria, *Letters to Serapion on the Holy Spirit* 1:25, in Khaled Antatolios, *Athanasius* (London and New York: Routledge, 2004), 225. Hereafter abbreviated as '*Ep Ser*'.
22. *Ep Ser* 1:31, Anatolios, *Athanasius*, 230.

fully Trinitarian act that enables a world of creatures to participate of the Word in the Spirit. It is only through this participation that individual creatures exist and interact in the community of creation. In Athanasius's theology, both creation and new creation occur through this structure of participation of the Word in the Spirit: 'The Father creates and renews all things through the Son and in the Holy Spirit.'[23]

This theology of God's creative presence to each creature through the Word and in the Spirit, enabling each creature to participate in its own way in the Trinity, already offers a foundation for developing a contemporary ecological theology. This is true, above all, when this theology of creation is held together, as it is in Athanasius's thought, with a theology of salvation as the deifying participation of creatures in God. Before moving forward to considering deification, however, I will explore three of Athanasius's further insights into creation that can open up new meaning in today's ecological context.

The immediacy of the Trinity to creation

In Athanasius's theology, each person of the Trinity is immediately present to each creature. It is astounding to think of the divine persons as immediately present to this starling flying by my window. But this is the clear implication of Athanasius's defence of the immediacy of the triune God to creatures.

The context for Athanasius's thought is his rejection of Hellenistic and Arian views that require created intermediaries between creatures and the Creator. In these views, God is so wholly other to creatures, that such a God could only be greatly diminished by any direct contact with matter and flesh. If creatures exist by participation in God, as many assumed, then there must be an intermediary between creatures and God that can enable this to happen.

Athanasius shares the model of participation in God borrowed from Platonism, but he develops it in a distinctively Christian way. He agrees with Arian thinkers about the complete otherness and complete transcendence of the Creator, and on the infinite difference between finite creatures and the Creator. How, then, is this gulf to be bridged? In standard Platonic views, the answer is through secondary intermediate figures, such as the Demiurge and the world of Ideas,

---

23. *Ep Ser* 1:24, Anatolios, *Athanasius*, 224.

or the Logos, or the Soul. Creatures participate in the intermediary, while the intermediary participates in God, but is not God.

Athanasius's Arian opponents see divine transcendence as meaning that there can be no direct relation between God and creatures. Not only would direct connection demean God, but finite creatures would never be able to stand the blazing touch of the infinitely other God. So, they reason, the Father creates the Word as a mediator to carry out God's purposes in creation and salvation. Peter Leithart summarises their view: the Word of God is a creature who 'serves as a buffer between God and creation'.[24]

For Athanasius, by contrast, there is no such buffer. This sharply distinguishes his thought not only from Christian thinkers like Arius, Eusebius and Asterius, but also from various forms of Platonism. Athanasius agrees with them on the radical otherness of the Creator and shares with other Christian thinkers the biblical conviction that the Father engages with creation through the Word. But he insists that the Word shares fully the Father's essence and, precisely as fully divine, bridges the gap between Creator and creatures by loving condescension. This word condescension does not have its contemporary suggestion of smug superiority, but its literal meaning of 'coming down to be with' creatures: 'For they would not have withstood his nature, being that of the unmitigated splendour of the Father, if he had not condescended (*sunkatabas*) by the Father's love for humanity and supported, strengthened, and carried them into being'.[25]

For Athanasius, no creature could ever be radically immanent to creatures. Only the God beyond all created being can bridge the gap. In Athanasius's thought, the very idea of divine transcendence is transformed in terms of the biblical categories of mercy and condescension. God is beyond all creatures precisely in the divine capacity to come down to be with creatures and in the divine generosity and loving kindness.

The Word and the Spirit, then, are in no sense created intermediaries, but share the one divine nature with the Father. Because Word and Spirit are one with the Father's essence, the Word's mediation in the Spirit also involves the immediacy of the Father's presence and

---

24. P Leithard, *Athanasius* (Grand Rapids: Baker Academic, 2011), 91.
25. Athanasius of Alexandria, *Orations against the Arians* 2.64, in Anatolios, *Athanasius*, 157–8. Hereafter abbreviated as 'C Ar'.

activity to creation.²⁶ As Athanasius puts it, the one who experiences the Radiance (the Word) is enlightened by the Sun itself (the Father) and not by any intermediary.²⁷

In Athanasius we find a fully Trinitarian theology of immediate presence of God through the Word and in the Spirit, by which creatures participate in God. They participate not in possessing the divine nature, but always from nothing. For Athanasius, then, the Word is a mediator, but a fully divine mediator of fully Trinitarian presence. Anatolios says that 'Athanasius's whole logic was averse to the notion of a created meditation between God and creation, since it is exclusively a divine characteristic to be able to bridge the distance between God and creation'.²⁸ Only God can relate the world of creatures to God's self.

What Athanasius brings to light is the idea that the true nature of the God-creature relationship, and its radical immediacy, can be understood only when Word and Spirit are understood as fully divine. Only a fully Trinitarian theology enables us to glimpse the immediacy of the relationship between God and creation. Because creation is participation in the life of the Trinity, this means that ultimately 'Athanasius's perspective is that of a relational ontology'.²⁹ I see this line of thought as offering a Trinitarian basis for a theology of the intrinsic value of each creature within the community of creation. Every creature on Earth, every whale, every sparrow and every earthworm exists by participation in the Father through the Son and in the Spirit—not one of them is forgotten in God's sight' (Lk 12:6).

The Universe of Creatures Springs from the Dynamic Fruitfulness of Trinitarian Life

A second insight with meaning for today's ecological context is offered in Athanasius's view of the dynamic fruitfulness of the Trinity. It is sometimes claimed that classical Trinitarian theologies, particularly Nicene theologies of the one divine substance, result in a static, lifeless view of God and of the God-world relationship. This critique

---

26. Anatolios, *Athanasius: The Coherence of his Thought*, 113.
27. *C Ar*, 3:14.
28. Anatolios, *Athanasius: The Coherence of his Thought*, 162.
29. Anatolios, *Athanasius: The Coherence of his Thought*, 208.

simply does not apply to the great theologians of the fourth century, Basil, Gregory of Nyssa, Gregory of Nazianzus, Hilary and Augustine, and it most certainly does not apply to Athanasius.

His view of the dynamic nature of divine life becomes apparent in his delight in bringing together the various biblical titles for Jesus Christ, the Word made flesh, such as those of Word, Wisdom, Power, Image, Radiance, Stream, Light and Life as well as Son.[30] He is particularly attached to the symbol of Christ as the eternal Radiance (*apaugasma* from Heb 1:3) of the Light. He interprets the fact that the Bible gives these names to both God and to Jesus Christ as pointing to their shared divine nature. He calls these names *paradeigmata* (symbols), interprets them intertextually, and sees them as giving some revealed insight into divine being: 'Since human nature is not capable of comprehension of God, Scripture has placed before us such symbols (*paradeigmata*) and such images (*eikonas*), so that we may understand from them however slightly and obscurely, as much as is accessible to us'.[31]

The different symbols qualify and correct one another. If unqualified, the Father-Son image might be thought to imply the physicality, and the beginning in time, of human birthing. When joined to the symbol of Light and its Radiance, it becomes clear that the Father must always have the Son, as Light always has its Radiance. As Peter Leithart puts it: 'The image of light and radiance thus assists in the apophatic purgation of our thoughts about God as Father and Son. One paradigm cleanses another'.[32] In the divine life, the Word is always generated by the Father, the Radiance always shines from the Light, the Stream always flows from the Fountain. This dynamic, eternal fecundity of the divine generation of the Word is the basis for all the diverse fruitfulness of creation.

One of Athanasius's arguments against his opponents concerns precisely this issue. He argues that the wonderful fruitfulness of God's creation must point back to the eternal generativity of divine life. Unlike Origen, he holds that creation comes to be as a free act of God in time, but he insists that it must be grounded in the eternal

---

30. Anatolios, *Athanasius: The Coherence of his Thought*, 98–100; Leithart, *Athanasius*, 41–50.
31. *C Ar* 2:32, Anatolios, *Athanasius*, 127.
32. Leithart, *Athanasius*, 46.

possibility of creating in the triune God. The fecundity of creation can only be grounded in the eternal dynamic fecundity of divine life.

If, as his Arian opponents suppose, the creative Word/Wisdom of God is a creature who has a beginning, then this completely undermines what Athanasius calls the eternal 'generative nature' of God.[33] Athanasius points to what he sees as the barren emptiness at the heart of his opponents' position:

> In accord with them, let not God be of a generative nature, so that there may be no Word nor Wisdom nor any Image at all of his own essence. For if he is not Son, then neither is he Image. But if there is no Son, how then do you say that God is Creator, if indeed it is through the Word and in Wisdom that everything that is made comes to be and without which nothing comes to be, and yet, according to you, God does not possess that in which and through which he makes all things (cf Wis 9:2; Jn 1:3; Ps 104:20, 24). But if, according to them, the divine essence itself is not fruitful but barren, like a light that does not shine and a fountain that is dry, how are they not ashamed to say that God has creative energy?[34]

God is a Light with its ever-lasting Radiance that enlightens us in the Spirit, a Fountain always pouring forth a River of living water from which we creatures drink in the Spirit, a Father eternally begetting the Son in whom we participate by adoption in the Spirit.[35] For Athanasius, those who deny the full and eternal divinity of the Word, deny the dynamic life of God that is the very ground of the creation and salvation of a world of creatures.

Again, Athanasius's thought, developed in response to the Arian challenge, can offer new and rich meaning in an ecological age. The Trinitarian God that he defends is a God of endless life and boundless loving. God is fruitful by nature. The fruitfulness of the natural world, the dynamic evolution of the universe from the Big Bang 13.7 billion years ago, the evolution of life on Earth, the existence of this blue wren I see in front of me, are grounded in the dynamic generativity and fruitfulness of the triune God.

---

33. C Ar 2:2, Anatolios, *Athanasius*, 111.
34. C Ar 2:2, Anatolios, *Athanasius*, 111.
35. Ep Ser 1:19 (Anatolios, *Athanasius*, 217–19).

Divine delight in creatures

A third insight that is rich in meaning for ecological theology is Athanasius's view of the divine delight in creatures. He points to the New Testament where we find Jesus testifying to the mutual knowledge of the Father and the Son, and to the joy this brings (Lk 10:22. See also Matt 11:27; Jn 10:15; 14:7). Athanasius interprets these texts with the aid of the beautiful image from Proverbs of God delighting in Wisdom (Prov 8:30). God rejoices in divine Wisdom, and with Wisdom takes delight in a world of creatures. In this context, Athanasius points out that God does not need a cause of rejoicing from outside God's self, because God eternally rejoices in Wisdom, who is eternally God's own:

> When was it then that the Father did not rejoice? But if he has always rejoiced, then there was always the one in whom he rejoiced. In whom, does the Father rejoice (cf Prov 8:30), except by seeing himself in his own image (*eikoni*), which is his Word? Even though, as it has been written in these same Proverbs, he also 'delighted in the sons of people, having consummated the world' (Prov 8:31), yet this also has the same meaning. For he did not delight in this way by acquiring delight as an addition to himself, but it was upon seeing the works that were made according to his own image, so that the basis of this delight also is God's own Image.[36]

Athanasius's central point is that in spite of the Arians' misuse of Proverbs 8:22: 'He created me as the beginning of his ways', God's delight in Wisdom does not have a beginning, but it is an eternal delight. The mutual delight of Father and Son in the Spirit is intrinsic to the divine being, and the biblical theme of God's delight in creatures is situated within this mutual delight. God's delight in human beings and other creatures, then, is not an addition to the divine being, but 'an inclusion of the creation into the eternal mutual delight of the being of the Father and the Son'.[37] God's relationship to creation is embraced within the divine joy of the Trinity.

---

36. *C Ar*, 2:82; Anatolios, *Athanasius*, 175.
37. Anatolios, *Retrieving Nicaea*, 153.

Creation takes place within the mutual love and delight of the divine persons. God's delight in creatures is enfolded within the mutual delight of the Father and the Son.[38] The Holy Spirit enables the mutual delight of Father and the Word to be sharable and brings about creation as the site of the extension of the Father-Word relation beyond the divine being. Anatolios comments: 'Such a Trinitarian account of creation speaks to our contemporary ecological crisis, leading us to see that a destructive posture towards creation is blasphemous in its dishonouring of the Father-Son delight and the Spirit's gift-giving of that delight'.[39]

Trinity in Act: Deification of Human Beings and of the Natural World

The deification of humanity

Why does the Word become incarnate? Athanasius sees human beings at their creation as being given the special grace of participating in the Word, and so being made according to the Image, and thus made sharers in eternal life. But humans wilfully sinned and lost the gift of eternal life. God's response was unthinkably generous: the Word in whom all are created would come in the flesh to bring about forgiveness of sin and to enter into death and overcome it in the power of resurrection. The overcoming of death, Athanasius tells us, 'is the primary cause of the incarnation of the Saviour'.[40] The second major reason is that we might now come to know 'the Word of God who was in the body, and through him the Father'.[41] The Word had long been teaching humanity about the Father through the Word's providence and regulation of the universe of creatures. Because humanity had neglected to hear this message spoken by the creation, the Word of creation is now made flesh.

The Word who is the Image of the Father comes to humanity to renew this image in us, to seek out the lost and to find them again through the forgiveness of sins. Christ's death abolishes our debt to

---

38. Anatolios, *Retrieving Nicaea*, 118, 153–4, 288.
39. Anatolios, *Retrieving Nicaea*, 288.
40. Athanasius of Alexandria, *On the Incarnation*, 10, Thomson, 159. Hereafter abbreviated as '*Inc*'.
41. *Inc*, 14, Thomson, 169.

death. Athanasius sees the cross in terms of a liturgical offering: he 'surrendered his body to death in place of all and offered it to the Father'.[42] In so doing, he liberates us from the evil one and, as Athanasius highlights, from the fear of death (Heb 2:14–15).

Athanasius makes use of a range of biblical images for the death of Christ which he finds in Paul and in the liturgical language of Hebrews. But he also offers a large overarching vision of what God does for us in Christ's life, death and resurrection with his theology of deification. He first speaks of deification in the well-known passage in his *On the Incarnation*: 'For he became human that we might become divine; and he revealed himself through a body that we might receive an idea of the invisible Father; and he endured insults from human beings that we might inherit incorruption'.[43]

In his later anti-Arian writings, Athanasius frequently uses deification language (the verb *theopoieō*, and the noun he coins, *theopoiēsis*) to defend the real divinity of the Word, who is made flesh that we might be made divine: 'So he was not a human being and later became God. But, being God, he later became a human being in order that we may be divinized'.[44] Athanasius builds on Irenaeus and others in his theology of deification. He uses this language more often than his predecessors, and helps to clarify its meaning, very often pairing it with words that function as synonyms, including adoption, renewal, salvation, sanctification, grace, transcendence, illumination and vivification.[45]

Athanasius insists, against his opponents, that the Word of God is not deified, but is the eternal divine source of our deification. However, it is central to his thought that the bodily humanity of Jesus *is* deified by its union with the Word. It is precisely this union that enables the deification of humanity: 'For the Word was not lessened by his taking a body, so that he would seek to receive grace, but rather he divinised what he put on, and, what's more, he gave this to the human race'.[46]

---

42. *Inc*, 8, Thomson, 153.
43. *Inc*, 54, Thomson, 153, modified.
44. *C Ar*, 1:39, Anatolios, *Athanasius*, 96.
45. See N Russell, *The Doctrine of Deification in the Greek Patristic Tradition* (Oxford: Oxford University Press, 2004), 177–8.
46. *C Ar*, 1:42, Anatolios, *Athanasius*, 99.

For Athanasius, deification is an ontological transformation in creaturely reality that occurs through the whole Christ-event, the birth, life, death and resurrection of Jesus and the outpouring of the Spirit. Because of the incarnation, there is a divine transformation already at work in humanity and in the world. But this divine gift of grace, given in principle, has to be accepted by the human recipient and embraced in a life of fidelity. For the Christian community, this divine life is transmitted in practice through baptism and growing in the life of the Spirit according to the Image that is Christ.

Athanasius's theology of salvation is fully Trinitarian. The Word, the true Image of God, repairs and renews the image of God in humanity. In the loving self-humbling of the Word in the incarnation, Christ becomes the receiver of the Spirit in his humanity, enabling us to become co-receivers of the Spirit through him:

> The Saviour, on the contrary, being God, and forever ruling the kingdom of the Father and being himself the supplier of the Spirit, is nevertheless now said to be anointed by the Spirit, so that, being said to be anointed as a human being by the Spirit, he may provide us human beings with the indwelling and intimacy of the Holy Spirit, just as he provides us with exaltation and resurrection.[47]

As Anatolios points out, this amounts to a Spirit Christology in that the Word of God who is the divine giver of the Spirit, in the kenotic self-humbling of his humanity becomes the receiver of the Spirit, that we too might become receivers of the Spirit. And this means that we too can become God's beloved daughters and sons. Born again of the grace of the Spirit, we are 'enfolded in the inner life of the Trinity', taken up in the position of the Word in relation to the Father, and are ourselves enabled to call God 'Father' and not simply our 'Maker'.[48]

The participation of the natural world in deification

How does this theology of deification relate to the rest of creation? Although his focus is not primarily the natural world, Athanasius clearly sees it as participating with humanity in its own proper way

---

47. *C Ar,* 1:46, Anatolios, *Athanasius*, 103.
48. Anatolios, *Retrieving Nicaea*, 125. See *C Ar,* 2:59, Anatolios, *Athanasius*, 152–3.

in transformation in Christ. So he writes late in his life, in his *Letter to Adelphius,* of Christ as 'the Liberator of all flesh and of all creation (cf Rom 8:21)', and as 'the Creator and Maker coming to be in a creature so that, by granting freedom to all in himself, he may present the world to the Father and give peace to all, in heaven and on earth'.[49]

Athanasius refers often to classic texts that include the creation in Christ, particularly Romans 8:19–23 and to Colossians 1:15–20. In his second *Oration against the Arians*, Athanasius refers explicitly to Romans 8:19–23 and Colossians 1:15–20, to include the whole creation in the liberation that comes through Christ's resurrection:

> The truth that refutes them is that he is called 'firstborn among many brothers' (Rom 8:29) because of the kinship of the flesh, and 'firstborn from the dead' (Col 1:18) because the resurrection of the dead comes from him and after him, and 'firstborn of all creation' (Col 1:15) because of the Father's love for humanity, on account of which he not only gave consistence to all things in his Word but brought it about that the creation itself, of which the apostle says that it 'awaits the revelation of the children of God', will at a certain point be delivered 'from the bondage of corruption into the glorious freedom of the children of God' (Rom 8:19, 21).[50]

In the following example, from Athanasius's defence of the divinity of the Spirit in his *Letter to Serapion*, he insists that the Word and the Spirit are inseparable, and that both are at work in the incarnation for the sake of the reconciliation of the whole creation:

> Thus is was that when the Word came to the holy Virgin Mary, the Spirit also entered with him (cf Lk 1:35), and the Word, in the Spirit, fashioned and joined a body to himself, wishing to unite creation to his Father, and to offer it to the Father through himself and to reconcile all things in his body, 'making peace among the things of heaven and the things of earth' (cf Col 1:20).[51]

---

49. Athanasius of Alexandria, *Letter 40: To Adelphius,* 4 (Anatolios, *Athanasius,* 103).
50. *C Ar,* 2:63, Anatolios, *Athanasius,* 157.
51. *Ep Ser,* 1:31, Anatolios, *Athanasius,* 231–2.

In these texts, Athanasius is fully explicit about his inclusion of the rest of the natural world with human beings in salvation. In other places, he speaks more generally of creation being deified, often in the context of the divine adoption of human beings. In defending the divinity of the Holy Spirit, for example, he reflects on the way we human beings are saved and sealed with the Holy Spirit: 'When we are sealed in this way, we become sharers in the divine nature, as Peter says (2 Pet 1:4), and so the whole creation participates of the Word, in the Spirit'.[52] In another instance, he insists that the Spirit in whom the Word adopts human beings and deifies creation cannot be a creature:

> Therefore, it is in the Spirit that the Word glorifies creation and presents it to the Father by divinizing it and granting it adoption. But the one who binds creation to the Word could not be among the creatures and the one who bestows sonship upon creation could not be foreign to the Son . . . Therefore, the Spirit is not among the things that have come into being but belongs (*idion*) to the divinity of the Father, and is the one in whom the Word divinizes the things that have come into being. But the one in whom creation is divinized cannot be extrinsic to the divinity of the Father.[53]

Through the incarnation of the Word, the Spirit binds creation to the Word made flesh that human beings might be forgiven, deified and adopted as beloved sons and daughters and to the rest of creation that it might be transformed in Christ in its own proper way. As the later Greek theological tradition makes clear, there are distinctions between creatures in their way of participation in Trinitarian life— they participate in the divine Communion according to their own proper capacity and their own proper nature. But in ways proper to

---

52. *Ep Ser*, 1:23, Anatolios, *Athanasius*, 223. CRB Shapland, in his translation of these letters, interprets 'creation' here as referring to the whole natural world rather than just to humanity. He notes that this reference to creation partaking of the Word in salvation seems to be a natural extension of the statement made earlier by Athanasius in his *Against the Greeks* (which I have quoted above) that all creation partakes of the Word for its very existence. CRB Shapland, *The Letters of Saint Athanasius Concerning the Holy Spirit* (London: Epworth Press, 1951), 124–5, 15.

53. *Ep Ser*, 1:25, Anatolios, *Athanasius*, 225.

each creature, the whole creation is to participate through the Word, in the Spirit, in the divine life of Trinity.

Conclusion: Where on Earth is God?

In these reflections, I have sought to outline a sketch for a Trinitarian theology of creation and deifying transformation in Christ that has meaning for today. I am conscious that making these kinds of claims about the triune God's engagement with the natural world immediately raises many issues that I am not dealing with here. One of the most important is the relationship between this view of God and the pain, death and extinction built into evolutionary emergence. Christopher Southgate's work in this volume is important here.[54] I have tried to offer some reflections on this fundamental theological problem elsewhere.[55]

In the creation theology of Athanasius, God continually creates the whole universe of creatures through the eternal Word in the Holy Spirit. The divine Source of All, the Father is *immediately* present, not only to the whole universe, but to each single creature, through the Word and in the Spirit. The diverse creatures of our universe give expression to the *fruitfulness* of the eternal generativity of the life of God—they all exist in and from the eternal generation of the Word and the eternal procession of the Spirit. This whole world of creatures exists *within the delight* of the mutual relations of the dynamic life of the Three.

The God of love dynamically empowers the emergent universe through the presence of the indwelling Word and Spirit. Earth and its creatures, its insects, birds and animals, its forests and seas, its habitats and bioregions, all exist because the God of love is closer to them than they are to themselves. The Trinity of love enables their existence, their interaction and their becoming in the community of creation. The relationship of creation is one by which each creature partakes of God through the Word and in the Spirit. Each is

---

54. See also C Southgate, *The Groaning of Creation: God, Evolution, and the Problem of Evil* (Louisville: Westminster John Knox Press, 2008).
55. D Edwards, *How God Acts: Creation, Redemption and Special Divine Action* (Minneapolis: Fortress Press, 2010).

loved, each is precious—'not one of them is forgotten in God's sight' (Lk 12:6).

However, the good news of Christianity is that the divine love for the world of creatures involves far more than the triune act of continuous creation. It centres on the radical self-giving of incarnation—a God who enters into matter and flesh, uniting the world of matter and flesh radically with God's self, and transforming it from within. In the incarnation, the eternal Word, in the power of the Spirit, is united not only with Jesus' creaturely reality, and not only with humanity, but also with the matter of the universe, with the evolutionary processes that constitute biological life on Earth, with all creatures. The eternal Word in whom all things are created becomes a creature of flesh and blood, made of atoms that are produced in stars, shaped by evolutionary history, subject to pain and death, in solidarity with the whole community of life on Earth.

Athanasius tells us that the incarnation is an act of radical revelation of what is in the heart of God—the Wisdom of God already manifest in the diversity of creation all around us now comes to us and meets us in our own humanity in the midst of biological life. But the incarnation is not only revelation, but also our forgiveness, healing and transformation. It is the beginning of the end of death. It is our deification and, with us, the deification and fulfilment of the natural world. God becomes a creature of matter and flesh in order that human beings and with them the rest of creation might be deified and transformed in God, participating in the life of the Trinity. This process has begun in our world through the resurrection of the crucified Christ, the beginning of new creation at work in our world.

This incarnational theology culminates in the bodily resurrection of the crucified Jesus. He is transfigured in glory, the promise and the beginning of the transfiguration of human beings and, with them, of the whole creation. The resurrection and ascension of the crucified Jesus show that matter and flesh are forever in God. In the incarnation and its culmination in resurrection, God commits God's self to this world, to this Earth and its creatures, and does so eternally. In the risen Christ, part of the biological community of Earth is forever transfigured in God, the promise and the beginning of the transformation of all things. God has committed God's self to this universe of creatures forever.

In pondering the triptych of creation, incarnation and the resurrection of the crucified Jesus, we come to know that we cannot love God without loving God's beloved creatures. We cannot follow Jesus, the Word made flesh, without embracing the matter and flesh embraced in his incarnation. The three Christian doctrines form the basis for a Christian commitment to this Earth and its creatures. Conversion to Christ involves love for this Earth and all its creatures, an ecological conversion.

I will conclude by focusing on a member of a threatened species, a small Australian marsupial, the bilby. It can be said that this bilby exists because it partakes of the Word of God through the indwelling Spirit. God is present to this bilby not through any mediation but directly. In boundless generosity, condescension and benevolence, the transcendent God reaches out directly to the creature, is immanently present to it, and directly confers existence upon it. Through the Word and in the Spirit it is immediately united to the Father in the relationship of creation. It lives from the divine Communion. It is the fruit of the fecundity of divine life—existing from the bounty and generosity of divine life. It represents in Australia in its own unique way the endless generativity of the Word. It is a creature in which God takes delight, existing within the mutual delight of the divine persons. Because of the Word becoming flesh, and entering into death to transform it from within, this bilby is part of the whole creation that will participate with human beings in the deifying transformation of the whole of reality. It will reach its proper fulfilment in the divine Communion.

Thomas Torrance, drawing on Athanasius's view of the incarnation, writes: 'God has decisively bound himself to the created universe and the created universe to himself, with such an unbreakable bond that the Christian hope of redemption and recreation extends not just to human beings but to the universe as a whole'.[56] We may hope that this bilby too 'will be set free from its bondage to decay and will obtain the freedom of the glory of the children of God' (Rom 8:22). This hope is based on the divine promise given us in Christ—in the transformation of death brought about through his death and resurrection.

---

56. TF Torrance, *The Christian Doctrine of God: One Being Three Persons* (Edinburgh: T&T Clark, 1996), 244.

As Paul says, however, our hope is not for something that we see—'we hope for what we do not see' (Rom 8:25). Karl Rahner long ago pointed out that we have no clear vision of our eschatological future.[57] What we have is the promise of God that we experience in the grace given now—which leads us to hope in the final fulfilment of ourselves, of bilbies, and the global community of life on Earth, and the whole creation in the incomprehensible loving mystery of the divine Trinity. In the meantime, we have the words of Jesus about sparrows and bilbies: 'Not one of them is forgotten in God's sight' (Lk 12:6).

References

Anatolios, K., *Athanasius: The Coherence of his Thought* (London: Routledge, 1988)

_____ *Athanasius* (London: Routledge, 2004).

_____ *Retrieving Nicaea: The Development and Meaning of Trinitarian Doctrine* (Grand Rapids, Michigan: Baker Academic, 2011).

Ayres, L., *Nicaea and its Legacy: An Approach to Fourth-Century Trinitarian Theology* (Oxford: Oxford University Press, 2004).

Behr, J., *The Nicene Faith: Part One: True God of True God. The Formation of Christian Theology*, Volume 2 (Crestwood N.Y.: St Vladimir's Seminary Press, 2004).

Bergmann, S., *Creation Set Free: The Spirit as Liberator of Nature* (Grand Rapids, Michigan: William B. Eerdmans, 2005).

Boff, L., *Trinity and Society* (Maryknoll NY: Orbis Books, 1988).

_____ *Cry of the Earth, Cry of the Poor* (Maryknoll NY: Orbis Books, 1997).

Edwards, D., *How God Acts; Creation, Redemption and Special Divine Action* (Minneapolis: Fortress, 2010).

Gunton, C., *The Promise of Trinitarian Theology* (Edinburgh: T&T Clark, 1991).

_____ *The One, the Three and the Many: God, Creation and the Culture of Modernity*. (Cambridge: Cambridge University Press, 1993).

---

57. Karlk Rahner, 'The Hermeneutics of Eschatological Assertions', in *Theological Investigations* Volume IV (London: Darton, Longman & Todd, 1974), 323–46.

Hanson, R.P.C., *The Search for the Christian Doctrine of God: The Arian Controversy* 318-381 (Edinburgh: T&T Clark, 1988).

Johnson, E. A., *Women, Earth, and Creator Spirit* (Mahwah, NJ: Paulist Press, 1993).

_____ *Quest for the Living God: Mapping Frontiers in the Theology of God* (New York: Continuum, 2007).

Kasper, W., *The God of Jesus Christ* (London: SCM, 1993).

LaCugna, C. M., *God for Us: The Trinity and Christian Life* (San Francisco: HarperSanFrancisco, 1991).

Leithard, P. J., *Athanasius* (Grand Rapids, Michigan: Baker Academic, 2011).

McFague, S., *Models of God: Theology for an Ecological, Nuclear Age.* (Philadephia: Fortress Press, 1987).

_____ *The Body of God: An Ecological Theology* (London: SCM, 1993).

Moltmann, J., *The Trinity and the Kingdom of God* (London: SCM, 1981).

_____ *The Way of Jesus Christ: Christology in Messianic Dimensions* (London: SCM, 1990).

Pannenberg, W., *Systematic Theology,* Volume 2 (Grand Rapids, Michigan: W.B. Eerdmans, 1994).

Pettersen, A., *Athanasius* (London: Geoffrey Chapman, 1995).

Polkinghorne, J., *Science and the Trinity:The Christian Encounter with Reality* (London: SPCK, 2004).

Polkinghorne, J., ed., *The Trinity and an Entangled World: Relationality in Physical Science and Theology* (Grand Rapids, Michigan: William B. Eerdmans, 2010).

Rahner, K., 'The Hermeneutics of Eschatological Assertions', in *Theological Investigations* Volume IV (London: Darton, Longman & Todd, 1974), 323–46.

_____ *Foundations of Christian Faith: An Introduction to the Idea of Christianity* (New York: Seabury Press, 1978).

Russell, N., *The Doctrine of Deification in the Greek Patristic Tradition* (Oxford: Oxford University Press, 2004).

Shapland, C.R.B., *The Letters of Saint Athanasius Concerning the Holy Spirit* (London: Epworth Press, 1951).

Southgate, C., *The Groaning of Creation: God, Evolution, and the Problem of Evil* (Louisville: Westminster John Knox Press, 2008).

Thomson, R. W., *Athanasius:* Contra Gentes *and* De Incarnatione (Oxford: Clarendon Press, 1971).

Torrance, T. F., *The Christian Doctrine of God: One Being Three Persons* (Edinburgh: T & T Clark, 1996).

Williams, R. *Arius: Heresy and Tradition* (London: Darton, Longman and Todd, 1987).

Weinandy, T. G., *Athanasius: A Theological Introduction* (Aldershot, Hampshire: Ashgate, 2007).

Zizioulas, J. D., *Being as Communion: Studies in Personhood and the Church*. Crestwood, NY: St Vladimir's Seminary Press.

―――― *Communion and Otherness* (London. T&T Clark, 2006).

Index of Authors

A

Ambrose of Milan, 46
Anatolios, Khaled, 6, 25, 26, 39, 69, 191, 192, 384, 395, 402, 406, 409, 410, 412, 424, 426, 429, 431, 440, 441, 443, 447, 453, 455, 459, 460
Anselm, 229
Assisi, Francis, Saint, 125
Athanasius of Alexandria, 6, 13, 24–27, 31, 39, 40, 45, 46, 50, 68, 69, 70, 71, 72, 187, 189, 190, 191, 192, 193, 194, 208, 383–466
Augustine of Hippo 106, 350, 374
Aquinas, Thomas, 10, 11, 12, 106, 108, 127, 128, 208, 209, 211, 214, 256–260, 266, 267, 270, 288, 289, 290, 300, 348, 350, 356, 357, 364, 374, 376, 377, 416
Arbib, Michael, 128, 213, 260, 298
Arius, 189, 383, 393, 402, 451, 466
Asterius, 393
Ayala, Francisco J, 76, 213, 272, 298
Ayres, Lewis, 192, 393, 424, 464

B

Balabanksi, V, 178
Barbour, Ian, 91, 214, 271, 298
Bartholomew, DJ, 210, 211
Bartholomew, Patriarch, 119, 120, 137
Basil, Saint, 148

Bauckham, Richard, 3, 67
Behe, Michael, 258
Behr, John, 385, 392, 393, 406, 407, 448
Benedict XVI, Pope, 99
Bergmann, Sigurd, 100, 446
Biallowons, Hubert, 349
Birch, Charles, 214, 298
Boesch, Christophe, 57, 63
Boff, Leonardo, 111, 125, 446
Bonaventure, Saint, 108, 127
Bouyer, Louis, 142, 143, 168
Brauer, Juliane, 66
Bradshaw, Paul, 143
Brosnan, Sarah, 66

C

Call, Josef, 66
Chysostom, Saint John, 148
Clarke, W Norris, 258
Clayton, Philip, 213, 229, 260, 298
Coffey, David, 342
Congar, Yves, 44, 45, 76, 153, 169
Conradie, Ernst, 92, 93, 100, 178
Consolmagno, Guy, 269
Costache, Doru, 413
Coyne, George V, 270, 398, 347
Crutzen, Paul, 102
Cuming, GJ, 140, 144, 145, 146, 147, 148
Cusa, Nicolas of, 247
Cyril of Alexander, 432

D

Dante, 249
Darwin, Charles, 11
Davies, Brian, 34, 208, 259, 260, 289, 290
Davies, Paul, 316
de Chardin, Teilhard, 86, 90, 126, 160–164, 317, 345, 346, 347, 348, 351, 353, 354
de Lubac, Henri, 35, 224, 348, 352
de Waal, Frans, 56, 57, 58, 59, 60, 61, 62, 63
Deane-Drummond, Celia 55, 100, 101, 181
D'Espagnat, Bernard, 278
Dillard, Annie, 17, 18
Dix, Gregory, 143
Dodd, CH, 75
Dweck, Carol, 61
Dych, William V, 318

E

Edwards, Denis, 28, 61, 82, 100, 101, 181, 195, 199, 200, 208, 218, 287, 297, 313, 340, 342, 424, 464
Edwards, Verity, 157
Egan, Harvey, 8, 196, 308, 349, 354, 371
Einstein, Albert 11, 173
Ellis, George, 87, 214, 230, 248, 271, 299, 342
Endean, Philip, 350
Eusebius of Nicomedia, 393
Evers, Dirk, 94

F

Fabel, Arthur, 160, 353
Feuillet, André, 5
Finch, Jeffrey, 20
Fiorenza, Francis Schüssler, 370
Fitzmyer, Joseph, 49
Flannery, Tim, 157
Fox, Patricia, A, 152, 166
Francis, Pope, 99, 103, 107, 108, 110, 111, 112, 113, 114, 119, 120, 121, 122, 125, 126, 127, 128, 130, 131, 132, 133.

G

Gavrilyuk, Paul 34
Gazzaniga, Michael, 282
Goodenough, Ursula, 79
Giraudo, Cesare, 143
Gregersen, Niels Henrik, 77, 79, 82, 101, 206, 419, 420
Gregory of Nyssa, 374
Gregory of Nazianzus, 427
Gunton, Colin, 446

H

Habel, Norm, 178
Hansen, James, 159
Hanson, RPC, 402
Happel, Stephen, 214, 271, 299
Haught, John, 92, 214, 348
Hawking, Stephen, 29, 269
Heidegger, Martin, 349
Heller, Mochal, 270
Heschel, Abraham, 17
Hines, Mary, E, 8, 20, 354, 370, 371, 374
Hipplytus of Rome, 147
Hopkins, Gerald Manly, 53
Horrell, David B, 178
Hubble, Edwin, 11
Hunt, Cherryl, 178

I

Imhof, Paul, 349
Irenaeus of Lyon, 45, 68, 147
Isham, Chris, J, 211, 260, 270, 298

J

Jasper, RCD, 140, 144, 145, 146, 147, 148
John Damascene, 432
John of the Cross, 115
John Paul II, Pope, 51, 99, 107, 126, 138, 161, 269
Johnson, Elizabeth, 17, 37, 55, 67, 73, 93, 101, 174, 179, 211, 424
Johnson, Maxwell, 143, 144

K

Kasper, Walter, 13, 14, 17, 38, 241, 297, 446
Kavanagh, Kieran, 115
Kelly, Anthony, 123, 128, 131, 155, 171
King, Thomas, M, 161, 162, 353
King, Ursula, 176
Kingsley, Charles, 27
Kirchner, U, 230
Kodikuthiyil, HK, 348

L

LaCugna, Catherine, 446
Lehmann, Karl, 349
Leithart, Peter J, 24, 189, 429, 432, 451, 453
Léon-Dufour, Xavier, 139
Lohfink, Gerhard, 291
Louth, Andrew, 50
Léon-Dufour, Xavier, 139

M

Marmion, Declan, 8, 20, 354, 370, 371, 374
Martano, Valeria, 119
Martyr, Justin, 146
Maréchal, Joseph, 349
Maximus the Confessor, 8, 405
Mayr, Ernst 275
McCabe, Herbert, 209
McDaniel, Jay, 90, 91
McFague, Sallie, 183, 184, 446
McMullin, Ernan, 347
Meier, John P, 254, 255, 256, 256, 290, 291
Metz, Johann, Baptist, 171, 233, 253, 264
Meyering, Theo, C, 129, 213, 260, 298
Moltmann, Jürgen, 34, 77, 90, 91, 92, 154, 229, 423, 445, 465
Murphy, Nancy, 101, 129, 213, 214, 260, 270, 271, 298, 299

N

Nissiotis, Nikos, 44
Newton, Isaac, 43
North, Robert, 351
Nyssa, Gregory of, 374

O

O'Donovan, Leo, 329, 348
Origen of Alexandria, 34, 35, 36, 410, 454

P

Page, Ruth, 88, 89
Palamas, Gregory, 413
Pannenberg, Wolfhart, 229, 446, 465
Paul VI, Pope, 99
Phan, Peter, 317, 337
Peacocke, Arthur, 129, 210, 213, 214, 271, 298
Peters, Ted, 85, 87, 94, 248, 296, 340
Pettersen, Alvyn, 383, 398, 439, 440, 465
Petty, Michael, 340, 379, 380
Polkinghorne, John, 77, 248, 260, 298, 446
Power, David, N, 138, 139, 141, 143, 145, 147, 148, 149

R

Rahner, Karl, ix, 6, 7, 8, 9, 10, 11, 12, 28, 47, 48, 51, 76, 86, 88, 90, 114, 149, 154, 169, 187, 195, 196, 197, 198, 206, 208, 209, 218, 219, 223, 224, 229, 234, 235–252, 253, 254, 265, 266, 291, 295–380, 405, 406, 414, 415, 416, 417, 423, 445, 464, 465
Ratzinger, Joseph, 162
Rees, Martin, 230, 231
Reid, Duncan, 81, 82
Richardson, Alan, 254
Rodriguez, Otilio, 113
Rolston III, Holmes, 18, 80, 81, 90, 366, 367

Russell, Norman, 394, 411, 457
Russell, Robert J, 76, 87, 92, 94, 101, 129, 213, 214, 215, 216, 229, 248, 250, 260, 270, 271, 272, 289, 293, 295, 296, 298, 299, 314, 340, 347

S

Schellnbuber, Hans Joachim, 119
Schillebeeckx, Edward, 15, 38, 39, 77, 184, 224, 233, 234
Schmemann, Alexander, 141, 150, 151
Schneiders, Sandra, 406, 418, 419
Schweigert, Rusty, 173
Scotus, Duns, 8, 47, 207, 236, 303, 318, 354, 371, 405
Serapion of Thmuis, Bishop 399–403, 425
Shapland, CRB, 45, 48, 50, 402, 409, 412, 424, 433, 435, 436, 459, 466
Silk, Joan, 61
Skinner, BF, 57
Skyrms, Brian 61
Southgate, Christopher, 18, 50, 77, 97, 178, 461
Spelke, Elizabeth, 61
St John, Donald, 160, 353
Stavrakopoulou, Francesca, 50, 178
Stix, Garry, 66
Stoeger, William R, 76, 101, 129, 213, 214, 230, 254, 260, 261, 262, 263, 264, 266, 269–291, 298, 299, 315, 347
Suchak, Malini, 57

T

Tacey, David, 176
Thomas, Gunter, 94
Thompson, RW, 6
Thompson, William M, 329
Thomson, Robert, 407, 408, 435, 456
Tomasello, Michael, 61, 62, 63, 64, 65, 66, 67

Torrance, Thomas, F, 416, 417, 446, 463, 466
Tracy, David, 234
Tracy, Thomas, 76, 214, 229, 271, 299
Trudinger, P, 178
Tugwell, Simon, 267
Turkson, Cardinal Peter, 119

V

van Fraassen, Bas C, 278
von Balthasar, Hans Ur, 34
Vorgrimler, Hebert, 348

W

Wainwright, Geoffrey, 144
Wallace, Alfred Russel, 11
Ward, Keith, 212
Watts, Fraser, 211
Weger, Karl-Heinz, 223, 244, 245, 301, 302, 307, 357
Wegter-McNelly, Kirk, 213, 229, 260, 298
Weinandy, Thomas, 34, 396, 399, 435
Welker, Michael, 87, 94, 2448, 296, 340
Westerfield, Karen B, 144
Whitehead, Alfred North, 91
Wienandy, Thomas, 34, 396, , 399
Wildiers, NM, 354
Wildman, Wesley, 418
Wiles, Maurice, 212
Wilkinson, David, 49, 50
Williams, Rowan, 402
Witherington Ben, III, 5
Woo, Carolyn, 119
Wurst, S, 178

Z

Zizioulas, John, 119, 120, 150, 151, 152, 158, 160, 164–170, 423, 446, 466
Życiński, Jósef, 30, 270

Index of Biblical References

Old Testament

Genesis
1:1–31	3
1:20–31	369
1:28	103
2:7	29
2:15	3
9:8–17	3

Exodus
23:13	103
23:25	139
3:2	29
32:32	94

Numbers
23:19	426

Deuteronomy
1:31	35
8:8	139
11:14	139
22:4–6	103

1 Kings
19:12	29

Job
19:23	94
34:14–15	29
38:1	29
38:2	116
38:39–12	3

Psalms
16:5	141
19:2	70
23:6	140
32	435
32:6	435
33:6	29
56:8	94
60:5	140
65:10	431
69:28	94
78:20	139
78:23–25	139
84:3	75
103:8	35
104	3, 73, 144
104:15	140
104:20	456
104:24	369, 398, 456
104:27–30	29
104:27–28	75
104:29–30	402, 436
104:30	87, 402, 435
104:31	104, 122
116:13	140
146:7–8	430
132:15	139
139:16	94

146:7	139	58:7	139
148	3, 73	61:1	436

Proverbs

8	431		
8:22–9:1	181		
8:22–31	5, 448		
8:22	69, 395, 457		
8:30	25, 89, 455		
8:31	455		
9:1–6	5		
9:5	32		

Jeremiah

2:13	429
31:12	140

Baruch

3:10	430
3:12	430

Ezekiel

18:7	139
37:3–10	29

Canticle of Canticles

1:2	140
4:10	140

Daniel

3:51–90	3

Wisdom

1:7	404
6:12–16	181
7:22	181
8:1–4	5
8:16–21	5
9:2	456
11:24–12:1	19
11:24	105, 369
12:1	402

Amos

4:6	139
4:13	427
9:14	140

Hosea

2:24	140

Zechariah

10:7	140

Sirach

1:9	70, 194
9:10	140
24:3–7	5
24:8–22	5
24:8	181
24:19	32
31:27	140
32:6	140
40:20	140

Malachi

3:16–18	94

New Testament

Matthew

1:23	4
6:11	139
6:22–23	181
6:23	219
6:25–34	75
6:26	219
10:29	75, 181
10:30	75

Ecclesiastes

10:19	140

Isaiah

5:12	140
11:2	437

11:27	455	6:43–46	32
11:28–30	32	7:37–38	32
12:40	416	7:39	400
26:29	140	8:26	433
28:19	441	10:15	455
		12:32	32

Mark

1:22–27	84	14:6	432
3:20	139	14:7	455
10:14	32	14:9	71
10:42–44	83	14:10–11	430
11:5	139	14:17	437
14:25	140	14:23	432, 440
14:36	221	15:26	437
15:17	139	16:13	437
15:34	221	16:14	433
		16:17	433
		17:4	433
		20:22	432

Luke

1:35	459
10:20	94
10:22	455
12:6–7	421
12:6	75, 192, 369, 454, 462
12:22–23	75
14:15	139
15:16	36
22:18	140

Acts

10:38	84
17:28	154, 179

Romans

1:19–25	71
1:19–21	194
8	397, 411
8:11	93, 400, 430
8:15	437
8:16	26
8:18–25	49
8:19–25	14
8:19–23	27, 89, 226, 298, 411, 459
8:19–22	85, 234
8:19	6, 27, 52, 459
8:21	6, 27, 31, 93, 180, 459
8:22–23	19
8:22	37, 89, 176, 463
8:23	37, 89
8:26	37
8:25	180
8:29	396, 411, 459
11:33–34	427
12:2	49

John

1:1–14	5, 49, 126
1:3	5, 31, 390, 396, 448, 456
1:5	431
1:9	429
1:12	430
1:14	31, 71, 81, 179, 188, 194, 398, 426
1:18	426
3:8	52
3:16	426, 433
3:18	426
4:14	400
5:43	433
6:5	5

15:18–19	430
16:27	430
19	397, 411
21	397, 411

1 Corinthians

1:23–24	84
1:24	5, 14, 116, 180, 181, 429, 430, 448
1:25	116
1:30	180
4:6	5
8:6	49, 448
10:4	429
10:16–17	169
10:17	140
11:25–26	140
12:13	429
15:28	112, 126

2 Corinthians

1:22	89
3:18	26, 49
5:5	89
13:13	154, 440

Galatians

2:19–20	432
3:2	426
4:4–5	7
4:6	437
4:7	26

Ephesians

1:13	438
1:8–10	31
1:9–10	8, 49, 85
1:10	169, 298
1:13–15	89
1:13	400, 436
1:17	430, 437
1:20–23	49, 85
1:20–22	6
4:6	440, 441
4:15	84
4:30	39, 89

Philippians

2:4–8	40
2:5–11	84
2:7	13, 76
4:3	94
3:21	49

Colossians

1:15–20	6, 27, 49, 85, 154, 169, 180, 182, 459
1:15	397, 411, 459
1:16	448
1:17	396, 431
1:18	397, 411, 459
1:19–20	31, 112, 126
1:20	52, 95, 226, 298, 444, 459

1 Timothy

3:16	35
5:21	427

Titus

3:5–6	400, 436

Hebrews

1:1–3	5
1:2–3	49, 448
1:3	429, 453
2:14–15	457

1 Peter

4:14	437

2 Peter

1:4	50, 377, 400, 411, 436, 460
3:13	49

1 John

1:5	429
1:27	436
2:27	400
4:6	437
4:8	36

4:9	426	16:19	140
4:12–13	432	20:12–14	94
		21:1–5	49
Revelation		21:5	226, 298
2:17	139	21:15	91, 95
5:13–14	49	21:27	94
5:13	369	22:13	49, 85

Index of Subjects

Autonomy,
   Creaturely, 9–11
   Word of God, 443

Christological, 76, 93, 112, 372
   'Confession', 258
   'Fullness', 162
   Hymn of Philippians, 40
   Teaching, 359
Christology, 7, 8, 12, 48, 100, 101, 149, 236, 237, 238, 240, 243, 303, 317, 318, 320, 322, 323, 354, 371, 375, 405, 445
   And the theology of salvation, 406
   Agenda for, 317, 345–359
   Creation and, 355
   Eco-Christology, 81
   Evolutionary, 207, 208, 239, 302, 304–306, 311, 321, 351, 351, 356, 378, 379
   Present-day, 352, 359
   Spirit-Christology, 46, 441, 458
   Unites God and the world of creatures, 384
   'Vision', 384, 403
Communion, viii, 67, 69, 72, 96, 126, 133, 151, 165, 313, 385, 395, 421
   And stewardship, 67
   As sacrament of, 120, 121, 155, 223
   Authentic, 111, 125
   Between creation and the Word, 46, 172
   Call to, 68

Divine, 36, 89, 95, 98, 153, 154, 170–171, 179, 251, 413
   God as, 130, 178
   In the life of the Trinity, 51, 96, 97, 131, 138, 156, 170, 171, 235, 252, 402
   Language of, 109
   Of all creation, 86, 98, 99, 102, 109, 114, 131, 162, 170
   Of Saints, 96, 97
   Sublime, 99–117, 121, 124–125
   Theology of, 109, 138, 149
   Universal, 107, 110, 112, 113, 121–124, 126, 132
Cosmology, vii, 87, 91, 101, 116, 213, 215, 216, 230, 231, 249, 251, 260, 269, 270, 272, 296, 298, 299, 314, 315, 317, 327, 337, 338, 340, 364, 379
Creation, viii, 28, 29, 31, 33, 37, 38, 40, 41, 43, 45, 67, 68, 69, 71, 73, 76, 79, 80, 86, 88, 89, 91, 92, 96, 106, 110, 112, 189
   Abuse of, 77
   Act of, 39, 88, 209, 211, 396, 407, 438, 449
   And deification, 24–27
   And redemption, 44, 47–52, 81, 84, 85, 95, 97, 99, 113, 114, 170, 180, 182, 329, 373, 399
   And suffering, 34, 76, 83, 102, 163, 198

477

And the Eucharist, 138, 143, 145, 146, 147, 148, 149, 151, 152, 154, 156, 158, 161, 164, 167, 168
And the incarnation, 101, 178, 191, 370, 371, 372, 391, 416
As gift of the Spirit, 46, 175, 192
Beauty of, 366, 367
Biblical accounts of, 103, 107, 108, 109
Blessings in, 142, 144, 166, 253
Communion of, viii, 46, 67, 68, 86, 96, 99, 102, 109–114, 116, 117, 120, 121–126, 131, 138, 151, 156, 162, 252, 402, 440, 463
Continuous, 40, 144, 191, 195, 212, 239, 243, 305, 448, 450
Divine wisdom in, 52–53
Doctrine of, 384, 386
Gifts of, 140,
Goal of, 377
God in, 23, 141, 194, 201, 205, 206, 207, 208, 201, 289, 291, 297, 299, 302, 303, 305, 309, 314, 316, 353, 376, 377, 388, 419, 451, 452
Groaning of, 18, 19, 33, 36, 37, 116, 176, 179, 397
Guidance of, 212–218
Harmony of, 390
Heart of, 82
Healing of, 93, 188
Lifting up of, 166
Love for, 37, 297
Order of love, 105
Ordering of, 190
Power of, 315
Resurrection as deifying transformation of, 357–359
Salvation of, 383
Seen in the light of Christ, 3–21
Self-bestowal as the meaning of, 236–239, 318–323, 337, 338, 354–355, 359, 374
Self-transcendence of, 306, 341, 342, 355–357
Spirituality, 98

Theology of, 272, 295, 406, 445, 446, 447, 451, 461
Transformation of, 308, 309, 312, 437
Trinity in, 423, 424, 425, 431, 432, 433, 440, 441, 456, 461, 464
Word of, 13, 24, 25, 31, 45, 46, 51, 68, 69, 82, 86, 88, 126, 147, 178, 188, 190, 191, 384, 393, 401, 403, 415, 457

Death, ix, 4, 5, 7, 14, 15, 16, 19, 26, 31, 32, 33, 37, 38, 41, 44, 50, 51, 69, 70, 75, 77, 78, 81, 82, 84, 85, 89, 90, 93, 96, 97, 101, 114, 116, 139, 140, 150, 154, 167, 168, 179, 178, 179, 184, 194, 198, 205, 206, 220, 221, 222, 223, 229, 233, 238, 247, 251, 252, 253, 255, 269, 295, 297, 306, 307, 308, 309, 310, 312, 313, 319, 324, 325, 326, 328, 329, 334, 340, 347, 354, 356, 357, 358, 366, 372, 373, 378, 384, 385, 388, 389, 390, 391, 393, 396, 398, 402, 403, 405, 408, 414, 415, 417, 447, 448, 456, 457, 458, 461, 462, 463, 464
Divine action, ix, 10, 31, 47, 84, 101, 205–226, 228, 236–250, 254, 260, 269–291, 296, 298, 300, 301, 302, 303–304, 311, 315, 323, 337, 338, 353, 355, 359, 374, 376, 377, 379, 380, 401, 420, 433, 434, 439
Special, 222–225, 270
Divine capacity, 252, 297
Divine communion, 170–171, 179, 251, 462
Divine forgiveness, 355
Divine image, 66–72, 424,
Divine influence, 289
Divine *kenōsis*, 76
Divine life, 90, 110, 171, 396, 431, 441, 443
Divine love, 31, 41, 307, 462
Divine mercy, 146, 191, 390
Divine nature, 242, 252
Divine power, 242, 290

Divine promise, 180
Divine providence, 376
Divine revelation, 287
Divine saving power, 84
Divine self-bestowal, 7, 9, 47, 207, 208, 212, 224, 239, 240, 244, 248, 251, 252, 291, 303, 322, 323, 342, 355, 356, 370
Divine self-communication, 7
Divine transcendence, 376
Divine wisdom, 31, 179, 180,

Ecology, 64, 99, 109, 113, 361, 445
   And theology, 340-342
   Eucharist and, 137-156
   Integral ecology, 11, 125, 132
Ecological consciousness, 361, 362, 363, 367, 379, 380
Ecological conversion, 112, 121, 130-133, 139, 445
Ecological destruction, 149
Ecological ethos, 156, 165, 166
Ecological hermeneutics, 361
Ecological praxis, 111
Ecological theology, 101, 102, 106, 124, 139, 141, 150, 151, 156, 164, 165, 338, 340, 361, 362, 364, 368, 373, 379, 380, 406, 445-466
Eucharist, the, 86, 96, 97, 113, 120, 124, 219, 223
   And the early Church, 256, 308
   Eucharist and ecology, 137-150
   Eucharist in a Time of Global Climate Change, 157-172
   Eucharistic theology, ix
Evolution, viii, ix, 8, 9, 11, 14, 55, 56, 58, 60, 61, 64, 66, 67, 68, 72, 90, 91, 93, 110, 116, 179, 185, 198, 201, 277, 341, 348, 366, 405
   Costs of, 37, 75-98, 101, 102, 175, 295-316, 380
   Cultural, 67
   Evolutionary biology, vii, 148, 154, 169, 205, 211, 213, 230, 253, 270, 298, 353, 364, 373

Evolutionary Christology, 12, 207, 208, 239, 302, 304, 305, 311, 317, 321, 337, 347, 351, 356, 359, 363, 378
Evolutionary consciousness, 100, 346
Evolutionary emergence, 11-13, 16, 18, 27, 28-33, 62, 79, 81, 86, 187, 207, 224, 225, 350, 357, 365, 427, 462
Evolutionary processes at work on Earth, 25, 52
Evolutionary universe, ix, 128, 130, 206, 212, 217, 227, 247, 252, 319, 455,
   Victims of, 97

Grace, 6, 7, 11, 26, 46, 47, 48, 50, 51, 60, 61, 69, 88, 105, 112, 144, 146, 154, 178, 179, 182, 185, 193, 195, 197, 205, 206, 208, 212, 218-222

Holy Spirit, the, 7, 12, 15, 24
   And Word are one, 25
   An ecological theology of, 43-53
   As breath of God that gives life, 76, 87, 155, 175, 217
   As breath of life of the Scriptures, 29,
   As breathing life into the laws of nature, 29, 39
   As energy of love, 23, 27-33
   As expressing the longing that is too deep for words, 37
   As life giver, 88, 104, 105, 122
   As midwife to the birth of the new, 89
   As power of the new, 31, 89, 142, 216
   As presence of God, 24, 127
   As present in the world as defenceless love, 39
   As transforming the gifts of creation, 152, 153, 156, 252, 308, 402, 441, 450, 461
   As unspeakable love, 200, 201, 235
   Binds creation to the Word, 13, 191
   Brings life to creatures, 46, 193, 402, 413, 417, 421

Deeply present in each creature, 127, 130, 139
Depends on human participation, 39
Divine love in person, 13,
Does not belong to the created order, 50
First fruits of, 19
Grace of, 26, 236, 247, 303, 308, 329, 342, 369, 370
Human experience of the Spirit, 195–198, 218–222, 225, 440
In the life of the church, 110
Joins creation to the Word, 46
Manifestations of, 258, 260, 264, 267
Operate through and within embodiment, 94, 179
Possesses infinite creativity, 126
Poured at at Pentecost, 222
Power of, 84, 85, 170, 430, 450, 462
Spirit of God, 4, 48, 154, 336, 339, 342, 399, 401, 402, 403, 413, 425, 428, 433, 435, 436, 456
Surrounds all with love, 97
Work in creation, 91

Incarnation, the, viii, 6–9, 13, 16, 26, 31, 33, 36, 38, 39, 40, 44, 46, 47, 48, 49, 51, 68, 72, 78, 81, 82, 100, 101, 102, 112, 113, 114, 116, 120, 126, 147, 151, 163, 164, 178, 179, 180, 183, 191, 207, 208, 209, 212, 222, 223, 237, 240, 249, 252, 272, 287, 291, 303, 305, 309, 310, 318, 320, 323, 324, 333, 338, 341, 342, 346, 354, 355, 358, 359, 370, 371, 372, 373, 384, 385, 396, 390, 391, 393, 394, 396, 397, 405–421, 441, 442, 443, 445, 447, 448, 456, 458, 459, 461, 462, 463

Participation, 9, 13, 14, 24, 33, 37, 39, 41, 50, 69, 87, 88, 95, 110, 153, 167, 170–171, 189, 191, 192, 252, 257, 310, 324, 402, 409, 413, 431, 435, 440, 448, 449, 450, 451, 452, 459–461

Resurrection, the, 4–6, 7, 9, 20, 31, 40, 84, 87, 92, 113, 114, 167, 168, 170, 180, 180, 182, 222, 223, 226, 236, 238, 247, 249, 251, 299, 396, 397, 449, 457
And divine power, 83–85, 405
And exaltation, 45
And hope, 229, 234
And laws of nature, 300
And love, 38, 40
And non-interventionist theology, 295–316
And the ascension, 414, 416, 463
And the Body of Christ, 392
And the Eucharist, 96, 169,
And the Spirit, 48, 51, 94, 154, 178, 221, 354, 421
And the suffering of creation, 316
And transformation, 50, 464
As beginning of communion of all creation with God, 86
As divine Attractor, 32, 34
As God's self communication, 76, 373, 390, 391, 403, 411
As ontological transformation, 309–311, 458
As penetrating into the ontological depths of creation, 417
As real symbol of salvation, 306–308, 372, 385
Bodily, 180, 462
Impact on the universe, 315
Participation in, 95
Power of, 170, 228, 242, 297, 408, 456
Promise of, 90, 93, 97, 106, 116, 169, 246, 250, 252, 253
Transforming power of, 14, 85–87, 296, 314, 317–343, 357–359, 403, 415
Within evolutionary Christology, 304–306
Within the *one* divine act, 303–304

Neuroscience, 129, 213, 260, 270, 272, 279, 298, 315

Quantum cosmology, 213, 272, 300, 317
Quantum mechanics, 230, 262, 272, 274, 280, 300, 317
Quantum theory, 283-287

Salvation, viii, 6, 26, 27, 43, 94, 100, 121, 122, 140, 146, 149, 153, 166, 167, 188, 205, 212, 221, 222-225, 236, 237, 245, 247, 250, 270, 301, 302, 303, 323, 326, 329, 334, 335, 339, 355, 357, 371, 373, 376, 378, 383-403, 405, 411, 412, 415, 433, 435, 445, 457, 458, 460
  As deification, 393-399
  As restoration of memory as life giving power, 151
  Economy of, 7, 423
  Creation and, 27, 41, 51, 88, 91, 168, 188, 244, 339, 364, 383, 384, 385, 423, 424, 426, 432, 434, 442, 448, 451, 454
  Resurrection as symbol of, 306-308
  Revelation and, 224
  Sacrament of, 224
  Theology of, 307, 309, 318, 324, 358, 372, 406, 447, 450
Science and theology, vii, viii, 8, 9, 10, 18, 28, 32, 33, 72, 76, 87, 101, 102, 130, 213, 215, 229, 230, 236, 239, 240, 260, 266, 269, 270, 272, 287, 290, 295, 297, 298, 305, 315, 316, 317, 318, 321, 322, 338, 339-340, 341, 348, 352, 355, 357, 362, 363, 364, 365, 377, 379, 380, 406, 445, 446
Secondary causes, 9, 10, 208, 209, 211, 213, 214, 215-216, 217, 219, 220, 221, 224, 232, 244, 256-260, 264, 266, 267, 286, 287, 288, 289, 290, 291, 299, 300, 301, 312, 315, 316, 348, 357, 375, 3786, 377, 379
Self-transcendence, 12, 28, 207, 208, 236, 239-240, 243, 248-50, 252, 305, 306, 315, 318, 321-323, 332, 333, 337, 339, 340, 341, 343, 350, 355-357, 359, 377, 378, 379, 445
Suffering, 16-17, 227-253

Transcendence, 16, 40, 92, 175, 191, 192, 196, 215, 234, 238, 286, 300, 320, 331, 332, 374, 379, 410, 451, 457
Trinity, the, 6, 7, 17, 23, 25, 26, 28, 36, 37, 51, 94, 95, 96, 97, 101, 108, 110, 113, 119-133, 156, 161, 167, 170, 171, 178, 180, 182, 188, 192, 287, 368, 396, 402, 414, 423-444, 445
Trinitarian
  Act of self bestowal, 47, 101, 355
  Basis for ecological conversion, 121
  Being and action, 429, 437, 441, 450
  Communion, 96, 112, 138, 233
  Divine action, 230
  Dynamism, 113, 131
  Eucharist as, 170,
  Image, 131
  Language, 424
  Life, 34, 179, 250, 251, 430, 453, 461
  Presence, 452
  Relational ontology, 446
  Self giving, 303
  Structure, 108, 127, 342, 440
  Theology, viii, 7, 16, 26, 27, 30, 34, 87, 95, 164, 198, 207, 299, 359, 393, 399, 401, 409, 417, 423, 424, 442, 443, 445, 446, 447, 452, 453, 455, 456, 458, 461

Universe, the, ix, 5, 6, 7, 8, 9, 11, 23, 24, 27, 29, 30, 32, 35, 36, 37, 41, 48, 49, 50, 67, 68, 76, 85, 86, 88, 89, 93, 100, 105, 106, 107, 110, 113, 114, 116, 123, 124, 125, 127, 130, 144, 148, 153, 155, 163, 164, 168, 169, 170, 171, 173, 175, 176, 185, 188, 190, 205, 206, 207, 208, 211, 212, 215, 217, 222, 224, 226, 227-253, 257, 259, 269, 277, 278, 280, 295, 296, 279, 302, 305, 306, 307, 310, 312, 313, 316, 318, 319-345, 348, 349, 355, 357, 358, 361, 365, 366, 367, 372-374, 376, 377, 379, 380, 381, 386, 387, 388, 391, 392, 393, 399, 404, 405, 407, 408, 409, 411, 416, 418, 419, 420, 421, 422, 429, 449, 450, 455, 457, 459, 463, 464, 465, 466.

Printed in Australia
AUHW011010221020
335979AU00003B/3

9 781925 643046